Cullercoats

A North-East Colony of Artists

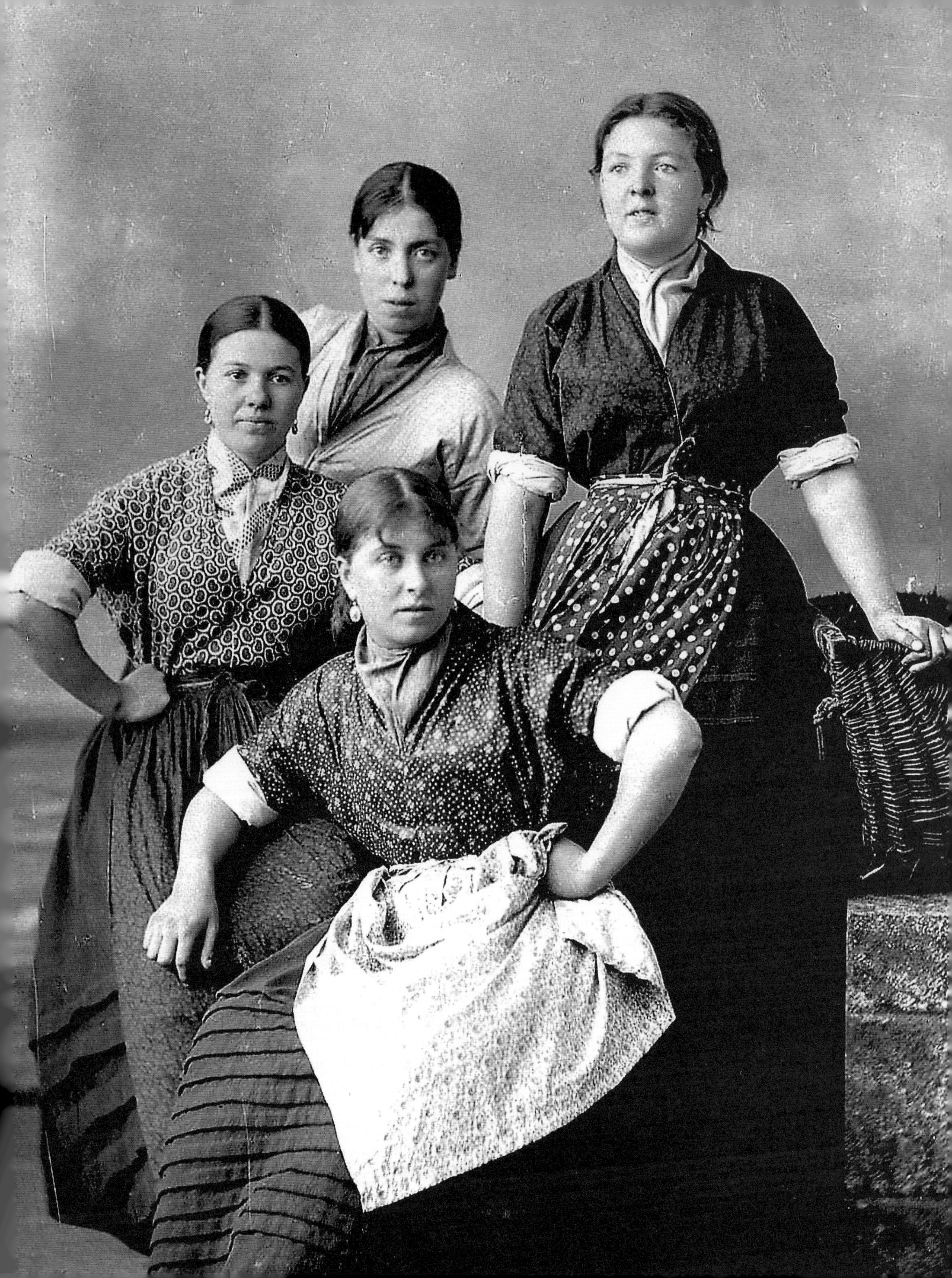

Cullercoats

A North-East Colony of Artists

LAURA NEWTON WITH ABIGAIL BOOTH GERDTS

First published in 2003 by Sansom & Company/Art Dictionaries Ltd., 81g Pembroke Road, Bristol BS8 3EA, in association with the Laing Art Gallery, Newcastle upon Tyne (Tyne & Wear Museums).

ISBN 1 904537 01 4

British Library Cataloguing in Publication Data:
A catalogue record for this book is available from the British Library.

Designed and typeset by Gendall Design, Falmouth, Cornwall and printed by HSW Print, Tonypandy, Mid-Glamorgan.

Text set in New Baskerville.

Contents

Frontispiece Fisher Folk, c.1900.

Foreword

We are pleased to welcome this book, which accompanies the exhibition at the Laing Art Gallery. The Laing has long had a role in curating exhibitions which place the art of the region in a wider cultural context, although it has been recognised for some time that a serious examination of artistic activity at Cullercoats was overdue. However, whilst the extensive research required remained incomplete, the project was unrealised.

Cullercoats: A North-East Colony of Artists was finally made possible by a partnership with the University of Northumbria at Newcastle following the completion, in 2001, of Dr Laura Newton's PhD on the Cullercoats colony. This research assessed the artists working at Cullercoats for the first time within the context of the British artist colony movement; it described the nature of artistic life at Cullercoats and explained its largely unrecognised status as arguably, the first British coastal colony.

The exhibition was curated by Ruth Percival, Assistant Keeper of Art at the Laing Art Gallery, and Laura Newton, a Post Doctoral Researcher at the University of Northumbria at Newcastle. The project has also greatly benefited from the advice of Professor Kenneth McConkey, Dean of the Faculty of Arts and Social Sciences at the University and Julie Milne, Curator, Laing Art Gallery.

We are tremendously grateful to Laura Newton for reworking her thesis into an accessible yet scholarly catalogue that preserves the essential core of her research. We are also most grateful to Abigail Booth Gerdts for her essay on Cullercoats' most famous visiting artist, Winslow Homer. This provides a welcome and reasoned assessment of the motivations behind Homer's visit to Cullercoats.

Visitors to the exhibition will see some of the finest works produced by artists identified with the colony, allowing a reading of familiar and less familiar works in a new light. The exhibition features work not only from the collections of Tyne and Wear Museums, but also paintings loaned by a number of private individuals, and from other public collections. We are indebted to all lenders for their co-operation and generosity.

Finally, we are delighted to acknowledge generous financial support. We are most grateful to the Friends of the Laing Art Gallery for their generous donation that has made this publication possible, and to Fentimans for their support. We would also like to thank Procter & Gamble for its continuing sponsorship of the Laing. Their financial support, together with that of Tyne and Wear Museums Business Partnership, has allowed this important project to be realised.

Councillor Barney Rice JP Chair, Tyne and Wear Museums Joint Committee
Alec Coles Director, Tyne and Wear Museums

Preface

In 1978, as one of its first projects, the then Newcastle upon Tyne Polytechnic Art Gallery staged 'The Restless Wave', an exhibition of marine and coastal *genre* paintings from the turn of the twentieth century. Drawn exclusively from the collections of Tyne and Wear Museums it demonstrated the impressive holdings in the region.

'The Restless Wave' quickly became important for a number of other reasons. It opened up an area of great interest which led to the splendid Charles Napier Hemy exhibition at the Laing Art Gallery in 1984. Hemy, although born in Newcastle, spent most of his life in Falmouth. From his floating studio, he dispatched impressive canvases to the Royal Academy in London every year. The Hemy exhibition was followed by other monograph shows devoted to the work of Ralph Hedley (1990) and Robert Jobling (1992). In each case these concentrated upon more locally-based artists who worked along the Tyne or at Cullercoats. They demonstrated that in the north east, we not only produced coastal *genre* painters for export to the other parts of Britain, but we also had the infrastructure to support them if they chose to remain.

It was clear from the earliest researches that in the 1880s the region also imported painters from the rest of Britain for brief periods to do significant work. However our most important catch was the great American painter, Winslow Homer, who stayed in Cullercoats for an eighteen month period at the beginning of the 1880s. 'The Restless Wave' brought us into contact with local Homer enthusiasts like John Boon who displayed his research at the Bay Hotel in Cullercoats in 1981. Boon's work paved the way to the Winslow Homer exhibition staged at Sunderland in 1988.

However, long before this notable American scholars who were conducting painstaking research on Homer's work were interested in the Cullercoats colony. Helen Cooper, Director of Yale University Art Gallery, researching the painter's watercolours, visited the region at that time, as did the important Homer researchers, Professor William H Gerdts and Abigail Booth Gerdts. William H Gerdts had just published his study of Homer at Cullercoats in the *Yale Bulletin* and Abigail was working on the complete record of Homer's work, following the pioneering scholarship of the great Americanist art historian, Lloyd Goodrich. This monumental task, based at City University of New York, is now nearing completion. I would like to express my own gratitude to Abigail for taking time out to write the thoughtful essay which accompanies the present catalogue.

Finally, all of this work is greatly enriched by the more recent research of Laura Newton. Laura began her work on the Cullercoats colony as a PhD student at Northumbria. In its course, she has not only been able to unearth new and original material on all of the Cullercoats artists, but she has also re-formed our understanding of the art economy in the region at the turn of the twentieth century. It comes as no surprise to discover that local networks, self-help societies and studio-based exhibitions were vitally important in sustaining the region's creative industry — its artist community — and to realize that much of the art produced *in* the region was also produced *for* the region. The points of comparison with other turn of the century artists' colonies are as clearly in her text, as the unique light and atmosphere of the north east.

Collaborations in the north east are often held up as examples for others in Britain to follow. In the case of the present exhibition, the expertise of Northumbria has once again fitted comfortably alongside curatorial skills of colleagues at the Laing Art Gallery. In this regard, Ruth Percival, Assistant Keeper at the Laing, has approached the task with great sympathy and imagination. There is now a generation's worth of such collaborations between the university and the Laing Art Gallery which have greatly enriched our understanding of the region's artistic heritage

Kenneth McConkey
University of Northumbria

Introduction

Less than two miles north of the river Tyne in the north east of England lies the former fishing community of Cullercoats, which was the location for a thriving colony of artists during the period c.1870-1920. This book, and the exhibition which accompanies it, examines the work of these artists and the conditions that fostered and maintained this colony. The focus will naturally fall on the main professional artists of the group — Henry Hetherington Emmerson, Robert Jobling, Arthur Hardwick Marsh, Isa Thompson, George Horton, John Falconer Slater and John Charlton — although occasional visitors such as John Atkinson, Ralph Hedley and Thomas Swift Hutton are also represented. Cullercoats also attracted a small number of more nationally renowned artists in its early years, including William Quiller Orchardson, John Dawson Watson, Frank Holl and, most famously, the American artist Winslow Homer. His 18-month sojourn in Cullercoats marked a turning point in his artistic development and provided material to which he returned throughout his career. For the first time the Cullercoats work of all these artists is brought together, revealing the richness of artistic life at Cullercoats at the end of the nineteenth century. But this project also has a wider purpose; that is, to compare the art of the Cullercoats colony with that of similar contemporary coastal colonies and to understand why Cullercoats has, until now, been largely forgotten.

The late-nineteenth-century phenomenon of the artists' colony has increasingly attracted the attention of academics and art lovers in recent years. Scholarship in Britain has focused primarily on the twin colonies at Newlyn and St. Ives, or taken the form of surveys of the more famous European colonies. This literature is very diverse in style and content, yet is united in its exclusion of Cullercoats and its artists. It is clear that part of the reason for this is that colony art has been appraised primarily in relation to international Naturalism and the 'avant-garde', with artistic worth gauged by the success or notoriety achieved at the major metropolitan venues in London, Paris and Munich. The Cullercoats artists, by concentrating on a regional marketplace, have hitherto slipped through the net.

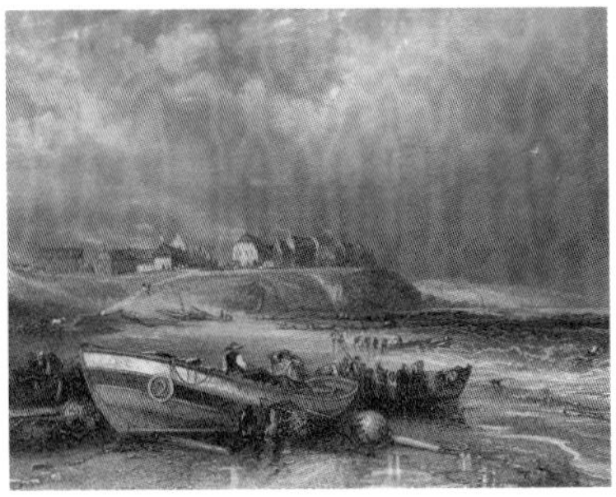

FIG.1
George Balmer, ***Cullercoats***, c.1820; engraving by W. Finden Laing Art Gallery

However, they have not been entirely ignored. The general reappraisal of Victorian art has revived local interest in a number of the region's foremost artists of the period, resulting in exhibitions of the work of John Atkinson (1981), George Horton (1982), Winslow Homer (1988), Ralph Hedley (1990), Robert and Isa Jobling (1992) and Henry Hetherington Emmerson (1995). But with the exception of the large body of mainly American scholarship on Winslow Homer, these north-east artists have been understood in splendid isolation, with little attempt to site them either in relation to each other, to contemporary British art or within the wider context of the colony phenomenon. Yet the most cursory examination reveals significant parallels between the subjects, techniques and styles found in the Cullercoats pictures and those of the colonies at Staithes and Newlyn particularly.

Cullercoats had a long tradition of artistic activity before the colony developed. Artists such as Thomas Miles Richardson, John Wilson Carmichael and Henry Perlee Parker regularly used Cullercoats as a sketching ground during the first half of the nineteenth century (fig.1). But this activity was too sporadic to be regarded as 'colony'-based. An art colony involved a group of artists living and working in a specific place over a significant period, whose work generally shared similar techniques and subjects presented by the particular location. The colony provided mutual support, sometimes leading to the formation of art schools, clubs and exhibition spaces. The late-nineteenth-century Cullercoats group seems to conform to this; but the first chapter will explore the more specific characteristics of coastal colonies, using contemporary accounts to understand Cullercoats' position in relation to other British colonies.

The second chapter will examine how the particular social and economic climate supported such a large body of artists working in one place. Who collected Cullercoats paintings and how did the artists resist the lure of London by stimulating and sustaining a market for their pictures over such a lengthy period of time?

In chapter three, the eminent Homer scholar, Abigail Booth Gerdts, uses her extensive knowledge of Homer archive material to provide a considered view of that perennial conundrum, 'why did Homer come to Cullercoats?'

Finally, the book will examine the Cullercoats pictures, following the subject categories of the exhibition. But, with an eye on the 'bigger picture', the groups of paintings are examined in terms of wider influences. It then becomes clear that issues of nationalism and regionalism, race and gender, and the impact of tourism, urbanisation and industrialisation, must all be considered as possible influences on, and points of entry into, the paintings produced at Cullercoats and other colonies.

Together, the book and exhibition confirm the place of the thriving colony of artists living and working at Cullercoats c.1870-1920 within the broader national and international colony movement.

1 Cullercoats and the Colony Phenomenon

Cullercoats had been recognised as a popular location for artists since the 1820s and developed into a thriving colony during the 1870s. It was arguably the first British coastal colony, yet it rarely features in the ever-growing body of literature on this phenomenon.[1] The neglect of Cullercoats seems to be largely bound up with its uniquely regional bias in membership, exhibiting sphere and patronage. This chapter will explore the common characteristics of colonies, how Cullercoats was perceived by contemporary audiences and whether the understanding of the north east in mainly industrial terms contributed to the marginalisation of the Cullercoats colony.

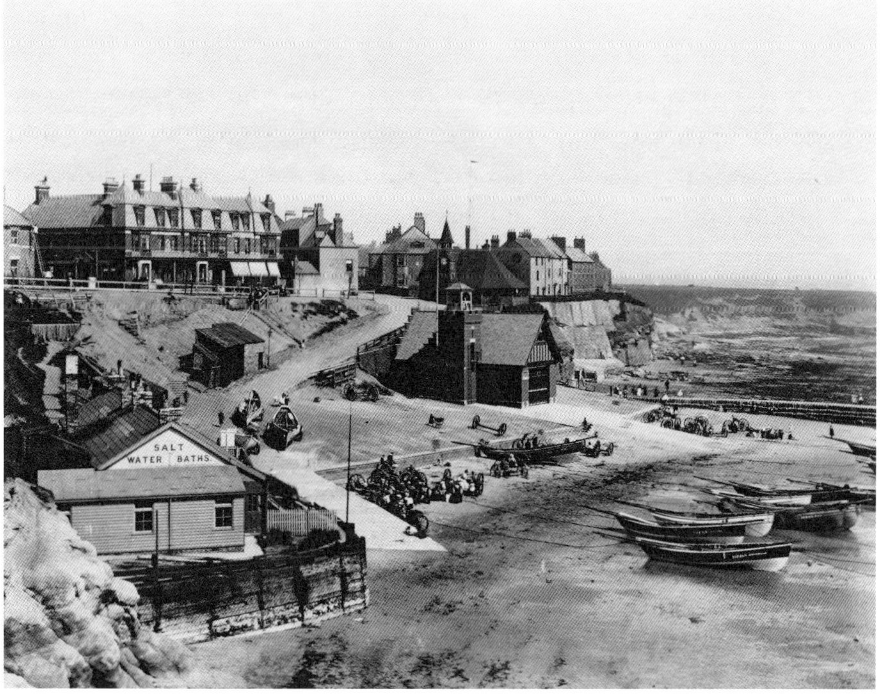

FIG.2
Cullercoats, c.1890; photograph; Newcastle Libraries & Information Service

Research on the formation of nineteenth-century artists' colonies in Britain and Europe has stressed the influence of the artists' student experiences at French colonies.[2] But, whilst the artists of Cullercoats and

Staithes had trained in Paris, Antwerp or London, there seem to be no links to any French colonies, suggesting that nostalgia for student experiences was not a factor in their subsequent emergence.[3] However, a number of other characteristics can be identified which are common to European colonies, which will be explored in relation to Cullercoats.

The Place

Location and People

Colony locations were invariably 'removed' from the urban landscape and provided opportunities for the artist to represent a 'pre-industrial' environment. A typical contemporary account declared, 'In Cullercoats everything is primitive ... [it] has been untouched by the waves of change.'[4] Coastal colony locations shared a common architectural feature of old fishing villages — the houses huddled together with their backs to the sea.[5] St. Ives' houses were 'Fortresses against Atlantic storms, strongly based, with no windows in their granite fronts except right up under the eaves.'[6] At Staithes 'the houses, instead of facing the sea, mostly turn their backs on it, and look out on one another, or on the steep cobble-stone-paved High Street.'[7] Cullercoats was also arranged in this way, with the cottages nearest the sea facing in on each other around a series of 'yards' (fig.3). The terraces of elegant town houses commanding sea views were a distinctly Victorian development which betrayed no concern with the practicalities of living so close to the sea all year round.

The indigenous workforce of these small coastal settlements were thought of as old-fashioned, hard-working, strong, usually of 'ancient stock', deeply religious, uncorrupted, living according to ancient customs and attuned to 'nature'. The Cullercoats fisherfolk 'might trace a direct descent from the Vikings' and had 'changed little in dress, in manners, or in speech' since the days of the Armada.[8] There are many contemporary accounts of fisherfolk described in such terms:

> *Endurance is not so much a necessity to fisher nature as courage. The men — and women too — have not only to bear with the elements, they have to battle with them for daily bread. They must perforce be quick, strong and self-reliant in their dealings with wind and wave. So perhaps they do gain that look of ... complete development, which, added to their fine, strong, robust looks, raises them above any other section of the working classes that I know ... They have a rugged independence which makes them intolerant of patronage.*[9]

FIG.3
Nancy's Yard, Cullercoats, 1915; photograph; Newcastle Libraries & Information Service

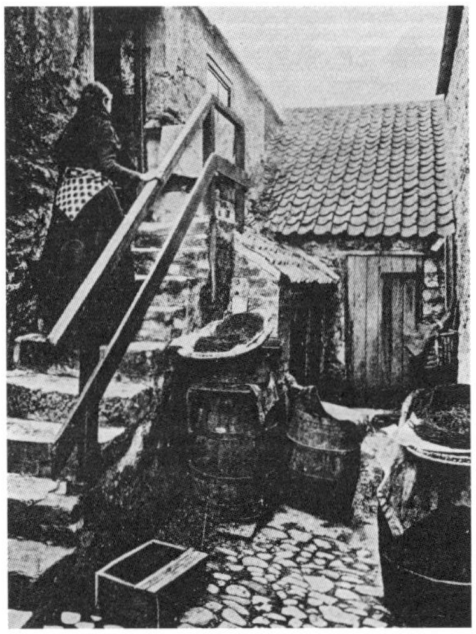

Similarly, the survival of traditional costumes, customs and superstitions was chronicled by contemporary writers such as Alice Meynell, Lillias Wasserman, R J Charleton and Laura Knight. Both Meynell and Stanhope Forbes praised the traditional dress of the Newlyn fishermen

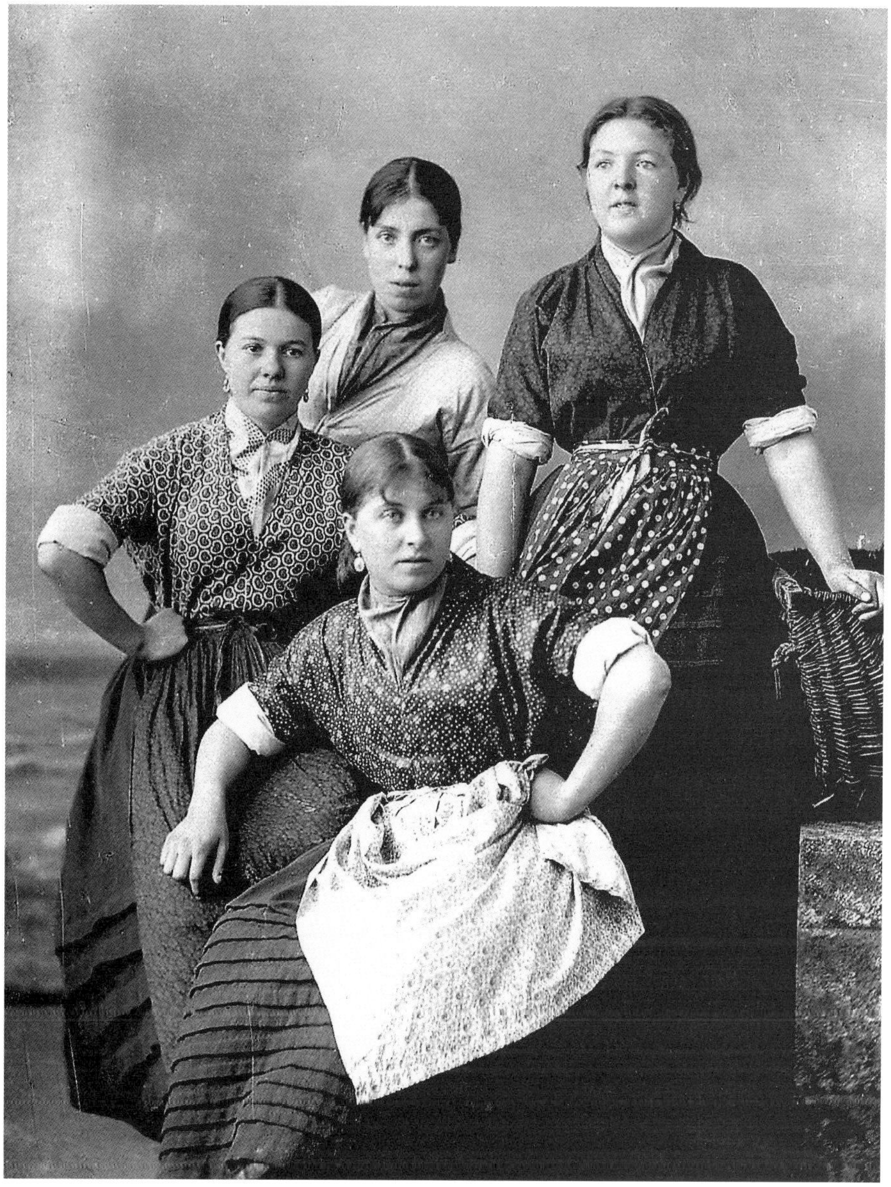

Fig.4
Fisher Folk, c.1900; photograph;
Newcastle Libraries &
Information Service

although they bemoaned the fact that the local women had taken to wearing, 'fringes, pigtails, crinolettes and other freaks of fashion all very well in a stylish London beauty, but appalling with these surroundings of sea, boats, fish, etc.'[10] This, however, was not a problem at Cullercoats or Staithes: 'They keep apart, intermarry amongst themselves, stick to their own ways, and wear their own particular costumes, just as their fathers and mothers, and grandfathers and grandmothers did before them.'[11] However, visible signifiers such as costume were often transposed by artists into surroundings in which they did not belong, to act as signs of status, i.e. a generic 'fisherman' rather than a particular one. At Cullercoats the distinctive blue 'tucked' skirt became an important signifier of location, ignoring the fact that it was a common garment in fishing villages all along the Northumberland and south-east Scottish coasts (fig.4).[12] The late-nineteenth-century focus on regional costume was fostered by the contemporary fascination with ethnographical study which has been linked to nationalistic tendencies throughout Europe. It was hoped that by capturing the 'essence' of the lives of peasants and fisherfolk in their 'pre-industrial' habitat this would help revive national identity and culture.[13]

Access

The accessibility of colony locations was also an important factor. The journey to a colony was always slightly more arduous than a day trip to the suburbs or seaside and, initially at least, always involved a change of trains and a walk or horse ride to the final destination.[14] This represented a symbolic shedding of the urban/modern for the pre-modern, part of the essential 'voyage of discovery' which was bound up with the contemporary rhetoric of the 'anti-tourist'. This rhetoric tried to assert a more 'authentic' experience of travel, a searching for a superior emotional/aesthetic experience from nature through a more total immersion in it. But even contemporary travel writers hinted at the ultimate futility of this quest:

> *The anti-tripper has left the breezy coasts and superb sands of the popular bathing towns and sought out-of-the-way villages ... Hence a vast number of new watering-places have been developed ... As they become popular, the ingenious anti-tripper moves on and opens up a new Filey for every Scarborough, a new Lowestoft for every Yarmouth.*[15]

Most colonies also ultimately underwent this appropriation, both by tourists curious to see for themselves the scenes portrayed so graphically year after year in annual exhibitions, and by the inevitable influx of amateur 'Sunday painters', lured by the promise of plentiful picturesque subjects. By 1890 one Newcastle critic noted, 'Mr. Jobling has made Cullercoats famous by his canvases, and by-and-by he will be the means of over-running the village with tourists.'[16]

Both the Cullercoats and Staithes colonies contained a high proportion of artists from surrounding towns and cities, thereby significantly lessening the sense of discovery. However, it is significant that artists travelling to Cullercoats by train would have experienced a journey which took them from the depths of urban Newcastle, through Tyneside's industrial heartland along the banks of the Tyne, before emerging into the fresh air of the coast. This journey was, therefore, still a sort of symbolic flight from the industrial landscape, almost a journey back in time.

Artists chose locations which had already been 'made safe', a tamed and reachable nature located 'in the past' rather than 'far away'. Part of the initial attraction for artists settling at Cullercoats or Staithes was that they could feed off the tourist trade for at least part of the year.[17] Yet their refusal to record signs of the tourist or the more famous local landmarks, helped perpetuate the 'anti-tourist' myth.[18]

NATURE

The 'natural' conditions of a location also played a part in artists' choices. The American artist Birge Harrison describing Concarneau said, 'The most agreeable season of the year ... is perhaps the winter and the early spring, for, owing to the proximity of the Gulf Stream, the climate is always mild, and the prevailing weather in the year's infancy is a beautiful silvery gray, without rain'.[19] This compares closely to Meynell's account of Newlyn: 'The possibility of painting out of doors all the year round is what principally has made this part of Cornwall famous and originated the 'Newlyn brotherhood'; this, and an equally grey climate which allows the study of the model in diffused daylight.'[20]

Whilst the east-coast colonists could not claim the benefits of the Gulf Stream, much was still written of the natural beauties of Cullercoats: 'In the fresh grey of morning, when the sunlight flashes back from the sands, and the receding tide has left behind it a series of shallow pools, such a scene ... lifts the fisherman's calling into the region of poetry, from which indeed it is seldom far withdrawn'.[21] Or:

> *The sea may not be so blue nor the skies so sunny as on the south coast of our island, but the horizon seems further off, the expanse of sky and sea grander, and the effects more striking ... There are few things so impressive as our gigantic panoramas of cloud, or so beautiful as our wind-swept seas, with their innumerable hues, fleeting and returning as the lights and shadows come and go.*[22]

Similar sentiments, praising a particularly 'north European' atmosphere, were recorded about Staithes by Laura Knight. Thus the output of these colonies, with their stormy seas or clear grey skies, echoes other writers' attempts to reclaim Britain's Anglo-Saxon or Celtic cultural past as part of a (re)defined national identity.

PRACTICALITY

Having chosen a location it was important that certain practical considerations could be met. The availability of co-operative models was crucial, a 'ready and willing' supply being more likely if a colony had a prior history as a sketching ground. Stanhope Forbes remarked that artists will congregate, 'in places where their oddities are known and their motives understood'.[23] This could explain the ease with which artists at Cullercoats were accepted into the community, since some of the older inhabitants (for example Joe Robinson, a favourite model of J D Watson and W Q Orchardson) had modelled for artists such as Henry Perlee Parker earlier in the century.

Even the notoriously insular inhabitants of Staithes seemed to accept the influx of artists fairly easily. Peter Phillips suggests that this was made possible by the serious dedication with which the artists worked, 'which appealed to the local population'.[24] Yet Laura Knight made it clear that artists provided an important source of income, in modelling fees, lodgings and studio rentals, for locals who were often poverty-stricken and starving.[25]

Local economies seemed to adapt quickly to artists' needs, both in terms of models, accommodation and studio space, and in providing materials and even exhibition space. Cullercoats artists could rely on supplies from either Newcastle or North Shields, and as well as setting up their own clubs, could use the growing number of commercial galleries and exhibition spaces which were spawned. For example, *Wards Post Office Directory for Newcastle 1863-4* (prior to the Cullercoats colony) lists two artists' colourmen, five picture framers and eight pictures dealers: by 1890 there were four colourmen, 22 picture framers, nine 'fine art' dealers and four picture restorers.

Colonists were often able to survive by being able to pay for their keep either heavily in arrears or by giving paintings in lieu. Anecdotal accounts suggest that this was particularly common at student-based colonies in France and Holland. There is little evidence of this happening at Cullercoats, although George Horton recalled exchanging pictures for food after being ejected from the family home, and anecdotes about Victor Noble Rainbird swapping sketches for alcohol in northern pubs are still common currency locally to this day.[26]

The Colony

Various accounts of colony life throughout Europe make it clear that no two colonies ever worked in quite the same way. Perhaps because of this Nina Lübbren defined them by what they were not, maintaining that colonies were not set up as alternative exhibition venues or schools to rival official ones, although these often developed later. They did not draw up manifestos or communal programmes, or publish journals. Also, the fact that, stylistically, their work was usually too dissimilar to be called a 'school' made classification difficult. She claims that colonies tended to be regulated by personal relationships between individuals who felt valued for 'who they were' rather than 'what they represented'.[27] However, this was true only of certain colonies, most particularly the French colonies and during the infancy of Newlyn, Skagen or Staithes. St Ives was unique amongst British colonies in maintaining this ethos, perhaps because its more fluid membership moved between St Ives and colonies in France, Denmark and elsewhere. At Cullercoats and Staithes a core of older artists settled with their families in, or near, the village, providing stability to the life of the colony. This allowed many of the younger artists at Cullercoats to live elsewhere, or share studio space in Newcastle.

Membership

All colonies had some degree of fluidity in membership, perhaps most obviously with the influx of urban-based artists during the summer months. However, even the most settled full-time members of colonies often left for prolonged periods, to fulfil commissions or go on sketching trips abroad. This fluidity played an essential part in the survival of colonies, not only in allowing for the stimulation which new horizons brought to long-term members, but also as a means of importing new ideas and 'fresh blood' to ward off the dangers of stagnation.

Another common feature of the colony was the 'father figure' or unofficial leader. Of the more stable colonies it seems that Staithes was exceptional in having no particular leader, although the more established artists such as Charles Mackie, Fred Jackson and Mark Senior acted as mentors to the younger ones, giving advice and passing on commissions.[28] Henry Emmerson was acknowledged by all in the north-east art world as the patriarch of Cullercoats, a reputation based not on age or skill, but on his ability to get on with everyone, giving him a very broad-based acquaintanceship and sphere of influence. This is made clear by a number of writers: 'Mr. Emmerson was perfectly at home in the drawing room of the great, the parlour of the middlemen, and the cottage kitchen of the humble. Utterly incapable of frigid formalities, he beamed as heartily in the company of a peasant or fisherman as in that of a lord.'[29] He was also one of the first artists to settle permanently at Cullercoats (buying a house there in 1866), where many of the early London-based visitors congregated whose works arguably helped bring Cullercoats to the attention of the art world. His kindnesses were legendary, often trying to secure commissions for impoverished artists from his patron Lord Armstrong.

Emmerson equally endeared himself to the people of Cullercoats. At a party in his honour he was presented with a silver spectacles case inscribed, 'Presented to H.H. Emmerson by the fisherfolk and his friends of Cullercoats, 12th July 1894'. At his death the following year, he was accorded the honour of a traditional fisherman's funeral. The true extent of his leadership was perhaps only appreciated after his death, whereupon factionalism threatened the very survival of the main exhibiting forum in Newcastle, the Bewick Club.

Support

Arguably the most important feature of any colony was the opportunity for mutual support. This could take many forms, from friendly criticism and discussion to the establishment of new exhibition venues, art clubs and art schools. Although uniformity was a potential problem, the benefits probably far outweighed the pitfalls, especially for younger artists. As Ralph Hedley maintained:

> *the great good that is got in working in classes is this — ... anyone can see other peoples [sic] bad drawing but cannot always see his own, but if he can point out the defects in others' work there is sure to be someone who can 'go for him' and point his out.*[30]

However, Laura Knight suggested that this type of mutual support and criticism was not so readily available to single female colonists. Until her accidental meeting with and subsequent lessons from Mackie, she claimed she was almost completely isolated from the main (male) body of artists at Staithes.[31] Her experience seems to have mirrored that of Isa Thompson, who, as a woman, was barred from the committee of the Bewick Club and, although she had been producing Royal Academy pictures at Staithes since the early 1890s (even before Knight's arrival), was only admitted onto the periphery of the group after her marriage to Jobling.

At Cullercoats it would seem that much of this mutual support came in the form of various art clubs set up around the area — at Newcastle, North and South Shields, Whitley Bay, Sunderland, Morpeth, Bedlington — some of which also served as art schools. A commentator on the Bewick Club noted:

> *Its classes, and the assistance which the members of the Club receive from and give to one another, have done much to raise the standard of excellence that characterises the local school of painters; and its exhibitions ... have undeniably helped forward that very useful attribute of modern civilisation — 'art culture'.*[32]

The importance of fostering patronage via local exhibitions is a factor which differentiates Cullercoats and Staithes from other colonies. The products of most European colonies were never primarily aimed at or intended for a local market. But at Cullercoats and Staithes local exhibition opportunities were vital to the colonies' survival. In 1901 the Staithes Art Club was formed to organise an annual exhibition at the Fishermen's Institute, moving to larger premises in Whitby in 1904. They also tried to send work to Bradford since it had a reputation for being more 'artistically-minded' than London and the dealers more readily bought 'pictures which were much in advance of their time.'[33] Still, both Cullercoats and Staithes artists recognised the need to acquire the kudos which went with a successful exhibit at the Royal Academy if they hoped to attract critical acclaim and (hopefully) a more secure patronage base.

Social Life

The social opportunities afforded by being surrounded by like-minded individuals played an important role in the survival of colonies. As H J Thaddeus recalled: 'The life in the open air, together with the absorbing, delightful occupation of painting from nature, followed by the pleasant reunions in the evening, constituted an ideal existence to which I know no parallel.'[34] In many colonies social gatherings took place in artists' homes, or involved sporting and social events arranged with the 'locals'.[35]

At Cullercoats, artists' social events were mainly organised around the clubs to which they variously belonged. The composition of satirical songs seems to have been especially popular. One, entitled 'Printed from a

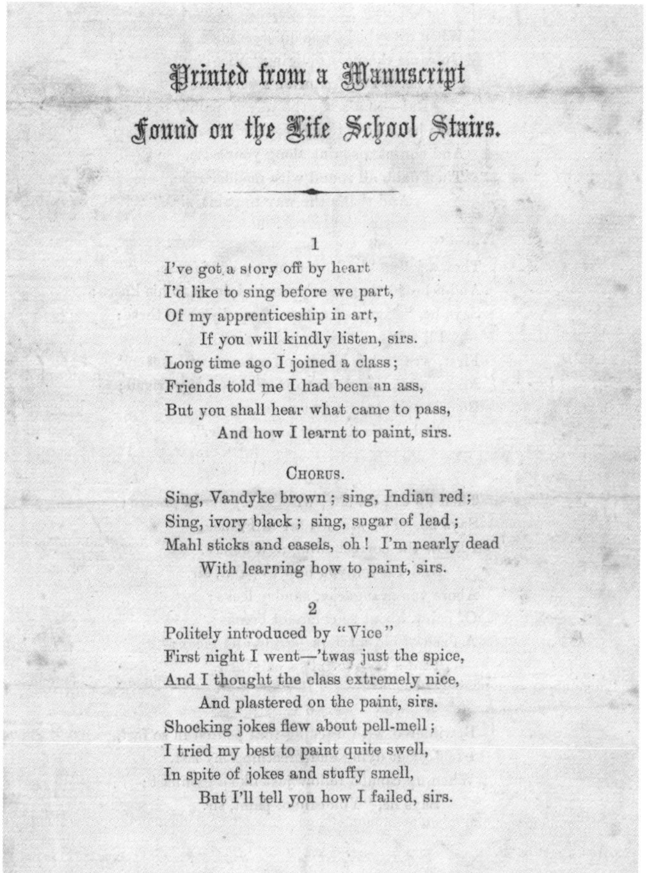

Printed from a Manuscript
Found on the Life School Stairs.

1

I've got a story off by heart
I'd like to sing before we part,
Of my apprenticeship in art,
If you will kindly listen, sirs.
Long time ago I joined a class;
Friends told me I had been an ass,
But you shall hear what came to pass,
And how I learnt to paint, sirs.

CHORUS.
Sing, Vandyke brown; sing, Indian red;
Sing, ivory black; sing, sugar of lead;
Mahl sticks and easels, oh! I'm nearly dead
With learning how to paint, sirs.

2

Politely introduced by "Vice"
First night I went—'twas just the spice,
And I thought the class extremely nice,
And plastered on the paint, sirs.
Shocking jokes flew about pell-mell;
I tried my best to paint quite swell,
In spite of jokes and stuffy smell,
But I'll tell you how I failed, sirs.

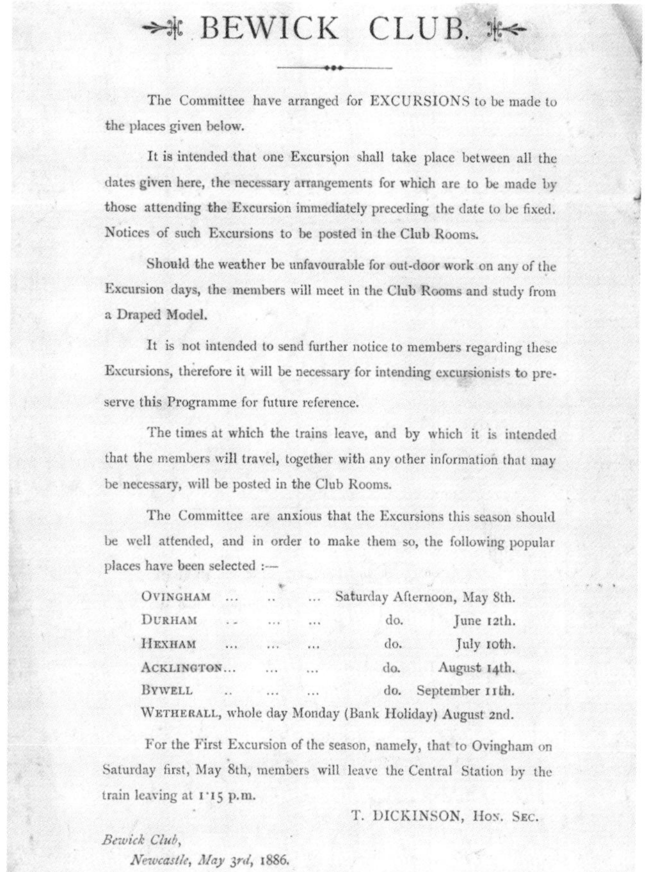

BEWICK CLUB.

The Committee have arranged for EXCURSIONS to be made to the places given below.

It is intended that one Excursion shall take place between all the dates given here, the necessary arrangements for which are to be made by those attending the Excursion immediately preceding the date to be fixed. Notices of such Excursions to be posted in the Club Rooms.

Should the weather be unfavourable for out-door work on any of the Excursion days, the members will meet in the Club Rooms and study from a Draped Model.

It is not intended to send further notice to members regarding these Excursions, therefore it will be necessary for intending excursionists to preserve this Programme for future reference.

The times at which the trains leave, and by which it is intended that the members will travel, together with any other information that may be necessary, will be posted in the Club Rooms.

The Committee are anxious that the Excursions this season should be well attended, and in order to make them so, the following popular places have been selected :—

OVINGHAM	Saturday Afternoon,	May 8th.
DURHAM	do.	June 12th.
HEXHAM	do.	July 10th.
ACKLINGTON...	do.	August 14th.
BYWELL	do.	September 11th.

WETHERALL, whole day Monday (Bank Holiday) August 2nd.

For the First Excursion of the season, namely, that to Ovingham on Saturday first, May 8th, members will leave the Central Station by the train leaving at 1·15 p.m.

T. DICKINSON, HON. SEC.

Bewick Club,
Newcastle, May 3rd, 1886.

FIG.5
'Manuscript of a Song found on the Life School Stairs'; Julian Brown

FIG.6
Bewick Club List of Excursions 1886; Julian Brown

Manuscript found on the Life School Stairs' (fig.5) satirises various club members and their different ways of working. Jobling is 'the Vice' and Emmerson 'a jolly old fellow' with 'a beard without end, [and] a wide-awake hat to inspire you'. These and others all offer a new member conflicting advice until finally agreeing that 'the best way to paint is to paint what you see.'[36] The Bewick Club also arranged regular excursions for its members (fig.6). In a letter from Richard Hesketh (secretary of the Bewick Club) to Hedley it is clear that an effort was made to foster camaraderie between different art clubs: 'the day we arranged for Hylton is the one on which the Sunderland Club goes there — we thought it would be nice to fraternize.'[37]

In 1900 a group of Cullercoats artists, together with local writers, journalists, musicians and intellectuals, formed the Pen and Palette Club, devoted purely to socialising.[38] Aaron Watson, the first President, explained: 'Men of various callings but kindred tastes, they wished to make a sheltered place where they could meet and enjoy each other's company; encourage each other if need be, and by chance, and when occasion offered, do some work for the world.'[39] Its activities included guest speakers (among early ones were George Clausen and Walter Crane), exhibitions of members' artworks, and two 'sketching nights' per month. Horton's reminiscences make much of the activities of the club, which he claims were based on the Savage Club in London, to which both Watson and Thomas Eyre Macklin were affiliated. This highlights a very interesting parallel with the activities of some of the Staithes artists. In 1897-8 the Leeds Savage Club was formed at a meeting in Owen Bowen's Leeds studio; the 50 or so members included Senior, Bowen and possibly other Staithes artists. The chief 'Savage', the Leeds art dealer and framer Edmund Bogg, explained the club as a 'gathering together of kindred spirits typical of the Bohemians for convivial and congenial amusement and recreation.'[40] The similarity to Watson's statement is striking. The Leeds group held their 'pow-wows' at each other's studios until the outbreak of World War One. Given Senior's connections with the London art scene, he may also have been a member of the club in London. It is possible that the intention in Newcastle was given impetus by the example of Leeds via Jobling's connections with Staithes. Perhaps most importantly, the existence of both clubs highlights the more self-sufficient nature of the art markets surrounding Cullercoats and Staithes, providing as they did excellent 'networking' opportunities.

Of all the Cullercoats artists it was, perhaps predictably, Emmerson who most involved himself in local social events. As well as being involved in the football and cricket clubs, he organised and took part in concerts for local charities.[41] At one event he, along with Hedley and other local 'notables', played members of the jury in a charity performance of *The Pickwick Papers* at Newcastle's Theatre Royal. However, as with other colonies, sketching trips also fostered camaraderie amongst the artists. Horton's writings chronicle sketching trips with various artists including the Ogilvie brothers, Robert Watson, Clive Blacklock and Aaron Watson. Jobling went on frequent sketching trips, staying with Emmerson at Tosson in 1879, around Northumberland with Stephen Brownlow, and to Holland with John Hodgson Campbell in 1907, as well as his annual trips to Staithes with Isa Thompson after 1895. Circumstantial evidence suggests Hedley went to Staithes with both Jobling (see plate 24) and W H Charlton in the mid-1880s. He also went to the Cornish colonies, although we do not know if he was accompanied.

Much has been made of Winslow Homer's notorious aloofness by a myriad of writers trying to account for his arrival in Cullercoats as evidence of some personal trauma. Some anecdotal evidence suggested that Homer found it easier to befriend the 'locals' rather than the artists — A B Adamson relates tales of billiards at the Bay Hotel (then called the Huddlestone, where Homer initially stayed) and friendship with the fisherman, Ralph Brunton.[42] However, W W Tomlinson referred to the fact that Homer 'met, and took an interest in a young artist of eighteen — Thomas Eyre Macklin'.[43] Given the reliability of the rest of Tomlinson's account, there is little reason to doubt this remark. Whilst a healthy scepticism must accompany the reading of George Horton's reminiscences, it is interesting that he never claimed to have truly met Homer. Instead, he seems always to have glimpsed him from afar. In his tale of seeing Homer coming out of a Cullercoats butcher's shop with a bullock's heart, it is Fred Ogilvie who recognises him and remarks, 'That's Homer! Get out of his way or we'll never get anything done. When he's in that state he'll keep us with him all day!'[44] The implication is, of course, that Ogilvie has been caught like this before and knew well enough to avoid Homer 'in that state'. There is nothing in the rest of Horton's article to suggest that this was alluding to Homer's alleged drink problem, or an attempt to bask in his reflected glory. But at a basic level it suggests that Homer did socialise with at least some artists at Cullercoats.

Belonging

Unlike artists of a number of European colonies who remained aloof from everyday village life, British colonists seem to have fostered close links with villagers. One critic writing of the Newlyners commented, 'So strong is their attachment to the old village that they are building themselves studios all over it. We have much to thank them for. They are circulating money and as a whole are ever ready to assist in anything which pertains to the wellfare [sic] of the town.'[45] In 1890 an Industrial Class was opened at Newlyn to teach the young fishermen other skills. Run by J D Mackenzie, the teaching staff included Thomas Cooper Gotch, Frank Bramley and Percy Craft.

The involvement of Staithes artists in the life of the village was well documented by Laura Knight. There is the impression that the community was so close-knit that active participation in all its events was not optional. Knight describes Sunday teas after Chapel and the elaborate preparations for the annual 'Love Feast' (fair). Hill had memories of more dramatic events:

> *Whenever there was a storm or a shipwreck we were always ready to give a hand launching the lifeboat, and we often gave shelter to fishermen from the cobles who had been forced to run for a strange harbour. I think it was that feeling of mutual help and camaraderie which fostered such a good feeling with the fisher folk.*[46]

Life at Cullercoats seems to have followed a similar pattern, with Emmerson even becoming a member of the Cullercoats Volunteer Life Brigade and accorded the traditional fisherman's funeral at his death. A H Marsh was also accorded the same honour in 1909, although it remains unclear whether he too was a member of the V.L.B. Although not a permanent member of the Cullercoats colony, J D Watson had become sufficiently attached to the fisherfolk that when the coble of his favourite model, Joe Robinson, was lost in a storm, Watson paid for a replacement.

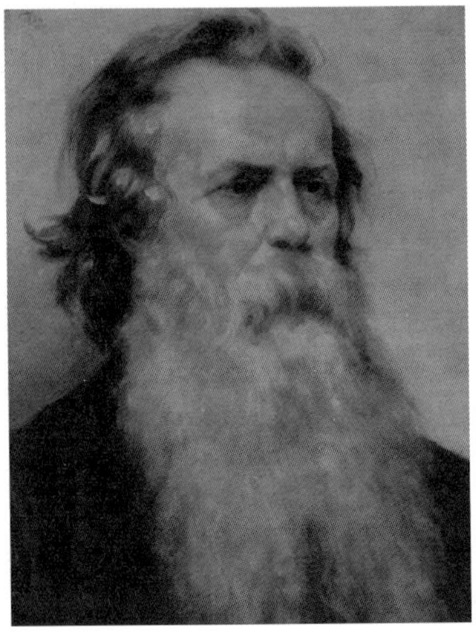

FIG.7
Ralph Hedley, ***Portrait of H H Emmerson***, 1884; Julian Brown

FIG.9
Robert Jobling, Bewick Club Illustrated Menu 1886; Julian Brown

Artists and Anecdotes

Colonists did not usually depict their own experience of colony life, but preferred to concentrate on the local people or scenery, to fulfil the urban audience's demand for images of pre-industrial life. This artistic 'non-presence' was reinforced by the artists' methods of depicting the locals — showing them engaged in everyday tasks rather than being obviously posed, implying that the artist was not intruding in any way, indeed was unnoticed

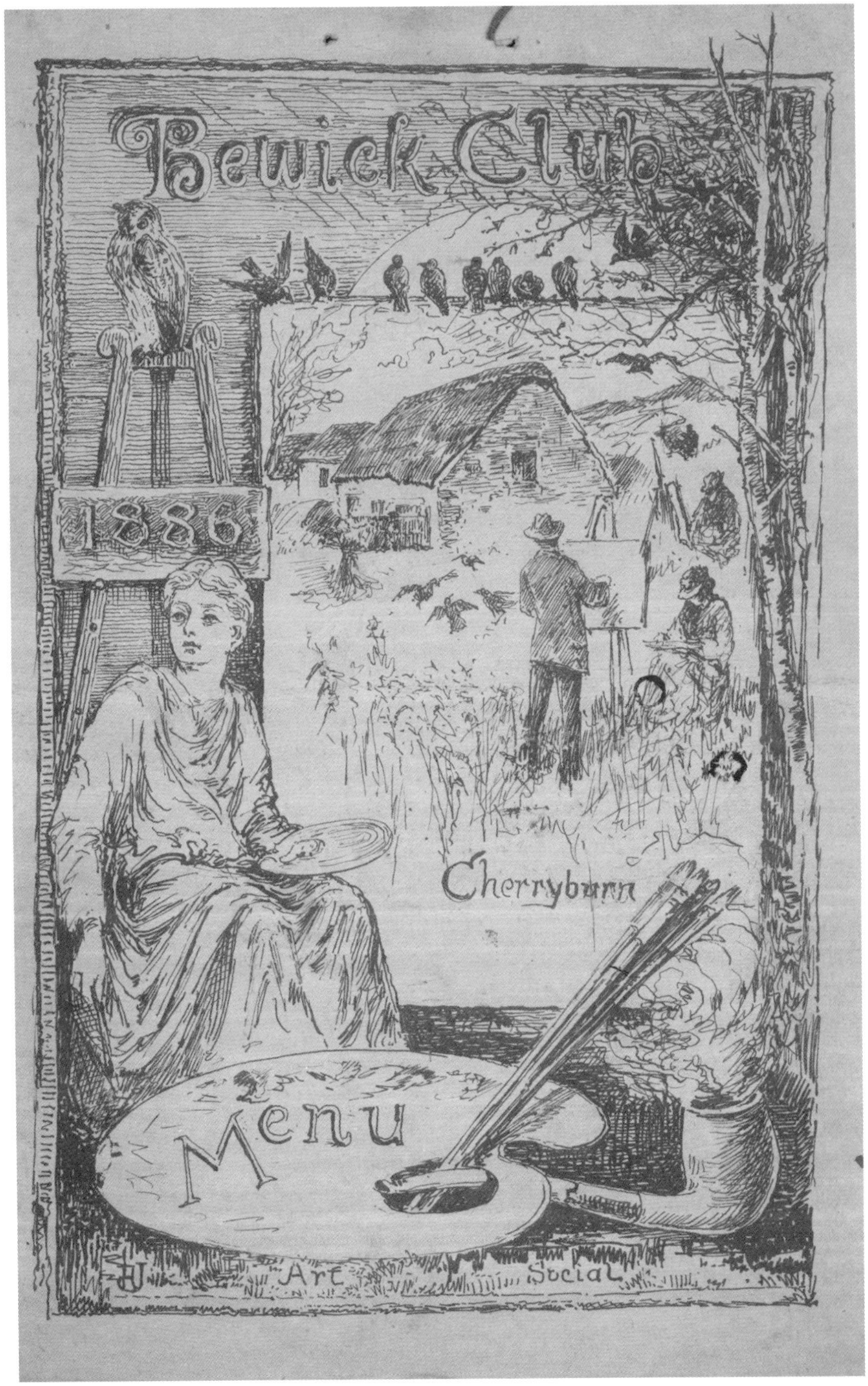

or invisible to the model/subject. There are exceptions to this: A J Munnings depicted Laura Knight painting at Newlyn; Mark Senior's *At Runswick* 1906, shows his pupil Gertrude Hudson painting *en plein-air*; and *A.G. Stevens Sketching* is a small picture by Ernest H Rigg.[47]

There are a number of sketches and portraits of Cullercoats artists, some showing the artist at work, but none of which directly links artist to location. There are several portraits of Emmerson: two by Hedley of 1884 (fig.7) and 1895, one by John Chambers and one by Watson. Watson also portrayed Marsh; whilst Hedley's *My Neighbour* c.1891-2 (fig.8) shows Stephen Brownlow working in his studio. The only group sketches seem to be those for the illustrated menus of the annual Bewick Club dinner. In 1886 Jobling produced one showing the club members sketching at Cherryburn (fig.9) and in the following year Hedley portrayed them working from a model (fig.10). In 1889 Chambers illustrated the menu with another sketch of Emmerson, surrounded by vignettes of Jobling, Hedley and Surtees (fig.11). Whilst these works may attest to the affection and esteem between the various artists, they tell us little about the experience of colony life.

There are, however, many more photographs which show the artists at various colonies, working and at leisure. Because they were probably intended as personal mementoes rather than for public consumption, it was safe to expose the presence of the artist in the landscape. But it is notable that, with the exception of a photograph of Jobling and friends sketching (fig.12), we never see the artist working from the model *en plein air*. This suggests that the photographs were not intended as records of artistic practice at the colony. It is tempting to think that, as with painting, to photograph an artist and his/her model was to expose the myth of an 'unmediated' portrayal of fisherfolk/peasant life.[48]

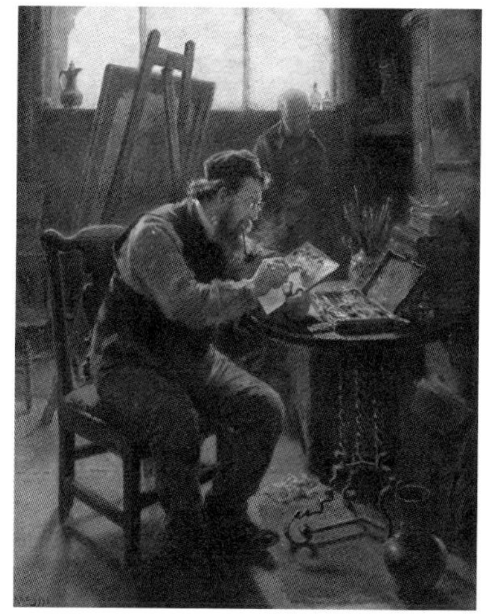

FIG.8
Ralph Hedley, ***My Neighbour***, 1892; Shipley Art Gallery, Gateshead

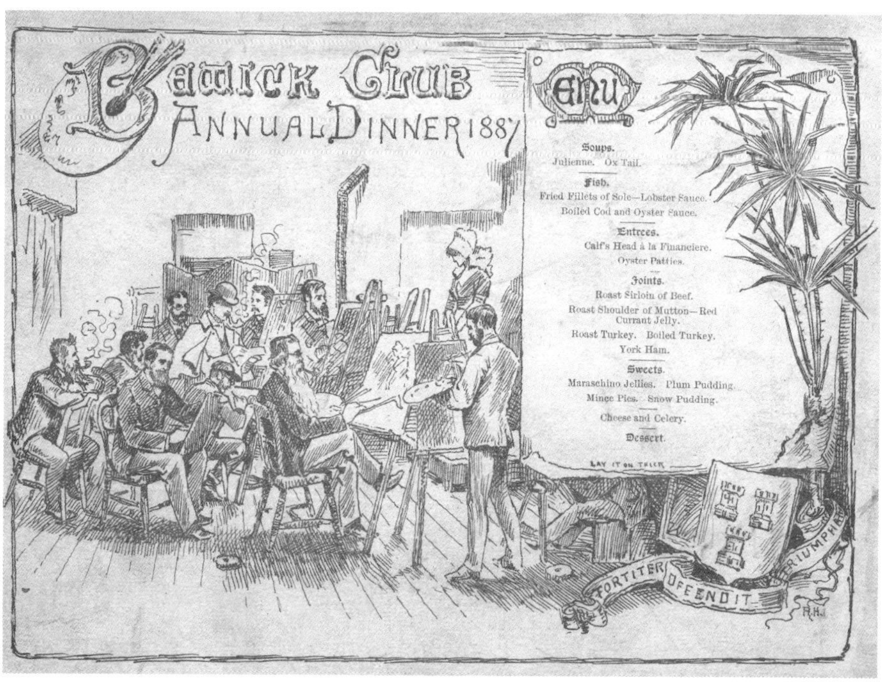

FIG.10
Ralph Hedley, Bewick Club Illustrated Menu 1887; Julian Brown

But if paintings of colony life are scarce, this is more than made up for by anecdotal personal recollections.[49] Taken together, they describe the regular events (such as Sunday night meetings at Staithes) which made up colony life, events for which there is little or no pictorial evidence. One particular theme that recurs in many accounts is that of the hardships endured to 'get that picture'. John F Slater relates how:

At first I used smaller canvases on which I made my sketches, because of the trying experiences with rain, sleet and snow … but further knowledge enabled me to work direct on the picture itself upon the spot, and so I obtained work

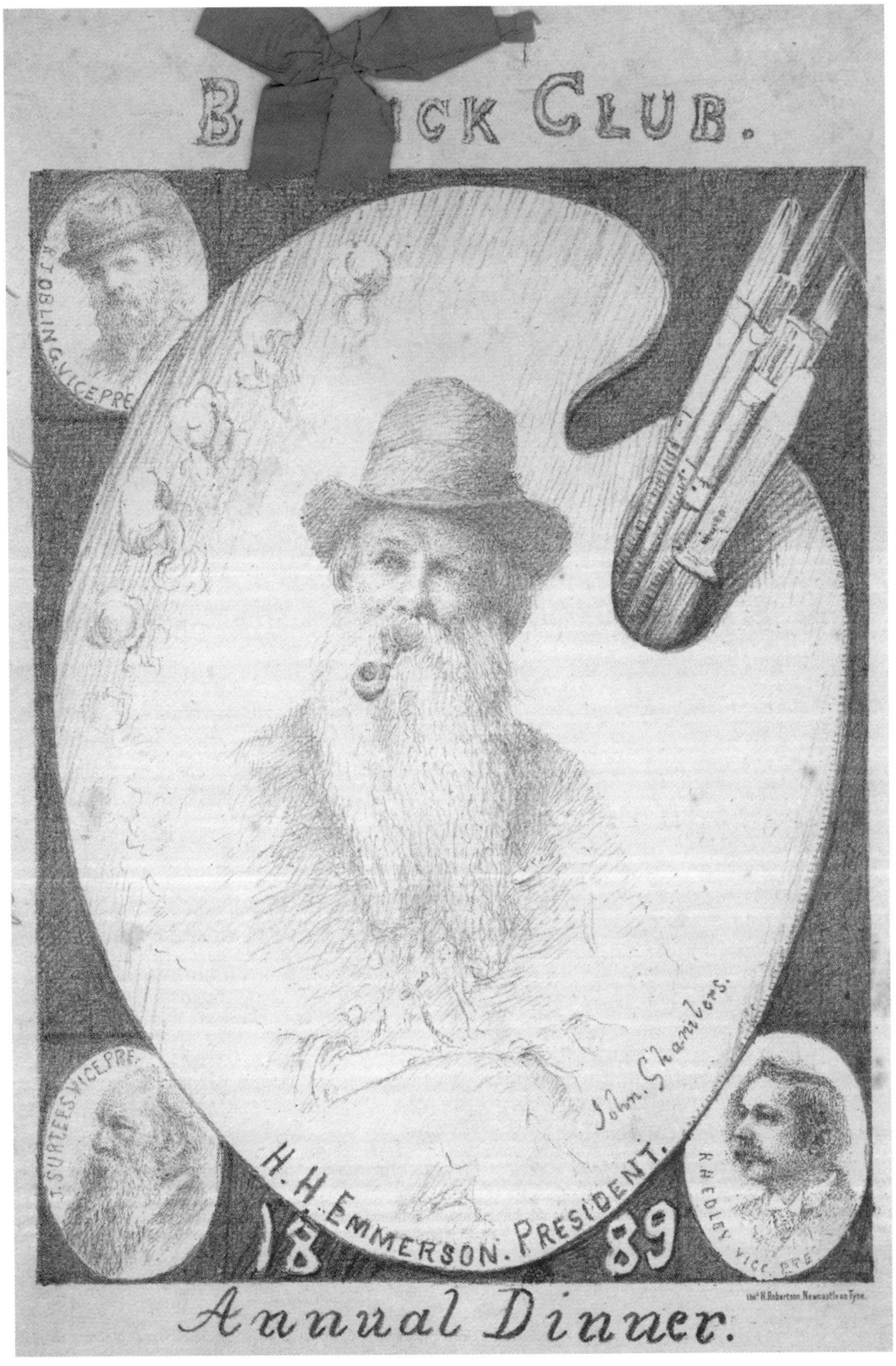

FIG.11
John Chambers, Bewick Club Illustrated Menu 1889; Julian Brown

which to me was better for possessing spontaneity, vim, and the truth of Nature's atmosphere.[50]

He goes on to describe the difficulties with one particularly large canvas which had to be secured by ropes around the rocks and weighed with stones, but adds, 'the wind, increasing in violence, nearly blew the canvas, easel and moorings away. I do not remember having had a harder or more thrilling tussle' (fig.13). Hill recounts a similar tale at Staithes,[51] verified by Laura Knight's memories of Fred Jackson: 'He painted out of doors in any weather. Under the mittens he wore, his hands were swollen, stiff and chapped, as were the edges of his ears and the wings of his nostrils.'[52] Horton's reminiscences and letters are full of references to bouts of bronchitis (the 'artist's complaint') caused 'because we sit out for hours at a time in all sorts of weather'.[53]

These anecdotes suggest that an essential part of the experience for these colonists was their 'immersion' in nature; enveloped by rain, mist, gales and grey skies: plein-airism with passion.[54] The implication is that the immersion in nature enabled the artists to render a more 'truthful' depiction of the scene, making their particular vision of the pre-modern landscape seem 'natural'. The beneficial effects of this communion with nature on the artists' work are also widely documented (see Slater's description previously), supposedly making it more 'continuous and sincere'.[55] There is of course nothing new in this; one only has to recall Turner lashing himself to the mast of the boat in a storm in order to translate that experience into his *Snowstorm — Steamboat Off a Harbour's Mouth* (1842). The difference is, I think, that this practice had become normalised, almost *de rigueur*, for late-nineteenth-century colonists as a means of perpetuating and valourising a particular anti-urban, anti-industrial message.

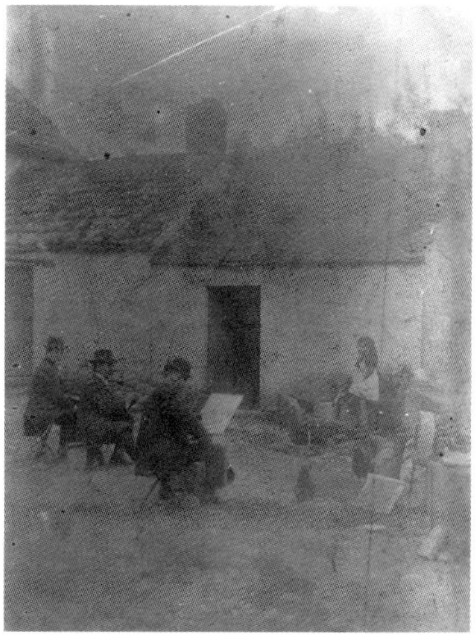

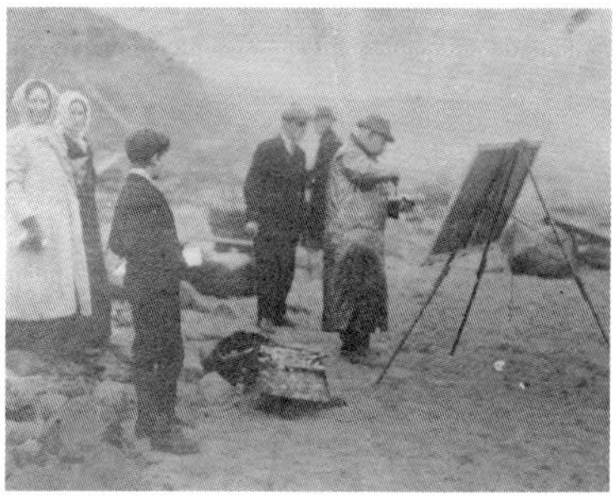

FIG.12
Robert Jobling and friends sketching; photograph courtesy Julian Brown

FIG.13
John Falconer Slater at work; photograph courtesy Marshall Hall

'Style but not Manner'[56]

In general, colonies are characterised by their lack of any one style. However, as the previous section suggests, there were certain common practices, such as the intermittent use of 'square-brush' technique and plein-airism. The latter was practised to a greater or lesser extent in all colonies, despite Forbes' claim that it was this practice which differentiated Newlyn artists from others.[57] The choice of subject, together with the experience of painting 'in nature' reveals a common desire to follow what the artists perceived or positioned as a purer or more 'honest' vision. Whether or not they succeeded is debatable, but what matters here is that it indicates a certain level of consensus.

The influence of Dutch art must also be noted. Whilst it is probably true to say that this affected Staithes and Cullercoats more than elsewhere, this was not exclusively so. Of the Newlyn artists Walter Langley had a particular affinity with the Hague School, easily recognised in his work in terms of palette, use of light and intimate interiors. Amongst Cullercoats artists, A H Marsh's work was likened to that of Josef Israels. George Horton's relationship with Holland spanned over thirty years. He modified his working methods to accommodate constant travel, developing from his laborious 'wash' technique to a 'mosaic' method (fig.14). *The Times* critic in 1922 noted his 'general affinity with the Hague School, practical feeling, refined observation, and sensitive execution.'[58] Horton would have seen Dutch pictures at the Bewick Club in the late 1880s which would have made him aware of the affinities between his interests and the possibilities offered in Holland. However, he did not seek out Dutch colonies as Laura and Harold Knight did, and his notebooks make clear that he was also heavily influenced by Whistler and Sickert. Other Cullercoats artists also worked in Holland, including Jobling, Campbell, Chambers, Rainbird and possibly Slater.

Many of the Staithes Group also sketched in Holland. Laura Knight talks of the revelation of seeing a Hague School exhibition whilst on honeymoon in London in 1903. The Knights made their first trip to Holland the following year, using Laren, a colony started by Israels, as their base. Fred Richardson had also been regularly visiting Holland since 1894, exhibiting the resultant work at Staithes exhibitions.[59] It is possible that Jobling was prompted to visit Holland by seeing the Dutch pictures of the other Staithes artists at their annual Art Club exhibition, where he too subsequently showed his Dutch pictures.

Holland's popularity as a sketching destination was probably due to its accessibility, and because it provided the types of subject the artists were

FIG.14
George Horton, ***Study in Holland***, c.1920; Laing Art Gallery

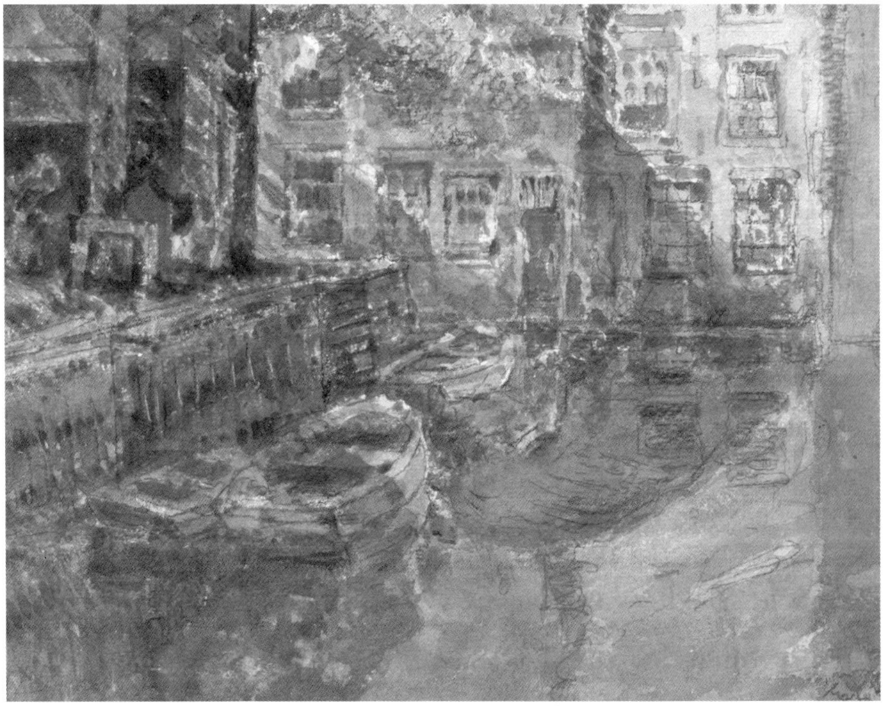

looking for — pre-industrial village communities in 'unspoilt' landscapes bordering the North Sea, where the indigenous population was both 'archaic' in dress and custom and yet familiar with the demands of artists — a 'home from home', a foreign land 'made safe'.

Contemporary Literature

It seems clear that there is little to differentiate Cullercoats from other British colonies, at least in terms of place, conditions and structure, suggesting that an explanation of Cullercoats' neglect lies elsewhere. Contemporary accounts of colonies and sketching grounds in a variety of media, when examined in the context of the 'north east' and other contemporary issues, make it apparent that Cullercoats' position was informed by wider debates, including regionalism and metropolitanism, the 'urban versus rural' and notions of 'difference'.

Colonies and Sketching Grounds

Throughout the 1880s and 1890s art magazines and illustrated journals produced regular features on suitable venues for painting, many of which have already been cited above. These articles tended to take two distinct forms; most commonly they were designed to suggest new or little-used sketching grounds to artists; the others were examinations of already-popular colonies of artists. They all used similar poetic language to evoke possible subjects, typically dwelling on scenery, indigenous population, history, etc and often including practical advice on how to reach the destination or where to stay. They usually included illustrations to depict specific parts of the text,[60] but only rarely were reproductions of actual paintings used.[61]

The Cullercoats artists attracted their fair share of press attention. Perhaps the first to explicitly talk of the artists was R J Charleton's article 'Cullercoats' in the *Magazine of Art* in 1886, which from the outset laid claim to the place as an artists' haven. 'There are not many places in England that can show a better record of service in the cause of art than can the comparatively unknown little fishing village of Cullercoats.'[62] A number of well-known artists and works associated with Cullercoats are mentioned, including J D Watson, Frank Holl and Winslow Homer. In the final paragraph, Charleton took issue with artists who have depicted scenes of rural labour as dehumanising:

> *We cannot see that there is anything essentially melancholy in the weariness which comes of labour undertaken and faithfully performed. There is, on the contrary, something noble and hopeful in the sight of the labour of tilling the earth … Yet, take it at its noblest and best, it lacks the fascination which the element of danger adds to the calling of the toilers of the sea.*[63]

This suggests he was aware of contemporary debates amongst British critics about the adverse influence of Bastien-Lepage's work. Obviously, if British artists also depicted fisherfolk/rural workers as dehumanised this would undermine attempts to offer them as working-class role models. So instead, the paintings of Millet and Jules Breton were championed, their work seen as ennobling and as embodying greater truths.[64]

Charleton used Jobling's illustrations for his article, including 'The Sands at Evening' (fig.15), derived from his 1886 Royal Academy picture, *The Day is Done and Darkness Falls from the Wings of Night.* Although the figures lend meaning to the images, Jobling concentrates on creating a sense of atmosphere and 'place' rather than depicting Charleton's idea of the heroism of their lives. The change of title of this image suggests an interesting anomaly. The verse of the Longfellow poem to which Jobling's painting seems to allude runs:

I see the lights of a village
Gleam through the rain and the mist,
And a feeling of sadness comes o'er me
that my soul cannot resist.

FIG.15
Robert Jobling, 'The Sands at Evening', pub. ***Magazine of Art*** 1886; Newcastle Libraries & Information Service

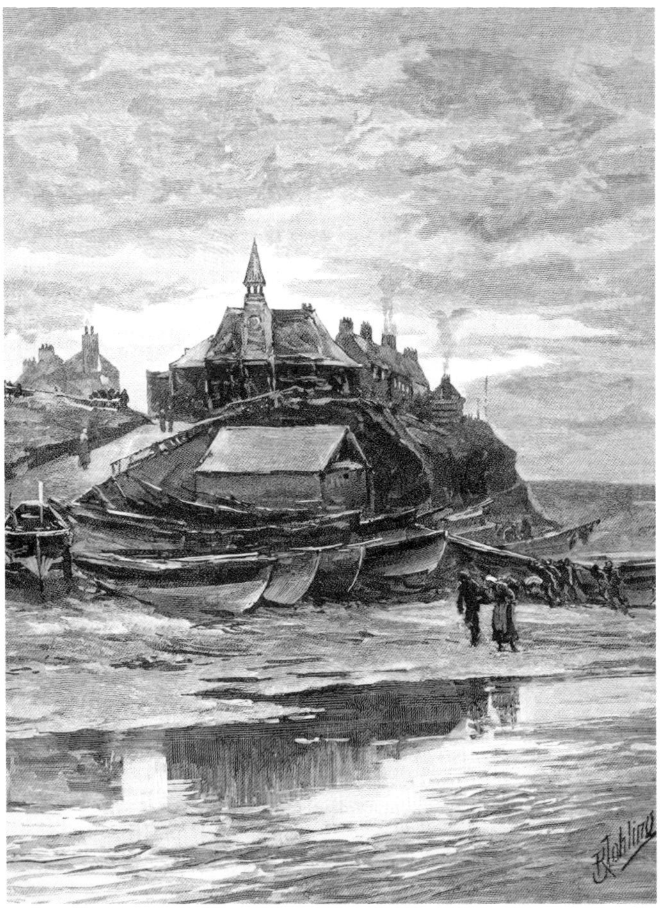

This sentiment contradicts Charleton's assertion that there is nothing 'essentially melancholy in the weariness which comes of labour'. By changing the title and the fact that the reproduced image was in black and white, the poeticism of the original was successfully converted into a more Naturalistic image of fisherfolk life, in keeping with the other illustrations and with Charleton's rhetoric.

At the end of 1886 and beginning of 1887 the writer/journalist Lillias Wasserman (widow of the merchant-turned-Cullercoats artist J C Wasserman), produced two related pieces of work on Cullercoats. The first took the form of a weekly serialised story of an artist in Cullercoats, written for the *Newcastle Weekly Leader*[65] whilst the other appeared as a factual article in the *Art Journal.*[66] Both draw on the same material, yet her treatment of the themes is vastly different, in particular towards the artists of the colony. In the fictional account she rather unfairly demonises local art for its use of heroic types. Yet in the *Art Journal* Wasserman seems to be acting as an apologist for artists of 'heroic' pictures, stating, 'Nature and life being here of the heroic type, painters must needs paint heroic pictures. This necessitates the posing of the models in grand attitudes, whether their real natures correspond or not.' More confusingly, Jobling's pictures were used to illustrate the

Art Journal article, showing scenes typical of his naturalistic output — baiting lines, pulling up cobles, launching the lifeboat and fisherlasses performing the ritual of the moonlit promenade (possibly derived from *A Fisher Song*, shown at the Bewick Club, 1885) (figs.16-18). These illustrations suggest that, contrary to Wasserman's text, Jobling was deliberately demonstrating the potential of Cullercoats to Naturalist artists.

Cullercoats, its fisherfolk and its art colony continued to attract attention from writers of guidebooks, histories and semi-factual tales. For example, Tomlinson's *Historical Notes on Cullercoats, Whitley and Monkseaton* (1893) is a particularly refreshing account which outlined the main artists and works produced at Cullercoats and tried to account for the presence of non-local artists. He referenced other articles on the colony and its associations with writers and musicians, quoting Aaron Watson's description of Cullercoats as 'a little Bohemia-by-the-sea'. Robinson's *Illustrated handbook to the Rivers of the Tyne, Blyth and Wansbeck* (1894) also makes reference to Cullercoats as 'famous as the residence of popular artists' and goes on to outline the attractions of its scenery and inhabitants with the usual poetical lyricism.

W.G.Larkins' 'Reminiscences of Artistic Cullercoats' (1894) was unusual for combining the standard fisherfolk rhetoric with meaningful critiques of various artists' works.[67] It also made use of reproductions of paintings, including a seascape by J W Carmichael, Emmerson's *A Foreign Invasion*, a sketch of two fisher girls by Isa Thompson and two works by Jobling. Cullercoats artists also featured prominently in Rudolf Dircks' article 'Northumberland and Some Artists' in the *Art Journal* of 1904, in which he represented an overview of art in the county, starting with Bewick. Whilst admiring the qualities of 'sincerity, strenuous independence and industry' as exemplified by T M Richardson, Dircks noted the disadvantages for local artists:

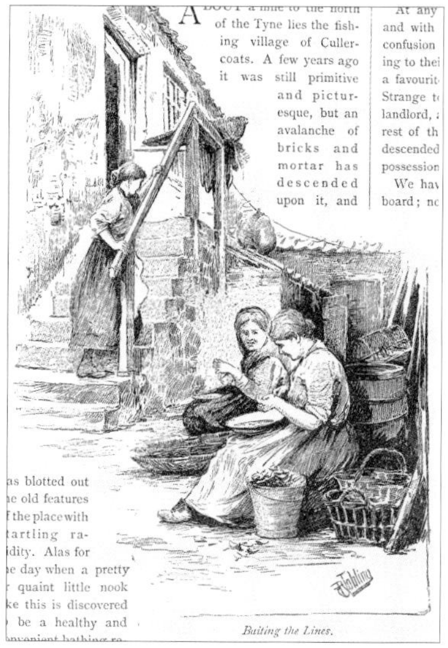

Fig.16
Robert Jobling, 'Baiting Lines', pub. ***Art Journal*** 1887; Newcastle Libraries & Information Service

Fig.17
Robert Jobling, 'Launching the Lifeboat', pub. ***Art Journal*** 1887; Newcastle Libraries & Information Service

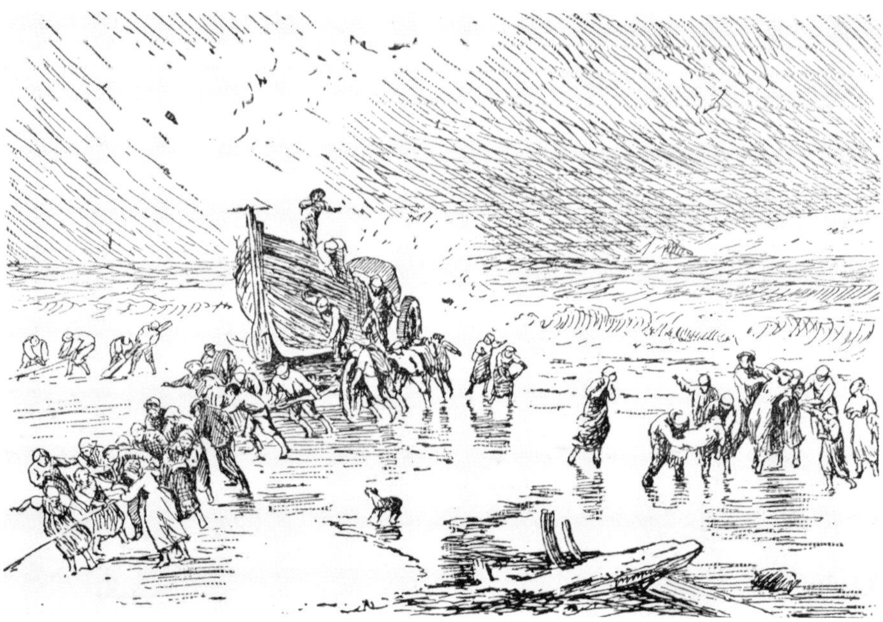

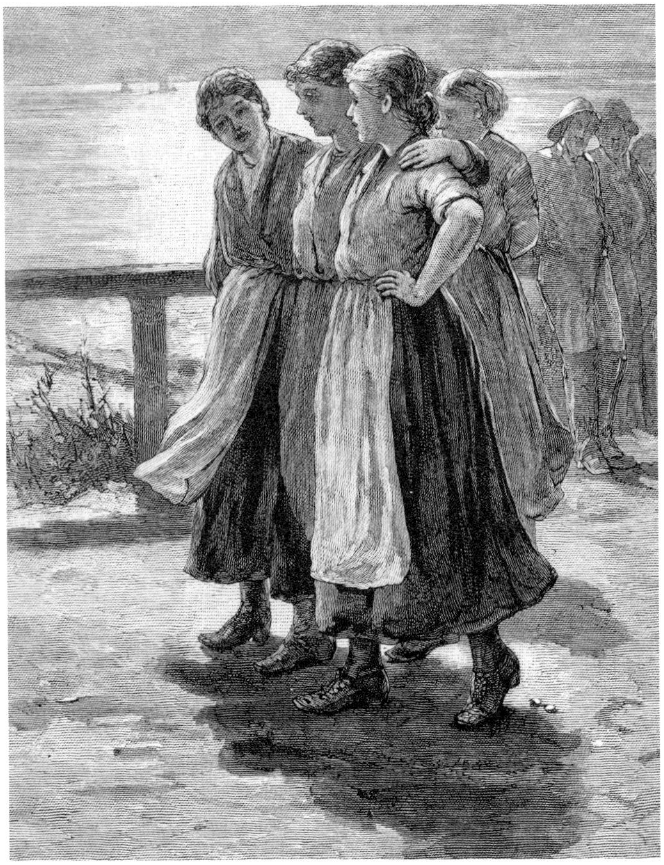

Fig.18
Robert Jobling, 'Singing Ballads', pub. ***Art Journal*** 1887; Newcastle Libraries & Information Service

Your Northumbrian student has … rarely sought London, as a French student seeks Paris. He has been self-reliant, largely content with what he could teach himself, not very impressionable, perhaps, to outside influences, and, in many instances, his art has had, as one says, to take the consequences.[68]

Dircks is guilty of exaggeration here, since many had trained in London and/or abroad, indeed Macklin, Surtees and Charlton were still based in the metropolis. Whilst the others could be described as self-reliant, it was only as a necessary result of their conscious rejection of the London art scene. But the charge of being closed to outside influences does not bear scrutiny, as we shall see later. Dircks contrasted Jobling's and Marsh's Cullercoats pictures. In *Cullercoats* (fig.19) Jobling 'looks upon the people with a poetic and sensitive eye, in their less intense moments. The simplest occasions provide him with all that is necessary'. But with *Winter Fuel Gatherers* (fig.20) Marsh 'is more deliberately concerned with the pathos of character, with the stress of incident; character at the psychological moment of intense energy'.[69] However, these pictures were used alongside examples by non-colonists such as Bertram, Lund, Spence, Hedley, Hatton and Hemy, to demonstrate the variety of northern art. So although the overall tone of the article was very positive, his stress on heterogeneity meant that Dircks failed to convey the existence of a community of artists at Cullercoats.

The Cullercoats colony did attract a wide variety of contemporary literature, usually designed to attract new artists by demonstrating the location's artistic possibilities through the reproduction of Cullercoats-inspired paintings. This follows the pattern of other contemporary articles on art colonies, suggesting that audiences/readers regarded Cullercoats as on a par with other British colonies.

The North East

When we compare the rhetoric of the Cullercoats articles with that of articles about 'Tyneside', the anomalies are starkly suggestive of an alternative agenda. Whilst 'Cullercoats lifts the fisherman's calling into the region of poetry … [and] has been untouched by the waves of change',[70] the Tyne at Newcastle is 'one of the most impressive of all spectacles, short of Hell'.[71] Vernon Lee's account of the 'leaden water, polluted with every foulness' and 'banks of blackish cinders, of white poisonous chemical refuse … of what was once pure live soil, now stained and deadened into something unnatural whereon the very weeds refuse to grow',[72] is echoed by numerous contemporary articles and books.[73] Metaphors of hell and death

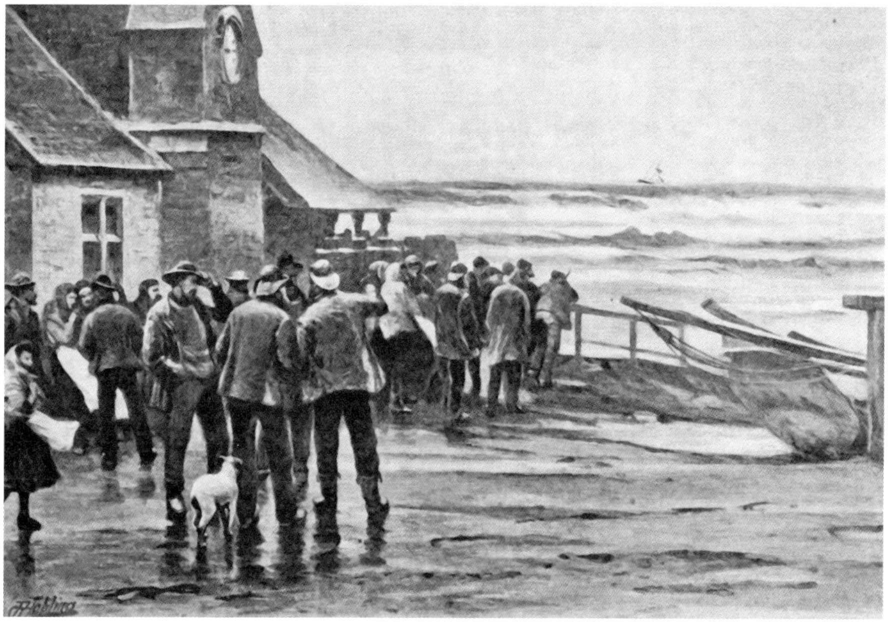

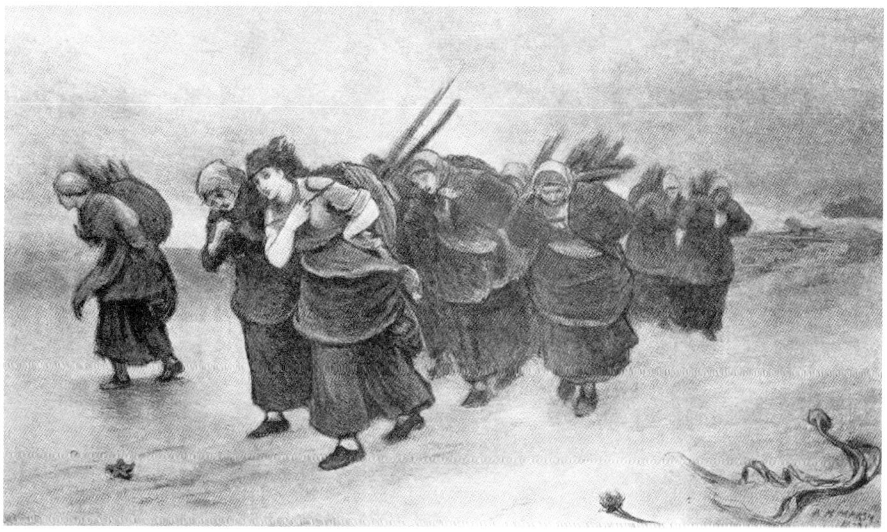

Fig.19
Robert Jobling, 'Cullercoats', pub. *Art Journal* 1904; Newcastle Libraries & Information Service

Fig.20
Arthur Hardwick Marsh, 'Winter Fuel Gatherers', pub. *Art Journal* 1904; Newcastle Libraries & Information Service

litter these accounts: 'tall chimneys belching sulphurous fumes; — black wooded erections, like gigantic scaffolds ... stunted trees gaunt in deformity':[74] 'stygian caves forlorn': 'Cyclopean industry ... Where the shipyard slopes down to the river in a row of iron skeletons'.[75]

Similarly, the 'fine, strong, robust looks' of the fisherfolk is replaced by the 'black, red-faced, and blistered, with flesh in pale creases under the grime, their clothes engrained with dirt, shiny with grease, often tattered, the filthy wisp of comforter round their necks'.[76] The 'habitual dweller' of industrial Tyneside becomes 'somewhat given to inflamed eyelids, a bloated countenance generally, and characteristic twitching at the mouth corners.'[77] So these accounts of Tyneside, written by both local and non-local writers for a national audience, seem to have descended into hackneyed responses to the industrial landscape into which the industrial worker was negatively inserted. Only Charleton, who wrote of the nobility of human toil in his 'Cullercoats' article, was equally positive of the industrial workers, regarding their work as 'labour for Titans'.[78] But crucially, although most of these articles are also illustrated, many again by Jobling, nowhere is the industrial worker depicted close up. Indeed, they are 'Lilliputians',[79] mere indicators of scale in the industrial panorama (fig.21). The artistic community refused to be provoked into any serious depiction of the industrial landscape and its inhabitants, such that the notion of the industrial north east could be maintained without taking on the threatening aspects which a naturalistic pictorial depiction of the industrial workforce may have unleashed.

Conclusions

'Difference'

The discrepancies between these two sets of accounts of the north east cannot simply be explained by ignorance on the part of the writers, since many were local, despite writing for national journals. This suggests that the separation was quite deliberate. During the nineteenth century 'the north' became increasingly equated with industrialism, reinforcing its 'difference' from the southern urban experience. Of course this notion was to a large extent a 'high culture' fiction, maintained in order to

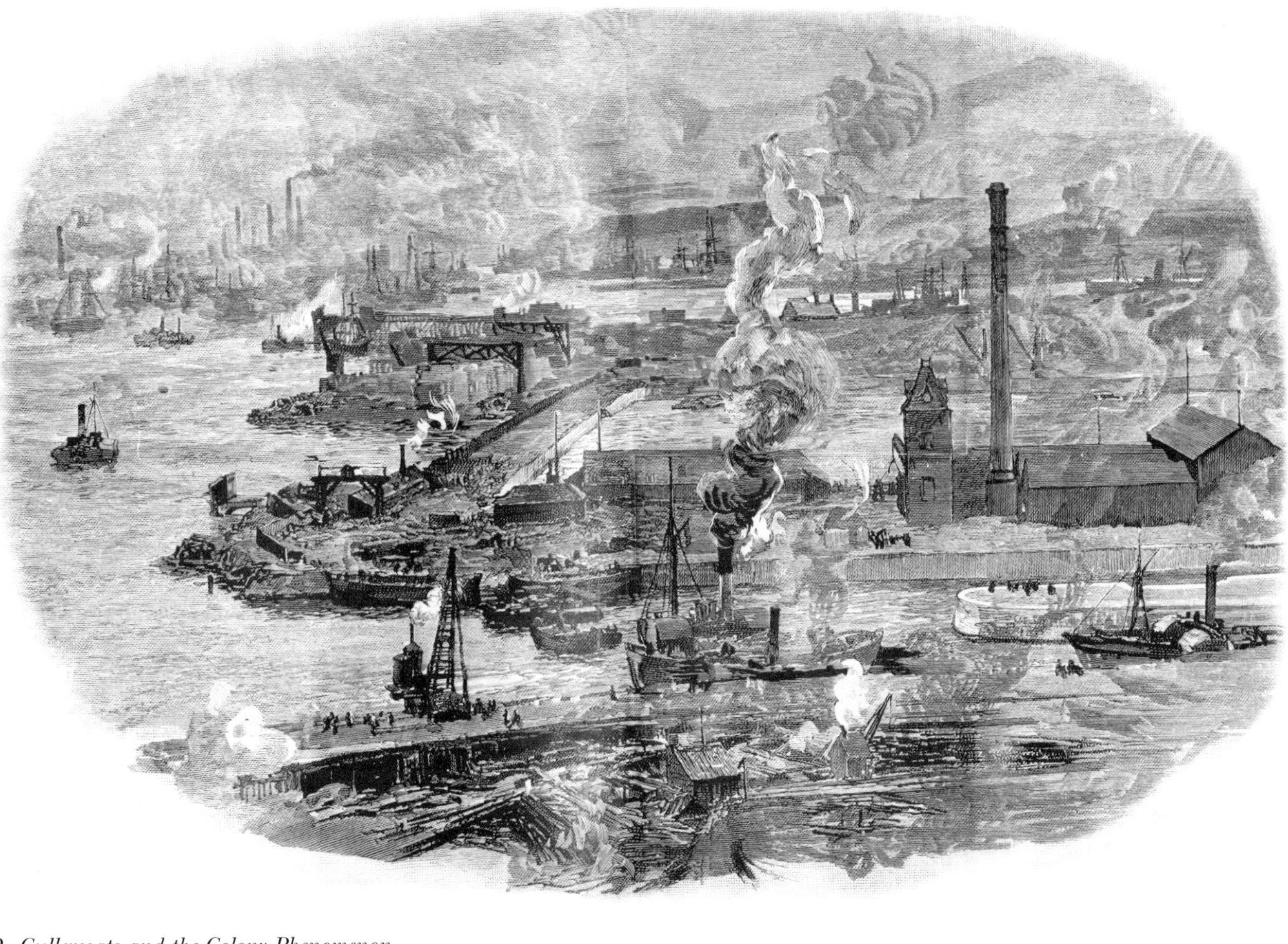

Fig.21
Robert Jobling/William Lionel Wyllie, 'General View of Albert Edward Dock', pub. ***The Graphic*** 23 August 1884; Newcastle Libraries & Information Service

displace the urban industrial experience to a location other than 'the south' or, more specifically, London. This helped to maintain the myth of London as the cultural jewel set in a southern rural idyll.[80]

However, the northern industrial stereotype could not be applied to Cullercoats. It was, of course, still 'northern' but this was of secondary importance. Rather, as the articles suggest, the Cullercoats imagery fitted into a larger, international genre — an 'acceptable' version of working-class life. In the fiction of Dickens, Eliot or Gaskell tales of working-class hardship or discontent could be resolved within the scope of the narrative. But painting does not offer this opportunity; so alternative strategies were developed, including putting the figures into 'the past' or depicting a single figure which could be 'aestheticised' or be made the object of pity.[81]

Faced with the unacceptability of naturalistic industrial imagery, the region's artists and writers turned to the acceptable face of working life — the fisherfolk. The nation's familiarity with Cullercoats was reinforced by a wealth of material from other media. In the first six months of its life *The Graphic* contained images and critiques of pictures on fisher life and sea rescues in virtually every edition. Photographers such as Frank Meadow Sutcliffe in Whitby and Lewis Harding in Cornwall produced images of fisher life which could be widely disseminated (fig.22).[82] Caricaturists, including George du Maurier of *Punch*, poked fun at the nation's obsession with fisherfolk (fig.23). Of course such subjects were also seen on the walls of the Royal Academy and in the pages of the art press from the appearance of the Hague School artists in the early 1860s to the large-scale works still being produced by Newlyn artists after the turn of the century. In a trip to the Yorkshire coast in 1864 to record fisher girls, Arthur Munby recalled: 'I found a civil photographer near the station, and had a talk with him. He often takes photos, he says, of Filey fishgirls, for artists, and sends them to London, even to Florence, to an English artist there.'[83] Similar photographs, aimed at tourists, are mentioned by J S Mitcalf in his *Guide to Tynemouth and Neighbourhood by A Native*, first published in 1880.[84]

The Cullercoats articles were therefore part of a larger body of material in a wide variety of popular and 'high art' media which fed off and informed each other. This suggests an astonishing level of complicity on the part of artists, writers, photographers, fisherfolk and public to maintain an acceptable image of the working class, which, despite regional fluctuations, was obviously a national phenomenon.[85] It was part of a general policy of inclusion, at once embracing yet marginalising (thereby neutering) possible disruptive groups such as the working classes, women, the Irish, etc.[86] During the 1860s Matthew Arnold put forward the idea that provincial cultures should be 'licensed as cultural contributions to English culture', but only as peripheral to the core 'metropolitan' English culture.[87] Newlyn colonists exemplified this relationship by positioning Newlyn fisherfolk within a Celtic framework, whilst ignoring the contemporary problems of mass emigration, the decline of tin mining and the

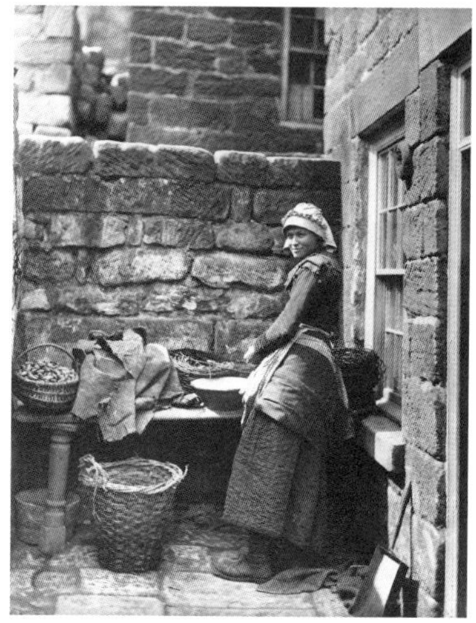

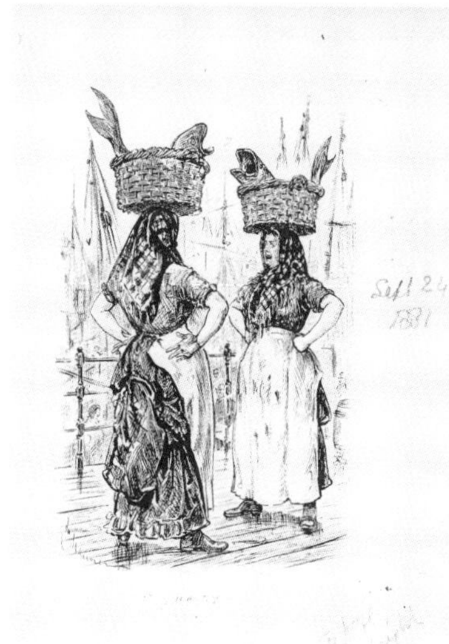

FIG.22
Frank Meadow Sutcliffe, ***Girl Baiting Lines, Runswick***, c.1880; photograph courtesy Sutcliffe Gallery, Whitby

FIG.23
George du Maurier, 'A Powerful Quartet', pub. ***Punch*** 24 September 1881; Trustees of the British Museum

decimation of the fishing industry by European competition. This 'framing' was 'the necessary complement of the artists' affiliation to metropolitan institutions, especially the Royal Academy.'[88]

Northernness

However, we must question the extent to which this also applies to Cullercoats imagery. The crucial difference between the artists at Cullercoats and those at other colonies was that the majority of them were local artists producing works to be exhibited and sold at regional venues. But to what extent did north-east artists deliberately set out to construct a 'northern' image, utilising Cullercoats? Was the choice of Cullercoats a conscious one, based on an awareness of similar subjects from other colonies, or dictated by a rejection of the other subjects to hand, i.e. the urban, industrial or rural? With the exception of a tiny number of privately-commissioned works, the urban and industrial seem to have been largely rejected.[89]

It has been claimed that colonies were often chosen because they filled a prior vision or expectation of particular available subjects. These preconceptions led to the creation of 'place-myths', whereby the artists, through repeated use of certain motifs, actually shaped the audiences' perception of that place.[90] Cullercoats, with its coble-filled harbour, the narrow streets of fishermen's cottages and the distinctive outline of the Lookout House, undoubtedly had plentiful subjects to supply a local market already well aware of similar French and Dutch paintings.

A dearth of first-hand accounts makes it extremely difficult to gauge if the artists actually saw themselves as working together to produce works that presented a coherent and particular image of a northern locality for local or national consumption. George Horton's reminiscences suggest a high degree of camaraderie amongst the north-east artists, and from contemporary press reports it is clear that the image of concerted effort was maximised locally in the push for exhibition spaces.[91] Yet the need to compete for the same small number of patrons was bound to foster individuality, counteracting attempts to portray Cullercoats as the local 'school' and accounting for the diversity of styles which hampered the development of one recognisable 'Cullercoats style'.

This brings us to perhaps the most crucial issue of all — who the Cullercoats artists were painting for. Most of the important north-east artists were regular exhibitors at the major British venues, but they never attempted to present themselves as a group to the outside world in the way that the Newlyn or Glasgow artists did. Their failure to bombard the London market with Cullercoats pictures year after year meant that its identity as a colony was never portrayed forcefully enough in the national art press. Rather than trying to overcome the problems inherent in their distance from London, the Cullercoats artists concentrated instead on building up a buoyant local art market via new clubs and exhibition spaces throughout the region during the 1880s and 1890s. In this respect

Cullercoats was part of a regional attempt to foster a 'northern' identity and culture.[92]

This alternative northern culture had its roots firmly in the past. Throughout the nineteenth century local newspapers, music hall, books, songs and poetry celebrated the region's dialects, often to recount tales of history and myth. ('The Lambton Worm' is one such famous product of the 1860s.) The recovery of the region's past was of crucial importance. The Society of Antiquaries and the Literary and Philosophical Society, and figures such as Dr. Bruce (editor of the *Archaeologia Aeliana*), Robert Spence Watson (who wrote a monograph on the Saxon poet Caedmon in 1877), James Clepham (journalist and antiquarian) and Richard Welford (historian), played a large part in this recovery. Magazines such as *The Northumbrian* and *Tyneside* carried articles on north-east history and tales of Walter Scott, Harry Hotspur, Johnnie Armstrong and border reivers. The

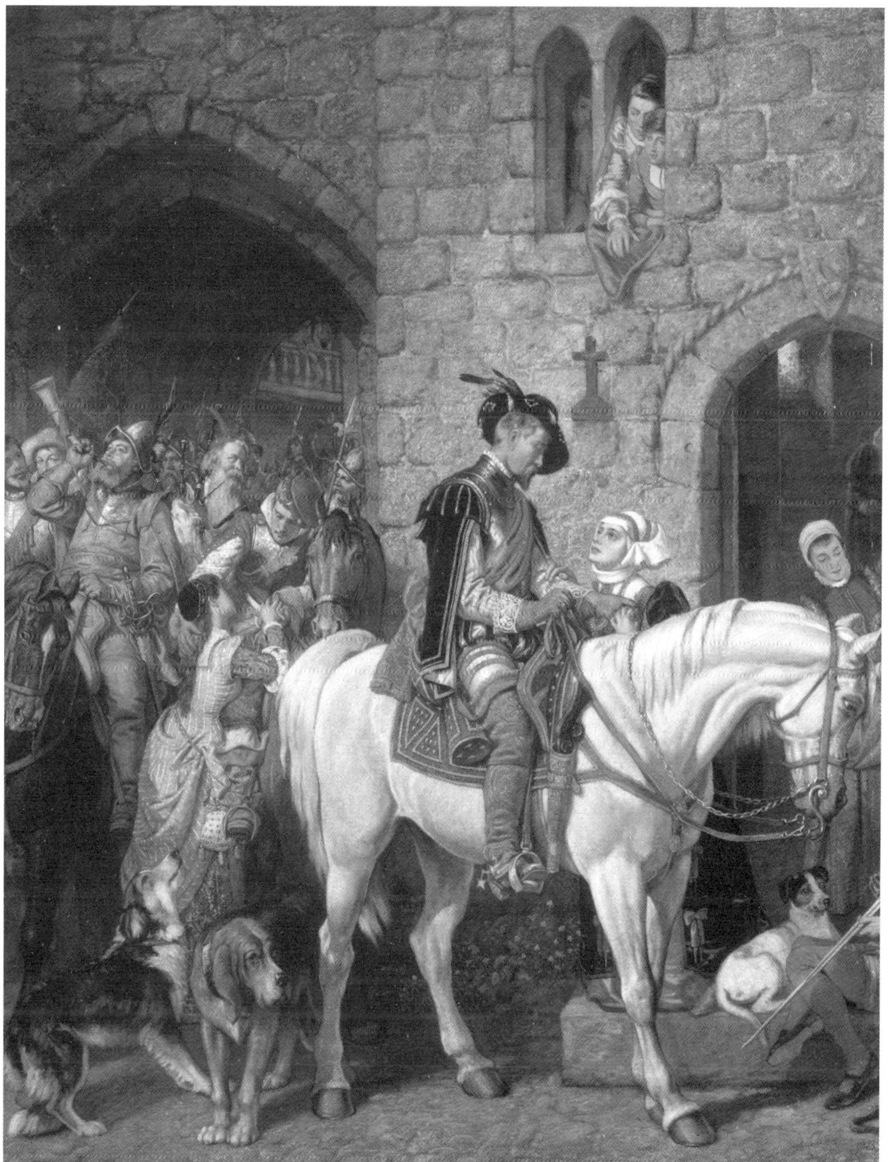

FIG.24
Henry Hetherington Emmerson, ***Johnnie Armstrong's Last Farewell***, 1886; Laing Art Gallery

industrial achievements of the north east were not ignored, but were celebrated either by heroising the inventors — Stephenson, Armstrong, Lowthian Bell, Palmer, Hawthorn — or fetishising the invention — the *Rocket,* the Armstrong gun, the High Level bridge, the steam turbine. Spence Watson's 1885 address to the Bewick Club drew attention to the plentiful supply of artistic subjects to be found in the region's history. This call was answered in particular by Emmerson with works such as *Johnnie Armstrong's Last Farewell* 1886 (fig.24) or *Grace Darling*; and by Ralph Hedley in *The Invention of the Lifeboat, Willie Wouldhave, South Shields 1789,* 1896 and *Scottish Prisoners in the Tower of St. Nicholas* 1899.

Can it therefore be mere coincidence that the writings on Cullercoats which most foster the notion of a coherent artistic colony are those written by locals for a local audience? The colony members' close relationships with local patrons, writers, historians, politicians, inventors, industrialists and businessmen meant that they were inevitably drawn into and bound up with this local drive to promote the north east in the national league of regions. The recovery of so many historically-based local cultural manifestations, including Cullercoats imagery, must be seen as an attempt to create an alternative 'northern' image to counteract the industrial stereotype. But in order to deny the urban, industrial Tyneside, the alternative image was regressive and inward-looking.

The Cullercoats artists subsumed the need for national recognition which, whilst highly laudable, ultimately led to obscurity. Whatever the similarities in subject matter, the art produced at Newlyn was never intended for local consumption, but was part of the appropriation of Cornwall by mainstream metropolitan culture as a site of 'difference'.[93] This different agenda is reflected in the size of the pictures produced — Newlyn producing large-scale 'history paintings' demanding attention and gallery space, whilst Cullercoats works were smaller to accommodate the local domestic market.[94]

However, by the end of the century there was a shift of 'the fulcrum of economic life away from the northern provinces to London, away from manufacturing industry to international finance.'[95] Culturally and intellectually this meant that 'Local art was to become synonymous with inferior and unimportant art in direct correlation to the deterioration in the significance of the regions.'[96] The art of all these British colonies lost much of their relevance as regionalism gave way to a new British urban identity focused firmly on London.

Despite the recent rehabilitation of the art of the Newlyn, Staithes, Walberswick and other coastal colonies, it would seem that the (re)appraisal of Cullercoats has been delayed because of its specifically local nature. The wealth of contemporary literature on the north east and the Cullercoats colony reveals the extent to which Cullercoats imagery played its part in the local construction of an alternative regional identity, and suggests a broader contribution to the wider cultural and ideological changes of the nation.

Notes

N.D.J. = *Newcastle Daily Journal*
N.D.C. = *Newcastle Daily Chronicle*
N.W.C. = *Newcastle Weekly Chronicle*
N.W.L. = *Newcastle Weekly Leader*
N.D.L. = *Newcastle Daily Leader*
S.D.N. = *Shields Daily News*

1 See for example C Fox & F Greenacre, *Artists of the Newlyn School*, Newlyn Orion Gallery, 1979: P Phillips, *The Staithes Group*, Phillips & Son, 1993: K Varnedoe, *Northern Light*, Yale University Press, 1988: A Meynell, 'Newlyn', *Art Journal*, 1889, p.97: R L Stevenson, 'Fontainebleau: Village Communities of Painters', *Magazine of Art*, 1884, p.253: R A M Stevenson, 'Grez', *Magazine of Art*, 1894, p.27: M Jacobs, *Good and Simple Life*, Phaidon, 1985: N Lübbren, *Rural Artists' Colonies in 19th Century Europe*, unpubl. PhD thesis, University of Leeds, 1996 and *Rural Artists' Colonies in Europe 1870-1910*, Manchester University Press, 2001.

2 The practices at Grez, Pont-Aven and Concarneau were indebted to the mid-century colonies at Barbizon and Fontainebleau. See L Newton, *The Cullercoats Artists' Colony c.1870-1914*, unpubl. PhD thesis, University of Northumbria, 2001, pp.96, 117.

3 However, some made friendships with other 'avant-garde' artists during their student days abroad. Jackson met Edward Stott, William Stott and La Thangue; Mayor met Brangwyn, Steer and Sickert; Senior (at Slade School of Art) met Steer, Clausen and Whistler. Henry H Emmerson, John Charlton, J D & T J Watson, G W Brownlow, V N Rainbird and T E Macklin studied in London; John Chambers, Emmerson, Isa Thompson, T B Garvie and Macklin in Paris; and C N and T M Hemy in Antwerp. Most were initially trained by William Bell Scott or his successor at the Newcastle School of Art.

4 A Watson, 'After the Herring', *Magazine of Art*, 1882, p.455.

5 S Howell, *The Seaside*, Cassell & Collier Macmillan Publishing Ltd., 1974.

6 Meynell, op.cit., p.98.

7 'Round and About Whitby', *The Graphic*, 6 September 1884, p.246.

8 Watson, op.cit. See G Allen, 'On and Off Shore', *Art Journal*, 1883, p.287 for a similar description of the Hastings fisherfolk.

9 L Wasserman, 'Some Fisher Folk', *Art Journal*, 1887, p.38.

10 Stanhope Forbes cited in Jacobs, op.cit., p.146.

11 Wasserman, op.cit., p.37. Similar claims were made for other fishing villages including Staithes, Hastings, Whitby, Clovelly and Eyemouth.

12 I am grateful to Adrian Osler for this information.

13 See Jacobs, op.cit., p.15.

14 Colonies that were fed by stations at a distance include Pont-Aven (Quimperlé), Worpswede (Lilienthal), Barbizon (Melun), Skagen (Frederikshaven), Staithes (Whitby), Newlyn (Penzance), Volendam (Edam), Cullercoats (Tynemouth), Walberswick (Southwold).

15 Bernard Becker, *Holiday Haunts*, Remington, London, 1884, cited in Howell, op.cit., p.103.

16 *N.D.J.* 7 May 1890, p.5.

17 See Janet Dunbar, *Laura Knight*, Collins, 1975, in which she claims that Harold Knight used to drink at the local pub in the hope of selling works to tourists.

18 For example, Newlyn colonists did not paint St. Michael's Mount even though it was just across the bay. Similarly, Cullercoats artists rarely depicted the picturesque Tynemouth Priory and Castle.

19 B Harrison, 'Quaint Artistic Haunts in Brittany; Pont-Aven and Concarneau', *Outing* v.XXIV, April 1894, p.30, cited in D Sellin, *Americans in Brittany and Normandy 1860-1910*, Phoenix Art Museum, 1982, p.43.

20 Meynell, op.cit,. p.98.

21 Watson, op.cit., p.455.

22 Wasserman, op.cit., p.37.

23 S A Forbes, 'A Newlyn Retrospective', *Cornish Magazine* v.1, 1898, p.83.

24 P Phillips, 'Britain's Impressionists', *Art and Antiques Weekly*, 9 June 1979, p.23.

25 Laura Knight cited in Phillips, 1979, op.cit.

26 See Horton reminiscences, Horton Archive, Tyne & Wear Archive, courtesy David & Marjorie Redpath.

27 Lübbren, op.cit., 1996, p.32.

28 Roland Henry Hill mentions this of Senior (R H Hill, 'A Seaside Colony of Painters', *Yorkshire Evening Post*, 30 August 1939) and Laura Knight claims to have been given her first commission, passed on to her by Friedenson.

29 Unnamed newspaper account dated 29 August 1895 in the *Oxberry Scrapbook*, 1918, Newcastle City Library.

30 R Hedley, Notes for lecture, 'The Schools of Painting of Today'. MS., J Brown.

31 See L Knight, *The Magic of a Line*, Kimber & Co, 1965, p.131.
32 *N.D.C.* 23 December 1896.
33 Hill, op.cit..
34 H J Thaddeus, R*ecollections of a Court Painter*, London, 1912, p.25, cited in Lübbren, op.cit. 1996, p.22.
35 See Hill, op.cit., for a description of Staithes activities.
36 'Printed from a Manuscript found on the Life School Stairs', a song in 11 verses, MS., J Brown.
37 Letter from R Hesketh, Hon. Sec. Bewick Club to Hedley, dated 10 May 1912. J Brown.
38 Minutes from the first meeting report the presence of A Watson, Macklin, T M Hemy, F S Ogilvie, G Hatton and Horton, with letters of apology from Charlton, F D Ogilvie, Niels Lund and W Hepple. The first committee included Jobling, Watson, Macklin and W C Way. Taken from A G M Sinton, *Pen and Palette Club 1900-1990*, n.publ.
39 ibid.
40 E.Bogg, 'Souvenir of the Savage Club' talk at AGM, 6 January 1899, cited in *Mark Senior 1862-1927*, Wakefield Art Gallery, 1983.
41 These include 'Tableaux Vivants' at Tynemouth in 1886 to raise money for the Village Homes orphanage in Whitley Bay; and arranging the tableaux vivants for Rockliffe Cricket Club's 1887 concert at the parish church hall in Cullercoats.
42 See A B Adamson's memoir of Homer in T Knipe ed., *Winslow Homer. All the Cullercoats Pictures*, Northern Centre for Contemporary Art, Sunderland, 1988. The Studio Gallery of Art, Detroit, U.S.A. has Homer's portrait of Ralph Brunton.
43. W W Tomlinson, *Historical Notes on Cullercoats, Whitley and Monkseaton*, 1893, p.111.
44 G Horton, 'Artist with Craze for Clocks', *Sunday Sun*, 5 March 1939. For the original version see Horton archive, op.cit.
45 *The Cornishman*, n.d. cited in C Fox, *Stanhope Forbes and the Newlyn School*, David and Charles, 1993, p.21.
46 Hill, op.cit.
47 The Danish artist P S Krøyer often portrayed the social events of the colony at Skagen, but I know of no similar pictures by British colonists.
48 G P Weisberg refers to the 'deliberately hidden' methods of naturalist painters who wanted to disguise both the level of orchestration in a composition and the reliance on photography as an aide-memoire, both of which would have exposed the artist's presence and selectivity of image. See G P Weisberg, *Beyond Impressionism. The Naturalist Impulse in European Art 1860-1905*, Thames & Hudson, 1992, pp.8-10, 24-25.
49 As well as those already drawn upon, see for example Frank Richards 'Newlyn as a Sketching Ground', *The Studio* v.29, 1895: W H Bartlett, 'Summer Time at St Ives, Cornwall', *Art Journal*, 1897: E Simmons, *From Seven to Seventy*, New York/London, 1922: W H Low, *A Chronicle of Friendships*, New York, 1908: Sir J Lavery, *The Life of a Painter*, London, 1940: Carl Larsson, Jag, Stockholm, 1931: M Menpès, 'In the Days of My Youth', *Mainly About People*, 6 July 1899.
50 J F Slater, *Odds and Ends from an Artist's Note Book*, Hewitt & Rudge Ltd., 1914, chapter 2.
51 Hill, op.cit.
52 Knight, 1936, op.cit., p.133.
53 'George Horton, Shields Artist, yearns for his home town', *North Shields Evening News*, 24 November 1948.
54 This is similar to the 'sous-bois' experience and work of artists at Barbizon in the mid-nineteenth century, their subjects literally 'under the trees'.
55 Low, op.cit., p.115, cited in Lübbren, 1996, op.cit., p.212. Other examples of this claim are found in L Wasserman, 'Where the North Wind Blows', *N.W.L.* 15 January 1887; W C Symons, 'Newlyn and the Newlyn School', *Magazine of Art*, 1890, p.205, as well as in many of the articles already mentioned.
56 Meynell, op.cit., p.99.
57 Forbes, 1898, op.cit., p.83.
58 *The Times*, October 1922, cited in *The Times* 14 Sept 1957, recording the acceptance by Queen Juliana of two watercolours by Horton, *On the Steiger Canal* (exh Paris Salon 1914) and *The Minister's House, Rotterdam*.
59 Bagshawe, Hill, Friedenson, Mason and Jackson also went to Holland. See Phillips, 1993, op.cit.
60 These included, 'Walberswick', *Art Journal*, 1880; 'Clovelly', *Magazine of Art*, 1880; 'Little Known Sketching Ground', *Art Journal*, 1881; 'Artist Strolls in Holland', *Harpers New Monthly*, 1883; 'Round and About Whitby', *The Graphic*, 1884; 'Lady Hilda's Town', *Art Journal*, 1885; 'Norfolk Broads', *Art Journal* 1886; 'A New Ground For Artists', *Art Journal*, 1886; 'Cambridge as a Sketching Ground', *Art Journal*, 1890; Richards, op.cit.; Bartlett, op.cit.
61 See for example Meynell, op.cit.; Allen, op.cit.; 'On the shores of the Zuyder Zee', *Magazine of Art*, 1893; 'South Holland as a Sketching Ground', *The Studio*, 1897 with pencil drawings by George Horton; R L Stevenson, op.cit.; Symons, op.cit.; R.A.M Stevenson, op.cit.
62 R J Charleton, 'Cullercoats', *Magazine of Art*, 1886, p.456.
63 ibid., p.461.
64 See Alistair Ian Wright, 'Bastien-Lepage and English Critical Taste', *Gazette des Beaux Arts*, September 1990, pp.94-104.

65 L Wasserman, 'Where the North Wind Blows. Pt.VII, A Cullercoats Artist', *N.W.L*, 25 December 1886; 1, 8, &15 January 1887.
66 Wasserman, 1887, op.cit., p.57.
67 W.G Larkins, 'Reminiscences of Artistic Cullercoats', *Tyneside*, v.1 no.1, December 1894, p.41. The *Tyneside* magazine was a new venture aimed at a distinctly middle-class readership, for which the Joblings and others provided illustrations. This article can be regarded as a publicity exercise for the Cullercoats artists, targeting their 'niche' market. It may also account for Larkins' promotion of the Joblings at the expense of Homer.
68 R Dircks, 'Northumberland and Some Artists', *Art Journal*, 1904, p.305.
69 ibid., p.308. This is Marsh's picture *Driftwood*, exhibited at the O.W.C.S. in 1877.
70 Watson, 1882, op.cit, p.455.
71 V Lee, 'The Tyne at Newcastle' from *Juvenilia* (c.1878) in I Cooper Willis ed., *A Vernon Lee Anthology*, John Lane, 1929.
72 ibid.
73 See Richard Welford, 'Newcastle Upon Tyne', *Art Journal*, 1882: 'Down Tyneside', *The Graphic*, 23 August 1884, p.195: W.J Palmer, *The Tyne and its Tributaries*, London, 1882, p.261: Aaron Watson, 'The Coaly Tyne', *Magazine of Art*, 1883, p.115. Watson's chapter on 'The Tyne from Newcastle to the Sea' (*Rivers of Great Britain*, Cassell & Co, 1892) closely resembles the previous article and uses some of the same Jobling illustrations. In a separate booklet, *Down the Tyne* (1894), Watson again covered similar material, though without the illustrations.
74 *The Graphic*, ibid.
75 Watson, 1883, op.cit., p.115.
76 Lee, op.cit., p.118.
77 *The Graphic*, 1884, op.cit.
78 R J Charleton, *History of Newcastle upon Tyne*, W H Robinson, c.1885.
79 This analogy comes from Watson, 1883, op.cit.
80 This myth is exposed in the writings of socialists such as William Morris. See W Morris, 'Art and Socialism' (1884) in J Marsh, *Back to the Land*, Quartet Books, 1982, p.15.
81 For a discussion of this see A Woods, 'Doré's London: Art and Evidence', *Art History*, v.1 no.3, 1978, p.349.
82 Sutcliffe took many photos of Staithes and Runswick Bay which make useful comparisons to the art produced there.
83 From the diary of Arthur Munby, 31 October 1864, quoted in M Hiley, *Victorian Working Women. Portraits from Life*, Gordon Fraser Gallery, 1979, p.103.
84 J S Mitcalf, *Guide to Tynemouth and Neighbourhood by A Native*, (c.1880), 2nd. ed., T Todd, North Shields, 1910, p.89. This describes being able to have one's photo taken with a pretty Cullercoats fishlass.
85 For parallels with rural labourers see Newton, op.cit., p.135.
86 See P Dodd, 'Englishness and the National Culture' in R Colls & P Dodd eds., *Englishness. Politics and Culture, 1880-1920*, Croom Helm, 1986, pp.1-28.
87 *Matthew Arnold, Complete Prose Works III*, p.295-345, discussed in Dodd, ibid., p.12.
88 ibid., p.14.
89 These include T M Hemy's poetical rendering of the Elswick Works 1886 for Lord Armstrong and F M Brown's portrait of James Leathart (1863-4) showing Leathart's lead works in the background.
90 Lübbren, 1996, op.cit. She points to Stanhope Forbes' choice of Newlyn instead of Manaccan, for example.
91 See *N.D.L.* 28 May 1887 which mentions Cullercoats as the painting ground of the north-east coast. Or the *Newcastle Courant*, 9 January 1897 which talks of a 'northern school' which seems to include members of the Staithes Group who were also taking part in the Bewick Club exhibition being reported on.
92 See P Quinn, *Picturing Locality. Art and Regional Identity in the North East of England, 1822-1900*, unpubl. PhD thesis, University of Sunderland, 1997.
93 See James Vernon, 'Border Crossings: Cornwall and the English (imagi)nation', in G Cubitt ed., *Imagining Nations*, Manchester University Press, 1998, pp.153-172.
94 A local gallery at Newlyn was only established after the national reputation was secured, and therefore operated merely as part of the Cornwall 'tourist experience'.
95 J Harris, *Private Lives, Public Spirit: Britain 1870-1914*, Penguin, 1993, p.19.
96 Quinn, op.cit., p.375.

2 The Art Market: Exhibitions and Patronage in the North East

An artist's career is often perilous, infinitely susceptible to fluctuations in the economy, 'supply and demand' and taste. The previous chapter suggested that one of the main differences between the colonies at Cullercoats and Newlyn was that the latter produced work aimed at the London art market, whereas Cullercoats artists primarily fed a regional demand. This chapter will explore how the north east sustained such a large body of artists, the part played by the Cullercoats artists in stimulating and supplying this market, and their success in infiltrating a pre-existing circle of sophisticated art patrons.

Before 1850 the region had a strong tradition of art collecting amongst the gentry/merchant class, although their conservative tastes stifled successive attempts by artists to establish exhibition societies in Newcastle.[1] The regional economic boom and industrial expansion which took place after 1850 was crucial to the flowering of a sustainable art market. It created a new, relatively well-paid, well-educated, broad middle-class layer in north-east society, who were to prove far more receptive to contemporary art.[2] Furthermore, the region's working classes, who benefited from opportunities presented by Mechanics Institutes, free libraries and evening classes, were more intellectually curious than is often supposed.[3] However, when the erosion of the autonomy of the regional economy towards 1900 challenged the position of the industrial/mercantile elite, the new middle classes became crucial to the maintenance of regional arts patronage and production.

A series of 'loan' exhibitions selected from local art collections during the 1860s revealed the north east's connoisseurial core. These lenders were 'an elite within an elite' whose 'activity was often spread over a number of organisations'.[4] They included Isaac Lowthian Bell, Robert Sterling Newall, James Leathart, Thomas and Jacob Burnett, William W Pattinson, Thomas and Joseph Crawhall, George Crawshay, Edward and Miss Julia Boyd, Lord Ravensworth, Earl of Durham, Charles Palmer, Thomas E Smith and John Redmayne. All either owned or worked in the main industrial companies and were further linked by marriage, social and professional ties and civic duties.[5] Coming from the gentry or 'merchant' classes, most either inherited or married into the positions they held, so as second or third generation industrialists were able to enjoy the fruits of past labour by moving to country estates, buying art and being seen to be philanthropic.

The 1860s exhibitions show these collectors to have had similar, eclectic collections usually of contemporary or near contemporary British art, including a significant number of important Pre-Raphaelite paintings.[6] However, some distinctly middle-class patrons loaned works to the 1866 exhibition, usually paintings by local artists.[7] This subtle expansion of the patronage base was reflected in one newspaper editorial which, bemoaning the lack of a permanent gallery in Newcastle, claimed that:

> *An industrial community needs nothing so much ... as the means of cultivating the aesthetic faculty ... Whoever reflects upon the matter must recognise at once that pitmen, mechanics and puddlers would become better, broader men if they were brought more constantly ... into contact and communion with the beautiful.*[8]

But whilst Newcastle waited for its gallery, the 1866 exhibition successfully lured the working classes across its portals with cut-price tickets on Saturday afternoons.

The hiatus in exhibitions between 1866 and 1878 has been offered as proof of the apathy of Newcastle audiences for contemporary art.[9] However, the period was one of acquisition and consolidation by both established and newer collectors.[10] Furthermore, Newcastle was not without exhibition and sales venues during this period. In 1870 the Central Exchange Gallery opened in Newcastle, combining a showcase for local talent with a series of loan exhibitions. The first exhibition was a purely commercial venture, aimed at drumming up support and subscribers to the newly-refurbished gallery and newsroom, and included works for sale and on loan. The owners, Messrs Barkas and Tweedy, did their best to disguise this by encouraging the press to portray this as an almost philanthropic enterprise, carried out for the general good of the citizens of Newcastle.[11] Northern artists represented included John Charlton, John Surtees, George Blackie Sticks, Henry Emmerson and J R Mather; but there were also works for sale by Eastlake, Teniers, Gainsborough, Cox, Turner and A W Hunt.

Unfortunately we cannot tell how successful any of these early exhibitions were at achieving sales for the local artists. It can only be assumed that the signs were favourable enough for a group of collectors and artists to found a more long-term exhibiting forum in Newcastle, the Arts Association, with ambitions for both temporary exhibitions and the eventual founding of a permanent gallery with its own collection.

The Arts Association

The Arts Association set out with very clear aims and rules, defined in the catalogue of the first exhibition in 1878 and reported in the local press. The objects of the Association were described as promoting

> *a taste for art generally, the development and encouragement of local art, and the formation of a School of Artists for Newcastle-upon-Tyne. … the holding of annual exhibitions of works of art of the highest character obtainable from all sources, the proceeds from the sale and exhibition of which, assisted by private support and public subscription, may, it is hoped, ultimately lead to the establishment of a permanent Art Gallery for the town, … wherein works of art can be placed which may be preserved or bequeathed to the town by lovers and patrons of art.*[12]

It began with a show of strength; its list of patrons and committee members demonstrated that the organisers and lenders to earlier exhibitions were sufficiently confident to lend their names to this new venture.[13] To avoid accusations of favouritism no professional artists were to be directly involved in the organisation of the society.[14] For their part, the local press certainly did their best to promote the first exhibition:

> *Not a few artists of celebrity both in England and on the Continent have sent valuable contributions, and nearly the whole of our local artists are well represented … Local professional painters need not fear the comparison of their productions with those around them.*[15]

Having reminded the public that previous art societies in Newcastle were 'starved out of existence', the reviewer of the *Chronicle* looked forward to the Association 'introducing a new and better spirit, of widening the art culture of the district, and of encouraging struggling talent'. The critic declared the new generation of local artists 'distinguished by a healthy tone of work, a masculine vigour of handling, and a pure feeling for what is best and truest in art'. But he recognised that northern talent had not so far enjoyed monetary success and hoped that the exhibition would 'have a powerful influence in altering the balance of taste'.[16]

The first exhibition was dominated by 'establishment' artists, including J Faed, Clara Montalba, James Linnell, Hubert Herkomer, Arthur Hughes and J W B Knight. Paintings by Frère, Tissot, Alma-Tadema, G F Watts and Fantin-Latour all attracted praise. The younger face of British landscape painting was represented by Alfred East, Cecil Lawson and Mark Fisher. Predictably, there were a large number of sea pictures, including Henry Moore's *The North Sea* and C N Hemy's *St.Mawes.*[17] Notably, one critic took the then unusual step of comparing like pictures — Orchardson with A H Marsh, Moore with Jobling, Birket Foster with Hemy.[18] Marsh's Cullercoats

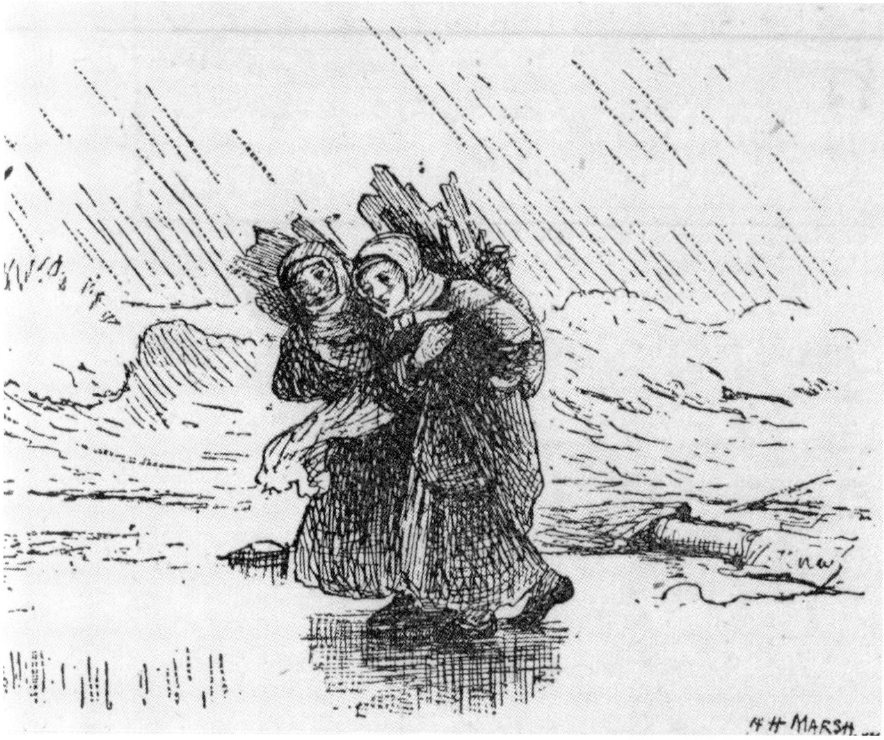

FIG.25
Arthur Hardwick Marsh, ***Hey Ho! The wind and the rain***, 1877; pub. Arts Association Illustrated Exhibition Catalogue 1878; Newcastle Libraries & Information Service

picture *Hey Ho! The wind and the rain* (fig.25) was greeted as 'a picture of the highest merit, well conceived, capitally executed, and conveying an admirable idea of our Northern coast on a dreary day.'[19] The catalogue noticed its affinity to the Hague School, describing it as a 'free, bold, genre picture, with seascape; something after the manner of Israels.' On the whole the other local artists working in and around Cullercoats also received favourable reviews, especially Jobling's *Wreck of the Last of the Seven Sisters*, although there was as yet no overt reference to Cullercoats as a colony.[20]

The success in attracting so many high quality pictures was perhaps due to the extensive connections of the exhibition's organiser, Joseph Crawhall, with the London art world. He was presumably aided by other committee members such as James Leathart, Alexander Stevenson, Charles Mitchell and William Armstrong, who also had strong links with many of the artists represented. Its success can be measured by sales of over £4,000 and attendance figures of 14,500 people.[21] Whilst many of the sales were achieved by the better-known artists, the critic of the *Chronicle* noted that, 'Many of our local painters have met with purchasers, and another element of the success of the exhibition has been the encouragement thus afforded to the art of the district'.[22]

In September 1878 the owners of the Central Exchange Gallery opened a rival exhibition devoted purely to north-east artists (fig.26). Many works were early-nineteenth-century paintings, but contemporary artists were also well represented, including Stephen Brownlow, John Chambers, Charlton, Emmerson, Hedley, T M Hemy, Jobling and Mather. As a purely commercial venture this gallery no doubt provided the artists with a valuable alternative 'shop window'.

FIG.26
Advance notice of exhibition, Central Exchange Art Gallery; pub. September 1878; Julian Brown

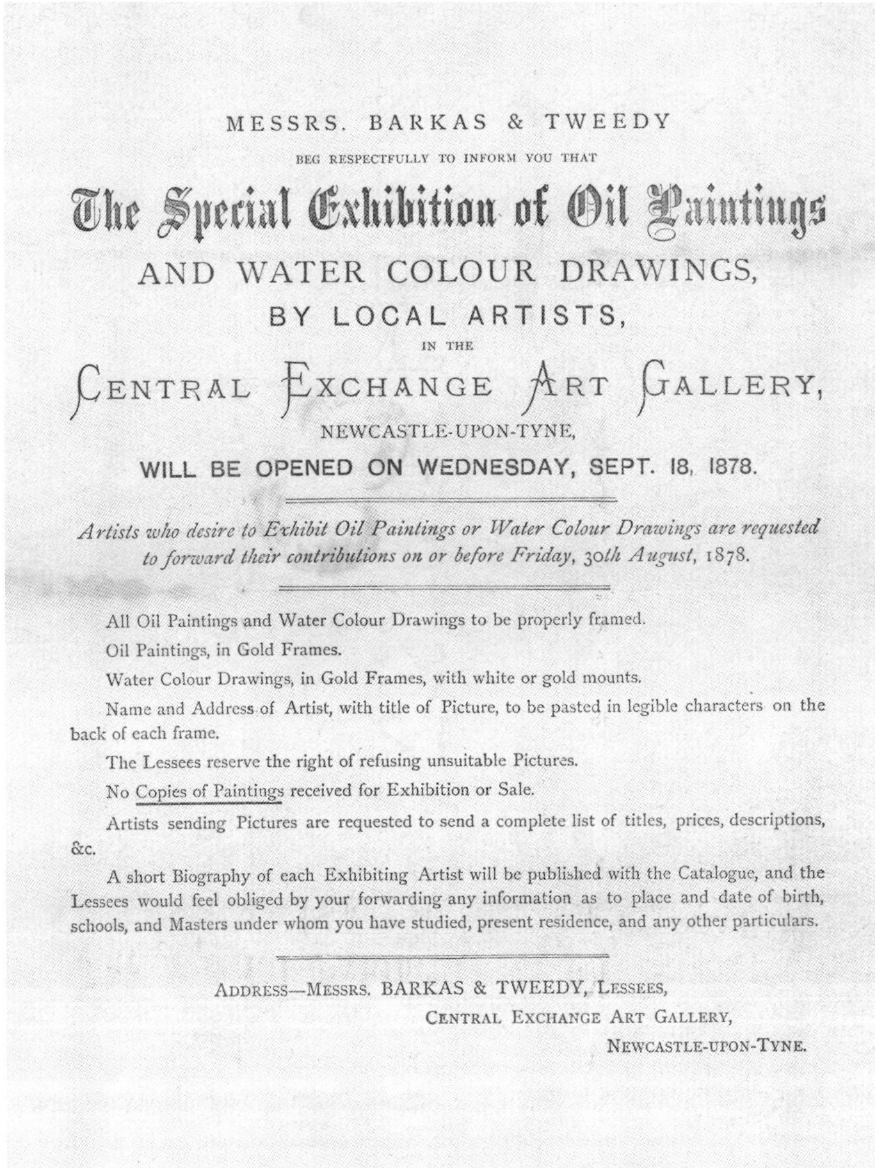
MESSRS. BARKAS & TWEEDY

BEG RESPECTFULLY TO INFORM YOU THAT

The Special Exhibition of Oil Paintings

AND WATER COLOUR DRAWINGS,

BY LOCAL ARTISTS,

IN THE

CENTRAL EXCHANGE ART GALLERY,

NEWCASTLE-UPON-TYNE,

WILL BE OPENED ON WEDNESDAY, SEPT. 18, 1878.

Artists who desire to Exhibit Oil Paintings or Water Colour Drawings are requested to forward their contributions on or before Friday, 30th August, 1878.

All Oil Paintings and Water Colour Drawings to be properly framed.

Oil Paintings, in Gold Frames.

Water Colour Drawings, in Gold Frames, with white or gold mounts.

Name and Address of Artist, with title of Picture, to be pasted in legible characters on the back of each frame.

The Lessees reserve the right of refusing unsuitable Pictures.

No Copies of Paintings received for Exhibition or Sale.

Artists sending Pictures are requested to send a complete list of titles, prices, descriptions, &c.

A short Biography of each Exhibiting Artist will be published with the Catalogue, and the Lessees would feel obliged by your forwarding any information as to place and date of birth, schools, and Masters under whom you have studied, present residence, and any other particulars.

ADDRESS—MESSRS. BARKAS & TWEEDY, LESSEES,
CENTRAL EXCHANGE ART GALLERY,
NEWCASTLE-UPON-TYNE.

Incredibly, the region accommodated another concurrent exhibition in the September of 1878, that of 'Amateur Artists native or resident in the Borough of Tynemouth' at R M Tate's Fine Art Gallery in North Shields. No catalogue survives, although a local newspaper article listed some of the subjects depicted, and with nearly 200 pictures it indicates the growth of interest and art practice in the region at all levels.[23]

The success of the first Arts Association exhibition, together with the offer of a loan of pictures from Sir William Armstrong, encouraged the committee to organise a loan exhibition in spring 1879.[24] This, and another in 1880, revealed the greater breadth of art collecting in the region, introducing Armstrong, Charles Mitchell, Alexander Shannan Stevenson, Sir John Swinburne, Earl Grey, S H Fraser, James Hall, H T Morton, Addison Potter, John Taylor and others to the list of collectors. As before, these men's lives intertwined on a business, civic and personal level, frequently finding reflection in their art collections.[25] Armstrong,

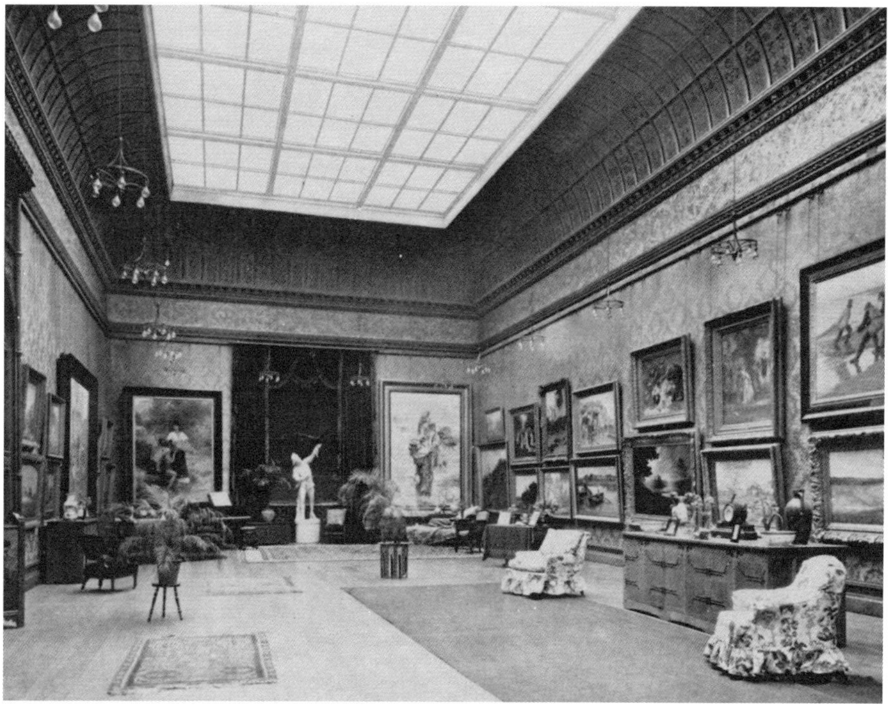

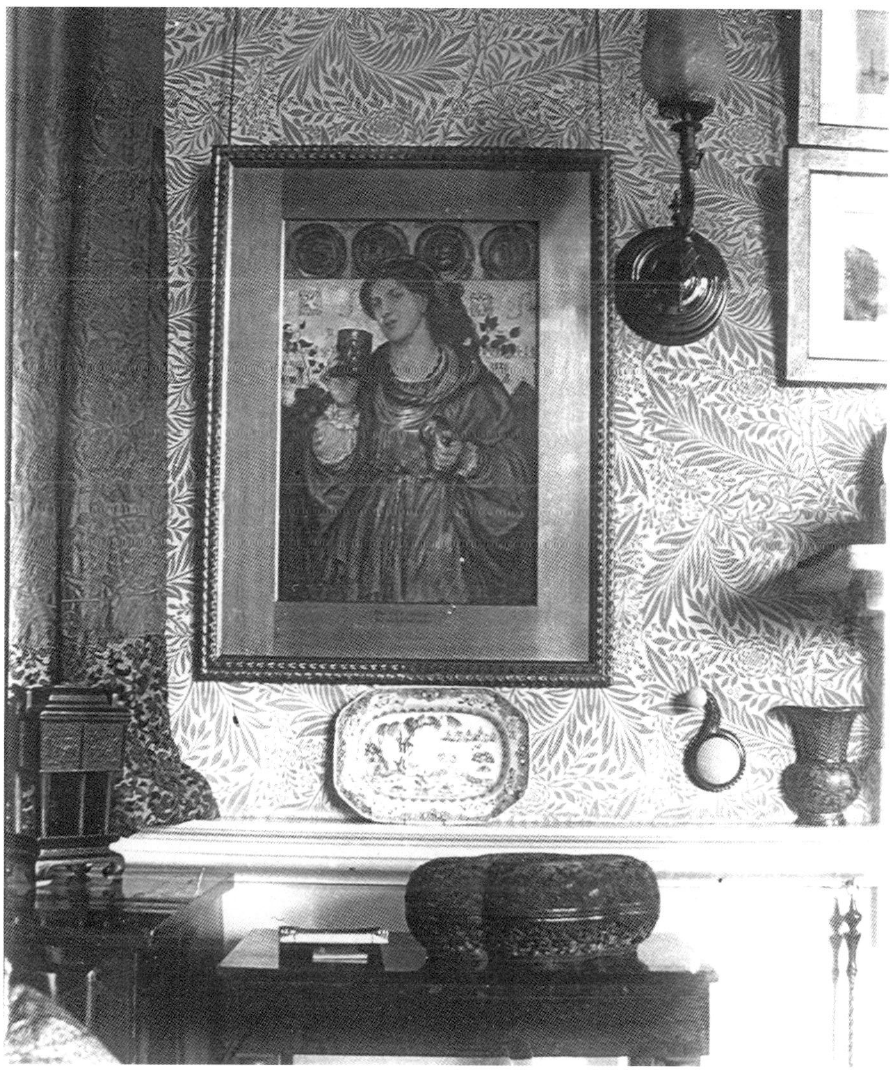

Fig.27
The Picture Gallery, Jesmond Towers, Newcastle (home of Charles Mitchell); photograph; Newcastle Libraries & Information Service

Fig.28
Interior of Oatlands Mere, Surrey (home of Alexander Shannan Stevenson) showing D G Rossetti's ***The Loving Cup*** of 1867; photograph courtesy private collection

Mitchell, Stevenson and Hall collected mainly contemporary British work, again with a strong holding of Pre-Raphaelite and Aesthetic Movement paintings (figs.27 & 28).[26] Early- to mid-nineteenth-century artists were favoured by most of the other patrons mentioned, except for Fraser who owned an impressive collection of Dutch and Italian Old Masters.[27]

With loans including Albert Moore's *Battledore* and *Shuttlecock* (fig.29), Millais' *Chill October* (fig.30), Whistler's *Lang Lysen*, Rossetti's *Lady Lilith* (fig.31) and *Penelope*, and others by Burne-Jones, Turner, Cox, Frère, Alma-Tadema and Fantin-Latour, it is not surprising that the response to the 1879 loan exhibition was emphatic: 'the Exhibition will have a good claim to be considered the best of the kind ever held in Newcastle. ... even a cursory glance at the pictures conveys the impression that nothing either of inferiority or mediocrity has been admitted.'[28] The Arts Association obviously served the philanthropic interests of the local collectors — an outing of their prized possessions not only fuelled their mutual self-esteem but also reminded the public of how public-spirited they could be. But more importantly, it showed the British art establishment 'the large number of splendid works of art in the possession of private collectors in the district, and should certainly be an inducement to good artists to forward works to the sale exhibition'.[29]

It seems to have worked, since the 1879 autumn exhibition was marked by both the better quality of paintings and by some very astute criticisms in the press. The journalist Aaron Watson demonstrated an intelligent understanding of contemporary art, giving in-depth commentaries on Aestheticism and recognising 'the new French school' (i.e. Impressionism). His newspaper critiques were also published as a

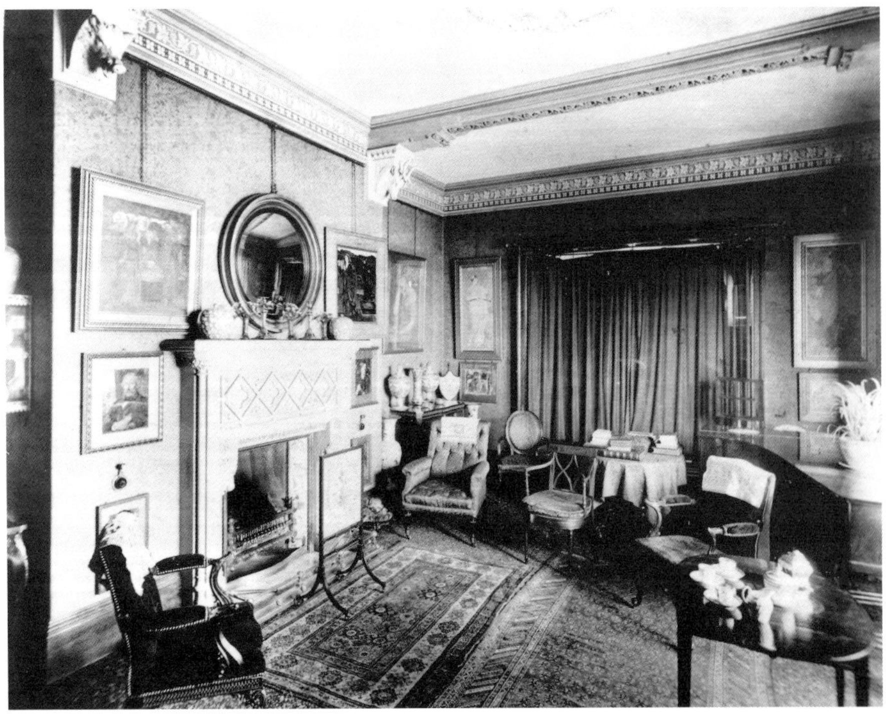

FIG.29
The Drawing Room, Bracken Dene, Low Fell (home of James Leathart), c.1895; photograph courtesy Dr Gilbert Leathart

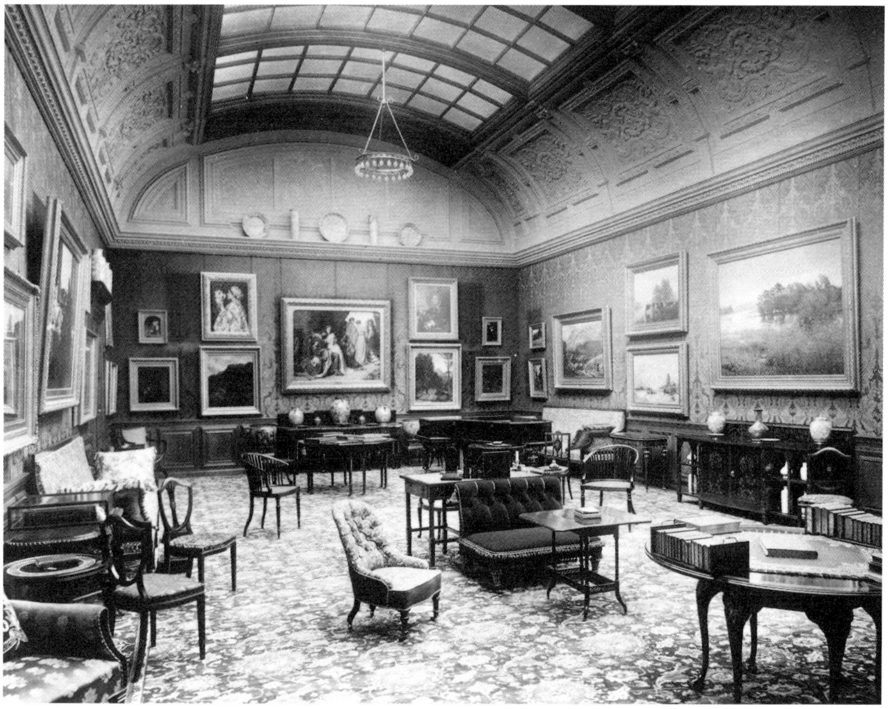

Fig.30
The Drawing Room, Cragside, Northumberland (home of Sir William Armstrong), 1891 showing J.E. Millais' ***Chill October***; photograph courtesy National Trust

pamphlet, along with an essay on 'taste', in which Watson showed his concern for educating the masses in the appreciation of art: 'The more opportunities there are of comparing good works with bad the more rapidly is there an improvement in the public taste.'[30] He goes on:

> *there are varieties of taste, even among those who have received the highest cultivation, and who have the finest natural instincts ... It may be taken for granted that the taste which is the broadest is most frequently the best. There are things worthy of admiration in Teniers, as well as in Michael Angelo; in a correct rendering of commonplace, as well as in the splendid deification of humanity.*

Watson's anti-elitist approach to exhibiting and collecting reflected Victorian collecting habits in ignoring the traditional hierarchies of art *genres*, but appreciating paintings on their individual merits.

Once again the local artists attracted a great deal of positive commentary, especially the paintings of Emmerson, Jobling, Chambers and Crawhall jnr. However, this exhibition was seriously marred by a war of words in the Newcastle press, centred around the fact that of the 395 artists represented, only about 50 were local. Perhaps in an effort to forestall the impending argument Watson's preview had already alluded to the more severe selection process, made necessary to avoid overcrowding and the 'skying' of many pictures.[31] This did not, however, stem the flow of recriminatory letters accusing the association of favouritism: 'It almost looks as if the Arts Association has already formed its "School of Artists", the school being composed of those artists who have been particularly favoured in this exhibition.'[32] Another writer attacked the snivelling rejected local artists, saying, 'From what I learn, somewhere above a hundred were returned to London; no complaint made, or a rush to *The Times*.'[33] The *Chronicle* editorial tried to put forward a balanced argument, but pointed out that the Association had to show works that would sell, 'or else somebody must be enormously out of pocket'.[34]

The Loan Exhibition in spring 1880 had an entirely different flavour to its predecessors, reflecting the collections of Old Masters and eighteenth-century works from alternative, often aristocratic, lenders such as the Earl of Durham and Sir Matthew White Ridley. But whilst the critical reception was very favourable, poor attendance showed that the general public was not equally enthusiastic for the type of art of the old cultural elite. This exhibition ultimately lost £169.

Anxious to avoid further losses, the committee and press were at pains to stress that if the next autumn sale exhibition was not a success, it would be the last. The *Art Journal's* advance notice commented that 'the association is now regarded by artists from all parts as one of the institutions of the country'.[35] But the *Art Journal* and the Newcastle papers hinted that in the worsening economic climate, artists could no longer expect to find patrons primarily amongst the industrial/mercantile classes, but must instead foster an alternative market by stimulating and educating the tastes of the masses. It is perhaps indicative of the changing marketplace that younger artists such as the 'Glasgow Boys' — Edward Walton, James Guthrie and Arthur Melville — made their first appearance, amongst an increasingly persistent local presence.[36] Unfortunately there was no repeat of the insightful critiques supplied by Aaron Watson the previous year.[37] Whilst there was no recognition of the Cullercoats artists as a group, they increasingly dominated critical attention. J D Watson's *Saved* (see fig.42 on page 81), one of his Cullercoats works which had been reproduced in *The Graphic*, was particularly well received.

The 'hard sell' approach of the press seemed to work, as pictures worth over £5,000 were sold, making an overall profit for the association of £36.14.8. Publishing these figures in December 1880, the committee was keen to attribute this success to the rise in the standard of works shown, vindicating their attempts to secure high quality (i.e. expensive) works for the exhibition.[38] Whilst Charles Mitchell continued to underwrite the Association, the public was urged to continue to support 'this very laudable effort to establish a permanent annual exhibition and art school in Newcastle'.[39] Of course there is a dichotomy here, for whilst there was a recognition that the traditional modes of patronage were under threat due to the worsening economic climate, the Association still expected to sell more expensive works to less affluent patrons. However,

FIG.31
Interior of Oatlands Mere, Surrey (home of Alexander Shannan Stevenson) showing D G Rossetti's ***Lady Lilith*** of 1867; photograph courtesy private collection

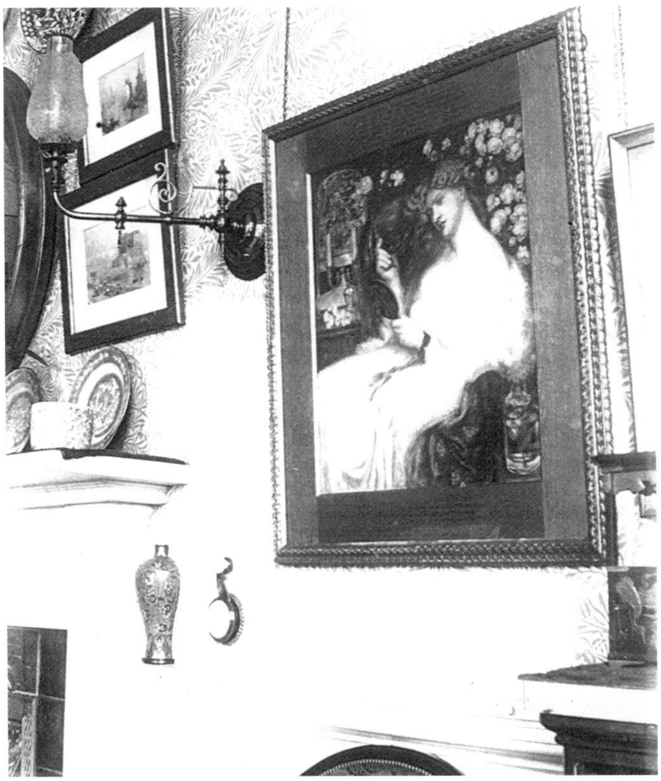

evidence suggests that some expensive works did sell; the *Journal* reported that paintings by Tissot and the Misses Montalba found 'eager buyers'.[40]

The 1881 exhibition showed no sign of falling support amongst the artists, with familiar names joined by Lhermitte and Adrian Stokes, as well as Guthrie and Walton once again. Even the *Art Journal* remarked that, 'considering the keen competition amongst the large provincial towns for high-class works of the modern school, the hanging committee have reason to feel proud of the fine specimens of English work that have been contributed by artists of established fame'.[41] They included Herkomer's *The Gloom of Idwal*, Legros' *An Old Wood Burner*, Lhermitte's *Le Cabaret* and Hunter's *A Day on Shore*, as well as paintings by Tissot, Fantin-Latour, Arthur Hughes, Walter Crane and Henry Moore.

But this exhibition was also significant in showing a number of new local painters, including George Horton, Thomas Eyre Macklin, J C Wasserman and Isa Thompson.[42] Winslow Homer also exhibited one of his recent Cullercoats pictures, *Two Cullercoats Fisher Girls*, which received a surprising amount of attention for such a previously unknown artist. The *Chronicle* noted, 'Mr. Homer's study does not go very far, but his description of two Cullercoats fish-girls is extremely natural'.[43] Whilst the *Courant* maintained, 'Winslow Heron [sic], an American artist, residing, we believe, at present at Cullercoats, contributes a charming sketch containing a couple of wonderfully drawn figures'.[44] The most intelligent critique came from the *Tyneside Daily Echo*:

> *"Two Cullercoats Fisher Girls" by Winslow Homer, ... is evidently influenced by the work of Jules Breton. There is an attempt to catch the noble forms and attitudes so frequently to be found in the toilers of the earth and sea, who are unfettered by modern conventionalities of costume. The aim is an admirable one, for on our English coasts and fields are to be found types of simple and noble beauty equal to those which inspired the old Greek masters when they gave to the world treasures of hewn marble.*[45]

This suggests a critical awareness of the affinity between the portrayals of Cullercoats fisher girls and those of French peasantry by Breton and Millet. It recalls also R J Charleton's rhetoric about the honest toiler reflecting a nobility of the soul, akin to the ideals embodied in classical statuary.

Buoyed up by the success of the 1881 exhibition (with sales of over £3,000) another was held in May rather than autumn of 1882. Of the 800 works on show approximately 250 were by local artists (as compared to 81 out of 774 in 1881), prompting the critic of the *Chronicle* to declare:

> *There can be no doubt that the previous labours of the association have influenced for the good the artists of this district. Some of the local work placed on view will well bear comparison with that of artists of metropolitan fame which is hung on the same walls, and more especially is this the case in regard to sea pieces and figure painting.*[46]

This was echoed by the *Art Journal:* 'the valuable influence of these exhibitions is clearly shown by the great advance in the technical work of the local artists. As the Association was formed in a great measure to foster local Art, this result is gratifying.'[47] By now Cullercoats pictures were commanding the majority of the critical attention devoted to local artists,[48] and their works were finding their way into the collections of Mitchell, Armstrong, Rogerson, Julia Boyd, Burnett, Crawhall, Hilton Philipson and R S Donkin. However, even works by Emmerson, Hedley and Jobling often reappeared periodically in various local exhibitions, still for sale after a number of years. Presumably for many local amateur artists, however, the prestige of being selected to hang alongside artists of national repute was reward enough.

However, by the third week of the 1882 exhibition the press was sounding alarm bells about the lack of attendance, due to good weather and the fact that column inches were dominated by political turmoil rather than the exhibition reviews. Unfortunately there is no clear reason why the Arts Association ceased to function beyond 1882. Sales figures for this final exhibition remain unknown, but if they were significantly lower than previous years, then this, coupled with poor attendance figures, would have incurred a loss.[49] John Millard has suggested that one reason for its failure was its elitism, both in its organisation and in the marginalisation of local art to the benefit of 'established' artists, therefore failing to win popular support. However, the opposite is equally possible, since the elite will abandon any process which becomes too democratic because it negates the (ideal of a) privileged position of the elite class.[50] The abandonment of the Association could be seen as just such a withdrawal by the elite, faced with the increasing strength of the local body of artists and their supporters. This, together with a failure to sell paintings by nationally renowned artists in the 1882 exhibition, would have amounted to a collapse of the spectacle of conspicuous consumption and elitist connoisseurship upon which the Association was based. The subsequent absence of many of the most familiar patrons from the succeeding Bewick Club list — including Armstrong, Leathart, Bell, Joicey, Burnett, Crawhall and the Earl of Durham — seems to support this hypothesis.

The vacuum left by the demise of the Art Association was filled in 1883 by an exhibition at North Shields and by the Gateshead Fine Art and Industrial Exhibition which opened in September 1883. These were very much local affairs, with no attempt to attract famous names from outside the region. The question of a new exhibiting forum in the region was, however, being discussed behind the scenes and through the letter columns of the north-east press. It was:

> *regretted that so important a city as Newcastle had no annual gathering together of works of art now that the Arts Association is no more. I notice that nearly every city and town of importance has its annual exhibition of pictures,*

... I trust the time is not far distant when Newcastle shall place herself side by side with other intelligent centres in the cause of art.[51]

This plea was answered almost immediately, not by the Corporation of Newcastle, but by the artists themselves.

The Bewick Club

In autumn 1882 members of the Newcastle Life School were already discussing a plan by amateur artist Thomas Dickinson for a new exhibiting society. The Life School had been set up in September 1878, providing two life classes per week, and had prospered despite constant haranguing from the Vicar of Newcastle at nearby St. Nicholas' Church. Millard claims, 'It laid the foundation of an energetic and influential group of artists on Tyneside'.[52] Certainly with Emmerson as president and Jobling, Hedley and Dickinson on the management committee the nucleus was in place for all of the most significant developments in the north-east art world for the rest of the century.[53]

After an enforced life in the shadows during the existence of the Arts Association, the artists disbanded the Life School and the Bewick Club was

FIG.32
Henry Hetherington Emmerson, Bewick Club Illustrated Menu 1885; Julian Brown

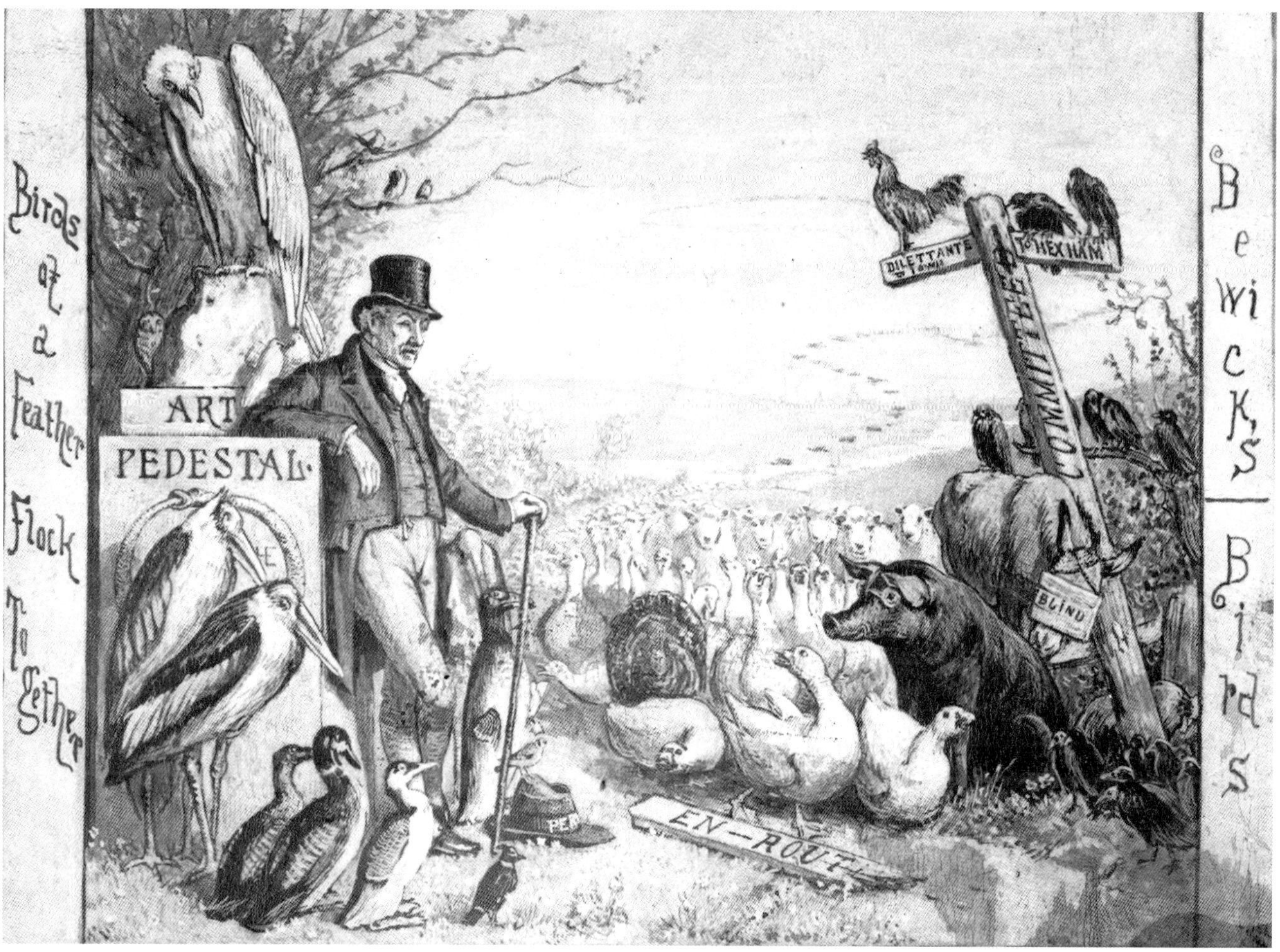

officially inaugurated in January 1883, taking over its premises and classes. The *Chronicle* noted, 'The present objects of the club are to bring together artists, amateurs, and persons interested in art generally, to whom opportunities will be afforded for intercourse and mutual encouragement and counsel such as cannot at present be obtained.'[54] The naming of the club after Bewick, perhaps the most famous local artist, 'was meant to provide a banner around which artists could rally to form a strong and independent local "school" of painters'.[55] This would seem to be supported by the illustrated menus designed for the annual Bewick Club dinners. For example, in 1885 Emmerson depicted Bewick surrounded by his 'birds' — an allusion to the artists of the club (fig.32). The following year Jobling's design showed the club's members sketching at Cherryburn, Bewick's birthplace.

The Bewick Club manifesto was outlined in a newspaper editorial in September 1883.[56] The club was to be controlled by artists because 'there is more direct appeal to the goodwill and co-operation of brother artists throughout the country, and also to the sympathy and support of the general public'.[57] An Art Union was proposed, based on the model at Dundee, in order that people could attain artworks at a reduced price whilst also boosting sales and receipts from the exhibitions.[58] The Bewick Club held its first exhibition in January 1884 at Joel's Auction Rooms on Pilgrim Street, Newcastle. With the exceptions previously mentioned, the list of patrons makes familiar reading, thus fostering some sense of continuity.[59] The local press gave the new club an enthusiastic, if cautious, welcome:

> *The importance of introducing the refinements of art culture into the influences which surround our daily lives is now insisted upon … A keen appreciation of art on the part of the many is an unmixed benefit to the nation, and in the development of this feeling lies the most important work which exhibitions such as that opened last night may perform.*[60]

There was a growing realisation, both locally and nationally, that the region's artists were worthy of serious consideration. Even without any large financial backing the committee had secured,

> *recent examples of many of the most eminent British artists, direct from the studios … the value of this collection, … is enhanced by the opportunity it affords of contrasting specimens acknowledged to belong to the best work of the time with the products of our northern artists. In conducting such a comparison the connoisseurs will not find it necessary to make any very serious allowances for the professionals of the locality, and it is clear that, despite all drawbacks, the natural art talent of the district … still continues to assert itself.*[61]

The first exhibition was made up of 600 works, including many national artists familiar through the Arts Association exhibitions.[62] A very strong local presence included Emmerson, Jobling, C W Mitchell,

Brownlow, Isa Thompson, Surtees, T R Spence, Hedley, Chambers, Charlton, Slater, Garvie, B B Hemy, Horton, Campbell and Dixon Clark, many showing subjects taken from the coast between Cullercoats and the river Tyne.[63] Other than Lady Butler, Thompson was one of the few women to be especially praised, for her Cullercoats work *The Pilot.*[64]

Strangely, the local press could not decide whether this exhibition was successful or not. The *Journal* declared, 'We are glad to learn that the Art Union, ... is proving a success far beyond that anticipated by its promoters ... The exhibition has been well patronised since the opening day, and we trust that the public will continue to give it their support.'[65] Then another newspaper doomed the Bewick Club and all like ventures to certain failure:

> *The local public has no taste for picture galleries. We said so last week because of the failure of the Arts Association, and because of the scanty encouragement received by the Bewick Club at their exhibition in Pilgrim St ... The fact is provincial galleries, unless they be free and maintained out of the rates, are a failure.*[66]

The following day another newspaper reported, 'The number of visitors at the Bewick Club Exhibition I understand, is increasing daily, which is a most gratifying proof, not only of the excellence of the display, but of the development of the artistic taste of the public.'[67] A sister newspaper also declared that the 600 subscribers to the Union had raised £300.

These diverse judgements reveal the essential dilemma at the heart of most provincial art exhibiting organisations. On the one hand, these independent bodies needed to be financially viable, both to survive and to demonstrate to their respective councils that there was sufficient interest in the arts to sustain a municipal gallery. On the other hand, success made municipal intervention less likely because seemingly unnecessary, whilst failure 'proved' there was no local demand to justify such expense. This problem was arguably underscored by the unusually fragmented nature of north-east society. Unlike other burgeoning northern industrial cities, there was little sense of any common social values fostering cohesive municipal projects to promote a particular civic identity. With the exception of the building of the Town Hall in the 1860s and the Free Library in 1880 there are few public buildings erected by Newcastle Corporation during the second half of the nineteenth century to match the splendour of Richard Grainger's urban developments earlier in the century. The reasons lie in the social structures of the north east — with the powerful industrialists mainly emerging from the pre-existing merchant/gentry class, therefore having little common bond with the new, very diverse middle classes. Whilst this diversity benefited a broad range of arts patronage, at a civic level there was no common ideology or shared vision of civic identity, and hence few civic projects to define and symbolise this identity.

Unlike the Arts Association, the Bewick Club also functioned as an educational establishment, expanding the number of life-model sessions to three evening classes per week. In 1885 there were 30 student and 105 ordinary members, multiplying to around 350 members by the 1890s. Generally during the 1880s and early 1890s the annual exhibitions maintained a core of regular regional and national exhibitors, with an increase in younger local artists working along the coast, centred around Emmerson and Jobling at Cullercoats. But in certain years particular 'schools' or groups of artists would come to the fore.

Following the showing of Israels' *Dutch Peasant* at the 1885 exhibition, there was a significant group of Hague School pictures on show in 1886,[68] and at the Jubilee Exhibition of 1887, both in the sale and loan sections.[69] For the first time two north-east collectors, Alexander Stevenson and Percy Westmacott, revealed their large collections of such works (fig.33).[70] Westmacott's collection included a pencil portrait of his two children by Matthew Maris, suggesting he knew Maris, perhaps through the dealer Daniel Cottier with whom Maris stayed in London. We can assume, therefore, that Westmacott bought some of his collection either directly from the Hague artists or through Cottier.[71] It is possible both collectors also bought in Glasgow, perhaps explaining loans of similar paintings to the 1887 exhibition by both Cottier and the Glasgow dealers Craibe, Angus & Sons.

From 1885 British naturalist painters such as Walter Langley and George Clausen could also be seen at the Bewick exhibitions.[72] Contemporary reactions suggest that north-east critics readily accepted these Naturalist works. The *Journal* declared, 'Mr. Walter Langley always sends something good to the Bewick Exhibition'[73] whilst in 1891 his *Knitting* was described as 'one of the gems of the room'.[74] These works not only helped to disseminate the newer French painting techniques being adopted by young British artists, but would have reinforced the acceptability of naturalistic images of working-class life, encouraging local artists to abandon any remaining vestiges of sentimentality in their work.

During the 1890s paintings by artists from other coastal colonies were increasingly shown, starting with Julius Olsson in 1888, followed by Fred Jackson and Blandford Fletcher in 1890; Fred Hall and Frank Brangwyn, 1891; Norman Garstin and H.M. Rheam, 1892; Arthur Friedenson, 1893; Gilbert Foster and Walter Osborne, 1894; Bernard Sickert, T.C. Gotch and Henry S. Hopwood in 1895. Again it seems that these artists were readily accepted by north-east critics.[75]

The frequency of Staithes artists at the Bewick Club exhibitions during the 1890s is testament to the

FIG.33
Interior of Oatlands Mere, Surrey (home of Alexander Shannan Stevenson) shows a family portrait by Etty and an unidentified Hague School landscape; photograph courtesy private collection

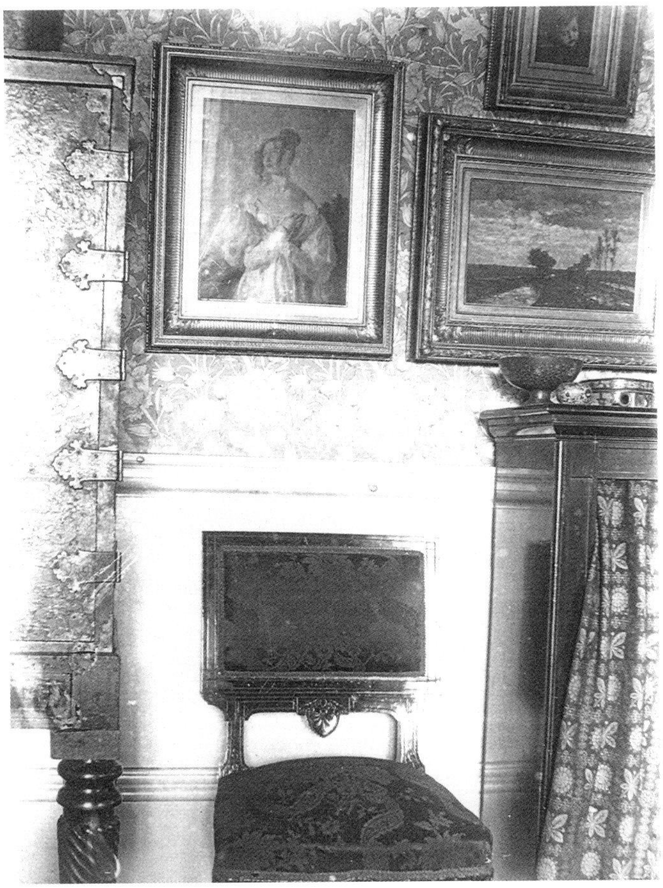

increasing involvement of north-east artists such as Thompson, Jobling, John Atkinson and Hedley with the artists working at Staithes and Runswick. This association undoubtedly affected their work. Hedley was probably the first to forge links with this group, perhaps serving as a channel for new ideas and techniques to the north east during the mid 1880s. The effect of the link on the technique and palette of Thompson and Jobling was noted even by contemporary critics.[76] Atkinson's art flourished after his move to Yorkshire where, although remaining preoccupied with rural themes, he became intimately involved with many of the Staithes group. Other Bewick Club members also used Staithes as a sketching ground, including James Watson, W H Charlton, T M Hemy, John Hodgson Campbell and H C Charlewood.

The primary objectives of the Bewick Club — to further art and artists in the north east — naturally found reflection in the exhibitions. Gradually these shifted from the type of 'crowd-pleasing' exhibitions previously held by the Arts Association, towards those designed primarily to foster local artists, both by showing more of their work and by attracting pictures from like-minded younger British artists. The benefits to local artists from the activities of the club did not go unnoticed, with Cullercoats and its artists often predominating.

> *Some of the old Life School students have made a vast advance in the practice of their art, and the younger or more inexperienced painters have shared to no inconsiderable extent, and with far from imperceptible effect, in the advantages of what has now become a local school of painting.*[77]

One particular critique, from 1887, declared Cullercoats as 'the great painting-ground of the north-east coast.'[78]

In October 1890 the Bewick Club inaugurated an annual exhibition of members' sketches, possibly in response to the Newcastle Sketching Club which had been set up in 1888.[79] By 1895 the Bewick Club was running five well-attended evening classes per week.[80] However, after the death of Emmerson in 1895 and the election of Hedley as president (resulting in the resignation of Jobling and his supporters), the club entered a period of general malaise and financial instability, exacerbated by the general economic depression.[81] When it became clear that Newcastle Corporation would not help out, the Bewick Club gave up its rooms in Pilgrim Street, hired rooms at the Geographical Institute in St. Mary's Place for its classes and the Academy of Arts for exhibitions.[82] From 1897 the cost of the exhibitions was reduced by restricting it to members only. But in 1902, when the club became more financially secure, the earlier pattern of annual exhibitions with an Art Union, plus separate exhibitions of members' sketches, was resumed at their new home at the Church Institute in Hood Street, Newcastle.

Other Local Exhibition Venues

The Bewick Club was not the only exhibiting venue in the region and whilst some of the others were sporadic or short-lived, taken together they represent a sustained attempt by local artists to further the cause of art and create a regional art market capable of supporting a significant number of artists. Crucially, it becomes obvious that the same 'core' of artists, predominantly those living and working around Cullercoats, feature in most of these ventures. The Tynemouth Fine Art Association (founded in 1879) seems to have developed from a purely loan-based exhibiting forum into a significant 'sales' outlet, although even as late as 1891 its primary aim was stated as encouraging 'the practice of the art amongst amateurs',[83] despite the fact that its committee and exhibitors included Jobling, F S Ogilvie, Horton, Dixon Clark and Aaron Watson.

Whilst this was a purely exhibiting association, another, the Borough of Tynemouth Art Club was centred round a regular painting club.[84] By 1891 the main organisers of this club had also undergone a major change since its inception in 1883. A report of the club dinner records Hedley as president, and attendance by Jobling, Emmerson, James Watson and W H Charlton amongst others.[85] By 1895 the club was even procuring pictures from artists outside the area.[86]

The art fraternity of South Shields also made several attempts to establish an annual exhibiting forum. The first, in conjunction with the Model Yacht Club, was held in March 1888, with another in 1890.[87] In 1891 the South Shields Art Club was established, with Aaron Watson as president and Emmerson, Hedley, Chambers and Jobling amongst the vice-presidents. Although there are no surviving catalogues after 1894, it must be assumed that the club survived for a number of years since there is evidence that it held a 'members' sketches' exhibition in 1896.

Prior to the inauguration of the Laing Art Gallery in 1904, only one other significant exhibition forum emerged — the Art Circle, which grew out of the Art Department of Armstrong College (the successor to the Newcastle School of Art). Contemporary newspaper reports of the exhibitions seem to provide the only surviving records. The first exhibition was held in January 1897 and aimed 'to cultivate the aesthetic side of art, ... thus a sort of local "New Gallery", in which conventionality is not a necessity. The members and students ... paint for art's sake, not for the sake of what art gives them ... The Circle is, in short, a striving after High Art.'[88] It was noted that 'the number of its members is few and select' and that whilst some exhibitors are already well known in local exhibitions, others were known only in 'more exclusive art circles'. The main exhibitors included Marsh, Jobling, Hedley, Charles W Mitchell, John Charlton, R G Hatton, Charles Spence and Ralph Bullock, as well as a number of students.

Of the second exhibition, in January 1898, a critic declared that, 'as those who contribute are free from the trammels occasioned by having to paint for public support, painting only for Art's sake, the exhibition has quite a unique interest'.[89] In this respect the Art Circle represented an important development in art exhibiting in the north east, being the first time artists were sufficiently free from financial shackles to be able to paint and show what they wanted, not what they thought would sell. But as well as being another vehicle for the already well-established Tyneside coterie, its object was 'to assist students over the critical period between their leaving the College and engaging art as a profession, chiefly by affording them the means of exhibiting their pictures'.[90]

The Central Exchange Gallery continued to exhibit art works throughout the years from 1870 until the mid 1890s. There seems to have been an almost continuous show of local pictures, which attracted notice whenever there were any significant new additions. A number of other privately-run galleries and dealers also sprang up during this period, offering a constantly varied spectacle for the region's art lovers as well as alternative exhibition spaces for local artists.[91] Successive auctioneers housed at the Academy of Arts building also featured many picture sales.

A number of artists held one-man shows in the region including Campbell and Surtees at Hay's Gallery in 1886 and 1895 respectively. Emmerson organised an exhibition of his own work in 1894 at Hellyer Bros. Gallery, and there was a further posthumous sale exhibition in December 1895 to raise funds for his widow. In 1905 Horton exhibited 23 works at the Pen and Palette Club. His other known one-man shows occurred after World War One and, with the exception of those at Trevor Stevenson's Gallery in Newcastle during the 1920s, they were not in the region.[92] But by far the most prolific one-man exhibitor was Jobling who from 1885 held exhibitions at his studio for many years, as well as being accorded a retrospective exhibition at Armstrong College in 1923, shortly before his death. An interesting insight into Jobling's *modus operandi*, and of the local art market generally, can be gleaned from a report of his 1885 exhibition.[93] Viewing was by invitation only, implying that this was not an exercise in broadening Jobling's patronage network but perhaps a more subtle 'peer pressure' approach. The article added that there was usually little opportunity to see Jobling's work because it never accumulated at dealers and the examples sent to the local exhibitions did not give a good overview of his output. The implicit message is that his works sold easily and quickly, and therefore must be desirable.

The crucial point about these diverse art clubs, societies, exhibition and sales venues is that they conform to a general trend of specialisation in which a variety of markets were created and served, 'reflecting a pluralism of taste and the commodification of art works as luxury items for mass consumption.'[94] It attests to the success of local artists to foster a much more widespread ethos of art collecting in the region, which was no longer dependent on a small minority of 'connoisseurs'. So whilst venues such as the Art Circle could make claims for exclusivity, their economic function was just as explicit as the more overt sales exhibitions.[95]

Non-Local Exhibition Venues

Despite the proliferation of new exhibiting venues in Britain, especially from the 1880s onwards, having a picture accepted for the annual Royal Academy summer exhibition was still an achievement loaded with symbolic meaning for most artists. And although the younger, more avant-garde artists clamoured for change to what they regarded as an outmoded, unrepresentative and elitist institution, they still, for the most part, submitted works to the Academy. One has only to consider the special railway carriage to take the Newlyn artists' works up to London, or Laura Knight's description of her wonderment and disbelief on receiving her first 'Varnishing Day' ticket.[96] Almost without exception the Cullercoats artists also exhibited regularly at the Academy, but not perhaps in such a concerted fashion as the Cornish artists.[97] From the late 1880s many of the region's artists featured in Blackburn's *Academy Notes*, an annual publication which passed brief comments (often with an illustration) on what were considered the best pictures at the Academy in any particular year. Jobling, Hedley, Charlton, T M Hemy, Emmerson, Garvie and F S Ogilvie all appeared, perhaps reflecting the rising status and higher profile of these artists on the national art scene.

This higher profile is perhaps also due to the increasingly diverse venues to which these artists individually sent works, including the Royal Glasgow Institute, the Walker Gallery, the Society of British Artists, the Royal Scottish Academy, the Grosvenor Gallery, the Royal Institute of Painters in Watercolour, the Dudley Gallery, the Fine Art Society, Manchester, Yorkshire Union of Artists, Staithes, Oldham, Leeds, Nottingham, Derby and Brighton. Internationally, it is known that Marsh was represented at the Paris Expositions in 1876 and 1889, whilst Horton exhibited at the Paris Salon and the International Society of Aquarellists prior to 1914, as well as in Holland during the 1920s.

It is difficult to assess the impact of non-local venues on the sales and reputation of the north-east artists. Examples from even the most successful Cullercoats artists suggest that their Royal Academy or other major-venue pictures often reappeared for sale at local exhibitions later. For instance, Jobling exhibited *Happy Days* (fig.34) at the Walker Gallery in 1885 but it was still for sale at the Bewick Club exhibition the following year. Similarly, Thompson's Academy picture of 1904, *In the Orchard*, appeared for sale at the Staithes Art Club exhibition in 1905. Hedley's main Cullercoats picture *Go and God's Will be Done!* (fig.35, untraced) was shown at the Bewick Club, the Royal Academy and the Walker Gallery in

1891, then at Leeds and the South Shields Art Club in 1892, still unsold. Similarly, Emmerson's posthumous sale in 1895 included at least four works previously shown at the Academy and elsewhere.[98] Why then bother to send to national exhibitions if they could not be relied on to produce sales? The only possible answer is kudos, both within the profession and, perhaps more importantly, with the art-buying public in the north east. It seems clear that these artists, unlike their counterparts in Newlyn, recognised that their primary market was in the region rather than London. They took advantage of the fact that the regional press rarely failed to

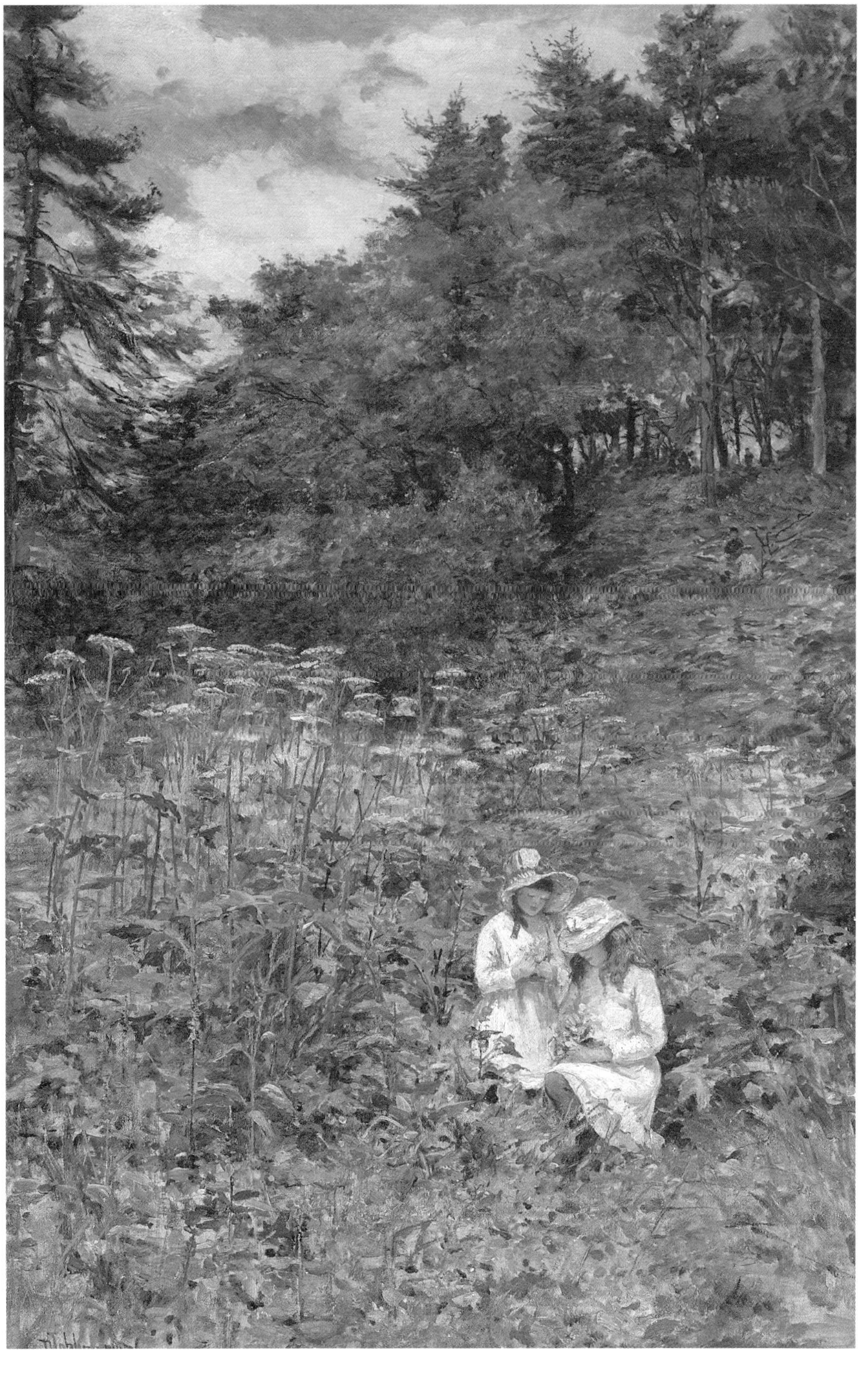

FIG.34
Robert Jobling, ***Happy Days***, 1885; oil on canvas; Joan L. Bell.

FIG.35
Ralph Hedley, ***Go! And God's Will be Done*** (untraced), 1891; photograph courtesy Julian Brown

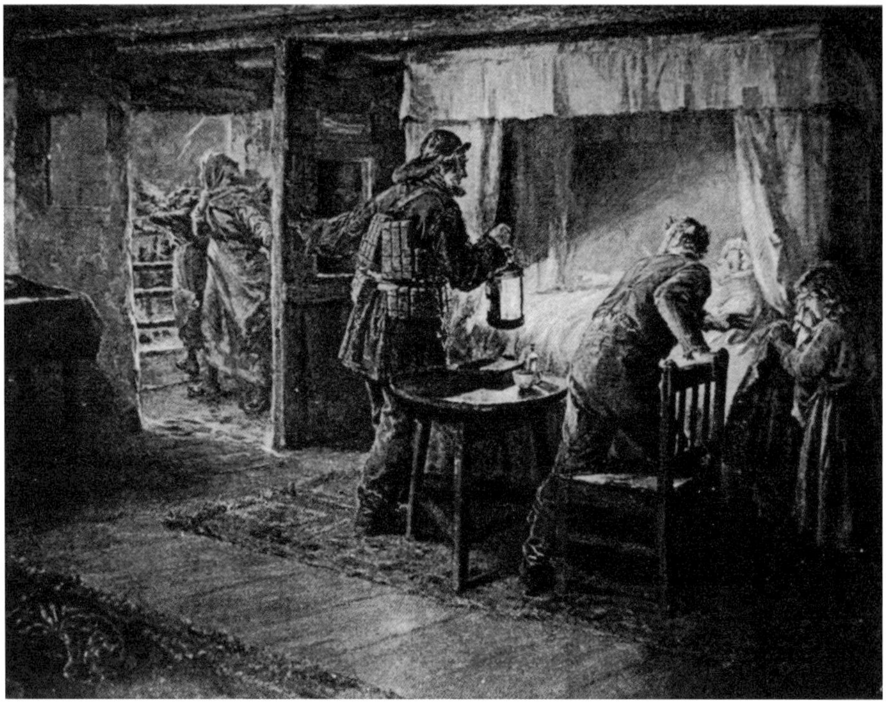

report on the summer exhibitions in London and other major venues; after all, what better advertisement for the Newcastle autumn exhibitions than for the region's press to announce that your Academy picture is hung in a prominent place, or, even better, sold.[99]

Patronage and Commissions

At times, even the region's more successful artists had to rely on commissioned work. For example, in a letter to his daughter Amy, Emmerson refers to two commissions: 'I think I will get the book home on Saturday and most likely to Cragside on Monday or Tuesday. Just finished Mrs Stewarts portrait and would not care if I had more to do in portrait as I find it the best way to get money at present' (figs.36 & 37).[100] Emmerson executed commissioned portraits throughout his career, starting in his student days in London during the early 1850s, indeed James Leathart was one of his earliest patrons. In another letter, however, Emmerson makes it clear that the patronage of Lord Armstrong has been crucial to his survival: 'I hope you will suit Miss Ware as times are frightfully hard in Art. I do not know what I should have done had it not been for Sir William's work. I expect every post to hear from him. [B]ut I hope for better times.'[101]

Jobling's commissions seem to have been mainly illustrative work for various publications.[102] But he was also careful to nurture wealthy patrons, as evidenced by an invitation to the Earl of Carlisle following the sale of two drawings to him: 'It will be a great pleasure to me to have you look in at my place any time you are in Newcastle. The intelligent interest in Art is unfortunately scarce enough here and I am always glad to compare notes, to say nothing of the great benefit of having fresh eyes seeing work in progress'.[103] In this at once grovelling yet self-important note Jobling seems to be deliberately setting up a 'them and us' scenario which is less than complimentary to his fellow artists. The blatant appeal to the Earl of Carlisle's vanity seemed to work, as a number of Jobling's pictures found their way into his collection.[104] Other wealthy patrons of Jobling's included Armstrong, Mitchell, Sir W J Noble, Sir A M Sutherland and Charles Williams.[105]

Horton also relied on commissions, especially early in his career, although these were for landscape subjects rather than portraits. A local chemist, Tom Binks, sent Horton on sketching trips to Wales and rural areas of Northumberland. Aaron Watson also provided crucial illustrative work for Horton at a time when he was trying to establish himself as a full-time artist.[106] However, Horton did not deliberately cultivate the patronage of the wealthy, although his works were bought by local collectors such as Jacob Burnett and Julia Boyd.[107] Many other local artists undertook portrait commissions, often as the 'bread and butter' income, including Thomas Bowman Garvie, F S Ogilvie, Campbell, Chambers, Marsh and Macklin. But this was common practice and does not therefore indicate that the region's artists were at any particular disadvantage.

Evidence from auction catalogues and bequests suggests that most of the major patrons bought large numbers of local artists' works to hang alongside their Royal Academy, Grosvenor Gallery and Aesthetic Movement pictures.[108] These sources also reveal many further patrons and collectors from a variety of social backgrounds — factory foremen, shop keepers, clerks, dentists, lawyers, politicians, journalists — whose collections ranged from Dutch seventeenth-century pictures to the contemporary paintings of Whistler and Clausen.[109]

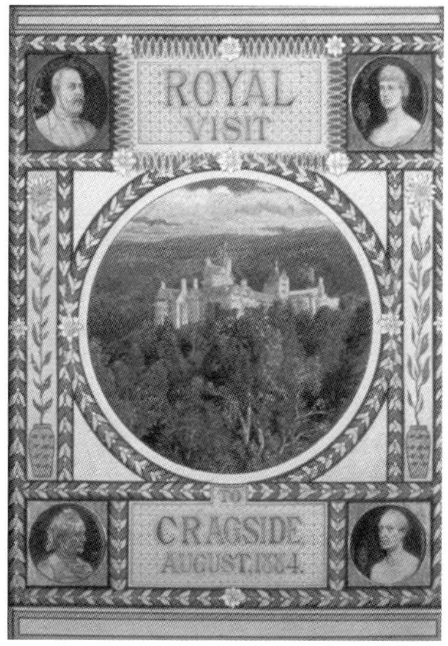

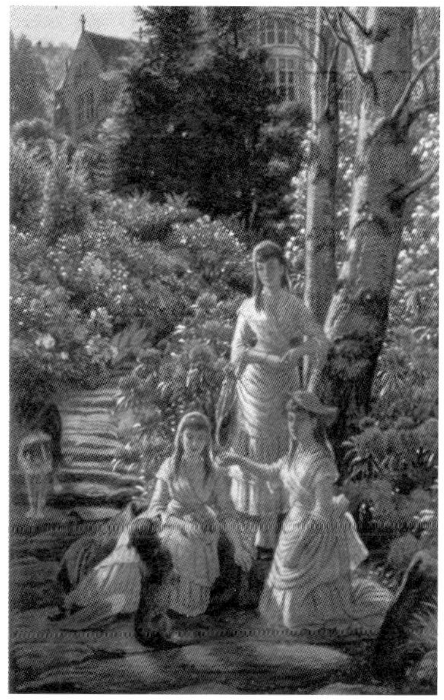

FIG.36
Henry Hetherington Emmerson, Cover of Presentation Book Commemorating The Visit of the Prince and Princess of Wales to Cragside in 1884, presented to Lord Armstrong by the people of Rothbury; National Trust

FIG.37
Henry Hetherington Emmerson, ***Princesses Louise, Victoria and Maud at Cragside***; watercolour in Presentation Book Commemorating the Visit of the Prince and Princess of Wales to Cragside in 1884, presented to Lord Armstrong by the people of Rothbury; National Trust

Conclusion

The exhibitions reveal that there was an increasingly sophisticated art market in the north east towards the end of the nineteenth century, recognised by metropolitan artists and dealers who were willing to send works to the Newcastle exhibitions. This culture of collecting was undoubtedly encouraged by those industrialists and businessmen whose eclectic collections, displayed in the loan exhibitions, fostered a broad critical engagement in the regional press, thereby providing fertile ground for the growing numbers of artists attracted to the Cullercoats colony. Local critics also took seriously their role in educating the public in art appreciation, encouraging a wider art audience and market.

Seizing the initiative, the region's artists capitalised on the relative success of the Arts Association to establish a crucial exhibiting and educational forum, the Bewick Club. Through this and other art clubs, the Cullercoats colonists supported each other, encouraged new members and, most importantly, supplied and nurtured a socially diverse patronage base. The centrality of the Cullercoats artists — Emmerson, Jobling, Thompson, Marsh, Horton, Slater — to the maintenance of the region's art market cannot be over-estimated. Similarly, they played a crucial role in the agitation for a municipal gallery in Newcastle. Whilst ultimately, the Laing Art Gallery was the result of an almost arbitrary decision by Alexander Laing to donate money, nevertheless the prolonged and concerted effort of local artists helped keep the dream of a permanent gallery alive.[110]

As a postscript it is worth considering the effect of the opening of the Laing in 1904 on the other exhibition venues. There is no evidence that either the Tynemouth or South Shields art clubs survived after 1900. South Shields held two loan exhibitions in 1911 and 1912, but these seem to be isolated examples. The Bewick Club continued to hold exhibitions but its vitality was terminally sapped by the Great War. J F Slater helped establish the North East Coast Art Club after the First World War, but this attracted mostly amateur artists. Other organisations emerged; the Benwell Art Club (1919) and the Northern Society of Artists — yet another initiative of the School of Art under R G Hatton. But the main annual exhibiting venue was undoubtedly the Laing's 'Artists of the Northern Counties Exhibition' which attracted all the older artists, as well as encouraging newer talent. C B Stevenson, first curator of the Laing, developed friendships with many of the local artists, not only buying their work for the new gallery but asking their advice on other acquisitions.[111] Whilst the Laing undoubtedly continued to encourage local art, the end of the struggle for the older artists seemed to dissipate the sense of community. This was exacerbated by the death of some of the key figures — Emmerson (1895), Marsh (1909) and Hedley (1913). It was also reflected in the broadening of horizons in terms of sketching grounds and exhibition venues. Unfortunately the negative effect of this dissipation was that many of the younger artists had to accept that the heyday of provincial art communities was over and that the new challenge could only be met in the metropolis.

Notes

1 See Paul Usherwood, *Art for Newcastle. T.M.Richardson and the Newcastle Exhibitions 1822-43*, exhibition catalogue, Tyne & Wear Museums, 1984.

2 See Norman McCord 'Some Aspects of change in the 19th century North East', *Northern History*, vol.31, 1995, and *North East England. The Region's Development 1760-1960*, B T Batsford Ltd., 1979, p.147.

3 See Vernon Lee, op.cit., p.118.

4 Michael E Rose, 'Culture and Philosophy and the Manchester Middle Classes' in A J Kidd & K W Roberts eds., *City, Class and Culture. Studies of social policy and cultural production in Victorian Manchester*, Manchester University Press, 1986, p.113.

5 Newall and Bell both married daughters of Hugh Lee Pattinson, Bell taking over Pattinson's Washington Chemical Co. Redmayne and W W Pattinson worked at H L Pattinson & Co. chemical works and later sold their art collections together in 1886. In the early 1860s Leathart, Newall and Redmayne lived in the same street. Leathart's wife, Maria, was the daughter of Thomas Hedley whose soap business depended on alkali produced at local chemical companies such as Pattinson's. Leathart, Crawshay, Newall and Redmayne served on Gateshead Council. Bell, Palmer and Smith served as Liberal MPs. Leathart, Newall, Boyd, Bell and Jacob Burnett were local JPs.

6 For details see Laura Newton, op.cit., chapter 1 & Appendix I; and F G Stephens, 'Private Collections of England', *The Athenaeum*, 13, 20, 27 September & 18 October 1873.

7 They included Henry Dixon (tailor), W H Budden (agent), J. Davison (auctioneer), C K Reid (agent), R B Bowman (worked at Washington Chemical Co.) and Stephen Stout (draper). For critiques of younger artists — Robert Jobling, John Charlton, Charles Napier Hemy, George Blackie Sticks and William Cozens Way — see *Newcastle Daily Advertiser* 25 & 29 September 1866, *Northern Daily Express* 22 September 1866 *Newcastle Courant* 21 September 1866 and *North of England Advertiser* 29 September 1866.

8 *N.D.C.* 8 March 1866. See also *N.D.C.* 13 September 1866 for similar sentiments.

9 D S Macleod, 'Private and Public Patronage in Victorian Newcastle', *Journal of the Warburg and Courtauld Institutes*, v.52, 1989, p.201.

10 Established collectors such as Leathart Newall and Burnett continued to add to their collections, whilst newer patrons such as William Armstrong, Alexander Stevenson and Charles Mitchell invested heavily during the 1870s. Armstrong bought key works from the succession of high-profile sales throughout the 70s, either directly or through Agnew. Mitchell's purchases seem to have been influenced by his artist son, Charles W Mitchell. Correspondence from Rossetti, Orchardson, J W North, Colin Hunter, Charles Keene and others suggests that Stevenson was building up his collection from the mid-1860s onwards; see Newton, op.cit and Stevenson family papers.

11 *N.D.J.* and *N.D.C.* 16 November 1870. Even the Mayor's opening speech adopted this tone.

12 *N.D.J.* 2 September 1878. For a more detailed discussion see Newton, op.cit., p.48.

13 Patrons: Sir W Armstrong (President), Duke of Northumberland, Marquis of Londonderry, Earl Percy, Earl of Tankerville, Earl Grey, Earl of Durham, Earl of Ravensworth, Rev. F R Grey, Sir John Swinburne, Sir M W Ridley. Committee: J Cowen, I L Bell, C Mitchell, Col. Joicey, T Bell, J Taylor, W Cochrane, A Reid, A S Stevenson, J Burnett, H Philipson, W G Woods, J Hall, J G Sowerby, J Leathart, S Holmes, W Pattinson, J Cartmell Ridley, J Crawhall (sec).

14 A number of artists had to help with the final hanging after Crawhall was badly injured in a gas explosion at the Assembly Rooms just before the opening of the exhibition. For this and the resultant outcry see *N.D.J.* 2 & 4 September 1878.

15 *N.D.J.* 2 September 1878.

16 'Art Exhibitions in Newcastle', *N.D.C.* 6 September 1878.

17 There were others by O'Neil, J H S Mann, R Simpson, Dever, E Edwards, E Hayes and E W Cooke; for critiques see *N.D.J.* 23 August 1878. Emmerson, D F McLea, C Richardson, G B Sticks, R Watson and J R Mather were amongst the north-east exponents of this genre.

18 *N.D.C.* 7 September 1878.

19 *N.D.C.* 12 September 1878. See also *N.D.J.* 2 & 10 September 1878: *N.D.C.* 7 September 1878.

20 See *N.D.C.* 7 September 1878 in which this work is described as 'exquisite', and *N.D.J.* 7 September 1878. Other Cullercoats works to attract attention include Emmerson's *Nearing Home* and *Preparing a Bait* and J H Campbell's *A Study of the Coast.*

21 Letter from Crawhall and Cartmell Ridley in *N.D.J.* 1 February 1879.

22 *N.D.C.*, op.cit.

23 *S.D.N.* 16 September 1878, p.2. The subjects tended to be local — the river, the coast, street scenes and picturesque places such as Bamburgh and Barnard Castle.

24 Armstrong's offer was possibly prompted by the example of London's Grosvenor Gallery which combined sale and loaned works from 1877. Armstrong, George Howard (Earl of Carlisle) and Charles Mitchell frequented the Grosvenor: Mitchell's son achieved acclaim there with his picture *Hypatia* in 1885.

25 Both Sir John Swinburne and Earl Grey served as Liberal MPs for Northumberland. Stevenson, Swinburne, Morton and Hall were JPs for Northumberland and/or Durham. Addison Potter served as a Liberal councillor for Newcastle, becoming mayor and alderman; see Newton, op.cit., Appendix I.

26 Stevenson also had a significant number of Barbizon and Hague School pictures. See Newton, ibid.

27 S H Fraser's collection, sold in 1904, included Murillo, Rubens, Lippi, Metsu, Ruisdael, Steen, Teniers and Vermeer.

28 *N.D.J.* 27 March 1879. See Newton, op.cit., pp.20-21 for more detailed critiques.

29 ibid.

30 See 'Art and the Public Taste', in 'Notes on the Principle pictures at the Arts Association Exhibition', 1879, also published in *N.D.C.* 29 September 1879.

31 *N.D.C.* 30 August 1879.

32 Letter from 'Turps', *N.D.C.* 6 September 1879. See also letter from 'L.J.C.', *N.D.C.* 2 September 1879 and *N.D.J.* 2 September 1879.

33 Letter from 'Savto', *N.D.J.* 9 September 1879.

34 'The "Condemned Cell" at the Assembly Rooms', *N.D.C.* 5 September 1879.

35 'Newcastle Arts Association', *Art Journal* 1880, p.339.

36 Their works included Walton's *A Summer Morning, At Clynder-Gare Loch, A Surrey Lane;* Crawhall's *Sleeping Dog;* Melville's *Comin' thro' the Rye;* Guthrie's *A Gallant of the Terror* (1879) and *How Sweet the Hour.*

37 For a discussion of non-local artists in this exhibition see Newton, op.cit., pp.56, 88, fn.48.

38 *N.D.C.* 21 December 1880.

39 *N.D.J.* 21 December 1880.

40 *N.D.J.* 24 September 1880.

41 *Art Journal,* 1881, p.318.

42 John Millard identified the 1883 Gateshead exhibition as Isa Thompson's first. But I suggest that *Group* (no.449) and *Venetian Teacher* (no.469) by 'Miss J Thompson' are Isa's. The substitution of I for J was a common publishing error, and this artist's address was given as 6 Wentworth Pl., Newcastle — Isa's address.

43 *N.D.C.* 25 August 1881.

44 *Newcastle Courant* 26 August 1881.

45 *Tyneside Daily Echo* 31 August 1881. This echoes a critique in the *Art Journal* in 1860 of Breton's *The Reapers.*

46 *N.D.C.* 5 May 1882.

47 *Art Journal* 1882, p.191.

48 For critiques of Cullercoats works see *N.D.C.* 5 May & 10 June 1882: *Newcastle Courant* 19 May & 9 June 1882: *N.D.J.* 22 May 1882.

49 *Newcastle Courant* 25 January 1884 reported that Mitchell had incurred £2,000 costs, despite having bought £4,000 worth of pictures during its lifetime.

50 See C Denney, 'The Grosvenor Gallery as a Palace of Art' in S P Casteras & C Denney eds., *The Grosvenor Gallery. A Palace of Art in Victorian England,* Yale University Press, 1996.

51 Letter from 'A Lover of Art', *N.D.J.* 19 September 1883.

52 J Millard, *Ralph Hedley. Tyneside Painter,* Tyne & Wear Museums, 1990, p.18. The Life School was based at 3 St. Nicholas Buildings, Newcastle.

53 Other members of the Life School committee included local councillors and men of industry, and some were also members of the Arts Association committee. An article on the South Shields Art Club (*N.D.L.* 11 November 1891) states that Aaron Watson referred to the Life School as having been set up by Emmerson, Jobling and himself.

54 *N.D.C.* 25 January 1883, p.3.

55 Millard, op.cit., p.33.

56 'Local Art' editorial, *N.D.J.* 24 September 1883.

57 Bewick Club Committee for 1884: J Blagburn, C Burlison, J H Campbell, A Carse, J Chambers, W H Charlton, J Clark, W Connell, T Dickinson (secretary), J W Dyson (treasurer), H H Emmerson (president), A J Farnia, J Grabham, W Hayward, R Hedley, J Hedley, W Hepple, W S Hicks, R Jobling (v-president), J Rock Jones, W H Knowles, T Mackay, W Mathieson, C W Mitchell, J Moses, Dr Newton, J Noble, J J Potts, J Reay, W Richardson, W B Ridley, J Robson, R Routledge, J Smith, J G Sowerby, F Spence, T R Spence, J A Stephenson, J Surtees, W S Vaughan, J Wallace, G A Waterston, J Watson, R Watson.

58 Like a raffle, prize-winners could select a picture up to a certain value, or pay the difference for a more expensive work.

59 Patrons of the Bewick Club exhibition in 1884: Earl of Scarborough, Earl Grey, Earl of Ravensworth, Bishop of Newcastle, Rev. Grey, Mayor of Newcastle (Dr Newton), Sir M W Ridley, C M Palmer, Sir F Leighton, Joseph Cowen, Sir W Fettes Douglas, J Morley, J Rogerson, W H James, A S Stevenson, Col. Johnston, W B Scott, C Mitchell, J Hall and R S Donkin.

60 'Our Local Academy' editorial, *N.D.C.* 19 January 1884.

61 ibid.

62 For critiques of these works see *N.D.J.* 19 & 30 January 1884: *Newcastle Courant* 25 January & 8 February 1884: *N.D.C.* 11 February 1884.
63 For critiques of local artists see *N.D.J.* ibid: *Newcastle Courant* ibid: *N.D.C.* ibid.
64 *N.D.J.* 30 January 1884 and *Newcastle Courant* 8 February 1884.
65 *N.D.J.* ibid.
66 *Newcastle Courant* 8 February 1884.
67 'Literature, Art and Drama' column by Puck, *N.W.C.* 9 February 1884.
68 These artists included Mauve, Mesdag, Neuhuys, J & W Maris, De Bock, and Artz.
69 Works for sale included Mesdag *Beach Near Schevinengen,* Neuhuys *Bedtime,* J Maris *Near Amsterdam,* Mauve *After the Rain,* W Maris *Cattle Watering.*
70 This part of Stevenson's collection was not included in the sale of his pictures in 1919, and remains untraced.
71 Westmacott was a partner at Armstrong's Elswick Works and a key organiser of the Jubilee Exhibition. His collection was sold at Christie's, London on 10 May, 1918 and included works by Blommers, Bosboom, Harpignies, Jongkind, Lessore, J, M and W Maris, Mauve, Sam Bough, Rowlandson, Turner, W L Wyllie, Corot, Dahl, Daubigny, Decamps, Diaz, Frankl, Israels, Monticelli, Thaddeus, Cuyp, Hals and T M Richardson — 84 works in all, realising £36,475.8.6.
72 Langley's works at the Bewick Club: 1885 — *A Quiet Pipe:* 1886 — *Idle Moments:* 1888 — *Tired Out:* 1889 — *The Evening Hour:* 1890 — *A Reverie:* 1891 — *Knitting:* 1892 — untitled. Clausen's works included: 1887 — *Woman of the Field:* 1889 — *A Toiler Still.*
73 *N.D.J.* 2 February 1892. This critique describes in detail Langley's untitled work, suggesting that it could be *Woman by a cottage door* (c.1889), illustrated in R Langley, *Walter Langley. Pioneer of the Newlyn Art Colony,* Sansom & Company/Penlee House Gallery and Museum, 1997, p.43.
74 *N.D.J.* 14 February 1891.
75 It was reported by *N.D.L.* 11 February 1890 that the Bewick Club members were so impressed by Blandford Fletcher's *Evicted* that they tried to buy it for the club. See also critiques of Walter Osborne in *N.D.L.* 27 February 1892 and *N.D.J.* 2 February 1892, or the *N.D.J.* 26 December 1896 for his *Atlantic Shores:* F W Jackson in *N.D.L.* 9 February 1892: Gilbert Foster in *N.D.J.* 23 December 1896.
76 See *N.D.C.* 20 November 1895 and *N.D.L.* 20 November 1895 for critiques of Jobling's studio exhibition.
77 *N.D.C.* 8 February 1889.
78 *N.D.L.* 28 May 1887.
79 The Newcastle Sketching Club was established in 1888 primarily as a self-help group for amateur artists.
80 *N.D.C.* 31 October 1895. The *N.D.L.* 31 October 1895 further states that the classes were held under the direction of Jobling, Hedley, Hepple, Dixon Clark, Atkinson, J Brown, J W Gilroy, J J Potts and W D Wild.
81 See L Newton, 'The Bewick Club and the Cullercoats Connection', *Cherryburn Times,* special issue, forthcoming 2003.
82 Millard, op.cit., p.67.
83 *S.D.N.* 25 March 1891.
84 *N.D.J.* 21 November 1889 stated that there were between 20 and 30 members and a new painting room in Tyne St., now also open to ladies.
85 *N.D.L.* 11 November 1891.
86 *S.D.N.* 4 November 1895 also claims that there were nearly 300 works on show.
87 The 1888 exhibition showed works by Chambers, Hedley, Jobling, Emmerson, C N & B B Hemy, Macklin, G B Sticks.
88 *N.D.C.* 6 January 1897.
89 *N.D.C.* 3 January 1898.
90 Amongst those students who exhibited in 1898 were Ethel Richardson, R J Bertram, Hannah Sandemen, Sophia Atkinson, Phyllis Lovibond and Mary Watson (daughter of Aaron Watson). Phyllis Lovibond, daughter of Thomas Watson Lovibond (head of Newcastle Breweries and benefactor to the Laing Art Gallery) did make the transition to professional painter.
91 These included Hay & Sons, carvers and gilders, which held regular exhibitions from the 1860s; Moretons, Turners, Mawson, Swan and Morgan, Rutherford, Carter's (the Nag's Head pub in Nun St. Newcastle), Hellyer Bros in South Shields, E Hardy & Co and T Rushworth both in Durham.
92 See Newton, 2001, op.cit, Appendix II.
93 'Mr. Robert Jobling's Pictures', *N.D.C.* 5 December 1885.
94 J F Codell, 'Artists' Professional Societies: Production, Consumption and Aesthetics' in B Allen ed., *Towards a Modern Art World,* Yale University Press, 1995, p.170.
95 ibid., p.182. Codell also points out that by the 1890s it was recognised that art consumption was addictive, ie. the more one bought, the more one bought in the future. This further encouraged small-scale works and year-round opportunities to buy.
96 See L Knight, 1965, op.cit., pp.119-20.
97 See appendix.

98 These were *The Sick Child* 1866, *Sir Joshua and His Models* 1867, *Enoch Arden* 1870 and *The Shepherd's Family* 1893.

99 For example, the *N.D.C.* 30 April 1887 report on the Academy exhibition which gives enthusiastic reports on the works of Hedley, Jobling, Marsh, T M Hemy, etc., whilst the *N.D.J.* of 3 May 1887 notes that Jobling's work had found a buyer.

100 Letter dated 11 November 1885 to Amy Emmerson, courtesy Mrs. Pat Bolam. The book referred to is a collection of watercolours compiled to commemorate the visit by the Prince and Princess of Wales to Cragside in 1884, which was presented to Lord Armstrong by the people of Rothbury.

101 Letter dated 10 June 1886 to Amy Emmerson, courtesy Mrs Bolam.

102 This included for Wasserman in *Art Journal* 1887; numerous illustrations for *The Graphic* and for the *Tyneside* magazine; for R J Charleton's *Newcastle Town* (1885) and 'Newcastle-on-Tyne (Old Bits in a New City)' in *The English Illustrated Magazine* (1885-6), and for A Watson's *Rivers of Great Britain; Rivers of the East Coast.* (1892).

103 Receipt 4 December 1893 to George Howard, 9th Earl of Carlisle. (Howard Archives J22/111) quoted in J Millard, *A Romance with the North East*, Tyne & Wear Museums, 1992, p.36.

104 As well as the two drawings in 1893, there is another receipt for three watercolours dated 17 October 1894 (see Howard Archives), and a Howard sale by Sotheby's in November 1991 included Jobling's *Woman at Work in a Back Lane.*

105 *Newcastle Courant* 27 February 1885 comments that Jobling's large picture, *When the Boats Come In*, was sold to Lord Armstrong at the Bewick Club exhibition of that year. They all lent works for Jobling's retrospective exhibition at Armstrong College in 1923.

106 These included a tour of the Tees valley, probably in connection with the same project for which Jobling produced illustrations, (note 102). He also illustrated other Watson publications including the *Gossiping Guide to South Shields* (1892).

107 Horton carefully maintained contact with his most valued patrons and friends, usually drawn from the middle and lower-middle classes — often people with a genuinely deep interest in art but whose income could only accommodate the small watercolours or etchings produced by Horton. See Horton Archive, op.cit.

108 Collectors of local artists included Leathart, Burnett, Stevenson, Armstrong, Mitchell, Bell, Newall, Julia Boyd, Rogerson, Lamb, William Cochrane, Hall, Adamson, Taylor, Atkinson, Crawhall and J W Barnes. Many families retained local works when the rest of their collections were sold, including those of Leathart and Armstrong. For detailed discussion of their buying patterns see Newton, 2001, op.cit, pp.29-36.

109 ibid., pp.27-29.

110 For a fuller discussion of the founding of the Laing Art Gallery see ibid, pp.78-85.

111 Horton recalled accompanying Stevenson to buy works in London. See Horton archive, op.cit.

3 The Winslow Homer Connection

There is something odd about an American painter choosing, in the 1880s, the village of Cullercoats on the north-east coast of England as his place of residence and work for nearly two years. American artists went primarily to Paris, or to Munich in this period; certainly, if they went abroad for an extended period of time, it was to the major urban centres where there were schools, exhibitions, museums, patrons, and especially, their own kind. No documentation on Homer's motives for removing to such a spot is known, and it is not likely any existed. The family members, friends and colleagues who might have been privy to his intentions in leaving America lived in New York City at the time, as did Homer. Such confidences as he might have shared would have come in conversation. Commentators on Homer's life and work consequently have been left free to speculate on the puzzle of his choice of Cullercoats. Some have simply stepped over it as a distraction to be avoided; some have taken it on as a challenge; and in some cases, it has served as inspiration to creative imagination.

Homer's first biographer, William Howe Downes, relied heavily on the artist's younger brother, Arthur and Arthur's two sons for information on Homer's life up to about 1885. As Arthur and his family had lived in Galveston, Texas, until their repatriation to the Boston area in 1900, their knowledge of Homer was limited and vague. This fact did not prevent their being generous and assured in responding to all enquiries about their celebrated relative. It might not, therefore, be surprising that Downes's summary introduction to his review of Homer's English period is the least informative, let alone least reflective, of all the published discussions on this turning point in his career:

> *In 1881 a happy chance directed the steps of the painter to the east coast of England, where he worked with his customary zeal for two entire seasons at Tynemouth, in Northumberlandshire, a well-known watering-place... In a suburb called Cullercoates [sic] he was fortunate enough to find a dwelling which just suited him.*[1]

Alan Adamson was the twenty-year-old son of a Cullercoats solicitor in 1881. He emigrated to the United States in the spring of 1882, carrying a letter of introduction from Homer. His memoir of his brief acquaintance with Homer, written from a distance of some forty years, might not be accepted as reliable. Yet the explanation he gives for Homer's arrival in his hometown may be precisely what Homer told him. Given Homer's propensity to tweak questioners, however, it may have been a tale Homer knew would satisfy Adamson and avoid further comment, but had nothing much to do with the case:

> *It was by mere accident he had chosen the village of Cullercoats from among the many other in England that are better known to artists both English and American. On the voyage over he met a man, who, when Homer mentioned his object in crossing the Atlantic, told him to go to the village, I have previously named, where he would find just the subjects for his brush that he was seeking.*[2]

Whatever brought Homer to the north-east coast of England, it wasn't 'chance' or 'accident'. Homer was forty-five years of age in 1881. He had family to whom he was closely attached, and certainly he had friends. Although Homer might not have agreed with them, his peers would have considered him highly successful in his career, in terms of public recognition as well as sales. There was nothing in his situation or known habits to suggest he would wander off without purpose and destination. More significantly, Homer was a thorough professional. He was dedicated to his career, and any action that affected it was planned. Adamson — probably unintentionally — caught the essential truth of Homer's behaviour in 1881: he had an 'object in crossing Atlantic . . . there were subjects for his brush that he was seeking'.

Homer's whole career — that is, his whole adult life — may be described as a search for a subject vehicle which would at once satisfy his aesthetic and expressive needs, and find favour with critics and patrons.

It is well known that Homer began his professional life as an illustrator; wood engravings after his designs appeared regularly in popular journals, especially *Harper's Weekly*, from 1857 into the 1870s. Although he achieved considerable success in this field, it is clear he never intended to limit himself to commercial art. One of the reminiscences gathered by Downes for his biography tells of Homer visiting a Boston picture gallery in company with several of his fellow apprenticed lithographers (therefore, in about 1855), and taking particular interest in a painting by Edouard Frère, a celebrated French artist. 'After a little, Homer said: "I am going to paint". Wight asked him what particular line of work he was intending to take up. He pointed to Frère's *genre* painting, and said: "Something like that, only a [damned] sight better".'[3]

In 1859, sure of being able to earn a living by his illustrations, Homer left his native Boston for the wider opportunities of New York. One of those opportunities was a few rudimentary lessons in painting in oil colours; these he had sometime in 1861. Apparently Homer recognized that the dramatic turn in American history provided him with just the sort of striking subject material with which to launch his career as a painter.

It is commonly assumed that Homer's experiences of the American Civil War was as an artist-reporter on assignment for *Harper's*. However, only his first contact in the autumn of 1861 — which lasted about a week, and was limited to the settled camps around Washington City — was made on *Harper's* business. When he returned to the Virginia outskirts of Washington in the spring of 1862, it was on his own initiative. This time he stayed with the Union Army for about five weeks as it moved towards (but never near) Richmond, a hard experience not embraced without good reason. The scores of pencil sketches Homer produced in these weeks were the groundwork for the paintings with which he made an auspicious debut in the New York art world. The first of these were small, sometimes comic, *genre* scenes of camp life. But Homer's reputation was established with the highly serious *Prisoners from the Front* (The Metropolitan Museum of Art, New York), introduced at the National Academy of Design annual exhibition of 1866, and promptly acquired by a major New York collector.

Where a lesser artist might have settled for this success and begun producing a steady flow of variations on the painting, Homer turned — as his audience did — to images of peace. Following a stay in France of less than a year which made no noticeable impact on his art, Homer spent the next thirteen years creating gentle scenes of American life at fashionable resorts, on farms, in the school-room or school-yard. Children and pretty young women populated these scenes almost exclusively.

The work of these years, 1868 through 1880, brought Homer a reasonable income, and more admiration than denigration in the art press. But even as they praised, critics repeatedly lamented that he seemed unable to equal the high concept and intellectual gravity of *Prisoners from the Front*. The only significant departure from the essentially trivial subjects Homer pursued in these years were the four paintings exploring the theme of the life of former slaves in contemporary Virginia: *The Cotton Pickers* (Los Angeles County Museum of Art) and *The Visit from the Old Mistress* (Smithsonian American Art Museum, Washington, DC), both of 1876; *Sunday Morning in Virginia* (Cincinnati [Ohio] Art Museum) and *Dressing for the Carnival* (The Metropolitan Museum of Art), both of 1877. These canvases met with considerable critical success, but did not attract American buyers. Besides the discouragement of these works' failure to find patronage, it is unlikely Homer would have found it easy or personally satisfying to sustain exploration of Southern life, a cultural context foreign to his New England sensibility. However, this excursion into what was essentially exotic subject territory may be seen as a symptom of Homer's seeking to break into a new mode of work.

That Homer showed signs of being troubled and restless in the later 1870s is well recognized. As usual with Homer, changes in mood and behaviour can only be inferred from some of his personal and professional actions, and from comments in the press — not necessarily well-informed, or free of bias. By the end of the 1870s Homer's prickly temperament had become so conspicuous that a writer felt free to couple with enthusiastic praise of his work the observation, 'he is posé in the extreme, and affects eccentricities of manner that border upon gross rudeness. To visit him in his studio, is literally bearding a lion in his den; for Mr. Homer's strength as an artist is only equalled by his roughness when he does not happen to be just in the humour of being approached.'

Explanations for this change put forward at the time were that Homer was bitter over negative press criticisms, or the failure of his work to sell well. Modern commentators tend to offer more intricate — and equally unsupported — theories, a favourite being that Homer was pining over a lost love.

Homer's 1880 summer-long stay in the light-house on Ten Pound Island at Gloucester, Massachusetts, is widely interpreted as demonstration of this undefined emotional crisis. It is characterized as a retreat from normal day-to-day life to self-imposed isolation. The connotation of 'light house', a solitary tower standing some remote distance from a bleak and dangerous coastline, reinforces this fantasy. In fact the light on Ten Pound Island is best described as a stationery buoy, necessary to maritime safety because the island is in the middle of what was a heavily trafficked harbour. As for being isolated, the island is a few oar-strokes from the centre of the town. However, when cast as melodrama, Homer's 1880 summer serves to prefigure his removal to England some six months later, and makes the departure for England a continuation of a flight from society, into scenery and climactic conditions congenial to his supposedly stormy emotional state.

Homer's commitment to Gloucester for the summer of 1880 may have had a pragmatic connection to his departure from America. Beginning in 1879, with his especially numerous — twenty-seven sheets — contribution to the American Water Color Society's 'Twelfth Annual Exhibition' Homer may be seen orchestrating a series of sales of blocks of watercolours and drawings, presumably to accumulate the money needed to support an extended stay abroad. The next of these events after the Water Color Society's spring 1879 show, was a one-man exhibition culminating in an auction presented at a Chicago gallery in December 1879. Then followed an auction of seventy-two works mounted at a New York sales-room in March 1880. The last of these fund-raising ventures occurred in December 1880, and took a novel form: a one-man exhibition mounted by an art dealer, and extending approximately two weeks. One hundred and twelve watercolours and drawings were on view and for sale on this occasion; all were the product of Homer's stay in Gloucester the previous summer. It is more probable Homer put himself to work in Gloucester in preparation for this sale exhibition, than that the exhibition was the result of Homer happening to have worked prodigiously over a few months, and assembled a large, homogeneous body of work.

The body of summer 1880 work is not without symptom of Homer's aesthetic restlessness. A handful of sheets among the approximately one hundred surviving works from these months are radical in technique and subject treatment. They are dramatic renderings of the last rays of sunset against skies already night-dark, and the extraordinary *Sailboat and Fourth of July Fireworks* (Fogg Art Museum, Harvard University, Cambridge, Massachusetts), all executed in broad strokes on wet paper.

Homer had made an extended stay in Gloucester once before — undramatically passed under the roof of a downtown hotel — which may be more pertinent as a model for his English venture than the 1880 visit. From June into August 1873 the usually peripatetic Homer stopped in Gloucester for dedicated practice of what was a new medium to him; that autumn he returned to New York an accomplished watercolourist. This example of Homer's rigorous approach to attaining an artistic goal parallels his removal to the north-east coast of England for nearly two years, and the major changes in the style and content of his art he effected in that place and period of time.

There are ample clues that Homer was disaffected with his life in the later years of the 1870s. This may have been because of personal disappointments, certainly, but given Homer's devotion to his work, it is more plausible that his frustration was professional. He turned forty in 1876. Real distinction in his career seemed to have eluded him. It was in these years he began to be counted by the critical press as among the 'older men', as the next generation of French-trained painters drew their attention. Homer's temporary expatriation was less likely a flight from some personal hurt, than a fundamental part of a well planned programme to reconstitute his art, and propel his career forward. Accomplishment of these goals required separation from familiar company and responsibilities, and new subject matter radically different than that he and his public was accustomed to.

The visual drama of the rugged terrain and storms of the Northumbrian coast offered vivid subject material, but the hazards created by the combination of these natural elements was more likely what attracted Homer. Just as the special risks of sailing its north-eastern coast were famous well beyond England, so was the institution created to contend with them: the Tynemouth Volunteer Life Brigade. Homer was drawn to the Tynemouth area to see Nature threaten, and man fight back. His 'object in crossing the Atlantic' was the pursuit of marine disaster.

The subject, in his life as well as art, was not entirely strange to him. Homer's design for a wood engraving published in the 24 June 1865 issue of *Leslie's Chimney Corner*, captioned 'The Cold Embrace — "He Sees the Rigid Features, the Marble Arms, the Hands Crossed on the Cold Bosom"' featured an artist — who does not in the least resemble Homer — among a small group of onlookers lifting a sheet to reveal the neatly posed, drowned beauty. Homer touched on ocean traffic and seamen's lives in two more illustrations: 'Winter at Sea — Taking in Sail Off the Coast', published in *Harper's Weekly*, 16 January 1869, and 'At Sea — Signalling a Passing Steamer', published in *Every Saturday*, 8 April 1871. Neither of these is concerned with the dramatic tension of a threat of disaster. However, his powerful drawing, 'The Wreck of the Atlantic — Cast Up by the Sea', published in *Harper's Weekly* 26 April 1873, may reflect a sympathetic response to a genuine tragedy fresh in everyone's mind. The White Star Line's steamer *Atlantic* sank off Nova Scotia in the early hours of 1 April 1873. It carried over 900 passengers and crew; 562 of these lives were lost, including all but one of the women and children, and all the married couples among the passengers. The *Atlantic* was found to have sailed with insufficient provisions and fuel; its captain was condemned for negligence, and the crew for its brutal behaviour when the ship went down. It is arguable that the *Atlantic* sinking was only overwhelmed in American memory by the loss of the *Titanic* forty years later.

No New Englander was untouched by maritime disaster in this period. Every port town's cemetery held cenotaphs listing entire crews lost. Gloucester's losses, as the most active fishing port along the north-eastern coast, were legendary. (The hold on the American imagination of the hard, dangerous life of Gloucester men reaches into our own time with the film *The Perfect Storm*, released in 2000.) Even by Gloucester standards, the storm of 24 August 1873 took a terrible toll: nine vessels with crews totalling 128 men were lost. Hardly a family in the town was not affected. This devastation fell on Gloucester just before Homer ended his first summer-long stay in the town. It is difficult to believe his sympathies were not deeply touched by this experience. It most likely underlies the unusual, poignant mood of his watercolour, *Waiting for Dad* (Mills College Collection, Oakland, California), probably done immediately before he left Gloucester in 1873, and the oil version of the subject, *Dad's Coming!* (National Gallery of Art, Washington, DC) developed in his studio that winter.

Gloucester is a deeply sheltered harbour; its fishing boats go out to work on the open sea, and if they come to grief, it is far from home. If Homer wanted vivid experience of the storms and the havoc they wreck, Gloucester would not serve.

The Tynemouth area, however, was well known to be immediately exposed to the violence of the sea, and for its pioneering rescue service. Exactly this reputation probably made Tynemouth Homer's destination when he went abroad in 1881. However, Homer would probably have expected to explore the Tynemouth area for just the location and accommodation that suited him. He may well have known of the summer artists colony at Cullercoats: American artists, especially those living and working in New York, were not naive provincials; they got the current European art journals, and natural preoccupation with their profession assured they were well read. The small scale of Cullercoats, its easy proximity to Tynemouth, that artists were a *genus* known to the local population, and thus he would not be a curiosity, all would have contributed to his choice of the village over the city. But the fact that Cullercoats had a life brigade of its own — something he could not have known until he got to the region (unless he really did meet a passenger on the voyage from New York to Liverpool who was from Cullercoats) would have sealed his choice.

That Tynemouth had a resonance for Americans, where Cullercoats did not, is borne out by the titles of the English subject watercolours and drawings Homer put into exhibition. He knew just where particular scenes had served to inspire a particular drawing or painting, of course, but of those which include specific place identification in their titles only the watercolour he showed at the Art Association of Newcastle-upon-Tyne's Autumn Exhibition of 1881 made a local distinction in being titled *Cullercoats*. The works he sent back for exhibition in Boston in February 1882, and that formed the bulk of one-man shows he mounted in 1883 and 1884, carried generalized titles such as *Fishing Fleet Coming In* and *Inside the Bar*, but if a place was named, it was Tynemouth or Newcastle, never Cullercoats.

Immediately after his return from England in November 1882 Homer began to pursue the goal he probably had intended: to apply to American subjects the understanding of a violent sea and newly enlarged skill in its rendering he had attained at Cullercoats. In the summer of 1883 He went to Atlantic City to witness a demonstration of the breaches buoy; *The Life Line* (Philadelphia Museum of Art) of 1884, was the result. An incident he is said to have witnessed at Atlantic City, rescuers dragging two drowning or drowned women out of the surf, was transformed into the monumental *Undertow* (The Sterling and Francine Clark Art Institute, Williamstown, Massachusetts), begun in 1883, but not completed until 1886. The culmination of this period in Homer's art is generally recognized to be his informal series on the Grand Banks fishermen, three oils completed in 1885. The first, *The Herring Net* (The Art Institute of Chicago), is a sunlit scene of a team of fishermen pursuing their working routine. Its juxtaposition with *The Fog Warning* (Museum of Fine Arts, Boston) heightens the dramatic tension of that scene of a solitary fisherman rowing his dingy toward the safety of his home-ship, hoping to outrun the fog bank seen in the distance. The series concludes with *Lost on the Grand Banks* (private collection) in which two fishermen find themselves in the desperate situation the solitary oarsman of *The Fog Warning* may, or may not, have avoided; they are immersed in limitless fog.

No oil painting by Homer is dated 1887, 1888, or 1889, but there is no reason to suppose Homer did not work in oil in these years. *The Signal of Distress* (Fundacion Coleccion Thyssen-Bornemisza, Madrid), in which a ship's crew prepares the rescue effort for a disabled vessel seen nearby, was originally dated 1890, and was first shown in 1891. However, it may have been begun several years earlier, and have been a close successor to the Grand Banks series.

It is arguable that after 1890 when Homer virtually eliminated the narrative element from his major oils — that is, the presence of figures — in favour of pure seascape, he was reducing this theme of the danger inherent in the northern sea to its essential element. Yet his preoccupation with the theme of maritime disaster lingered long. In *The Wreck* (The Carnegie Museum of Art, Pittsburgh), of 1896, only a rescue team is seen pulling its life boat across dunes toward an unseen shoreline. (The masts of the sinking ship had been seen beyond the dunes, but Homer painted them out before exhibiting the picture.) And in the same year that he finished *The Wreck*, 1896, Homer reworked *The Signal of Distress*, mainly to make the distressed ship into a derelict.

The ultimate expression of Homer's fascination with the theme that had drawn him to Northumbria may be *The Gulf Stream* (The Metropolitan Museum of Art), of 1899. In this, his only oil painting set on a southern sea, the subject is a single soul, helpless to prevent being swept into the great current which connects America and England.

Abigail Booth Gerdts, Director, The City University of New York Graduate Center, Spanierman Gallery, Lloyd Goodrich and Edith Havens Goodrich, Whitney Museum of American Art. Record of Works by Winslow Homer.

Notes

1 William Howe Downes, *The Life and Works of Winslow Homer,* Cambridge, MA: Riverside Press, Houghton Mifflin Company, 1911, p.99.

2 Alan B. Adamson, 'The Homer That I Knew', in *Winslow Homer: All the Cullercoats Pictures* (Sunderland, England: Northern Centre for Contemporary Art, 1988), 16.

3 Downes, op.cit. p.29.

4 *The Cotton Pickers* was introduced at a private reception held at a prominent gentlemen's club in New York in March 1876. It was immediately purchased by a member's English guest, and was said to have been still wet when it left the country a few days later. The buyer's name has never been discovered but it is known he was in the cotton business — doubtless the reason for his enthusiasm for the painting. Apparently it commanded respect for something beyond the topicality of its subject matter. It was shown in the Royal Academy of Arts spring exhibition of 1878, as '*Cotton Pickers — North Carolina* by Winslow Horner'.

5 'Art Interchange Artists', *Art Interchange* 5, 22 December 1880: p.130.

6 Over the next approximately one hundred years owners and dealers of Homers dating — or thought to date — from 1881 and 1882 awarded them titles which tied them to Tynemouth. The 1977 publication of William Gerdts's article elucidating Homer's connection with Cullercoats led to immediate and sweeping changes in the titling of works in museum and private collections, substituting 'Cullercoats' for 'Tynemouth' in those which already had been made geographic specific, or adding 'Cullercoats' to previously neutral titles.

4 The Cullercoats Pictures

Late nineteenth-century coastal imagery is complex and problematic. It is tempting to read naturalistic pictures of fisher folk simply as 'snapshots' of a particular way of life, or as perhaps a commentary on the part of artists about the threat posed by 'modern life' to these picturesque pre-industrial workers. However, these paintings were not so straightforward, and were instead intimately bound up with contemporary notions of nationhood, imperialism and regionalism.[1] National identities are often largely defined by what Stephen Daniels termed 'legends and landscapes' — stories of a Golden Age, traditions, heroic deeds — which give shape to the 'imagined community' of the nation.[2] To this end poets and painters have, consciously or not, helped express, depict and shape ideas of national identity. Hence the Cullercoats output — encompassing subjects of heroism, shipwrecks, virile masculinity, female stoicism, traditional customs and costumes and pre-industrial scenery — fed into a much wider attempt by British intellectuals to construct certain notions of 'Britishness' during the late nineteenth century. From the bullish imagery of the 1870s reflecting the expansionist 'New Imperialism', to the subdued pictures of fisherfolk at leisure or children at play by the turn of the century, Cullercoats imagery seems to reflect the wider cultural and ideological changes of the nation as it reacted to Britain's loss of status as *the* global economic power.

Before 1870, none of the artists later identified with the colony exhibited any works specifically produced at or showing Cullercoats. Henry Emmerson's first Cullercoats-inspired works to be exhibited, in 1870, coincided with Cullercoats-based pictures by the better-known artists William Q Orchardson, Frank Holl, John D Watson and Arthur H Marsh. In 1869 Orchardson, Watson and Marsh had stayed with Alexander Stevenson in Tynemouth, using Emmerson's studio in which to work.[3] Yet, despite a rash of pictures at various London venues during the 1870-72 seasons, there is no contemporary evidence that critics realised that they shared a common location.[4] This is understandable, however, given that few of them carried any overt reference to Cullercoats, either in the title or pictorial detail. The

Lookout House, which became the most significant topographical feature of Cullercoats pictures, did not figure as it was not built until 1879. But these early paintings did set up certain themes — the fishermen's cottages, the watching/waiting figures in a storm, the heroic fishermen, the land-based activities of fisherwomen and children — which became entrenched in Cullercoats imagery.

Beyond this initial influx of painters it is difficult to assess the level of local artistic involvement at Cullercoats at this point, although it is clear from London exhibitions that Watson and Marsh continued to work there throughout this period. It is likely, therefore, that the flowering of the colony was heavily indebted to this early investment by non-local artists.

The catalogue that follows is arranged by the following groupings — Heroic pictures; Waiting/Grieving Women; Work; Leisure; Topography and Fish Quay; and Seascapes. These categories are extremely fluid, but it is clear that none is unique to Cullercoats, and no subjects tackled by coastal colonists elsewhere were not also attempted by Cullercoats artists.

Heroic Pictures

The strength of Britain as a maritime nation has long found reflection in the paintings of its artists, particularly in times of prosperity or war. North-east artists — Richardson, Carmichael, Ewbank and Clarkson Stanfield — all had reputations for maritime subjects during the early nineteenth century. Yet their storms and shipwrecks are characterised by a detachment from the human element, in favour of the most effective rendering of sea and sky that academic convention would allow. This element of

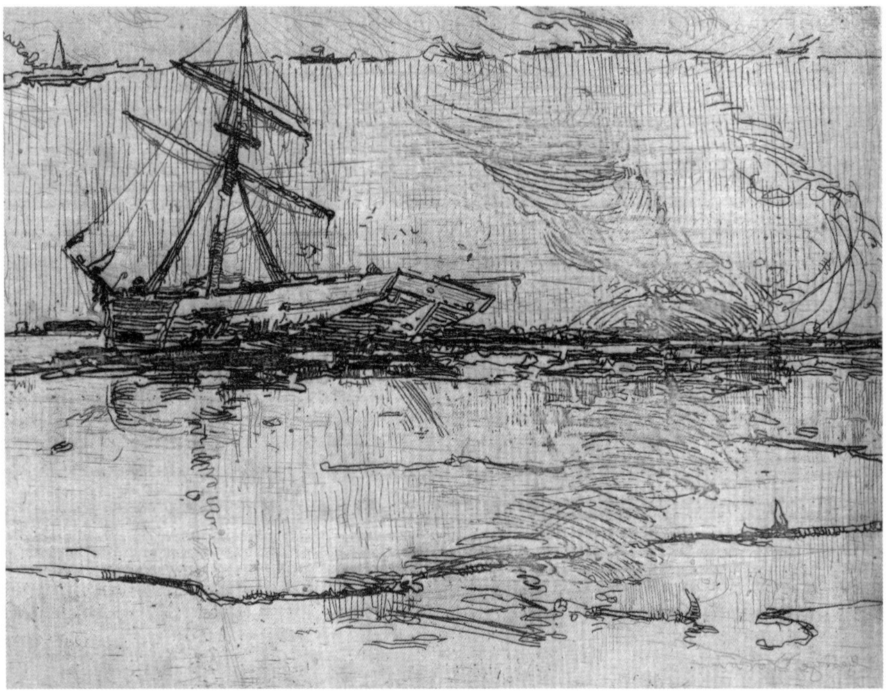

FIG.38
George Horton, ***Wrecked beneath the Cliff***; Tyne & Wear Archive, reproduced courtesy D & M Redpath

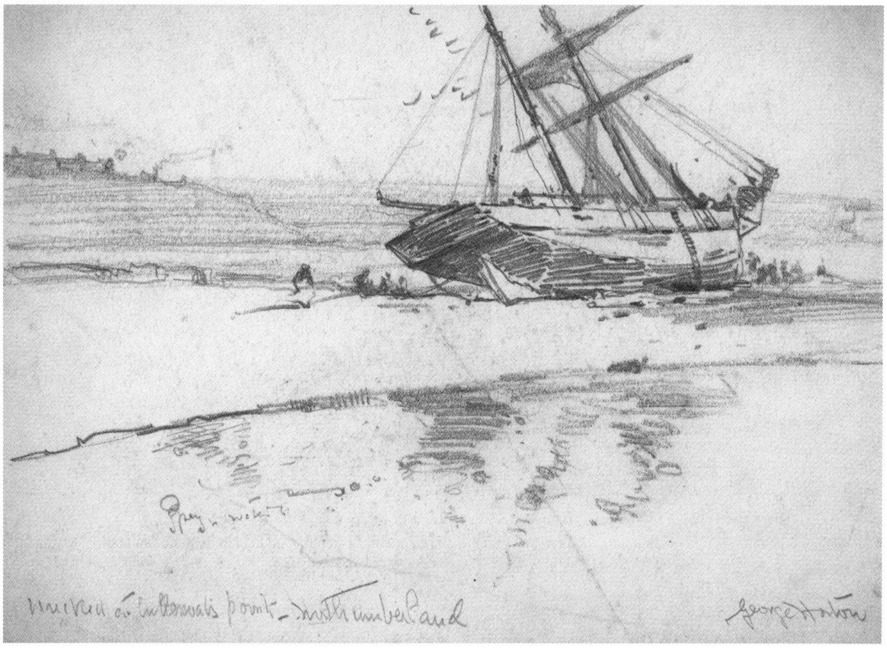

Fig.39
George Horton, ***Wrecked on Cullercoats Point***; Tyne & Wear Archive, reproduced courtesy D & M Redpath

detachment persisted throughout the nineteenth century, in the 'wreck' picture, although this subject became less common as the century wore on. Regional practitioners included Jobling, John Chambers, W T N Boyce and A J Sticks. George Horton produced numerous wreck pictures and etchings during his early career, including *All that was Left of Her, Wreck of the Peggy* (both 1892) and *The Wreck of the Salween* c.1895 (plate 1). However, whilst a fastidious draughtsman, Horton's lack of interest in the particularities of his wrecks is evident by the number of images which seem to use a similar ship in a number of different settings (figs.38-40). Thus the wreck was a stereotype, a prop which he used in his pictures of atmosphere and

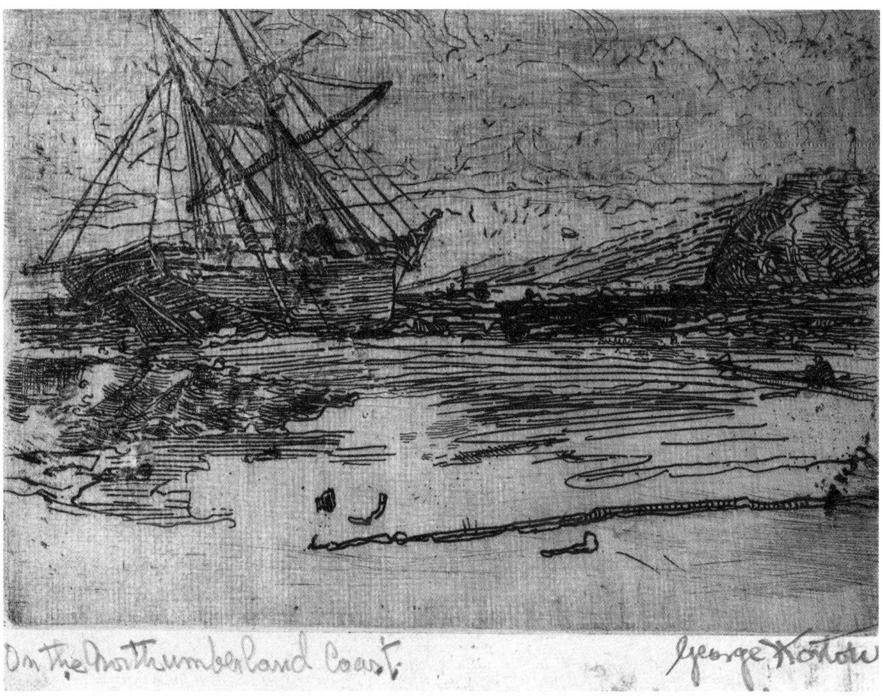

Fig.40
George Horton, ***On the Northumberland Coast***; Tyne & Wear Archive, reproduced courtesy D & M Redpath

light. His is perhaps an extreme example, but it underlines the strangely dispassionate nature of this genre. The ambiguity of response to such an emotive subject can perhaps be partly explained by the ambivalence felt by those witnessing such scenes. On the one hand loss of life was tragic and avoided if possible, but on the other, the driftwood of a wrecked ship and a washed-up cargo were welcome gifts to struggling fishing communities. Those artists most deeply involved in the life of a community like Cullercoats must surely have shared this ambivalence.

However, from the 1860s 'heroism' was an increasing theme in this genre, perhaps encouraged by works such as Israels' *The Shipwrecked*, whose appearance at the Royal Academy in 1862 was acclaimed as a 'thrilling tragedy, ... admirable in pathos, yet bold in heroism'.[5] A clue to the reason for this change may also be found in the same edition of the *Art Journal*:

> *the free life of our fellow-countrymen is ever bursting into the picturesque and the passionate because ... Britain is a land of action and of progress, trade, commerce, growing wealth, steadfast yet ever changeful liberty; a land and a people, therefore, wherein a contemporary Art may grow and live, because in this actual present hour we act heroically, suffer manfully, and do those deeds which, in pictures and by poems, deserve to be recorded.*[6]

This passage echoed Charles Baudelaire's notion of the 'heroism of modern life',[7] and signalled a profound ideological shift in the iconography of shipwreck paintings; from Nature as God's instrument of retribution or spiritual testing, to the celebration of heroic man in Nature.

Fisherfolk 'drama' pictures have been regarded as peculiarly British, encouraged by both the 'literariness' of British art and the traditional role of the sea as a stage upon which to act out notions of British heroism.[8] But, whilst they did enjoy immense popularity with the British public, these pictures were not confined solely to British artists. Hague School artists such as Israels and Mesdag produced similar works, as did some of the artists of the Skagen colony in Denmark.[9] This 'literariness' — whereby a particular story was enacted at a specific location — was often further enhanced by the use of titles taken from literature or poetry, most often from Kingsley, Longfellow, Tennyson or Shakespeare. This undoubtedly strengthened their didactic nature, making them popular subjects both for the walls of the Royal Academy and for illustrated magazines such as *The Graphic*.

However, this appropriation of the sea by both art and literature as a vehicle for metaphors of British heroism cannot simply be taken as a 'given'.[10] Not surprisingly, the flowering of this type of subject coincided with a period of colonial expansionism and international conflict. Britain's imperialist pretensions, together with events such as the Crimean War and anxiety over the Franco-Prussian War, seem to have fuelled this appetite for heroic fisherfolk subjects. But it does not explain why fisherfolk in particular came to epitomise notions of British heroism.

During the nineteenth century our contemporary constructions of masculinity took shape and entered into 'culture'. Victorian ideals of 'manliness' included courage, virility, stoicism, fortitude and patriotism.[11] These ideals were traced back to Elizabethan times by many Victorian writers, who promoted hero figures as aspirational models,[12] prompted by the realisation that the nation's manhood — actual and metaphorical — did not measure up in this time of need. The nation's conquerors and cannon-fodder were perceived to have degenerated pitifully as a result of industrialisation and urbanisation. It is easy therefore to understand how those qualities of endurance, stoicism, hardiness and bravery, which were part of the daily lives of the fisherfolk, were held up as the epitome of British manhood. However, the fisherfolk were 'ideal' in another crucial

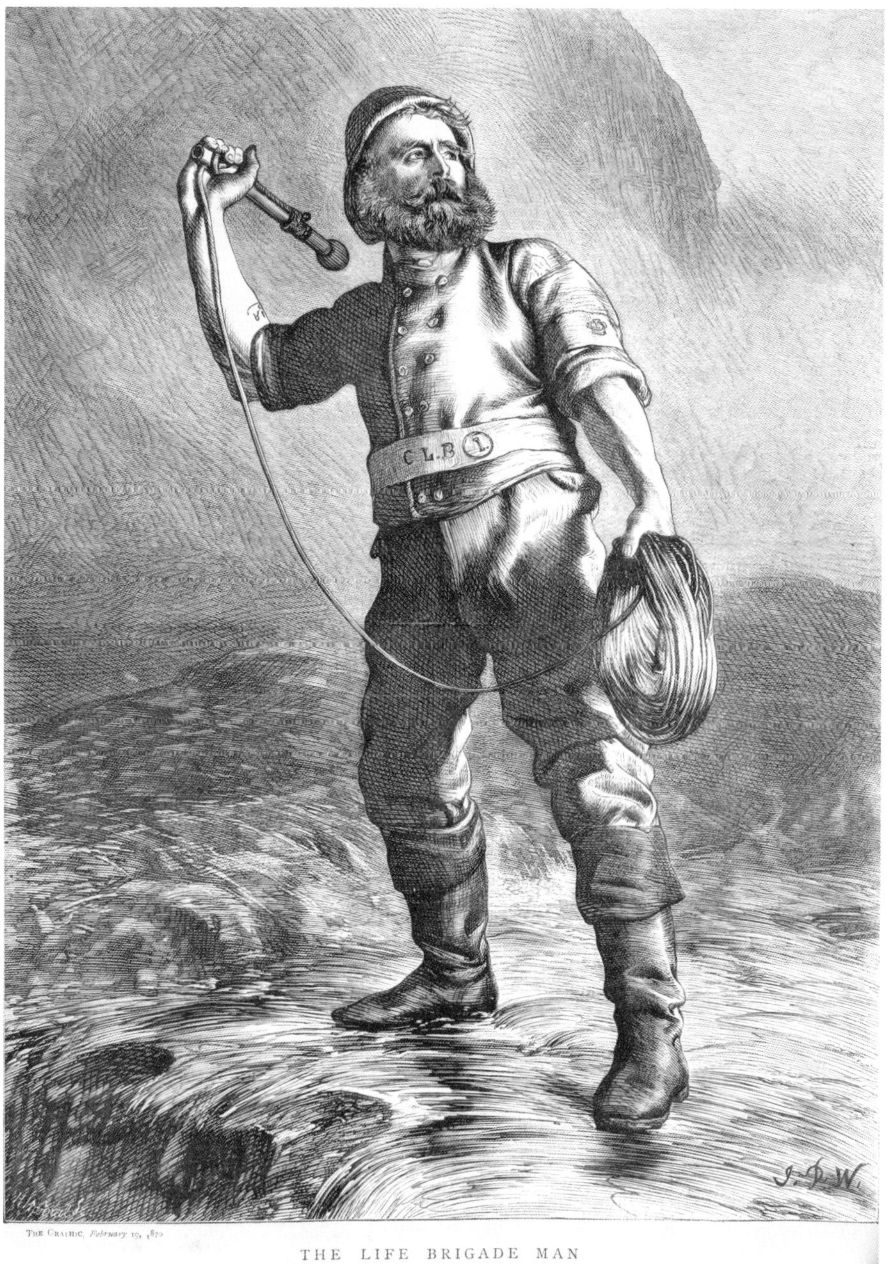

FIG.41
John Dawson Watson, ***The Lifebrigade Man***; pub. *The Graphic* 1870; Newcastle Libraries & Information Service

way, being able to trace an unbroken ancestry back to the Vikings or Jutes. This again echoes a much broader cultural concern to establish the racial superiority of the Anglo-Saxon race, in step with Britain's colonial exploits.

Art therefore helped to constantly validate these ideals of British masculinity as part of the hegemonic process. Cullercoats images such as J D Watson's *The Lifebrigade Man* 1870 (fig.41) fulfilled this demand, and by appearing as both 'high' art painting at the Royal Academy and as an illustration in the popular magazine *The Graphic*, this, and images like it, were guaranteed to reach a wide-ranging section of the populace. This image offers us the epitome of bravery, endurance and strength, its 'truth' secured by its site-specificity — this is a real Cullercoats lifebrigade man/fisherman, not an idealised studio model in fancy dress.

Painted at the same time as Watson's image, Orchardson's *Toilers of the Sea* (plate 2) is a more ambiguous treatment of the 'heroic' theme. Although he was renowned as a portraitist and painter of upper-class social commentaries, Orchardson's picture received mixed reviews at the Royal Academy in 1870. The *Art Journal* noted, 'The old man at the helm is a fine study. There is amazing dash in this work: the subject and style are apparently in emulation of Mr. Hook's stormy seas.'[13] The critic of the *Athenaeum* also alluded to Orchardson's indebtedness to Hook and conceded that it was a 'comparatively wholesome work'. But this is as fulsome as his praise got: 'One may dismiss the sea here at once, because it is vilely painted ... The execution of this work is flimsy to a wonder; there is no natural light about it; all is shadowy and insubstantial, dim and weak in colour.'[14] This critic did have a point; the rendering of the sea is utterly unconvincing and it is unclear whether the sharply-dipped angle of the boat is a result of rolling waves or merely a high vantage point.

Toilers of the Sea seems to have little connection with Orchardson's usual output, pictures in which he often made use of spatial distance between figures as a sign for psychological or emotional isolation. But it seems that the very claustrophobia of this image creates its own isolation. It would have been an obvious cliché for Orchardson to have set this small boat in a vast expanse of ocean. Instead, the lack of any definable boundaries — horizon, sky, land, other craft — gives the work a feeling of entrapment. You cannot even see the full extent of the boat's boundaries. Orchardson succeeded in suggesting the terror, acceptance and isolation of the experience through his use of space and the placing of figures. Even the lukewarm critic of the *Athenaeum* had to admit that 'while Mr Orchardson is unable to paint a wave, he can observe or realise in imagination the action of a lad in the circumstances. Of course one sees that this is the boy's first voyage'.[15] Yet even this is ambiguous, and the barefooted boy again suggests a debt to Hook's *The Luff Boy*. Orchardson's picture has little to do with the faithful rendering of a fisherman's work; as the *Athenaeum* pointed out, 'the very title is a misnomer'. Yet the 'heroic' reading is unconvincing and difficult to sustain because of the presence of the terrified boy. Perhaps it is the ambiguity of *Toilers of the Sea,* the inability to pigeonhole it, which exacerbated the contemporary critical confusion.

It is notable that by far the vast majority of dramatic fisherfolk pictures revolve around 'the rescue' idea. Parallels can be drawn with the late-nineteenth-century obsession with the rescue stories of classical mythology — Hercules and Alcestis, Perseus and Andromeda or Orpheus and Eurydice — which were appropriated by artists and writers as paragons of male superiority and heroism. This was part of the use of classical mythology to provide affinities with imperial and cultural objectives.[16] It was hoped that

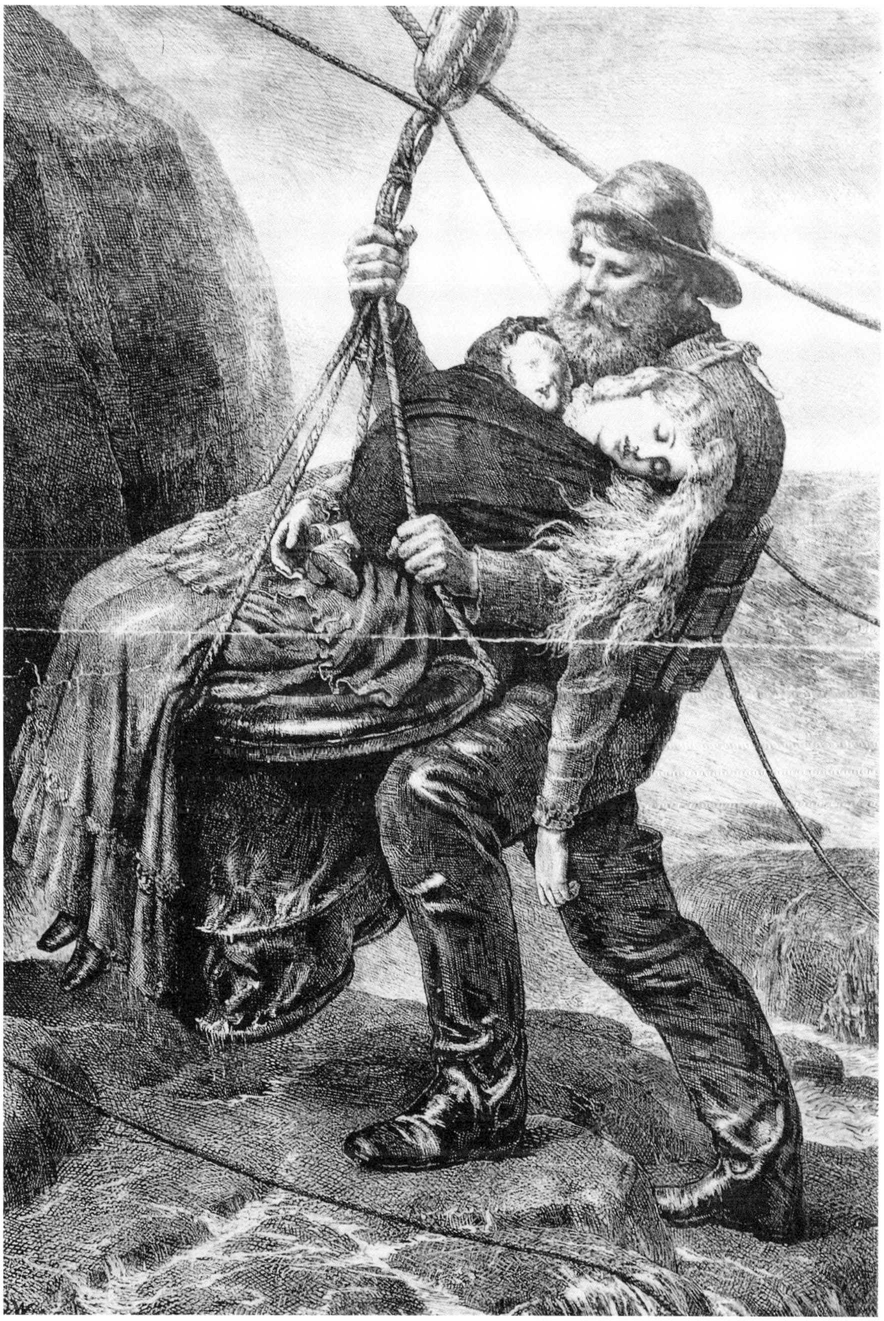

FIG.42
John Dawson Watson, ***Saved***; pub. 1871 ***The Graphic***; photograph courtesy South Shields Voluntary Life Brigade

the classical attributes of virtue, self-control, 'greatness' and patriotism would be mirrored by contemporary British manhood. Similarly, the cultural obsession with the 'rescue compulsion' reinforced notions of male superiority and female passivity and helplessness.

The influence of the classical ideal can be seen in the previously mentioned *The Lifebrigade Man* whose figure is posed like some latter-day javelin thrower, his mind and body totally focused on the unseen object of his gaze. But the rescue element of this picture is not particularly strong. In Watson's *Saved* 1871 (fig.42), the rescue/heroic ingredients are epitomised.[17] The powerful male, the swooning (sexually-experienced) female and defenceless child, are all typical ingredients. Although helpless, the virtue of Watson's Pre-Raphaelitesque female is never in any doubt.[18]

The efforts of the Lifebrigade man remained a popular subject for many British artists into the twentieth century. In A H Marsh's *First from the Wreck* 1894 (fig.43), the heroism of the Lifebrigade man is secondary. For Marsh the real drama resides in the faces and gestures of the women, each one a portrait of a discernible individual. He seems uninterested in creating an image of grand pathos or conveying some greater message on the power of nature or the fragility of life. It is instead an image 'full of tenderness and compassion'.[19] But it is also an image of unswerving realism — the rendering of the women's clothing, the wet oilskins of the man and child, the wetness of the sea-washed blocks of stone on the pier — all are treated with an almost photographic precision. This allies it much closer to the work of Newlyn artists such as Forbes or Bramley rather than the painterly concerns of many of the Staithes artists or the contemporaneous paintings of the Joblings.

This theme largely lost its appeal for Cullercoats artists after the early 1880s, but was substituted by a subtly different form of rescue picture — the lifeboat scene. In these images individual heroism was usually replaced by collective endeavour. North-east artists and audiences would have been familiar with such dramatic images through the work of J H S Mann, Birket Foster, J W McIntyre and Henry Moore at the Arts Association exhibitions 1878-82. However, in Jobling's *The Wreck of the Iron Crown* 1882 and Winslow Homer's 1881 picture of the same incident (plates 3 & 4) a certain ambivalence reappears. In both images the presence of a lifeboat offered the potential for an emotional/heroic reading, but this opportunity is negated in preference for the concerns of composition and 'atmosphere'. The

FIG.43
Arthur Hardwick Marsh,
First from the Wreck (untraced),
1894; photograph courtesy
private collection

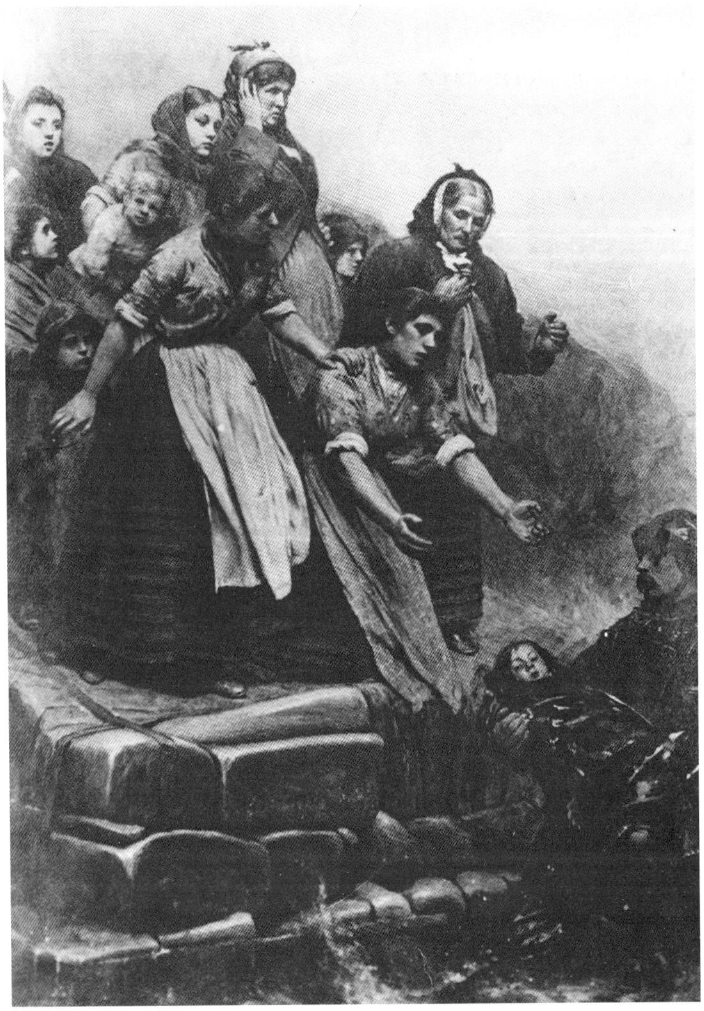

similarity of the images is unmistakable and it is possible that Jobling saw Homer's picture before completing his own, since Homer decided 'to exhibit *Wreck of the Iron Crown* soon after its completion in the window of a Newcastle art dealer' before sending it to his Boston dealer in February 1882.[20] Both watercolours are highly-finished studio works intended for exhibition, but based on *plein-air* sketches.[21] Some critics have suggested that Homer's work is the first in the long line of marine epics which he completed during the 1880s and 90s. But it seems more akin to other contemporary British works on the same theme. And although it is a distinct development in his own watercolour technique, its detachment from the emotional nature of the subject links it more closely to his Gloucester watercolours of 1880 than to the intense psychological dramas of his later sea pictures. His odd direction to his Boston dealer Chase, that 'If you like you may cut off the life boat'[22] again seems to reinforce the notion that he was primarily concerned with atmosphere rather than the contemplation of heroic endeavour.

In 1884 Jobling showed *Storm — Lifeboat Off* at the Bewick Club (plate 5) which proved very popular with the local audiences, as one critic noted that 'the faces of the scared women rivet the eye of the observer'.[23] Although the title suggests a subject of great drama, Jobling chose to play this out as much in the depiction of the natural as the human elements. Greater prominence was given to the storm-riven twilight, the eerie glow cast over the figures on the beach and reflections on the wet sand, and the expert handling of the raging seas. Millard suggested that works such as this signal Jobling's refusal to portray the true hardships of the fisherfolk's lives, and instead cast 'a romantic glow over the harsh, cold and wet reality of the scene.'[24] Whilst it is undoubtedly true that Jobling often pandered to the Victorian taste for poetic renderings of tragic/dramatic scenes, this picture more successfully balanced the human drama with that of Nature. The displacement of the heroic element, now implied by gestures and features rather than overt actions, allowed Jobling to concentrate on the light and colour of the ensemble. In this respect it signalled a shift in Jobling's concerns, bringing it closer to the slightly later Staithes works of Fred Jackson (plate 6) and Ernest Dade, where the figures are reduced to dark shapes on the edge of the picture, whilst the fundamental concern is with the depiction of the elements, and the effects of sky and sea. Yet no-one could accuse Jackson of trying to cast a 'romantic glow' over the scene. The issues surrounding the lot of the fisherfolk are of no concern here. The people are literally marginalised, signalling the sacrifice of social concerns to the growing preoccupation with the formal qualities of picture-making. As the century drew to a close these preoccupations increasingly pervaded all subjects of the coastal colonists. Until now the work of Cullercoats artists has always been regarded as firmly entrenched in the Victorian 'social realist' groove. Yet it seems clear that the shift in Jobling's treatment of these themes, from his early slightly sentimental images to the late experiments with colour and brushwork, started in his works of the mid-1880s.

Jobling's shifting perspective can be taken as symptomatic of a much broader change, partly brought about by a period of relative stability in Europe which meant that the stimulation of nationalistic fervour was no longer so urgent. The out-pouring of patriotic sentiment prompted by Queen Victoria's Jubilee in 1887 proved short-lived as the nation became gripped by an ever-deepening economic depression by the late 1880s. This depression created working-class unrest, erupting in events such as the 'Bloody Sunday' Riots (1887) and the London Dock Strike (1889). There was a 'crisis of masculinity' in the 1890s caused not only by the increasing impact of industrialisation/urbanisation, but by the emergence of the 'New Woman' and the waning of Victorianism.[25] In the arts this not only deflected attention away from nationalist and imperialist imagery, but forced artists to reconsider how working-class 'heroic' images could be couched. In the face of anxiety over the working classes it became difficult to project an idealised version of the British worker. There was a growing awareness that the heroicisation of fisherfolk could not be sustained as a contemporary role-model.

However, the didactic properties of heroic fisherfolk pictures, eagerly seized upon by town councillors desperate to fill the walls of their new municipal galleries with morally-uplifting artworks, ensured that some coastal colonists continued to produce a steady trickle of works, such as J W Gilroy's *Hauling up the Lifeboat* (plate 7), Walter Langley's *Disaster! Scene in a Cornish Fishing Village* 1889 (plate 9), C.N.Hemy's *Wreckage* 1898-1901, Harold Knight's *The Last Coble* 1900 (plate 8) and Stanhope Forbes' *A Rescue at Dawn* 1904. Even Jobling returned to this theme in 1902, when he was commissioned to paint *Launching the Cullercoats Lifeboat* (plate 10).[26] This returned to the heroic ideals of the earlier lifebrigade pictures, but although the figures play a prominent part in the composition, their treatment, like that of the sea, is much looser which enhances the sense of movement, urgency and drama. There is an unsettling, claustrophobic feel about this picture — wrought by the relative largeness of the boat, almost enclosed by people, the cliffs, the front of the picture plane and a lack of sea into which it must go.

But it is at this point, when the majority of coastal colonies seemed to have finally dispensed with the type of dramatic narratives so readily adaptable to nationalistic jingoism, that Cullercoats produced arguably its most exceptional heroic work. In some ways John Charlton's *The Women* 1910 (plate 11) represents the summation of the heroic/lifeboat genre at Cullercoats, and yet it is problematic for a number of reasons. Charlton had maintained a house at Cullercoats for many years and, despite finding fame and fortune in London, continued to exhibit works regularly in north-east exhibitions. But, except for a small amount of illustrative work, there is no evidence that he produced any major Cullercoats picture until *The Women.*[27] Its large size, dramatic content and striking composition were enough to ensure its success at the Royal Academy. The *Chronicle* noted that it:

> *occupies an equally conspicuous position, as it catches the eye of the visitor on entering through the vestibule and draws attention to itself first of all in the exhibition .. In this work Mr. Charlton has made an entire departure from the style which has earned him so high a reputation in the past, and the success he has achieved fully justifies the change he has made.*[28]

The *Art Journal* described it as 'a spirited rendering of a buffeting storm of snow and sleet with the strenuous figures of heroic women dragging a lifeboat.'[29] One cannot deny the strength of the composition; the way in which Charlton has used the contours of the land, the lines of women and the stormy skies to produce a spiralling maelstrom effect. The dramatic composition is capped by the lifeboat, silhouetted against the sky, placed where the lines of women converge.

The Women seems to conform to the notion of the literariness of fisherfolk pictures; indeed the picture is based on an actual incident in Cullercoats' recent past.[30] This fits both with the alternative imaging of the region identified in chapter one and with Daniels' 'legends and landscapes' notion of a constructed national identity. As such, *The Women* could be regarded as fitting into Charlton's 'portfolio' of paintings recording historical events, and as part of the more widespread recovery and recording of the north east's past.[31] Yet as a 'heroic fisherfolk' genre painting, it is clearly an anomaly.

In subject and treatment this picture was arguably thirty years out of date. As a history painting its place stylistically was amongst the 1880s productions of Stanhope Forbes and the other Newlyn artists. Amongst its contemporaries at the Royal Academy it must have seemed hopelessly dated. And yet no contemporary critics seem to have noticed, probably because of the picture's subject matter and its historicity. Recalling the points made about nineteenth-century masculinity, the classical ideal and the 'rescue compulsion', it would seem that *The Women* almost parodies these ideals. The assertion of nineteenth-century manhood was based on the disparagement of women and on male claims of difference from and superiority to women and other races.[32] Yet Charlton's heroic women have assumed all those attributes normally reserved for men. Indeed, Charlton seems to exacerbate this role reversal by depicting the men mostly huddled together near the boat, regaled in waterproofs, whilst the Amazons' strength and endurance is enhanced by their bare arms and heads, despite the weather conditions.

Could this perhaps be a reflection of the *fin-de-siècle* 'crisis of masculinity' referred to earlier? It is easy to see how *The Women* could be linked to notions of the 'New Woman', with moves for new political and social freedoms, the rejection of Victorian ideals of propriety and the woman's 'place', and the emphasis on healthy bodies and practical clothing. Charlton's picture seems to almost embody these ideals. Whilst there is little pictorial evidence that the work is set in the past, it was accompanied by an explanatory text at the Royal Academy exhibition. But, the specifics of the story would have been relatively unimportant to the contemporary audience, since its subject, together with Charlton's comparatively old-fashioned technique, would have been of a sufficiently familiar type to have effectively neutralised any possible contentious readings for the contemporary viewer. In other words, the 'New Woman' reading could only have been convincingly applied if the subject had been more obviously contemporary and given a more avant-garde treatment. For those who did notice, the fact that the drama was set at a distant geographical location would have diminished the threat still further. Thus, *The Women* was made safe by its historical and geographical distance. Further, it could be argued that Charlton reinforced the traditional ideas of 'difference' by fetishising the female forms — the risqué element of being bare-armed and bare-headed being enhanced by the clinging draperies of the soaking costumes — fulfilling the male viewer's ability to 'take possession' and, by implication, maintain male dominance. The obvious distance of time and place between these women and contemporary urban working-class women avoided the more sinister sexual anxieties that this latter group provoked. Instead, the women, acting together, reinforced the traditional role of women as the mainstay of the community.

In common with national trends, the heroic themes which were common during the early years of the Cullercoats colony (c.1870-85) were integral to constructing a role-model for the nation's manhood and reflecting the glory of its maritime prowess. The frequent use of literary references in titles or accompanying text reinforced this nationalistic message, perhaps to counterbalance the site-specificity of many of the images. However, there was rarely any reference to the true human hardships and cost implied by these scenes. Gradually these subjects were even emptied of any heroic/dramatic content until, by the 1890s isolated examples of the genre, such as painted at Staithes, usually focused on the formal qualities of the picture rather than the subject as narrative or the embodiment of nationalistic ideologies. Hence, as the summation of the heroic impulse, Charlton's *The Women* stands as a glorious anachronism.

Waiting/Grieving Women

The imagery of waiting or grieving women was the complement to the 'heroic' imagery. In this sense it supports the dual Victorian ideals of female behaviour in depicting women as either stoic and supportive of their men folk and each other, or as the grief-stricken fairer sex mourning the loss of their brave providers. However, it also has resonances with earlier imagery, particularly works such as Jacques-Louis David's *Oath of the Horatii* 1785 or *Brutus* 1789, in which the women have similar supporting roles to the heroic actions of the men. This again draws attention to the influence of classical role models, used by both David and late-nineteenth century artists to underscore ideals of nationhood.[33] In these images, and those of 'working women', the classicism of female forms and poses is particularly notable in the work of Winslow Homer and Marsh.

But there is clearly another lineage which runs through this sub-genre; that of religion and the imagery of the pietà. The combination of Christianity and classical ideology may seem uneasy, but again has antecedents in the neo-classicism of David and Canova, as well as the more obvious Renaissance works of Michelangelo, Raphael, etc. Theological doctrine is relatively unimportant: more fundamental are the notions of morality, belief and codes of behaviour which inform and contain the acceptable demonstration of hope and loss which unite these different belief systems.

The strong religious beliefs of the fisherfolk were reiterated again and again in artistic reminiscences and the contemporary literature about the fishing villages adopted by the artists' colonies. The reasons for this are bound up with middle-class anxiety about the irreligion of the urban working classes, which seemed to foretell the breakdown of social and moral values in society.[34] It is therefore understandable that the religiousness of the fisherfolk was seized upon as yet another aspect in the creation of this working-class ideal. On another level, the physical strength and idealisation of fisherfolk bodies in the literature and imagery not only connects with a classical ideal but with the Christian conflation of spiritual and physical strength.

Emmerson was perhaps the first at Cullercoats to explore this subject, in his picture *Waiting for the Boats* (plate 12), which was shown at the Central Exchange exhibition in 1870, priced £10 and subsequently bought by Hugh Taylor of Chipchase Castle.[35] In this splendid large oil Emmerson set the precedent for countless subsequent pictures on this theme, with the juxtaposition of youth and age — the old mother and young wife awaiting the return of their loved one. His superb portrait technique is given full rein in the characterisation of these women. The old woman, Betty Donkin (see fig.44), gazes into the distance, back across the years. She is stooped and needs a walking stick, but still sits with a creel on her back, awaiting the catch. The young woman, Meggie Arthur, sits knitting. Her classically

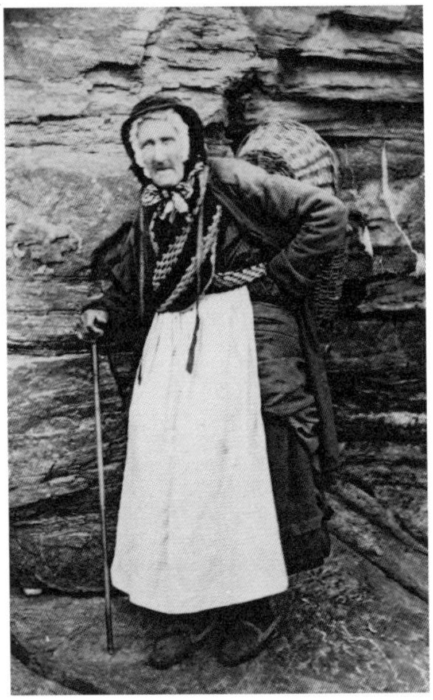

FIG.44
Betty Donkin, 1873; photograph; Newcastle Libraries & Information Service

beautiful face, silhouetted against the grey sky, is as yet unlined by care. Although we can identify the place as Cullercoats from the cliff-top houses, Emmerson has not emphasised this by putting the fisherwomen in the tell-tale pleated skirts, suggesting that in these early days of the colony, artists were still unconcerned with the specificities of place.

This is borne out by the more famous picture, Frank Holl's *No Tidings from the Sea* (plate 13), also painted at Cullercoats during the summer of 1870 and shown at the Royal Academy the following year.[36] Perhaps because it had been commissioned by Queen Victoria, the painting received a quantity of diplomatic praise. The *Art Journal* noted that it 'tells a pathetic story; the execution is as earnest as the thought.'[37] *The Graphic* went into more detail:

> *The materials are of a thoroughly homely kind, and the execution is somewhat gaunt and crude … The poor, famished-looking creatures, nervously alert to every sound, clung together oppressed by sorrow too great for words. There is no more touching picture in the whole collection than this.*[38]

However, when a posthumous review of Holl's career appeared in the *Art Journal* in 1889, the picture was compared, perhaps unfairly, to Frank Bramley's *Hopeless Dawn* 1888 and described as 'ill drawn … grotesquely out of proportion … the central figure of the fisherman's wife, the abandon of grief is certainly not visible in her attitude.'[39] The central figure does seem hugely out of proportion to the rest of the picture. The poses of both women are slightly stagy and unconvincing, although the child clinging to the old lady's skirt in startled incomprehension at her mother's despair is a more successful passage. But by isolating the grieving figure in the centre of the picture Holl helps to convey the sense of loss and loneliness felt by the bereaved.

Perhaps the most successful Cullercoats picture to tackle this subject of grief and which must certainly owe a debt to Holl's picture is Emmerson's 1888 painting *Bereaved* (plate 14), which was shown at the Royal Academy in 1889. Its resemblance to Bramley's *Hopeless Dawn* (fig.45) begs the question of whether Emmerson had seen Bramley's work or at the very least been inspired by its huge success. Bramley's picture was based on a quote from Ruskin, the religious content of which is reinforced in the picture by the open Bible and the print of Raphael's cartoon for *Christ giving the Keys to St. Peter* on the wall to the right. These features are echoed in Emmerson's picture, but in this case the Bible is closed, whilst the print (Watson's *Saved*) alludes to the bravery and danger faced by fishermen such as the dead man — an obvious connection with Peter the fisherman and Christ as a 'fisher of men'. The religious connotations are reinforced in Emmerson's picture by the vicar reciting over the coffin and by the symbolically charged baby in the crib, placed in the centre of the painting and lit up by the full force of the sunlight coming through a gap in the curtain. Bramley's snuffed out

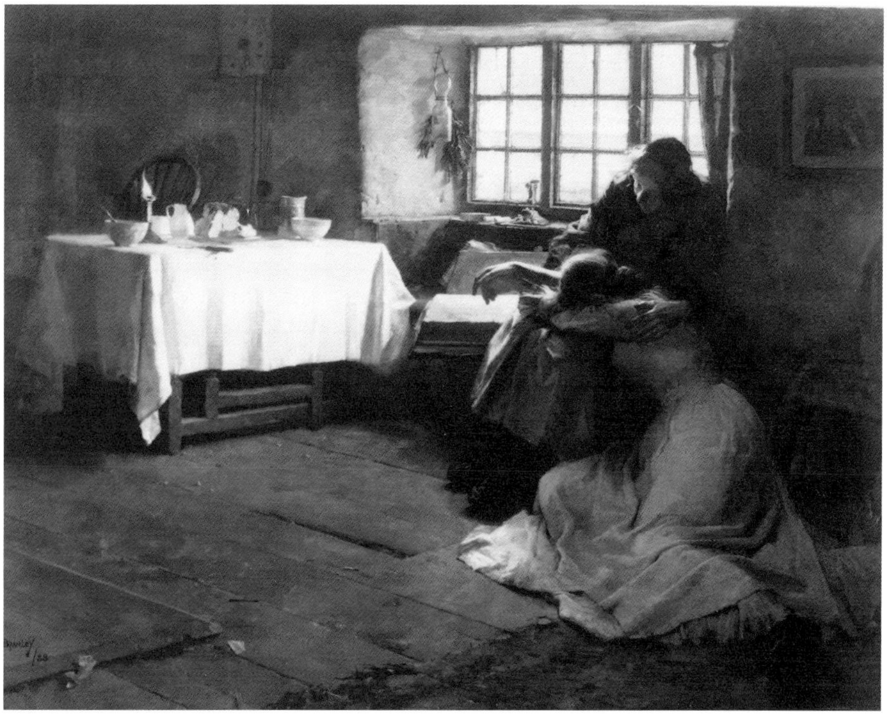

FIG.45
Frank Bramley, ***Hopeless Dawn***, 1888; Tate, London 2002

candle in the window, symbolising the expired fisherman, is mirrored by the empty flowerpot on the window-ledge of Emmerson's cottage. The similarity of pose of the grieving women — both arms stretched out, cradling the head — and the halo effect created by the light coming from the window, is striking, and recalls the grieving Madonna.

Like Bramley, Emmerson paid careful attention to every detail of the cottage interior, rendering the furnishings, the still-life elements and the sleeping baby with painstaking fidelity. The almost hyper-realism is continued outside, with the face of every fisherman being an identifiable portrait, including the white-bearded figure of Emmerson himself. The high degree of care and finish given to every aspect of this work is more remarkable still when considering its small size. When it was shown at the Central Exchange Gallery in Newcastle in 1889 it was picked out by the *Art Journal* critic H V Barnett as an example to which Hedley should aspire: 'The chief figure in "Bereaved" ... is most moving, a real achievement in pathetic expression.'[40]

Emmerson's carefully considered composition also uses pictorial arrangements to hint at the very different gendered reactions to death. The women are contained within the interior, surrounded by reminders of the dead man — his oilskins hanging up, his jumper dangling from the 'Sheila Maid', his child blissfully unaware in its crib. The widow's outward display of grief will be replaced by an internalised one, held in place by the signs of his absence. The men are squeezed into the pictorial space to the left of the wooden partition, and are engaged in the acceptable form of the public display of grief. Even the boy of the family stands at the door, identifying with the men outside, symbolically on the threshold of manhood.

Although they are out in the open air, the men's true feelings are internalised, pictorially contained within the narrow space, expressed only through ceremony and ritual. The young girl peers out from behind the curtain, perhaps curious to witness the display. But no man enters the realm of the women. The picture records local funeral customs — the resting of the coffin outside the home before being carried to the burial place by the fishermen in their lifebrigade uniforms, and the fact that the women of the family were not expected to take part in the funeral ceremony (still common practice locally). Emmerson was himself given just such a funeral when he died in 1895, as a mark of the respect and esteem in which he was held by the local fishing community.

One of the crucial details in which Emmerson's picture differs from Bramley's is that the grieving young widow is being comforted by an equally young woman and is surrounded by her supportive family. Indeed, the sense of community is very strong, despite the fractured space. The presence of the baby, a clear reference to the infant Jesus, also acts as a symbol of hope and regeneration. By comparison, and in common with many similar works, for example Langley's *But Men must work and Women must weep* 1882 (fig.46), Bramley's grieving woman is comforted by an older woman — mother or mother-in-law — whose grief is just as great but whose experience has taught resignation. To me, these images are truly hopeless.

FIG.46
Walter Langley, ***But Men must Work and Women must Weep***, 1882; Birmingham Museums & Art Gallery

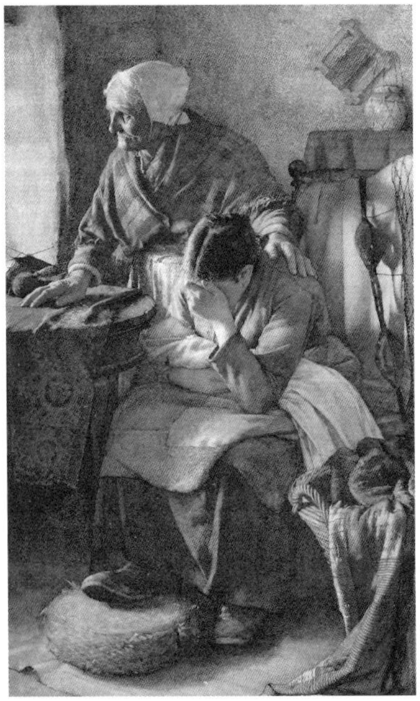

The juxtaposition of young woman and old is a common thread running through the 'waiting women' theme and includes Jobling's *Old Betty Laidler and Mary Lisle* 1886 (plate 16)[41] and Marsh's overtly religious *For those in Peril on the Sea* 1896 (fig.47, untraced). V N Rainbird's 1919 picture, *Waiting* (plate 15), is evidence of the continued popularity of this theme with the second generation Cullercoats artists. With great economy Rainbird captured both the wistful gaze of the younger woman and the grim watchfulness of the old woman as she fidgets with her hands. Their surroundings are similarly loosely worked in. Like Homer's *The Gale* and Thompson's *Fisher Folk*, the angry sea is suggested by a streak of white, whilst the figures are similarly placed against a forbidding, unbroken sky. The use of the much-reduced palette is a bold yet effective device echoing the sentiment of the picture — stark and uncompromising. The figures may be timeless in their waiting, but they are not monumental, only isolated.

The 'waiting women' theme abounds in the Cullercoats work of Homer, perhaps culminating in the reworking of *The Coming Away of the Gale* 1882 into the monumental *The Gale* in 1892-3. However, in *Under the Cliff, Cullercoats* 1881 and *Fisherwomen* 1881-2 there is little of the drama or sense of foreboding of the later work. Instead, in both, the women watch as the boats make for the shore; their wait is almost over.

Under the Cliff (plate 17) is typical of his earliest work at Cullercoats in revealing a significant amount of topography; in this case the headland at Tynemouth with its distinctive Priory forms the backdrop. But *Fisherwomen* (fig.48) is more akin to the later monumental works in dispensing almost entirely with topographical detail to concentrate instead on Homer's characteristic groupings of women. The unusual viewpoint, looking slightly up at the foreground group, makes the picture depth very shallow; the cliff is no more than a thin slice and depth is suggested only by the different scale of the two groups of women and the distant boats. The vast blank sky further flattens the image, producing the classical frieze-like quality noted by many Homer scholars. The monochrome washes of this sketch further enhance this 'marble relief' effect. The affinities with Rainbird's *Waiting* are particularly striking.

Jobling's 'waiting women' pictures include *Anxious Times* 1889 (plate 21), whose loose paint-handling again demonstrates his technical developments at this period. The moonlit backdrop of *Three Fisher Lasses* (plate 18) lends a less frantic atmosphere to the subject. Isa Thompson also addressed this theme but, as with much of her Cullercoats output, works such as *Women must Weep* 1885, *Looking for the Sail* 1886 and *Sudden Squall* 1888 are now untraced. Thompson's *Storms*

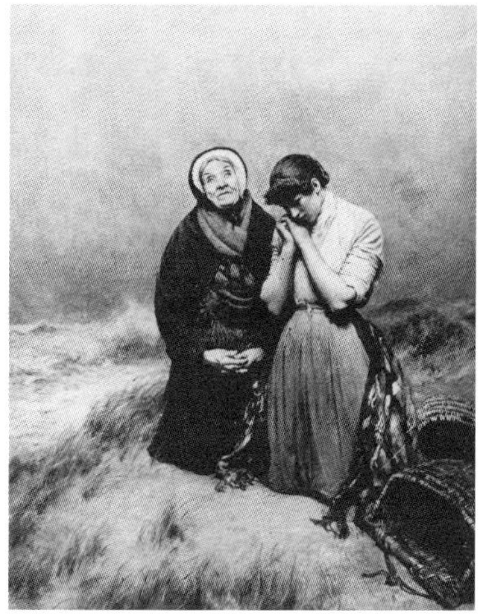

Fig.47
Arthur Hardwick Marsh, ***For those in Peril on the Sea*** (untraced), 1896; photograph courtesy private collection

Fig.48
Winslow Homer, ***Fisherwomen***, 1881-82; Courtesy, Museum of Fine Arts, Boston. Bequest of John T Spaulding, 1948 (48.728) © 2003 Museum of Fine Arts, Boston

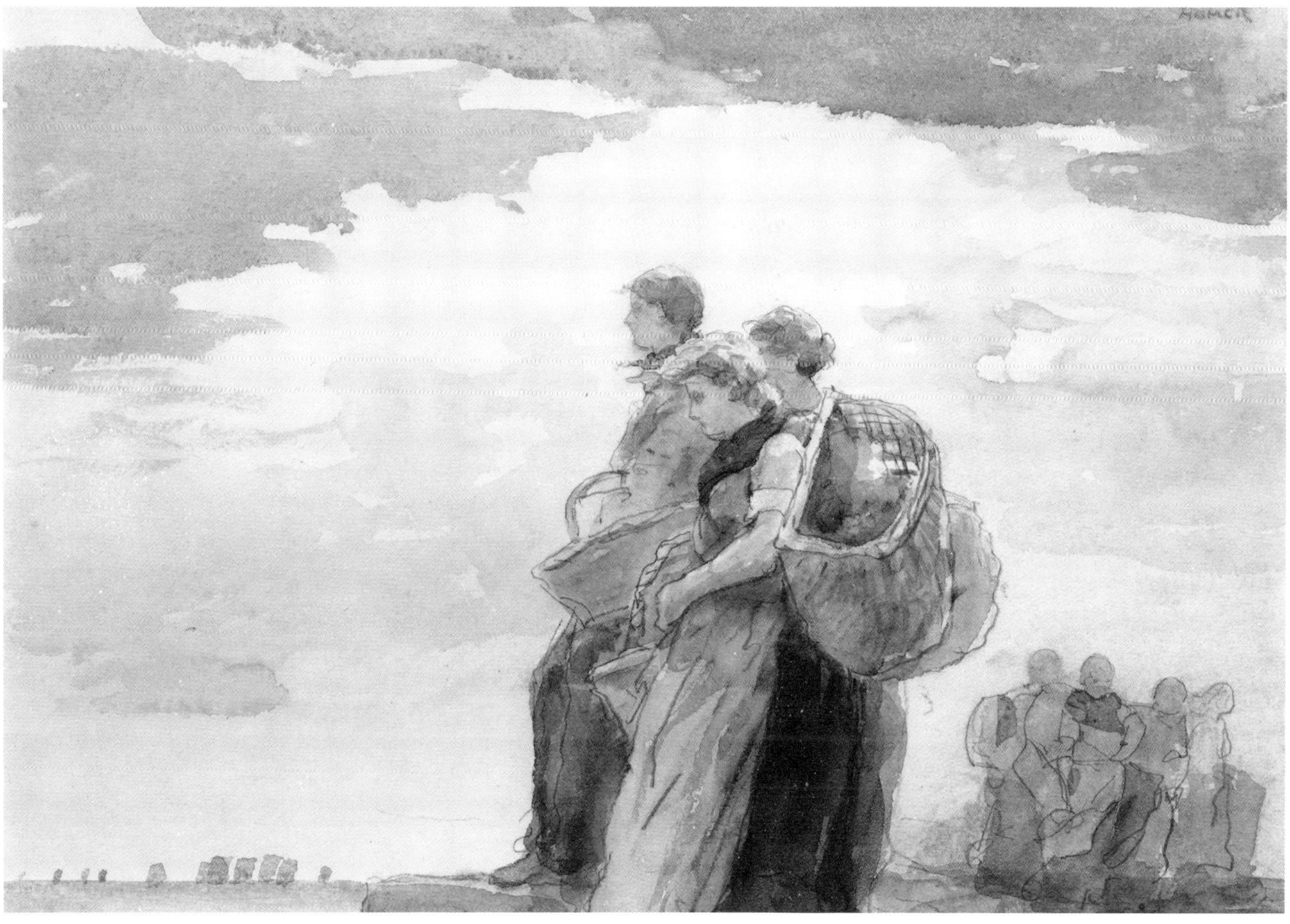

be Sudden 1887 (plate 19) bears the hallmarks of her early style and technique. Yet her minute attention to the details of the figures whilst leaving the background almost blank, does suggest the influence of Homer rather than Jobling. There is little in the surroundings to suggest the danger of an approaching storm, but we are asked to empathise with the wistful, longing looks of mother and child as they await the hoped-for return of husband and father.

In 1887 Marsh exhibited a large watercolour, *Men must Work and Women must Weep*, at the Royal Society of Painters in Watercolour. Subsequently renamed *Lighting the Beacon* (plate 22), the picture is a more literal translation of Kingsley's poem from which it took its original title than, for instance, the more emotive version by Langley of 1882 (fig.46).[42] When Marsh's work was subsequently shown at the Bewick Club in 1891 it received a very positive reaction: '"Lighting the Beacon" is a really fine study of figures, beyond which the general conception of the picture is stunning, and the execution is effective in the extreme'.[43] And:

> *A subdued scheme of colour permeates this remarkably dramatic and stirring picture. The principal group of comely women gazing seaward is admirably modelled. The artist has conveyed into their faces and eyes an agonised look of despair which tells its own tale. How "men must work and women must weep" were adequately told by this group alone ... To face such a storm is to be stung by salt spray and pelted by sand and shingle until the blood comes, as we know by experience.*[44]

Although seemingly flattering, this latter critique highlights the equivocal nature of the image. We are told that it is 'dramatic' and 'stirring', which seems to be supported by the notion that these women risk being pelted 'until the blood comes'. Yet this sits uneasily with the 'agonised look of despair' and the inference that they can only weep. Perhaps the change of title was an attempt by Marsh to dispel some of the ambiguity, to downplay the melodrama of the poem in favour of a more restrained exploration of the theme. We are spared the display of grief being enacted by the girl on the left, and are instead invited to consider the feelings of anxiety, fear, hope, fascination and even excitement, that the girls must be experiencing. Although a lone girl stands on the rock, silhouetted against the sky, she has none of the monumental qualities of Homer's girls but rather seems dwarfed by both the beacon and the enormity of the task. Strangely, despite its obvious dramatic possibilities, there are few Cullercoats works which use the beacon as a focal point, making this picture quite unusual. However Marsh has retained the distinctiveness of location by the clear use of the characteristic Cullercoats pleated skirts.

But there are obvious parallels with Homer's Cullercoats work, especially in the three-woman grouping and the idealised classicism of poses, figures and faces. However, Marsh handles watercolour more as if it were oil, giving the whole composition a greater sense of solidity. The greater modelling makes the figures seem more statuesque than frieze-like. Such use of the medium was constantly criticised by the *Art Journal*, who noted of Marsh's *The Messenger* in 1893 that it 'rather trespasses beyond the proper attributes of watercolour.'[45] The earth palette provides compositional unity whilst also maximising the brooding sense of the coming storm without being over-dramatic. The vast expanse of pictorial space given over to the sky further suggests the smallness, futility even, of human effort when confronted with the power of nature. Thus parallels can be drawn with the lifeboat pictures in the idea of the heroic, perhaps futile attempts to save 'those in peril on the sea'. Peering out to sea, the women/nation watch, wait and mourn the heroic explorers of the foreign and the unknown.

The 'waiting' paintings share many features with those of 'working women', but had roots in a much richer tradition of Christian and (neo)classical imagery. This provided opportunities to explore and affirm certain notions or anxieties about the woman's place in relation to men, to society and to the nation. But the high degree of specificity in many images has hitherto encouraged a more straightforward reading of these paintings as exercises in presenting an unmediated, 'truthful' account of fisherfolk life. For example, Walter Langley's *Time moveth not* and *But Men must work* were described as demonstrating 'his deep understanding of the role of women in the Newlyn community ... in Newlyn women faced a lifetime of hard work and patient reconciliation to a portion in life that promised, and often gave, nothing.'[46] This suggests that the reasons for this subject's universal appeal are obvious — lying in its ability to provoke feelings of sympathy or fortitude in the viewer.

However, the longevity of this *genre* resists a mere sentimental/narrative reading of these pictures. Indeed the reason for its timeless and universal appeal lies not only in its religious and classical motifs, but in the implicit associations binding women, the shore and the sea, embedded in the iconography of the waiting/grieving women pictures. These associations concern notions of boundaries, of insularity and nationhood. The sea itself is an obvious marker of boundaries: it limits and contains island nations yet also insulates and protects them.[47] Similarly, the French theorist Alain Corbin talks of the beach as 'that uncertain, ephemeral, luminous boundary.'[48] As these comments imply, the boundary is not fixed, but is prey to erosion or attack. The role of the female figure as the marker of national boundaries and symbol of the nation is also important here, and when considered alongside the idea of vulnerability it is clear how powerful the iconography of this subject becomes.[49]

> *This combination of apparent fixity and latent uncertainty helps to give borders and the frontier regions that adjoin them an often remarkable symbolic importance*

in the defining of national identity. It is at borders that nationality is checked, and national difference most formally asserted; it is in frontier regions that national belonging, being most at risk, is often most persistently invoked.[50]

The waiting woman, sited at the edge, facing the unknown, embodies both the nation and its vulnerability.

Yet this *genre's* survival, long after national and imperial imperatives had shifted, suggests that other readings were possible. In his survey, Corbin notes, 'The Romantics made the sea-shore the favourite spot for self-knowledge ... The ocean's vastness became a metaphor for the individual's fate ... They came in search of themselves'.[51] So in the later 'waiting women' pictures the associations with national insularity were often overtaken by notions of a more personalised insularity. In pictures such as Rainbird's *Waiting*, the sea maintained its role as definer of identity, but of the self. The sea was the visualisation of the internal; the women became a symbol of the ultimate paradox — how we are united in our insularity.

Work

The 'work' theme evokes many of the same concerns as the 'heroic' paintings. However, this category enjoyed a period of development during the most productive years of the colony (c.1880-95) which was not shared by the heroic pictures. This development locked into the pan-European adoption of Naturalism, characterised by the 'truthful' rendering of the rural/coastal worker in his natural habitat, the often meticulous detail of place, costume, customs, work implements, etc., and the frequent method of working *en plein-air* using the 'square-brush' technique. But, despite the internationalism of Naturalism, the individual groups of images from the various colonies still fed into the 'national identity' machine, albeit in a subtly different way to the heroic imagery. Instead of creating a model of British manliness, these images placed high value on age-old ways of life which were to be treasured as unique elements contributing to the construction of the nation. Also, as has been previously discussed, the fisherman provided an ideal example of the British working class at its best, thereby circumventing the problems associated with the depiction of this class in high art.

In common with other coastal colonies, the naturalistic representation of men working comprised a significant proportion of Cullercoats' output during the 1880s and early 1890s. Images of men working on shore, getting ready to sail, or boats arriving home with the catch were common. Pictures such as J F Slater's *Cobles* (fig.49) and Jobling's *Sea Fret* 1884 (plate 20) or *Hauling the Boats* 1890 (plate 23) can be regarded as 'typical' of this *genre*, sharing a number of common features. Heroic content and anecdote have

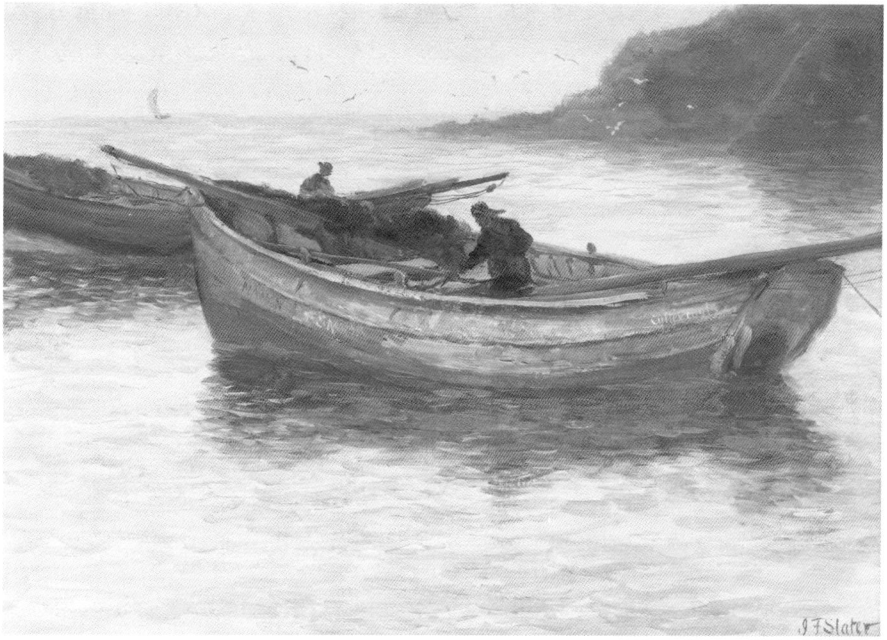

FIG.49
John Falconer Slater, ***Cobles***; South Shields Museum and Art Gallery

been largely emptied out. Instead, the artists were concerned with specificity of place, task, costume and the naturalistic rendering of objects and people, a preoccupation clearly understood by contemporary critics.[52] These characteristics signalled an ideological shift that permitted the representation of this particular working-class group without recourse to anecdote, overt narrative, heroicisation or the soft focus of poetic allusions. In this respect these Cullercoats works found reflection in the work of other coastal colonists, suggesting a widespread acceptance of images which were simultaneously extremely particular yet oddly universal. Yet by the late 1880s and 1890s this subject became less site-specific. For example, Jobling's *Fishermen at Staithes* (plate 24) could, despite the title, have been painted anywhere; there are no specific signifiers of place.

Emmerson's *Early Morning off the Coast* 1888 (plate 25) seems to embody many of the diverse ideologies and practices which had been, and were being, attached to coastal subjects. It is a small oil showing figures working at the shoreline at daybreak, watched by a group of children.[53] Although we can be fairly certain that it was painted at Cullercoats there is nothing in the picture or title to confirm this; the dress of the women and the shape of the boat — two possible clues — are too indistinct to help us. The group of workers unloading the catch at first seems only to be a minor detail; their thinly-painted sketchiness suggests that perhaps Emmerson added them as an afterthought. Yet our attention is drawn to them, rather than to the group of children in the foreground, precisely because they are the objects of the children's gaze. The more substantially-treated group of children belies Emmerson's roots in the more sentimental realm of mid-Victorian *genre* painting; and whilst their treatment is convincing, the transition of scale between them and the middle-ground group is not entirely successful. It could be argued that the elimination of one or other of the groups would have provided a more satisfactory composition. But doing this, as Emmerson probably realised, would have made the picture seem very old-fashioned. The composition without the workers would have left the children gazing out over an empty sea, setting up the typical Victorian mawkishness often attached to pictures of children. To have eliminated the children however, would have presented us with an out-of-date pseudo-Turner. Thus both groups are needed to establish a more contemporary message.

There are other contradictions in this work. The importance of the figure groupings is secondary to Emmerson's treatment of the seascape. This seems to conform to the general movement towards a more integrated Naturalism in which man is seen 'in nature'. Emmerson has used the traditional vehicle of a sunrise to explore the effects of sand seen through shallow water and to achieve the atmospheric glow of mist-filtered light on water. His 'hot' colouring can again be linked to Turner. This effect gives the group of workers an ethereal quality. They seem no more substantial than the shadows they create, always threatening to evaporate with the morning mists. The foregrounded children, though more solid, are not enough to upset this other-worldly quality. Perhaps it is this element which led Kenneth McConkey to declare this work as 'strikingly reminiscent' of the contemporary work of Philip Wilson Steer.[54] But Emmerson used a more traditional method of handling and brushwork. The effects of shadowy figures and boats at the shoreline, silhouetting them against a sunrise/sunset, are devices to be found in the works of H W Mesdag, an artist with whom Emmerson would have been familiar through the Bewick Club exhibitions in 1886 and 1887.

Despite the charming informality achieved with the group of children, the overall sense is that this picture somehow belongs to a previous age. It shares neither Steer's avant-garde approach to the 'childhood nostalgia' theme, nor Marsh's partial adaptation of square-brush technique for *Cockle Gatherers* 1885 (plate 26). Marsh's picture is a finely-balanced exploration of tones and colour values which superbly captures the particular luminosity of sky and shallow water at this time of day.[55] The obvious parallels between these works only serve to reinforce the ambiguities and tensions in Emmerson's picture. In this sense, the uneasy change of gear between foreground and middle-ground figures, which at first appears to be only an unconvincingly-handled perspective problem, becomes symbolically loaded. *Early Morning* thus embodies many of the tensions in art of this period — the balance between Victorian *genre* and Naturalism, between sentimentality and nostalgia, the poetic and the 'realistic', 'finish' and spontaneity, the real and the ethereal.

The representation of working fishermen at Cullercoats continued throughout the lifetime of the colony, and, broadly speaking, would seem to have been in-step with developments of the genre in other coastal colonies. But from the late 1880s the emphasis shifted subtly from the accurate representation of figures in a specific environment, to the depiction of an often less-specific environment of which figures were a part, in many cases accompanied by more experimental techniques. This can be seen in works such as Horton's *Coast Scene with Beached Fishing Boats* (plate 27) where, whilst figures are present, the picture is not about fishermen at work, but about the formal concerns of shape and colour. Similarly, Harold Knight's *Fishing Boats, Evening* (plate 28) takes a more distanced, almost ethereal view of the Staithes fishermen putting out to sea. The shadowy figures in the twilight are a far cry from the close-up drama of *The Last Coble.* These examples represent the continued fascination which this subject held for artists into the twentieth century.

The pictures depicting working women present both a broad range of styles and treatments and ideological ambiguities. Many images of working women would seem to embody those ideals traditionally associated with Victorian womanhood, in which the woman's role was one of homemaker and helpmate. Mid-Victorian intellectuals frequently used this ideal to set up a male/female opposition as part of the promotion of a positive masculine image. As Ruskin stated in 1865:

> *The man's power is active, progressive, defensive. He is eminently the doer, the creator, the discoverer, the defender ... But the woman's power is for rule, not for battle, — her intellect is not for invention or creation, but for sweet ordering, arrangement ... Her great function is Praise ... wise, not that she may set herself above her husband, but that she may never fail from his side.*[56]

It is easy to see how the image of the working woman as helpmate, such as Jobling's *Sharing the Burden* 1881 or *Sea Fret* 1884, fits well into this pattern.[57]

However, the images of fishergirls frequently present us with other possible readings. To the contemporary viewer pictures of Cullercoats fishergirls could have suggested a strong sexual undercurrent; the girls were often depicted bare-armed, bare-headed and with skirts short enough to show more than a glimpse of ankle and calf. Practicality dictated they be uncorseted, yet their comeliness was emphasised by the way the shawl was crossed tightly over the chest and tucked in at the waist. These factors would have provided a tantalising hint of sexual availability which could give 'helpmate' pictures an ambivalent quality. Furthermore, these images often combined a sexual undercurrent with depictions of the women as almost manly in their strength, stance or gait, conveying a message of independence or a reliance on each other rather than on men.[58] This, of course, was much closer to their life experience, since fisherwomen had to do work which required enormous physical strength and also to manage home, family and money alone during some seasons of the fishing calendar. Obviously, all this represents the epitome of what Victorian womanhood was *not* supposed to be. Therefore, the ways in which various artists negotiated this ideological minefield — to be true to their Naturalist principles without upsetting the sexual *status quo* — is telling.

Diversity of subject, style and treatment characterises this theme. At Cullercoats two of the main exponents of the working woman subject were undoubtedly Jobling and Homer. At the Arts Association exhibition of 1881 Homer showed a watercolour of two Cullercoats fishergirls that was likened to the work of the French artist Jules Breton.[59] The informality of his 1881 watercolours was noticed immediately by his American critics: 'we do not believe he has ever shown us any works so spontaneous in appearance and delightful in effect as these'.[60] They were admired for their 'blending of vitality, vigor, and enthusiastic feeling'.[61] They were not intended as mere studies, but in comparison to the larger 'exhibition watercolours' they are less idealised, more spontaneous and therefore have a heightened sense of veracity.

This is amply illustrated in *Fisherfolk on the Beach, Cullercoats* 1881 (plate 29) in which Homer used the device of separating the activities of men and women into distinct areas of the canvas. In this, and *Coast Scene with boats on the beach* 1881 (plate 30), the men occupy the shoreline, directing the beaching of the in-coming boats, whilst the women stand apart in groups, mostly separated from the men by the boats. *Fisherfolk on the Beach*, though, is more closely related to pictures such as *Two Girls on the Beach, Tynemouth* 1881 or *Four Fishwives* 1881, with the women waiting to load their empty creels. They share other stylistic traits; the silhouetting of at least one figure against the sea; and the use of wet sand and puddles to act as a mirror, allowing for the echoing of shapes and colours as well as the play of light on water.

Coast Scene is closer to works such as *Summer Cloud* 1881 or *Beach Scene, Cullercoats* 1881 in that the sea is all but blocked out by boats and figures. The women and children are at rest or watching the activity rather than working, though in *Coast Scene* work goes on around them. This is a curious watercolour — the woman and older children, each carrying a small child on their backs, are looking seaward, yet the object of their gaze is ambiguous as the line of boats seems to block their view. This gives a heightened sense that it is a spontaneous *plein-air* sketch, an uncomposed snapshot, rather than one of his more 'designed' pictures. In a rare interview given the year before his trip to Cullercoats, Homer extolled the virtues of working *en plein-air*:

> *I prefer every time a picture composed and painted outdoors ... it is impossible to paint an out-door figure in studio light with any degree of certainty. ... This making studies and then taking them home to use them is only half right. You get the composition, but you lose freshness; you miss the subtle, and, to the artist, the finer characteristics of the scene itself.*[62]

The sense of spontaneity also contributes to this notion of Homer almost deliberately recording every aspect of these fisher women's lives, no matter how 'picturesque' or mundane. As one critic noted: 'Mr Homer seems to have observed the fish-wives of the little seaside town unusually closely.'[63] Homer's identification with them is reinforced by his viewpoint — placing himself on the beach, amongst them, rather than observing them from afar or from an elevated position.

This is repeated in *Mussel Gatherers* 1881 (plate 31), where again the rock pools balance the colour values. But this picture is surely also a direct reference to Millet — Homer's stooping figures are a mirror image of Millet's *Gleaners* 1853. As such, Homer overtly appropriates notions about the nobility of toil and of the fisherfolk as 'belonging' or being 'at one' with their surroundings. Homer achieves this formally by making the lasses appear to meld with the rocks, anchoring them in place, yet also silhouetting them against the sea and sky. So whilst their stooping pose denies them the statuesque quality of his figures in works such as *Hark! Hark! The Lark!* 1882, they nevertheless are imbued with a certain classical timelessness. Rather than contradicting this message, the presence of the steamship amongst the cobles provides further commentary on the survival of this traditional way of life despite the encroachment of the modern world.

The tendency of Homer, Jobling, Thompson and Marsh to classicise or monumentalise their fishwives provokes many of the same issues as Charlton's *The Women*. What is crucial here is that these fisherwomen, although 'real', were so obviously 'removed', so sufficiently 'different' from the contemporary viewer's experience of working-class womanhood that the usual negative connotations did not come into play. The fishwife's 'difference' was distinctly marked — her archaic, unfashionable costume; her unfeminine stance; her position in an untamed landscape rather than protected from it or in a controlled/urban environment; the impossibility of an overt sexual reading despite her class.[64] Her obvious physical and mental strength can be accepted as a necessary attribute to her survival (and that of her 'ancient race') rather than an emasculating threat. Thus her figure, like that of the fisherman, can assume mythical status as part of the appropriation of time-trapped enclaves of past greatness into the confection of Britishness. The fisherwomen are the 'authentic body of national tradition (inert, backward-looking and natural), embodying nationalism's conservative principle of continuity.'[65] Also, the widespread fetishisation of the working-class woman in late-nineteenth-century imagery and literature embodied a myriad of social and national concerns which could be expressed and, to some extent controlled, through the fetish.[66]

For Homer, however, the national concerns cannot apply. His Cullercoats pictures signalled his intention to bring a new aesthetic to his work. Yet in drawing on the associations from classical mythology of the analogy between the mysterious and dangerous attraction or power of women and the sea, Homer's idealised fisherwomen become a personalised fetish. Tellingly, Christopher Reed suggests that Homer's identification with the fisherwomen corresponds to Leslie Fiedler's notion that bonding with the 'other' usually occurs 'when we have been cut off, or have cut ourselves off' from our usual associations.[67] Clearly, in coming to Cullercoats, Homer had deliberately done just that.

The influence of Homer on other Cullercoats artists is difficult to quantify, although from 1882 it is evident that Jobling was already beginning to dispense with the narrative content in his fishergirl pictures. In *The Day is Done and Darkness Falls from the Wings of Night* 1885 (plate 32), as with *Storm — Lifeboat Off*, the human interest is subordinated to the desire to create an atmospheric representation of the twilight effects on sky, buildings and wet sand. By using a quote from Longfellow as the title Jobling not only maximised the poetic evocativeness of the work but counterbalanced the specificity by stressing the universality of the image. When it was first shown at the Bewick Club exhibition in January 1886 it received laudatory critiques: 'We regard his large picture of Cullercoats beach at evening as the best work he has, as yet, produced.'[68] And:

> *the work stands the severe test to which the hanging committee have subjected it. At one side of it is the large painting "The Return from Communion" by Mr P. Morris A.R.A. … at the other side is the finest work sent from the continent, "The Fisherman's Family" by D.A.C. Artz of Holland; and near to is Mr B.J. Blommer's capital work, "On the Downs". The high merit of these works only tends to bring out more boldly the merits of Mr Jobling's picture, and to prove more evidently the high position he has attained among artists. The picture of Cullercoats is a piece of bold and vigorous painting, and true to nature.*[69]

It received similar praise when it was shown again, at his retrospective exhibition at Armstrong College, Newcastle in 1923.[70]

As these critics pointed out, much of the picture's success is due to its technical achievement. Perhaps for the first time, Jobling had succeeded in overcoming earlier technical difficulties with palette, composition or draughtsmanship. In reducing the figures to a subordinate role he avoided the usual problems of proportion and characterisation. Whilst the palette is still dark and subdued, Jobling has countered the usual muddiness by keeping the sky quite bright, the blue counterbalancing the yellows and browns of the buildings, an effect which is mirrored by the reflections coming off the puddles on the beach. These are positioned to reflect the Lookout House as well as the bright sky. The compositional importance of the Lookout House is verified by the perspectival lines running through the image converging at the apex of the tower (or its reflection). The line of beached cobles forms a dividing line between nature and man, both a barricade against and a retreat from the sea. But it also presents a barrier to the fishwives, isolating them on the beach. This provides another echo of Homer's work in his tendency to separate the working women from the men.

Whilst at first glance this work would seem to be a highly-finished one in the Academic manner, closer examination reveals that Jobling laid on the paint in broad strokes with little attempt at gradation or seamless blending. He created a harmonious whole based on tonal relationships without sacrificing any of its 'truth to nature'. In this sense the work perhaps marked the beginning of the shift in Jobling's preoccupations, away from 'realistic' representations of fisherfolk life, towards the aesthetics of composition and modes of representation. Ultimately this picture, like Homer's *Inside the Bar*, has little to do with the lot of the fisherfolk, but as a faithful rendering of Longfellow's poem it asks us to connect on a deeper emotional level.

Indeed, it could be questioned whether the image would lose much of its effect and its message if the figures were removed from the composition: after all, the sombre atmosphere created by the twilight would remain the same. Yet without the figures the scene would be too cosy, too picturesque. The burdened fishwives remind us that whilst to us the scene represents a poetically-rendered twilight, to them it marks the end of a long day's work. As the lines of the poem suggest, even the prospect of going home cannot overcome the heaviness of spirit. This picture and its associations come dangerously close to sentimentality, yet this is avoided precisely because Jobling chose to put these figures in. In making them fairly small-scale and with their backs to us, we are given enough information to know why they are there but not what they are thinking or feeling. Furthermore, their compositional isolation suggests a psychological one, another reference to the poem. Their presence will not allow us to dismiss this image as a comfortable 'village by dusk' scene, but instead reminds us of the reason for the presence of the distinctive Lookout House. It seems to me that Jobling could not separate Cullercoats 'the place' from its *raison d'être*; they were, for him, one and the same. Thus, to attempt to use the topography of Cullercoats for the rendering of a universal poetic sensibility without reference to the fisherfolk would have been a betrayal and a failure.

Women gathering fuel along the seashore was a common subject for coastal colonists. A H Marsh produced many works on this theme, including *Driftwood*, *Harvest of the Sea* and *Hey Ho! the Wind and the Rain* (all 1877).[71] The unidealised figures in these works betray an indebtedness to Millet and Israels rather than to the Naturalism of Breton or Bastien-Lepage. It is also interesting to note the parallels between *Winter Fuel Gatherers* (see fig.20) and Walter Langley's later *Breadwinners* 1896 (fig.50). In *Harvest of the Sea* (plate 33) there is a suggestion of narrative, but there

FIG.50
Walter Langley, ***Breadwinners***, 1896;
Penlee House Gallery and
Museum, Penzance

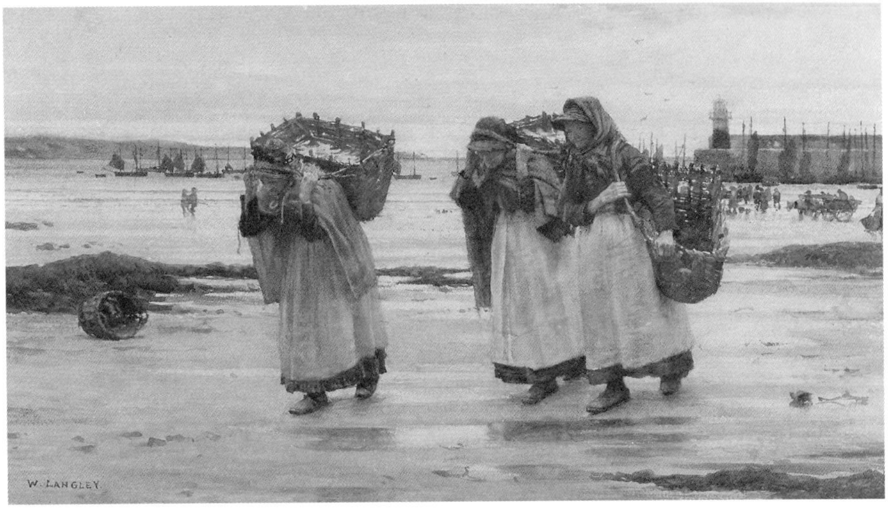

is little sense of Marsh trying to heighten the drama of the scene. Instead, there is an air of mundanity about this salvage operation. And although some of the women seem to be peering out to sea, there is nothing to suggest they are watching for human wreckage or loved ones, as a contemporary critic of the *Art Journal* maintained.[72] Instead there is a Millet-like feeling of acceptance of, and integration with, their surroundings, aided by Marsh's very restricted palette.

Isa Thompson's monumental picture *Fisher Folk* 1892 (plate 36) also deals with the subject of collecting driftwood. Dating from probably the earliest period of her association with Staithes, it retains the sombre earth-palette of her Cullercoats work, adding gravitas to the forbidding scene. Probably intended for the Royal Academy, the size of the picture obviously forced Thompson to abandon her use of square-brush technique, used on her previous Academy picture, *Blossom* 1892. Instead, *Fisher Folk* is built up with long strokes of colour which accumulate to form the suggestion of the texture and density of sodden sand and seaweed-covered rocks. Although a superficial look gives the impression of a very dark, almost monochrome canvas, closer inspection reveals touches of orange, green, red, blue and pink which bring the picture to life. As one critic noted,

> *"Fisher Folk" by Isa Thompson, is a very remarkable picture. Full of force and fine qualities, it is marked by earnest thoughtfulness and good solid work, which have resulted in one of the most noticeable pictures in the room, repaying the artist for the unstinted care which is apparent in every part of the canvas.*[73]

Borrowing Homer and Marsh's trait of silhouetting the figures against the sea and sky, Thompson has produced two formidable yet characterful women. The older woman in particular, hand on hip, basket on head, stares out at us, almost challenging us to get out of her way. Again we see the parallel with Homer's statuesque figures; in this case the figure, like the caryatids of the Acropolis, literally carries the burden on her head.

Wearing the characteristic Staithes bonnet (the colour signalling her widowed status), with what appears to be seaweed dangling from the basket on her head, her easy poise confirms that this is a task she has performed often. Unlike Marsh's driftwood gatherers, her toil has not bowed her. The younger girl is more difficult to unravel, seemingly caught up in some private reverie. Her very unconsciousness reveals how careworn her features have already become — the deep-sunk eyes, the grim downturn of the mouth. She cradles the wood in her arms like an absent infant. As one contemporary critic summed up, it 'is a successful attempt to deal with a rather unpromising subject, the return of two fisherwomen from the shore. They are shown walking across the wet slippery rocks. It is a sombre but effective piece of work.'[74]

There are many parallels between *Fisher Folk* and the more heroic of Homer's fisher women, such as *Inside the Bar* or *The Gale*, most obviously the unbowed poise and innate strength of the figures, and their defiance of nature. There are some important differences, however. Despite the monumentality of Thompson's women, there is little suggestion of timelessness or 'separateness' which often characterises Homer's figures. Thompson's restrained, harmonious palette, used for figures and background, ensures that these women are firmly located, almost rooted, in their surroundings. This is aided by a relatively high horizon and by the fact that Thompson has paid as much attention to the treatment of the background as to the figures themselves. Thus the almost graphic stylisation of *Inside the Bar* — with its blocks of colour and bold diagonals — is resisted in favour of a more organic quality which anchors these women in time and place.

It is also evident that Thompson's women are portraits of particular Staithes inhabitants whilst Homer's are of an idealised 'type'. This profoundly affects how we can read these images. Homer's alignment with classical hero(ine) 'types' both elevates his imagery to the universal but also removes any point of access or contact with the viewer via shared experience or sympathy. One may find the images ennobling, but it is of an abstract and elusive nature. Thompson's characterisation, however, provides access and makes connections on a human level possible, even if the subject itself defies the sympathetic eye. Further, unlike Homer, Thompson makes no compromises to Victorian notions of female beauty. Although their upright bearing could be described as 'noble', there is an asexual, almost masculine quality in the severity of their clothes and countenances. There are no bare arms, heaving bosoms, clinging draperies or picturesque costumes: no beautiful faces peering out to sea with just enough trace of anxiety to suggest that the real drama and hardship is going on elsewhere. There is no way that these women can be possessed as sexual beings or dismissed as minor characters in a larger narrative, therefore making Thompson's picture far more challenging for the contemporary viewer. It would have been difficult to simply accept it as some symbolic embodiment of the great 'traditional' British values of stoicism, endurance, the capacity for hard work or bravery in adversity. Instead, the viewer is challenged, forced to confront the awkward questions raised by the obvious deprivation of these women's lives. Their rootedness in time and place offers no grounds for hope or escape. Further, there is no attempt by the artist to negotiate the problems inherent in this challenge to the traditional male/female oppositions established during the nineteenth century. These factors, reinforced by the sheer size of *Fisher Folk*, suggests that this image must be regarded in the same terms as the more difficult rural figures by Clausen or La Thangue rather than either the poeticism of Jobling or the idealisation of Homer.

Laura Johnson's *The Fishing Fleet* 1900 (plate 34) shares the same uncompromising grimness of Thompson's picture, tempting speculation that Johnson might have seen the older artist's work. Here too the earthy palette binds the fisherlass to her surroundings; brine squelches underfoot and oozes from the canvas. The solitude of Johnson's lone female — already retreating into her private purgatory — is underscored by the backs of the other villagers, watching the fleet depart.

Women engaged in other tasks, such as baiting lines, mending nets and knitting ganseys, were also common subjects. Thompson uses the same motif of a girl baiting lines in at least three different works, *Dove Cottage, Cullercoats* (plate 35), *Fortune Telling* 1887 (plate 37) and *Women in the back lane, Cullercoats* (plate 38). These works are typical of her early output in terms of narrative content, palette and stylistic debt to Jobling.

Homer produced many images of fishergirls knitting which are united in their representation of the monumental female figure placed in windy/stormy conditions. Their 'unreal' quality counteracts any suggestion of sentimentality and reinforces the message of Homer's 'higher' preoccupations.[75] Jobling's *They are Coming* 1890 (fig.51) suggests how easily this subject could slip towards sentimentality. However in *Awaiting Sweethearts* (plate 39) Jobling captures a similar sense of quiet contemplation that characterises Homer's *Mending the Nets* 1882. But rather than emptying the background completely, Jobling used the crystal blue waters to reinforce the sunny stillness of the scene at Staithes. The foremost fishlass, her lips parted in mid-story, tells another tale. Her resemblance to Mary Lisle, one of Jobling's Cullercoats models, suggests that he was not averse to combining elements from Cullercoats and Staithes into the same painting.

The influence of Staithes seems to have reinvigorated Jobling's work at a crucial point in his career, convincingly illustrated by the small oil *Winter Fuel* 1910 (plate 40). The handling is broader and looser than ever before, and though the scene is a stormy one, the palette is of a much brighter key altogether. The lack of definition also serves to conceal some of Jobling's long-standing problems with figure work; indeed the main figures are convincingly being blown across the canvas from left to right. It is also unusual in Jobling's output for showing the fisherfolk actually engaged in hard physical labour, which again may suggest the influence of the Staithes artists, some of whom (for example Bagshawe and Knight) more consistently depicted the hard physicality of fisherfolk life.

A number of Cullercoats artists with associations with Staithes started to produce images of rural labour from the 1890s. The animal painter John Atkinson painted many rural scenes from the area around his home at Sleights, which are very similar in technique to work by Fred Jackson. James Watson and Jobling also included rural imagery in their Staithes work. This interchangeability between fisherfolk and rural subjects was not only ideologically feasible, but reflected a real-life exchange of workforces and economies.[76] Hedley, a long-time depictor of the urban poor, increasingly produced pictures such as *Gathering Potatoes* 1903 (fig.52), in which the presence of women in Staithes bonnets suggests this interweaving of workforces. Similarly, Marsh's *The Workers Out* c.1885 shows a group of Cullercoats fisherlasses on their way home after a day harvesting potatoes at a local farm.[77]

But this exchange of subjects was perhaps most noticeable in the work of Isa Thompson after 1890. The vivid palette and obvious use of square-brush technique in *Haymaking* (plate 41) seems to connect it with works such as *Blossom* of 1892, but the use of her married name of Jobling implies a date after 1900.[78] The stylistic qualities seem to be a far cry from *Fisher Folk*, yet essentially the concerns are the same; the representation of the female worker in a hostile environment. Despite the difference in scale, there are also many compositional similarities between the two paintings: the presence of the sea as a backdrop; the closeness of the figure to the picture plane, giving a high horizon which anchors the figure in the landscape; the distant gaze of the young women suggesting they have been captured mid-reverie. Yet the differences are important. Whilst *Fisher Folk* is uncompromising on a number of levels, *Haymaking* is not. Despite the scale of the figure, the picture is small, minimising any element of monumentality. Similarly, although working, the girl is gaily dressed, complementing the vivid blues of the sky and sea. This helps distract attention away from any grim associations with poverty and back-breaking work. The more avant-garde techniques and palette ally this decorative work much closer to the artists of the Staithes group such as Booth and Senior.

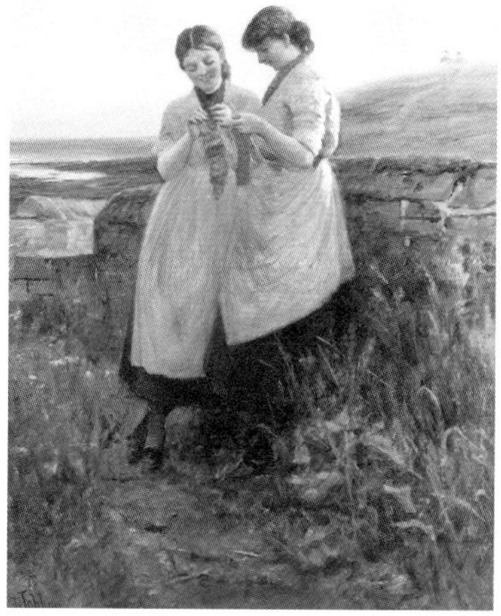

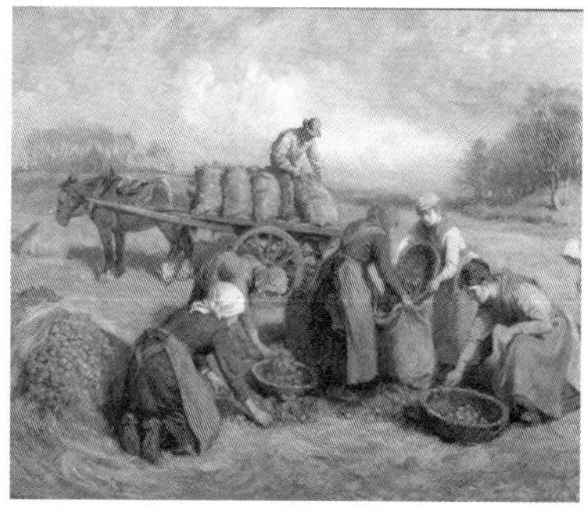

FIG.51
Robert Jobling, ***They are Coming***, 1890; private collection

FIG.52
Ralph Hedley, ***Gathering Potatoes***, 1903; Shipley Art Gallery, Gateshead

Early Cullercoats pictures on the theme of work tended to have an obvious narrative content, often reinforced by literary references which added a universal element to counterbalance the site-specificity of Cullercoats costume and topography. The changing emphasis in the 'working men' subject echoed contemporary ideological shifts. The idealised chivalric workmen promoted by Carlyle and Ruskin, which embodied the idea of the moral benefits of labour, were epitomised in the fisherman pictures of the 1870s and early 80s. But having answered the political and cultural need to project a model of the British worker, the overt nationalism gave way to a more subtle appropriation of fisherfolk imagery in the construction of nationhood. Seemingly straightforward, 'truthful' renditions of working fishermen dispensed with the need for poetical rhetoric, as the working figure became valued as an important subject in its own right. The quaintness of the pre-industrial workforce was to be preserved as a unique encapsulation of traditional British values, against the homogenising effects of a seemingly value-less industrial urbanisation. The untenability of this position towards the end of the century forced artists to abandon all narrative content, enabling the subject to survive primarily as a vehicle for aesthetic concerns and experimentation.

The pictures of female labour, however, invited widely differing treatments and ideologies throughout the lifetime of the colony. This embraced not only narrative but social commentary on female labour/poverty; a 'naturalised' classical nobility; interrogation of accepted notions of femininity and female beauty; as subjects of psychological insight; and as pretext for experimental techniques. The lack of uniformity promoted a versatility seemingly not possible in the subjects involving men, where the machismo of male imagery is ultimately limiting. This versatility could perhaps be partly explained by the willingness of female models to act as subjects in very different types of pictures. Practical factors such as the more readily available female models and economic necessity must also have played their part. This enabled artists to constantly reinvent the *genre* and thus maintain the interest of successive audiences.

Leisure

The paintings in this section fall into two distinct categories: the first reflects the subtle shift away from naturalistic depictions of working fisherfolk towards more experimental techniques. Here, the fisherfolk are presented at leisure, sitting around enjoying the sunshine or waiting for the tide. In the second are pictures of leisure-seekers and children, and the physical signs of their impact on the coastal topography.

As action and narrative content were emptied out of fisherfolk subjects, a small number of artists painted them at leisure. But perhaps the earliest example of this theme was Emmerson's *A Foreign Invasion* (plate 47), shown at the Royal Academy in 1871. The *Art Journal* remarked, 'H H Emmerson's "Foreign Invasion" comes in the not very formidable form of Italians with bagpipes; the picture wins a good place by fairly well-painted character and costume.'[79] This bizarre gathering was used by Emmerson as the excuse for character studies of some of Cullercoats' inhabitants including Betty Donkin once again. It is also interesting as a record of one of the more unlikely events in Cullercoats' social calendar; the arrival of an Italian dancing troupe was an almost annual occurrence.

Later, more typical examples of the leisure theme were painted by Ralph Hedley during the mid-1880s at Staithes and Runswick. It is said that *Fisherfolk at Staithes* 1886 (plate 42) includes the figure of Jobling on the right, and was painted whilst the two artists were on a sketching trip. He has adopted the distinctive sweater of the Staithes men to blend into the community. On a technical level it is interesting to note that Hedley has used the square-brush technique for much of this picture, demonstrating his awareness of the avant-garde techniques of the artists at Newlyn. Another picture, *Pleasant Memories* (plate 43) has also been dated to the period between 1883 and 1886, which the use of the same central male figure as *Fisherfolk at Staithes* would seem to support. Although Hedley does not use square-brush technique here it is interesting that the bright palette foreshadows that adopted by Jobling after he also started to work regularly at Staithes, from the mid-1890s. A number of Staithes and Newlyn artists also depicted fishermen at rest, including Henry Hopwood, Hannah Hoyland, Walter Langley and Harold Harvey.

The influence of Newlyn and Staithes artists is also clearly seen in Isa Thompson's first Royal Academy picture *Blossom*, 1892 (plate 44). In this seemingly narrative-less painting she used square-brush technique, inviting the viewer to feast the eye on the exuberant colouring of dappled sunlight on figure and foliage. It is possible to enjoy this picture purely for its decorative qualities. There is, however, an obvious symbolism at work here — the title referring not only to the vegetation but to the girl herself, poised at that bittersweet moment between childhood and adulthood. As if to press home the point, the colouring of the girl's garments echo that of the apple blossom — the virginal white kissed by the pastel hues of promised

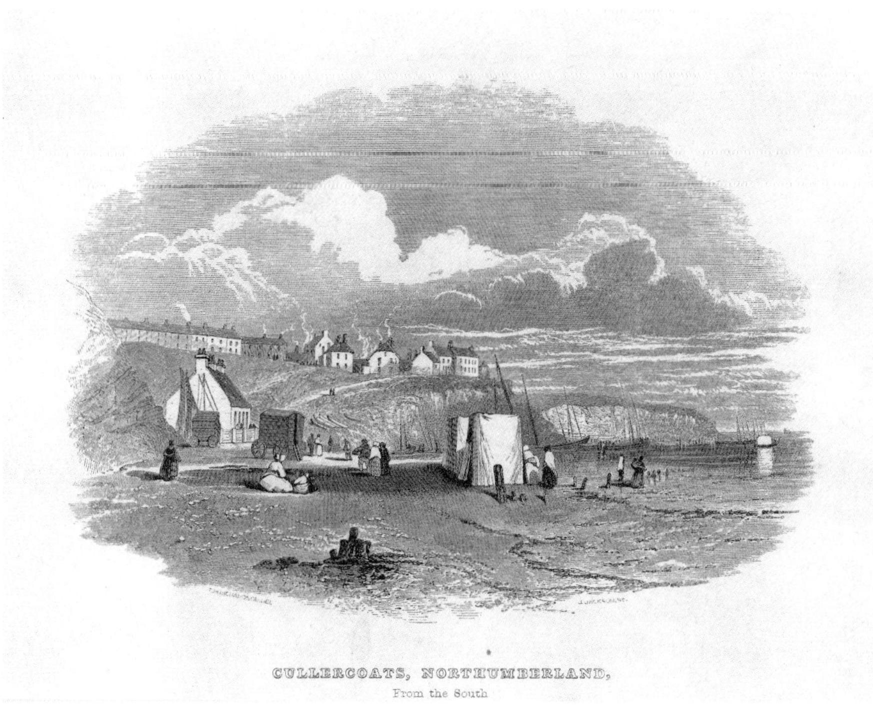

FIG.53
T. M. Richardson, ***Cullercoats***, c.1830; engraved by J. Jackson
Laing Art Gallery

fecundity. In this highly-decorative symbolism Thompson seems, consciously or not, to be allying herself with some of the more progressive artists at Staithes, in particular Mark Senior.

Sandwiched between the burgeoning resort/dormitory town of Whitley Bay and the upper/upper-middle-class bathing retreat of Tynemouth, it would be unrealistic to expect Cullercoats to have entirely escaped the summer invasion of holiday-makers and day-trippers, especially after the arrival of the railway in 1882. Cullercoats' history as a bathing place reaches back at least as far as the mid-eighteenth century and its popularity was such that sea-water baths were erected in 1807 for safer bathing (fig.53).[80] So by the late nineteenth century the large numbers of leisure seekers on the beaches and promenades between Tynemouth and Whitley Bay would have provided a high visual impact on Cullercoats and its surroundings (fig.54).[81] Why, therefore, is there a relative paucity of 'leisure' imagery by Cullercoats artists?

Pictures showing bathing machines and well-dressed figures mingling with fisherfolk on beaches were commonplace by the 1820s.[82] These early examples are significant because they showed upper-class leisure seekers, and because there was little attempt to downplay or ignore the signs of modern life. But both of these elements were incompatible with the 'Naturalist impulse' of the 1880s and 90s. Consonant with notions of the 'anti-tripper', depictions of middle-class holiday-makers, working-class trippers and signs of leisure-seeking (beach furniture, trams, piers, Winter gardens, etc.) would have contradicted the construction of Cullercoats as a pre-industrial landscape. It is only from the 1890s that leisure themes begin to creep into Cullercoats imagery, very much in line with other British coastal painters.[83]

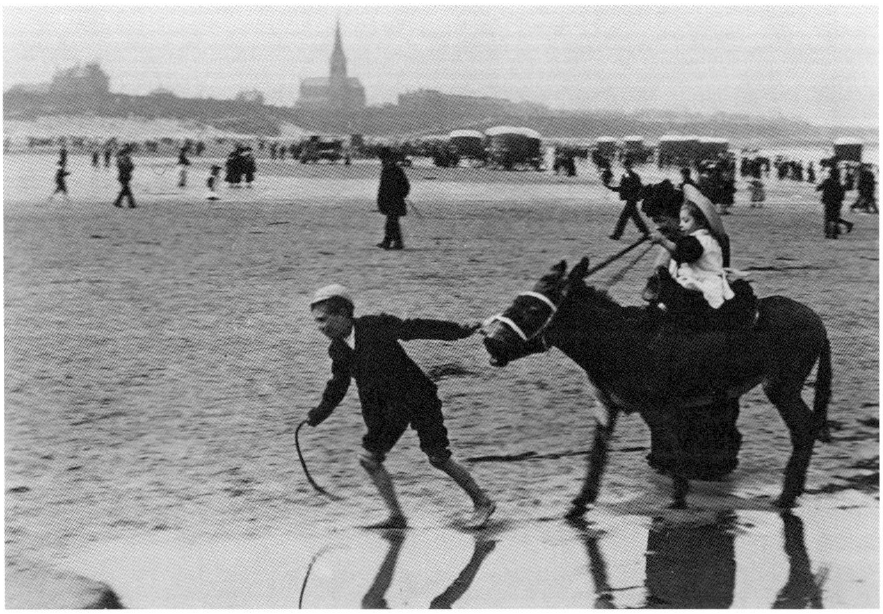

FIG.54
Donkey Rides, c.1898; photograph; City of Newcastle upon Tyne

Paintings by Charles Conder or Joseph Oppenheimer of the south coast seem to celebrate the contemporary middle-class passion for seaside leisure. But it is striking that a distinctly experimental or avant-garde technique was often adopted, suggesting an intrinsic connection between subject matter and mode of representation, a connection understood by artist and audience.

There are a small number of works by north-east artists which seem to support this idea. John Atkinson executed a number of beach scenes including *Tynemouth Sands* 1907 (plate 45). This is quite unusual for Atkinson because he has restrained his tendency to let animals dominate the scene, and has instead given us an Impressionistic account of middle-class mothers and children enjoying the seaside, using a muted palette to suggest the hazy heat of the day. The women wear large sun-hats or take refuge under parasols whilst children paddle or take donkey rides. The motif of mother and toddler in the left foreground, is echoed in Fred Mayor's *The Bathing Tent* (plate 46).

Jobling's *Promenaders on the Cliff above Cullercoats* c.1910 (fig.55) is a small oil, possibly an on-the-spot sketch for an intended larger work. The background of sea, sky and rocks have been broadly blocked in, the movement of the sea denoted by heavy impasto, the figures but loosely suggested, and yet the image captures that same essence of 'modernité' so apparent in the works of other British impressionists. The foreground figure of the dark-clothed woman holding a parasol/umbrella, silhouetted

FIG.55
Robert Jobling, ***Promenaders on the Cliff above Cullercoats***, c.1910; private collection; photograph courtesy Anderson & Garland Auctioneers

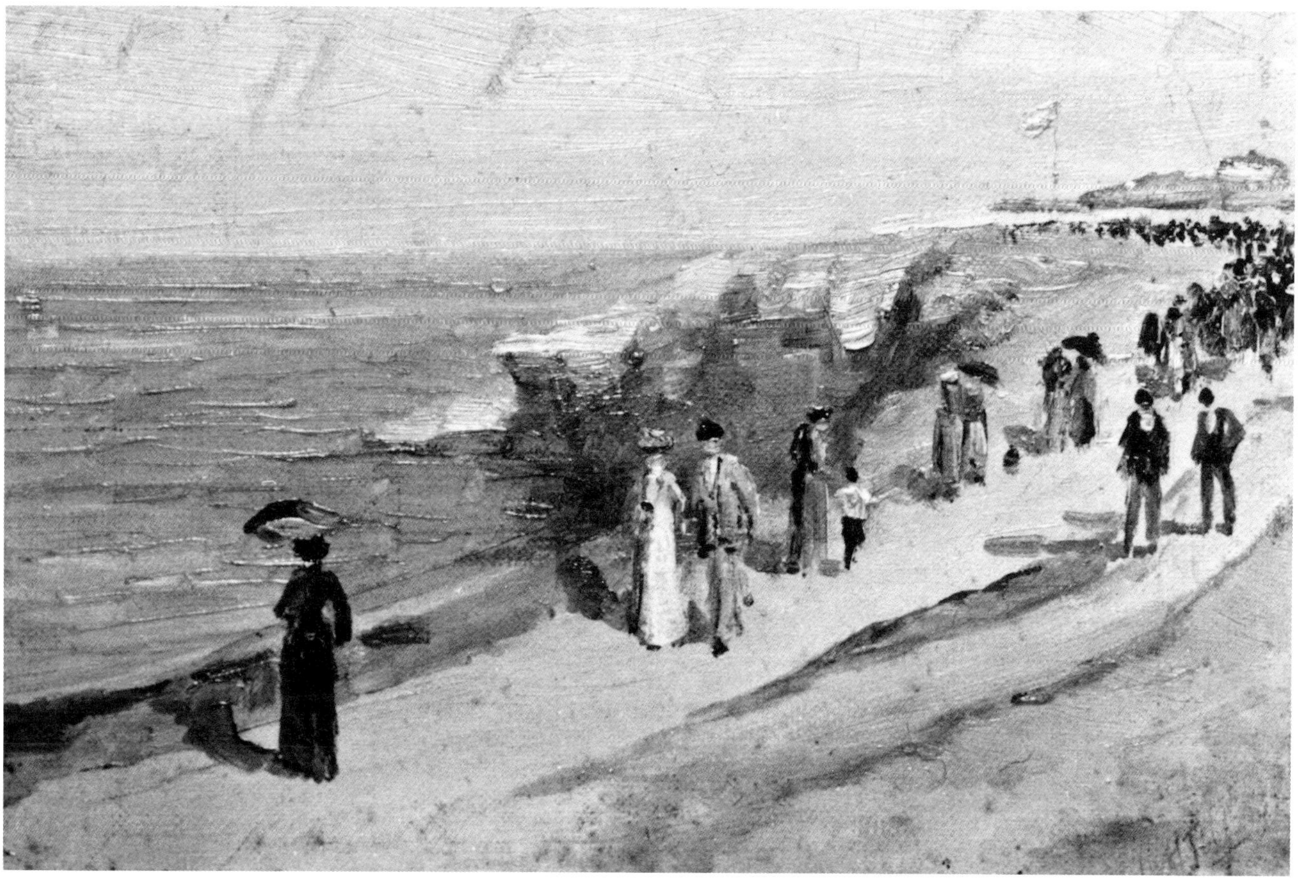

against the sea or promenade, is a motif to be found in many other contemporary works, from Garstin's *The Rain it Raineth Every Day* 1889 to W.L.Wyllie's watercolour *Berck Plage* 1891 (fig.56).

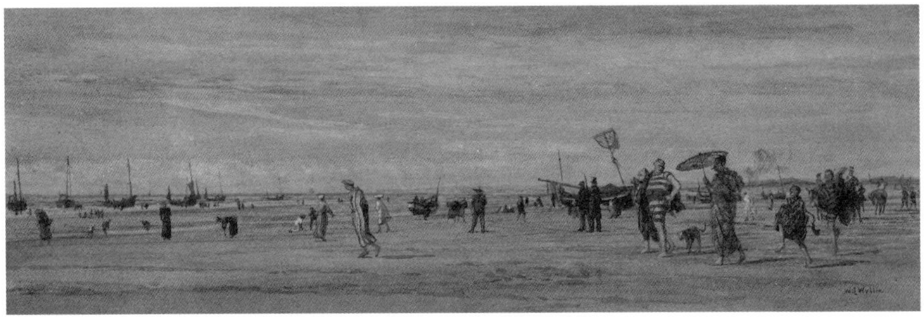

FIG.56
William Lionel Wyllie, ***Berck Plage***, 1891; watercolour 18.5 x 42.2 cms; © National Maritime Museum, London PA F0738

In Jobling's figure there is something melancholic, a sense of isolation despite the crowds. In her recent book Lisa Tickner argued that through Romantic literature the sea had 'ceased to represent the residual part of primordial chaos — something relentless, infinite, a source of terror and repulsion — and became a Sublime object of contemplation in the pursuit of self.'[84] Jobling's picture could be understood in these terms: the sea is certainly not a 'source of terror and repulsion' here, whilst the single figure would seem to be contemplating its empty expanse. Her modern apparel negates any suggestion that she is looking for her loved-one — the 'waiting women' are always the indigenous working-class women in traditional costume. It is possible that this lone figure is a projection of Jobling himself — drawing inner strength from his old subject, but all the time in danger of being swamped by the insistent signs of contemporary Cullercoats.

Other artists represented leisure at Cullercoats in a more distanced way, for example Slater's large gouache *Cullercoats* (plate 48).[85] Although a topographical view, the detail clearly shows that the figures on the beach are not fisherfolk but pleasure-seekers; children paddling, groups on the sand and a couple in a small rowing boat. The presence of the cobles further up the beach serves as a reminder of the more serious side of Cullercoats' existence, yet the bright and cheery atmosphere of this whole image seems far removed from the earlier sombre visions of Jobling and Homer.

George Horton revisited the subject of the sands between Tynemouth and Cullercoats throughout his career, examples appearing at exhibitions from the Bewick Club in 1891 through to his London exhibitions in the 1920s and the Laing Art Gallery in 1934. Unfortunately few are dated and Horton tended to use the same or similar descriptive titles for many works. *On Tynemouth Sands* (plate 49) shows a view taken from the Cullercoats end of Tynemouth Long Sands looking south, with the Aquarium on the right. A similar work was bought by the Shipley Art Gallery from the artist in 1943, so was presumably executed slightly before that date. There survive a number of sketches of this subject (figs.57 & 58) which seem to date from 1935, so it is possible that this watercolour stems from this same sketching

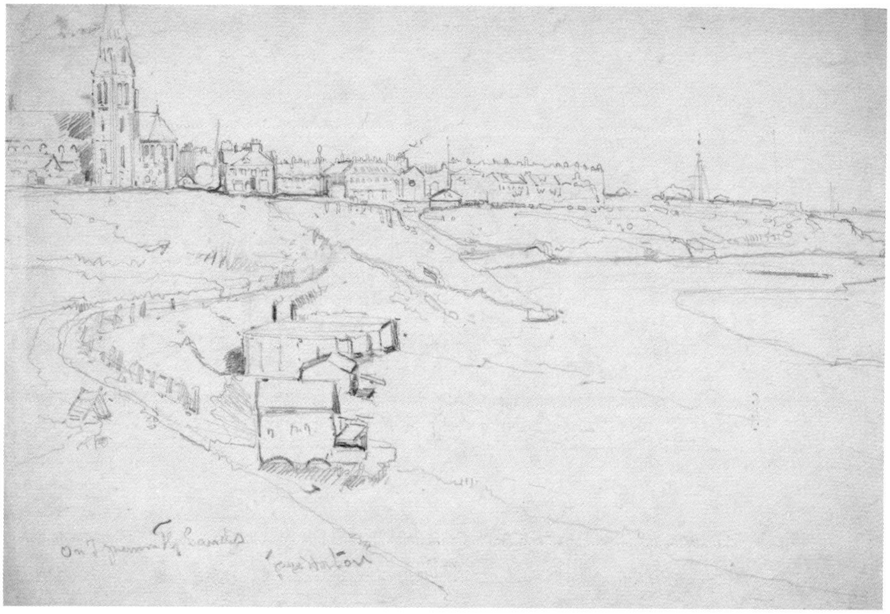

FIG.57
George Horton, ***On Tynemouth Sands***; Tyne & Wear Archive, reproduced courtesy D & M Redpath

FIG.58
George Horton, ***Aquarium, Tynemouth***; Tyne & Wear Archive, reproduced courtesy D & M Redpath

trip. Figure 57 bears the same title as the watercolour even though they are views taken from different vantage points. Sharing a view north with figure 57, another watercolour (plate 50) seems to complement the first watercolour. Another pencil and watercolour sketch (plate 51) again shows the view south. All of these works seem to be inter-related and all show the presence of leisure activities in the shape of beach huts, swings, carousels and figures on the sands. However, it would be misleading to suggest that Horton was primarily concerned with 'seaside leisure' as a subject, since his writings make clear that he was most interested in the formal concerns of picture-making — the capturing of light effects, tonal

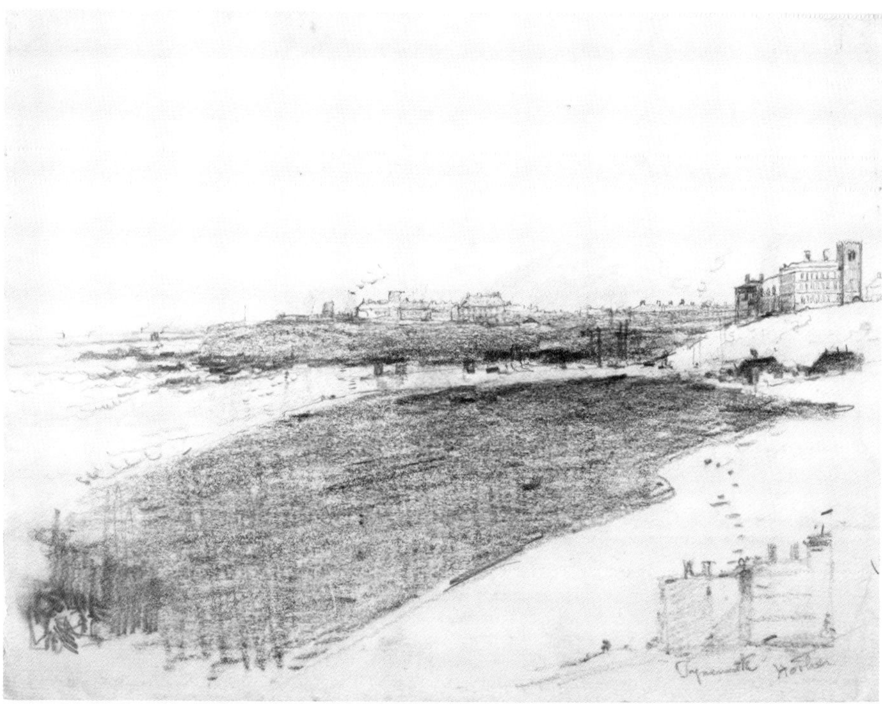

and colour relationships, shape and compositional harmony. But, these works show that, unlike many Cullercoats artists, Horton had no interest in editing out the signs of modern life in order to present a particular image of the area. As a 'younger generation' Cullercoats artist, Horton had no affinities with the Naturalist ideologies of the older artists. Even during the 1880s, when coastal Naturalism was at its height, his work eschewed the fisherfolk themes in favour of more atmospheric topographical or wreck pictures. Even in the early pictures there is the sense that the subject is merely a pretext for tonal experiments. Thus, in these later pictures the signs of leisure would merely have presented him with additional compositional interest of shape and colour.

Linking into the seaside leisure theme are pictures of children playing on the beach. Given that pictures of children were very popular in the nineteenth century, it is surprising that this subject was relatively rare amongst coastal artists until the late 1880s. At Cullercoats, earlier examples of children on beaches were usually anecdotal, showing them engaged in some sort of activity connected with fishing.[86] In such paintings the children are usually dwarfed by nature as a sign of God's over-reaching presence. Their pretend work prefigures their place in society as industrious, healthy adults — brave fishermen and domesticated, supportive females. As with the other leisure pictures, the full-blown Naturalism of the 1880s could not accommodate this subject, perhaps because paintings of children have always been overladen with symbolism, making a supposedly 'unmediated' image almost impossible. But by the late 1880s, pictures such as P W Steer's *Knucklebones* 1888-9 or *Children Paddling, Walberswick* 1889-94 used an avant-garde technique to signal a reinvestment of symbolic content back into this subject matter. These are images of nostalgia — nostalgia for the 'oblivion' and innocence of childhood, albeit a distinctly middle-class childhood.[87] So, although the language may be different, there is a desire, shared by much of the fisherfolk imagery, to somehow reach back into the past.

There is, however, little evidence that this subject was attempted by Cullercoats artists until much later.[88] Jobling painted a number of such works at Staithes after 1900, including *Minding the Bairn* 1915 (plate 52).[89] With seagulls hovering at the shoreline, the figures are set against the distinctive headland. The short strokes of pure colour give structure and texture to the whole, demonstrating that by this point in his career, detail and characterisation had given way to these concerns. It is interesting to compare this with Isa Thompson's, *Girl on the Quay at Staithes* (plate 53), which, although undated, was probably painted before 1900. Although the palette is not so high-key there is evidence of this same concern with texture and the play of light on different surfaces. In particular the use of streaks of lilac to denote the sunlit sea in the middle distance are 'borrowed' by Jobling in *Minding the Bairn*. There is also the same bold, almost choppy use of brushwork put to effective use in the rendering of stone-edged quay and swelling sea. This would seem to suggest that by this date perhaps Jobling was now learning from Thompson.

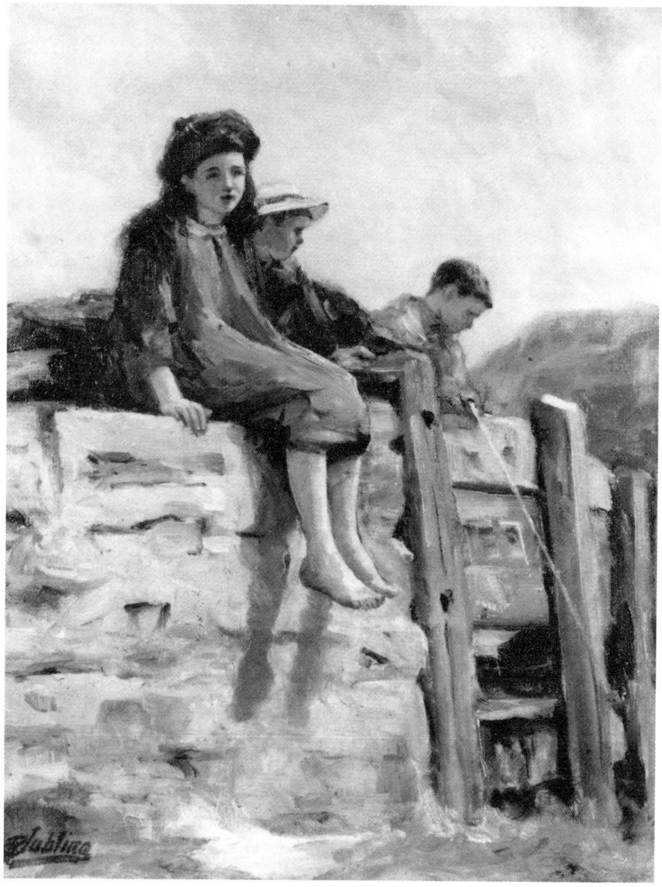

But these works differ from Steer's in one crucial way. These children are not middle-class holiday-makers but local children, at rest rather than at play. Instead of carefree oblivion there is an almost melancholic tinge to these works. In Jobling's pictures this sombre element may be accounted for by the external circumstances of the First World War, a mourning for childhood robbed. The contemplative nature of these works is also present in his *Sunshine — Children sitting on a wall* (fig.59) in which the children sit on the quay, fishing or looking out to sea.[90] Notably, the girl is not wearing the usual Staithes bonnet, but a tam o'shanter like one of the girls in *Knucklebones*, suggesting that the children were not local but holiday-makers. Whilst assumed to be a Staithes picture, there are no specific indicators to this effect — no recognisable topography or characteristic bonnet as sign. With its air of quiet contemplation and simple pleasures it is closely

FIG.59
Robert Jobling, ***Sunshine – Children sitting on a wall***, private collection; photograph courtesy Anderson & Garland Auctioneers

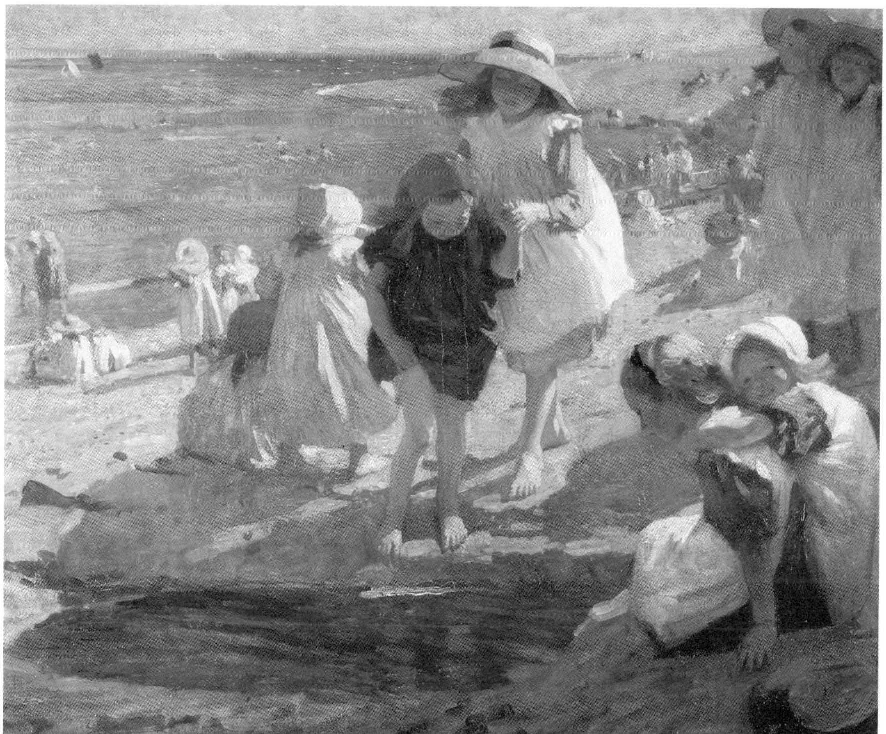

FIG.60
Laura Knight (née Johnson), ***The Beach***, exh.1909; Laing Art Gallery; Reproduced with permission of Curtis Brown Group Ltd, London on behalf of the estate of Dame Laura and Harold Knight. Copyright © Dame Laura Knight

aligned with works such as Harold Harvey's *A Quiet Paddle* 1913 rather than the oblivion of Steer or the hectic pleasure-seeking of Laura Knight's *The Beach* 1909 (fig.60).

It was not until after World War One that any of the regular Cullercoats artists attempted a truly avant-garde seaside picture. Slater's *Beach Scene* c.1920 (plate 54) is surely the artist at his Impressionistic best. Here we have all the ingredients that Cullercoats artists had avoided for so long — the gaily-coloured middle-class families on the sands and in the sea, the deck chairs and pleasure craft. All are painted with the same exuberant Impressionism of his large-scale seascapes, but here packed into this tiny oil. The painting was reproduced in *Drawing and Design* in October 1922, where Kenneth Glover likened it to Whistler and Manet. But with the figures set off against this intensely luminous blue it begs comparison with Steer's *Boulogne Sands: Children Shrimping* 1891, rather than the limpid atmospherics of Whistler's seasides.

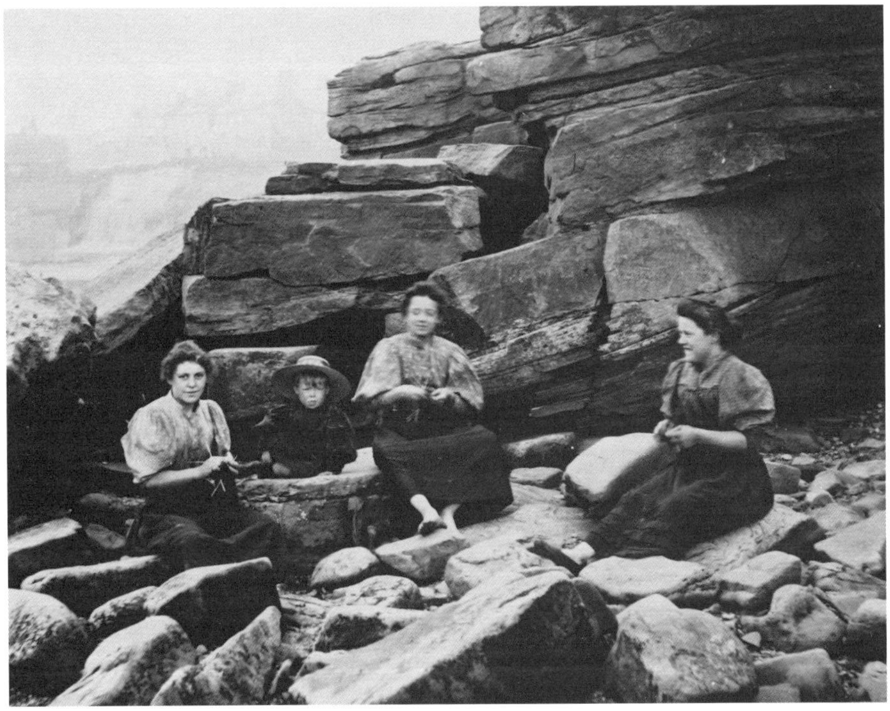

FIG.61
Brown's Point, Cullercoats, c.1896; photograph; Newcastle Libraries & Information Service

Despite photographic evidence to the contrary (fig.61), artists were reluctant to depict scenes of leisure at Cullercoats during the 1880s and 90s, this probably stemming from their attachment to fisherfolk imagery. In the first instance the precepts of Naturalism would have discouraged any recognition of the intrusion of modern life into the pre-industrial landscape of Cullercoats. Here, the beach was purely a site of work, worry and grieving. Even when Naturalism gave way to more avant-garde techniques, the older artists were unwilling to betray their loyalties. Jobling's late pictures of Staithes children reflect an uneasy attempt to assimilate newer techniques with fisherfolk imagery by tapping into the contemporary taste for nostalgic childhood pictures. Even in his single image of Edwardian promenaders at Cullercoats, he suggests a distance between himself and the pleasure-seekers in the figure of the single, contemplative woman. The younger artists, Slater, Horton and Atkinson seem to escape this dilemma, their post-1900 seaside pictures embracing old and new alike, if only because they had no particular attachment to the fisherfolk. It is only then that artists could admit that the beach was no longer the domain of the fisherfolk, but had become a 'domestic space, dominated by mothers, children and nursemaids'.[91]

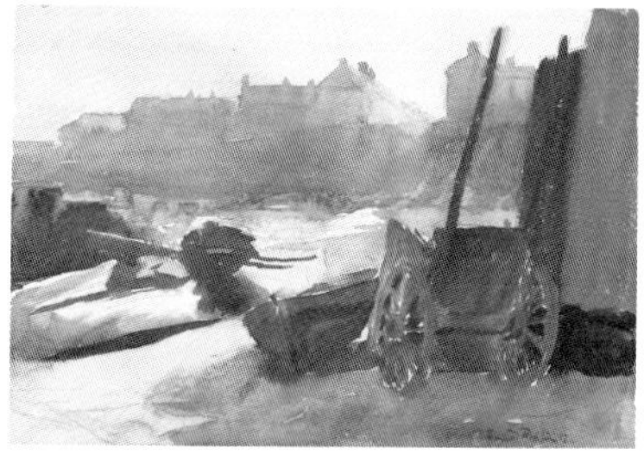

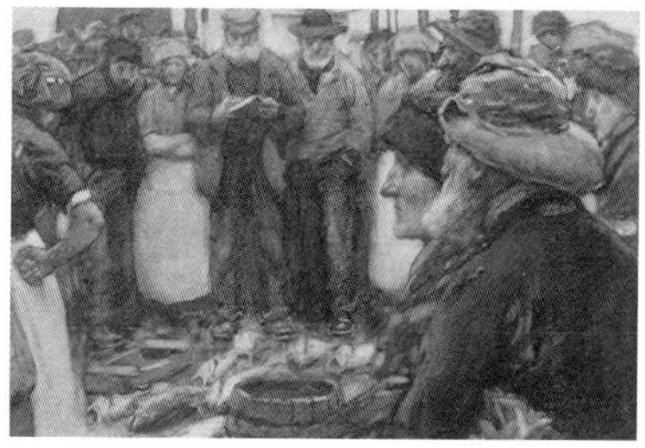

FIG.62
Ernest Procter, ***Old Newlyn***, 1913; Laing Art Gallery

FIG.63
Harold Knight, ***Fish Sale***, c.1900; private collection/ Reproduced with permission of Curtis Brown Group Ltd, London on behalf of the estate of Dame Laura and Harold Knight. Copyright © Harold Knight

Topography and the Fish Quay

This section explores the important shift in topographic subjects, from standardised views of what we might call 'Cullercoats signifiers', to more experimental explorations of nearby North Shields fish quay and its environs. This shift was part of the search for alternative subjects, another reflection of the colony's inability by the late 1890s to sustain the 'pre-industrial myth' of Cullercoats in the face of a dwindling coble fleet, the rising economic importance and visual impact of the tourist industry, and the geographical encroachments of Whitley Bay which had all but surrounded Cullercoats by 1900. With the corresponding decline in Naturalism, a number of Cullercoats artists turned their attentions to more modern subjects and experimental techniques.

As one of the busiest fishing ports in the country, the fish quay at North Shields could provide a host of modern subjects. It is telling, therefore, that none of these pictures could justifiably have been included in the 'working fisherfolk' section, but must instead be regarded as essentially topographical. Whilst I do not intend to dwell on the largely unexceptional topographical views of Cullercoats, it should be noted that their contemporary role in underpinning certain notions of Cullercoats — helping to create the 'place myth' — is crucial. This is attested by the fact that, long after the more important artists had moved on, others continued to try to bolster the place myth with countless topographical views.[92]

Views of Cullercoats had been popular since at least the beginning of the nineteenth century. In the early 1870s Watson painted a number of pictures of the fishermen's cottages and the old manor house, Sparrow Hall. The latter was a popular focus for artists' attention, appearing in the work of Jobling, Thompson, Homer, John O'Connor and F D Ogilvie. Many artists also produced standard views of the harbour. T S Hutton's *Cullercoats* (plate 55) is one of the better views of the village in stormy weather. But, with the possible exception of Horton, all the topographical pictures of Cullercoats seem to have used conventional techniques and by the turn of the century this theme was rarely tackled by the more important Cullercoats artists.[93] There seem to be no works to compare with, for example, Ernest Procter's *Old Newlyn* 1913 (fig.62), utilising a more avant-garde technique for what is otherwise a conventional view.

A marked unconcern with the figure is a noticeable feature of many of the pictures of the fish quay. Given the subject's potential one might have expected works more akin to Harold Knight's *Fish Sale* c.1900 (fig.63), where the Staithes fisherfolk stand grimly watching as the buyer makes his notes. But with few exceptions, this theme was largely ignored by Cullercoats artists. In an early Horton drawing, *Fish Quay* 1891 (fig.64), the figures play only a minor role, serving merely to add a sense of scale and some movement to the overall topography of the location. Horton is much more concerned with the communication of a particular atmosphere — dark, brooding, sublime almost, and above all, wet. In another drawing, *On the Fish Quay* (fig.65), Horton focused on the activity around the lamp-post, yet the figures are no more prominent a part of the composition than before. Again, the activities of the quay merely provide a vehicle for his exploration of shape and light, even though the boxes and barrels of fish are foregrounded.

This theme was evidently one of Horton's favourites throughout the 1890s, culminating in his 1896 Royal Academy work, the small oil *Fish Quay, North Shields* (plate 58). He rarely worked in oil but this medium

FIG.64
George Horton, ***Fish Quay***, 1891; Tyne & Wear Archive, reproduced courtesy D & M Redpath

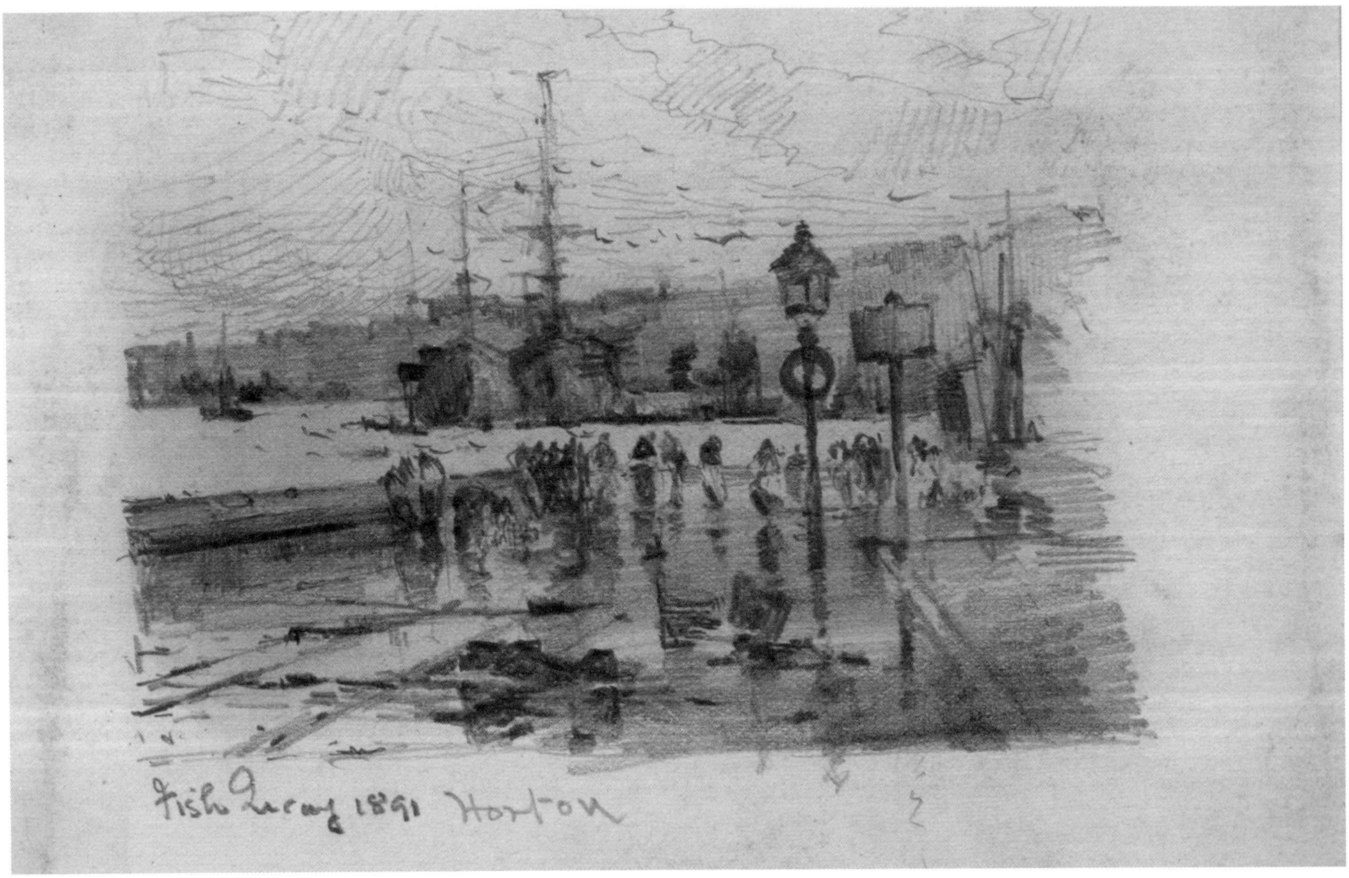

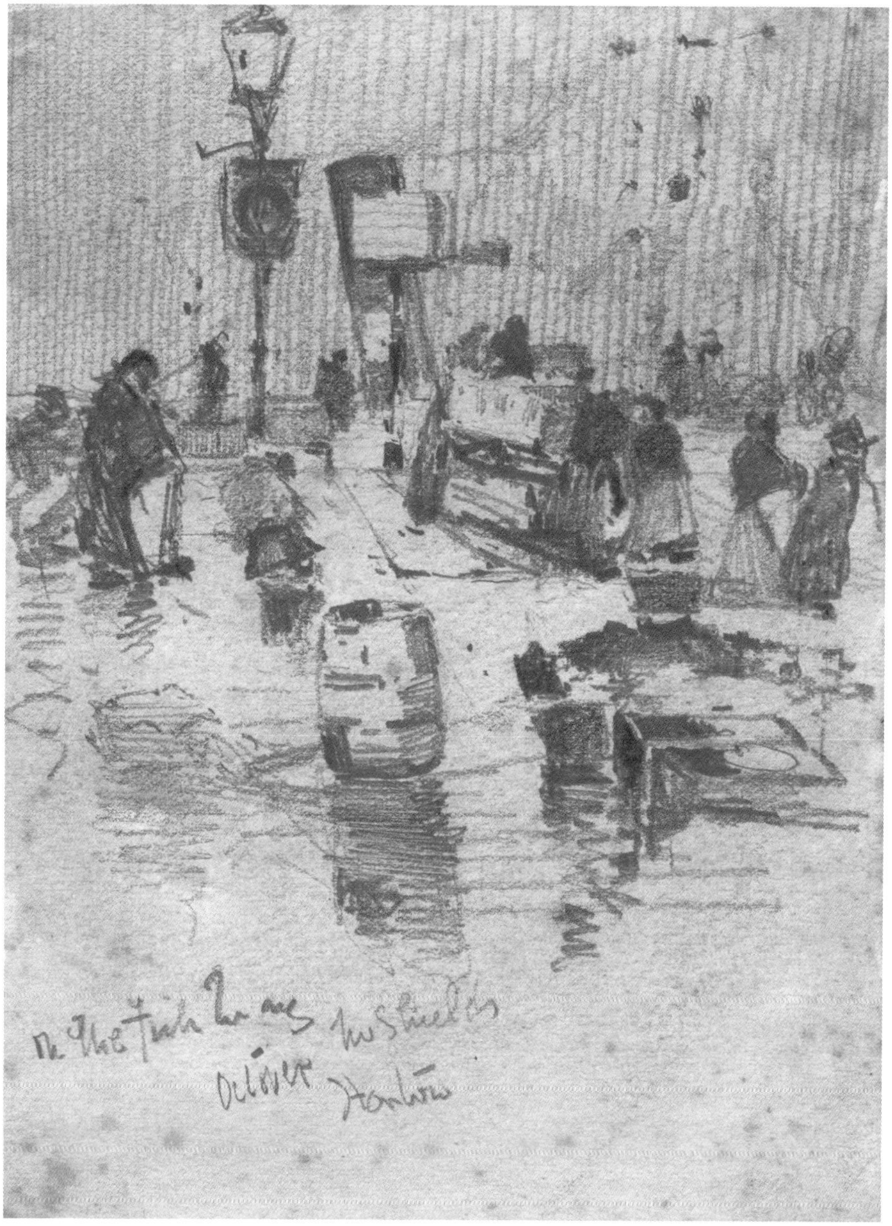

FIG.65
George Horton, ***On the Fish Quay***;
Tyne & Wear Archive, reproduced
courtesy D & M Redpath

seems to accentuate his over-riding interest in the formal qualities of the painter's art which this subject presents. The looseness of the paint handling and the economy with which he suggests his subject — the figures on the quay, the topography of the location, the boat alongside and the scavenging seagulls — flies in the face of the laborious multi-layered wash technique which he used for his watercolours of this period. The low horizon line, leaving a vast expanse of turbulent sky, accentuates the flatness of the composition. The distinctions between sky, sea and quay are blurred, reinforcing the two-dimensionality of the canvas.

But this picture is remarkable for more than just its technical features. The subject includes, quite clearly, a steam vessel of some kind on the right hand side of the canvas. This should be an unremarkable detail, since steam tugs had been in operation on the Tyne since the mid-nineteenth century. But it was still an unusual feature in the work of all British coastal colonists of the period, actively suppressing any signs of 'modern life' — machinery, telegraph poles, trains, steamboats — in order to perpetuate the pre-industrial myth. In the north east, steam-driven vessels stood for everything that the Cullercoats artists were trying to ignore or deny, because these vessels symbolised an end to the pre-industrial modes of fishing. Therefore, Horton's decision to include a steam vessel not only reinforces the modernity of the image but seems to embrace the future.

Perhaps not surprisingly, local critical reaction to its Royal Academy outing was mixed. The *Chronicle* noted, 'Mr.G.Horton ... has attempted in a very small canvas to depict the Fish Quay at North Shields, but there is a sad lack of definition in the work.'[94] However, the critic of the *Journal* was far more positive:

> *"The Fish Quay, North Shields" by Mr. G. Horton will doubtless be recognised by all Tyneside visitors as a familiar scene. One perceives the influence of Turner in this work, and its many good qualities encourage the hope of seeing further studious works from the hands of this artist.*[95]

These comments perhaps suggest that this critic was aware of the arguments of contemporary apologists for the 'London Impressionists' and their claim of affinity with, in particular, Constable and Turner.[96] It is easy to see how Horton's picture could be understood within this frame of reference. The sketchy, ethereal quality of the figures in particular invites comparison with the beach scenes of McTaggart or Steer. Noting that it was hung 'on the line' in the 'Gem Room', the critic of the *Newcastle Daily Leader* went so far as to call *Fish Quay*, 'a daring impressionistic sketch, holding its place most effectively in a room that is full of good work.'[97]

John Falconer Slater also embraced the pictorial opportunities presented by the fish quay. In *Quayside at North Shields* (plate 56) he combines an Impressionistic setting with precise topography and detailed treatment of foreground fishing vessels, including steam-driven boats. In *North Shields River Frontage, Snow* (plate 57) Slater turns his attentions to the tenemented buildings, warehouses and factories, smoke and steam spewing from chimneys along the waterfront.[98] Whilst the ramshackle buildings are undeniably 'picturesque', this facade takes little account of the human cost of living and/or working in such an environment. Slater prefers to play with the compositional possibilities of the multi-layered geometric shapes and the play of light on the facets of the snow-covered buildings.

John Atkinson also produced a series of works of the fish quay c.1905-10. Although never Cullercoats-based, Atkinson had worked there occasionally before his decision to turn to painting professionally.[99] In his watercolour of North Shields fish quay (plate 59), as with many of his other pictures, this subject is used as a pretext for the study of his beloved horses. Atkinson's fish quay pictures all share similar characteristics; a busy foreground full of movement and interest to engage the eye, with a hazy suggestion of background buildings and the strong verticals of ships' masts to give a sense of depth to the picture. These characteristics are also to be found in Rainbird's *Fish Market* c.1920 (plate 62). But Rainbird seems to be more concerned with suggesting the movement of the figures at work, using a sketchy, almost out-of-focus technique reminiscent of the ghostly shadows left by moving figures on old photographs.

The fish quay subject has been presented as a topographical one, yet without paying much attention to its distinctive features — the long, low, covered fish market and the tall 'High Light' and 'Low Light' buildings used to mark the safe channel to the quayside. These elements can be seen in a number of the works already discussed. Horton made frequent use of one or more of these buildings in many works, such as *Fish Quay* (plate 60), of which there are many versions. Hutton gives us a view of these buildings from the seaward side (plate 61). Even that most faithful depictor of the Cullercoats fisherfolk, Jobling, turned his attention to the fish quay from time to time; for example in 1901, when he produced a series of watercolours including *Low Lights, North Shields* and *Bank Top* in 1901 (plates 63 & 64). However, despite the distinctiveness and artistic possibilities presented by this topography, these images are far less site-specific than the Cullercoats pictures. Further, these signifiers of place were not used frequently enough to become instantly recognisable except to local audiences. This loss of specificity is a further sign of the shifting parameters of the colony's artists.

As well as the fish quay, Horton also turned to the streets of North Shields for new subjects, perhaps inspired by the urban scenes of Whistler and Sickert. But it is difficult to assess exactly when Horton started to paint such subjects since they were rarely shown, even at local exhibitions, although it is clear from his correspondence that they were often painted to order. It is possible that his interest in urban scenes was first awakened by his experiences in Holland since his first exhibited urban scenes were Dutch. His north-east works of this type were first shown at his one-man exhibition at the Greatorex Gallery in London in 1922. Dating these works is notoriously difficult, however. For example *The Kirkcaldy Arms* (plate 65) had become a butcher's shop by 1907, but it is likely that Horton painted the picture much later, reinstating a fictitious sign (see fig.66) in order to recapture the haunts of his youth. In another, *Wooden Bridge Bank* (plate 66), it is clear from contemporary photographs (fig.67 & 68) that Horton has reproduced a junction further up the street, rather than the one he thought. (It may be significant that both Whistler and Sickert used the memory training skills advocated by Horace Lecoq, which Horton may have tried to imitate.)

However, in many ways the topographical accuracy of Horton's street scenes is unimportant. As with his other pictures, these subjects merely provided the initial stimulus for his experimentation with shape, tone and

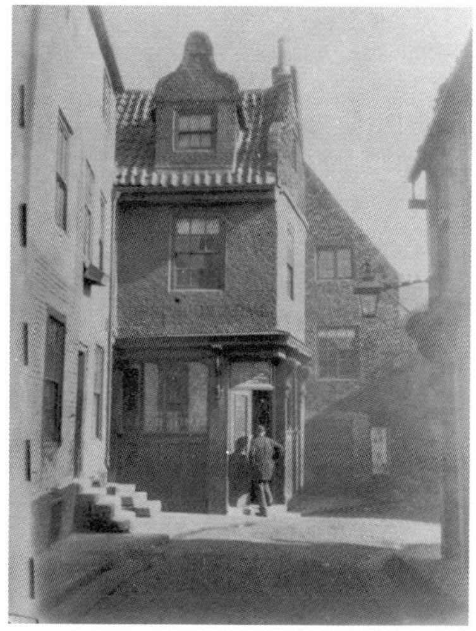

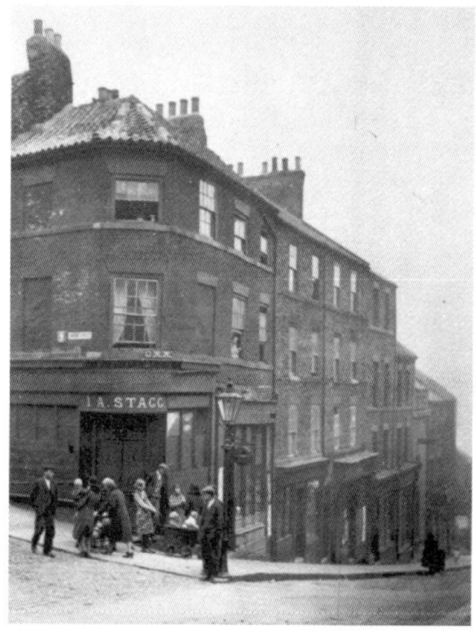

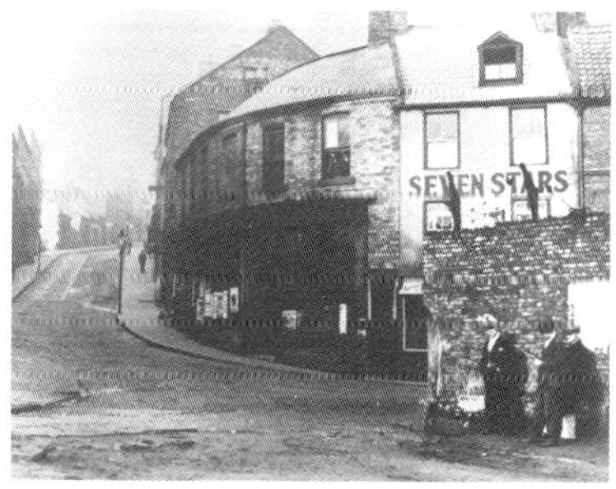

Fig.66
The Kirkcaldy Arms, North Shields; photograph; North Tyneside Libraries

Fig.68
Staggies', North Shields; photograph; North Tyneside Libraries

Fig.67
Wooden Bridge Bank, North Shields; photograph; North Tyneside Libraries

composition. However, it is noticeable that he found inspiration in a limited number of subjects. The street scenes were invariably of the older, ramshackle shops and back streets of the working-class area of North Shields near the river, what we would now think of as quaint in their dereliction. When compared with the previous paintings, pictures such as *J R Hogg's Shop, Comical Corner, South Shields* 1935 and *Winter, Clive Street*[100] (plates 67 & 69; fig.69) reveal the repetition of a number of compositional devices: the open foreground; the main building set at a slight angle to allow for a patch of deep shadow adjacent which leads the eye in and gives a sense of depth (reversed in *Wooden Bridge Bank*); the relishing of textures such as snow, cobbles and water; the same earth-based palette enlivened by touches of blue or red; the almost abstract emphasis on geometric shapes — each canvas is predominantly made of squares, triangles and rectangles. Many of these formal characteristics can also be found in the topographical work of the Staithes artist Roland Henry Hill, for example in *Runswick Cottages* (plate 68). With few exceptions, Horton's pictures are devoid of people, and even where they are present — in *J R Hogg's Shop*, for example — they fulfil compositional requirements rather than being the actual subject of the picture. But otherwise he emptied these busy streets. If these pictures were done from a distance, geographically and historically, perhaps these essentially melancholy images reflected his sense of isolation from his 'roots'.

FIG.69
George Horton, ***Winter, Clive Street***;
Tyne & Wear Archive, reproduced
courtesy D & M Redpath

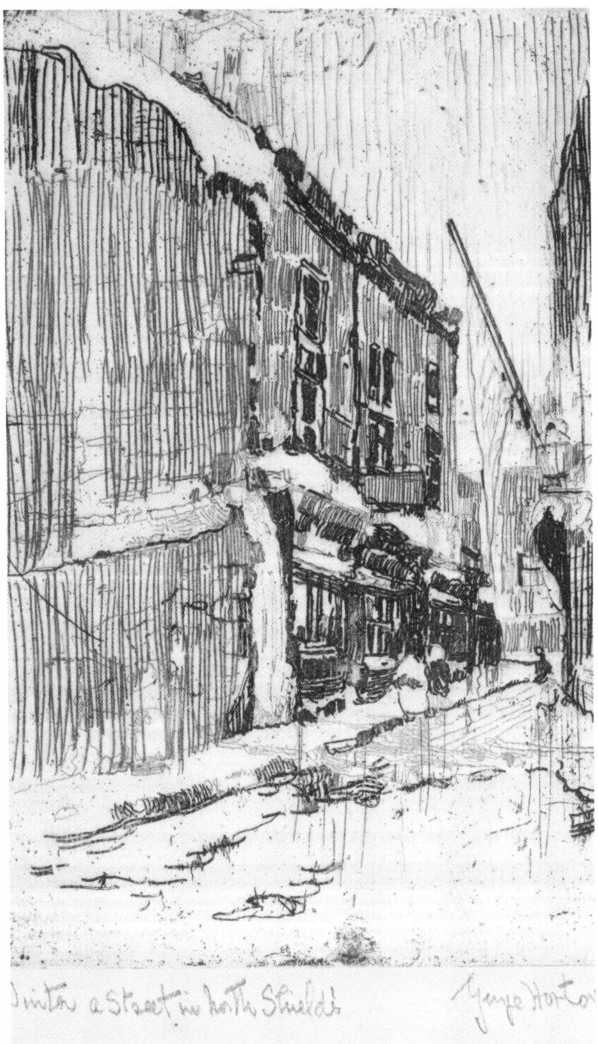

Faced with the growing irrelevance of the Cullercoats fisherfolk subjects and the unacceptability of adopting subjects from the industrial landscape, the region's artists sought fresh subjects and experimented with newer techniques. The younger artists explored contested sites: North Shields fish quay — a boundary between nature and the urban, a reference to the old fisherfolk subjects yet the reason for their demise: or seaside leisure — the beach as a site of middle-class leisure rather than fisherfolk workplace, yet the new source of income. However, there is nothing to correspond with the Baudelairean revelry in the urban working-class subjects found in the work of Sickert or Rothenstein. The modern worker is present, but reduced in size and significance — a mere signifier of scale or movement, an insertion for colour, shape or compositional harmony. Some artists, notably Horton and Rainbird, embraced the urban landscape more completely. However, these works remained strictly topographical; Horton's usually unpeopled; Rainbird's inhabited by ghostly signifiers of movement. For others, the fish quay subject represented the closest they ever came to exploring the modern urban landscape.

Seascapes

Historically, seascapes have resisted analysis. Even scholars of other well researched coastal colonies have by-passed the problematic presence of seascapists amongst artists seemingly devoted to recording 'ways of life'. Yet the pattern of seascape production at British coastal colonies is indicative of broader changes in the colonies' priorities. In the early nineteenth century the north east had a particularly strong seascape tradition, yet during the first decades of the Cullercoats colony this subject was rare, even despite the popularity of seascapes by Henry Moore or Colin Hunter at local exhibitions. Crucially though, neither Moore nor Hunter was affiliated to a colony. So, excepting a few examples by Jobling, seascapes were largely present only as the stage upon which human drama was played out in the period c.1870-90.

There are a number of factors at play here. The immense influence of Turner's patriotic yet atmospheric seascapes had allowed subsequent artists to successfully equate an empty sea with notions of Britishness; indeed, to paint the sea was seen as an artistic expression of patriotism. John Brett's *Britannia's Realm* 1881 exemplifies this attitude, where, as Charles Hemmings notes, it 'enumerate[s] each ripple as though each was a jewel in the Queen-Empress's crown'.[101]

But Brett's patriotism was not mirrored by the colonists; they preferred a more subtle patriotism. However, with the gradual abandonment of Naturalism in favour of more painterly concerns from c.1890, an increasing number of colonists turned to seascapes as an alternative vehicle for experimentation. The 1880s Impressionistic *plein-air* coast scenes of Whistler and McTaggart were adapted to fulfil more personalised or introspective reactions to the power of the sea. As Corbin noted: 'The sight of the boundless sea's emptiness creates a sensation without an object that encourages the imagination to plunge into the waters. The marine monotony is conducive to sleep, and it creates a temptation to let oneself be swallowed up.'[102] Seascapes painted at the shoreline, such as plate 71 by Slater, give the visual sensation of infinite horizontal space and of being engulfed, prompting simultaneous associations with the unchanging, infinite sea and with our mortality — the sea as grave. Here the seashore was transformed from the Romantic site for contemplation and self-knowledge, into the Jungian dream of regression and desire to return to the womb.

But how do seascapes fit with the other colony paintings? The definitive break with a human or topographical anchorage in Cullercoats seascapes was not universal. Slater's *Cullercoats Bay* (plate 70), and Harry Sticks' *Breakers, Whitley Bay* 1915 (plate 72) tie the seascape to a particular location associated with the colony. Other artists, such as Horton (plate 73) and Jobling (plate 75), use the distinctive topography of Tynemouth Priory and Castle, suggesting a continuity of the *genre* from the earlier nineteenth-century marine artists. Jobling's *Moonlit Bay c.*1922 also seems to nostalgically refer back to a Turneresque style, similar both to his own earliest riverscapes and to Steer's post-1900 tributes to Turner. This element of nostalgia mirrors developments in other subjects, as we have seen, but is perhaps especially poignant here, coming at the end of Jobling's own career. The shadowy figures walking along the shore are repeated in his watercolour *Dusk* (plate 74). His primary concern here, as in much of his work, is with atmosphere — indicated by the title and the lack of any topographical clues. Similarly, in another watercolour, *Seascape* (plate 77), he experiments with the medium to study clouds, sea and sandy rock-pools.

In all of the above pictures there is a link of some kind to the colony, either through topographical reference, association with past artists, or shared artistic concerns. This makes it more difficult to understand the later seascapes of Slater as part of the colony phenomenon. However, as has already been noted, there are long associations between women and the sea: indeed, Christopher Reed draws an analogy between the monumental fisherwomen of Homer and his later seascapes.[103] It is therefore possible to understand the unpopulated seascapes of Slater (plates 76 & 78) or Julius Olsson (*Off Cornwall,* plate 79) as encompassing similar notions of dangerous attraction, monumentality, introspection and the marking of boundaries as suggested by many of the fisherwomen pictures.[104] However, their formal aspects cannot be overlooked; the sheer exuberance of the brushwork and the heavy impasto of Slater's late seascapes seem to edge towards Abstract Expressionism, prompting the sensation of being engulfed by the medium as much as by the subject.[105] It is perhaps significant that Slater does not seem to have painted any seascapes until 1891, with his larger, increasingly expressionistic paintings dating from after 1900. This development equates with the search for new subjects and styles amongst the other Cullercoats artists at this period, and was perhaps a logical choice for an artist who had never specialised in figurative Naturalism. So, although we know that Slater worked mostly on the beaches of the north-east coast, his unpopulated seascapes are not accurate portrayals of this busy coastline, but are intensely personal reactions to the subject in all its guises.

Conclusion

> *Since the early nineteenth century, national identity has required having a heritage and thinking it unique. Heritage differentiates, we treasure most the things that set us apart.*[106]

Recent scholarship on European art colonies has persistently positioned them in relation to the 'avant-garde', whilst critical scrutiny of British coastal colony art has been resisted because of its connection with the maritime — commonly accepted as an unproblematic symbol of 'Britishness'. This 'given' has been compounded by a reluctance to problematise the connection between Naturalist subjects and Naturalist techniques, further shoring up the notion of these works as straightforward, natural, unmediated.[107] However, by situating the Cullercoats output within the discourses surrounding anxieties about urban life and the working classes, and the inter-related nineteenth-century constructions of nationhood/imperialism and masculine/feminine ideals, a much richer seam of readings can be mined.

Clearly there are strong parallels between the development of subjects and modes of representation at Cullercoats and those at colonies such as Staithes and Newlyn, although the earlier genesis and strong local presence at Cullercoats initially made it difficult to shed the vestiges of an earlier anecdotal narrative style. There are intimate links between the developments of subjects, techniques and audiences, and the dominant contemporary social, political and intellectual ideologies. Thus the subjects of the 1870s and 80s — the heroic lifebrigade man, the working men and women and waiting/grieving women — utilised a classically-inspired, Naturalistic technique to encourage an unproblematic reading of the British working class as hard-working, healthy, religious and racially pure. The apparent 'truthfulness' of this vision masked the true extent to which such imagery was part of wider ideological constructions of northern-ness and Britishness. These constructions, supported by a vast body of literature and other media, promoted a working-class ideal, based on a pre-industrial workforce and landscape which was historically and geographically on the margins. It was fed by a variety of needs and anxieties — imperialist pretensions, threat from foreign powers, the perceived degeneration of the urban working-classes, the role of women in society, and the failure of religion as a hegemonic tool, for example. Thus W J T Mitchell's assertion that landscape fulfils Marx's notion of a 'social hieroglyph' — that it is 'an emblem of the social relations it conceals' — can be equally applied to this imagery.[108] By appearing 'natural' or unmediated, these pictures constructed meanings and values which concealed their own artifice.

But as those needs and anxieties mutated, so too did the imagery. During the late 1880s and 1890s Britain's industrial and economic domination and imperial expansionism was tempered by foreign competition and colonial insurgence, industrial and civil unrest, the Irish Question, chronic rural depopulation, increased working-class leisure time and the emergence of the 'New Woman'. For coastal colony art this meant that the overtly nationalistic 'heroic' imagery of the 1870s and 80s became unsustainable. The 'working fisherfolk' imagery was similarly undermined by both practical and ideological changes — the decimation of small fishing communities by mechanisation, and the therefore untenable position of trying to perpetuate this 'pre-industrial' myth.[109] As a result, these themes gave way to others, often of an ambiguous, symbolic or nostalgic nature — fisherfolk at leisure, scenes of leisure or children playing, and rural scenes.

Even topographical views were affected, shifting from a preoccupation with establishing the main signifiers of the Cullercoats landscape to less site-specific explorations of more modern, semi-urban scenes.

Only the waiting/grieving women category and seascapes survived largely intact because of their ability to support a variety of readings. In the former, the religiosity and morality of the early works confirmed the ideal woman's subordinate and supporting role in Victorian society, and also served as symbol of the nation and its boundaries. Whilst the religious element may have become less overt, it nevertheless remained important. The nationalistic and patriarchal overtones of the 'waiting women' and seascapes were reworked to suggest retrenched horizons, internalised or psychological boundaries.

The dissemination and adoption of new styles and techniques at Cullercoats seems to have occurred in a number of haphazard and piecemeal ways. The artists who visited Cullercoats around 1870 had little lasting impact on subsequent developments but shared the *genre*-like, often anecdotal style of the earliest Cullercoats works, using an 'academic Pre-Raphaelite' technique.[110] This was ideally suited to the didactic nature of these moralistic and ideologically-loaded works. The development of a more Naturalistic style can be seen from the late 1870s. The initial influence of Millet and Jules Breton, followed by Homer's example, may have encouraged others to empty out narrative content from their subjects. A number of Homer's key stylistic traits are subsequently found in the work of other Cullercoats artists, most notably Thompson and Jobling. However, the Cullercoats interlude came at a crucial time in Homer's career, and the resulting idealised and classicised female figures were consonant with the quasi-Naturalistic images already being produced by Marsh and Jobling, undoubtedly revealing a shared indebtedness to Millet and Breton.

The impact of Bastien-Lepage and the Newlyn School is less certain since, although the square-brush technique was adopted sporadically from the mid-1880s, it was never consistently used by any Cullercoats artist. The Newlyn artist whose works the Cullercoats artists most resemble is Walter Langley — the first and most frequently exhibited Newlyn artist at the Bewick Club — who mostly worked in watercolour. Many Cullercoats artists encountered new ideas on style and technique through direct contact with London or European artists. Of course those local artists who pursued careers in London — John Surtees, John Charlton, Thomas Macklin, Thomas Spence, Charles W Mitchell and (later) Horton — also provided a channel for new ideas. But the primary conduit to the majority of local artists must have been the Bewick Club exhibitions in Newcastle. Over the years local artists were able to study at first hand works by a wide variety of well known artists including those of the Aesthetic Movement, the Glasgow Boys, Hague School, Newlyn School and Staithes group.[111] But this encouraged the haphazard adoption of various stylistic tendencies rather than the development of a uniform 'school' of thought and practice.

However, it is clear that from around 1890 the influence of the Staithes group was a crucial intervention at a critical period in Cullercoats' survival. The Staithes influence suggested alternative subjects and introduced more avant-garde techniques which encouraged a more painterly style with greater emphasis on the formal qualities of picture-making. The battle to abandon older subjects and styles was never satisfactorily resolved, but this reflects a wider debate which rumbled on in the art world throughout the 1890s.[112] After the relative uniformity of Naturalism, the variety of responses at the turn of the century perhaps reflects both the excitement and confusion at new possibilities.

If the Cullercoats paintings fulfil David Lowenthal's notions of a nineteenth-century heritage project, then this book and exhibition perhaps mark the next phase in this historical recovery. The process has revealed a large, thriving colony at whose centre was a core of mainly local artists. Their determination to resist the metropolitan-centred art market fostered self-sufficiency and the establishment of numerous art clubs, exhibition opportunities and educational facilities. The commercial success of the region's exhibitions was founded on the existence of a number of well informed art collectors, whose example stimulated the ethos of collecting amongst the increasingly broad-based middle classes, supported by a small but intelligent body of local critics. The existence of a regional art colony, whose work undoubtedly fed off associations with higher-profile colonies such as Newlyn and yet whose market was overwhelmingly local, challenges the hitherto normalised, metrocentric history of late-nineteenth-century British art. This study has, it is hoped, illuminated both the summations and the anachronisms which give measurement to the achievements of the Cullercoats colony.

Notes

1 See for example N Lübbren, 'Toilers of the Sea. Fisherfolk and the geographies of tourism in England, 1880-1900' in Y Holt, F Russell & D P Corbett eds., *The Geography of Englishness: Landscape and the National Past 1880-1940*, Yale University Press, 2002, which sees these works as a middle-class reaction to modernity.

2 S Daniels, *Fields of Vision. Landscape Imagery and National Identity in England and the U.S.* Polity Press, 1993, p.5. The phrase comes from Benedict Anderson's *Imagined Communities: Reflections on the Origin and Spread of Nationalism*, Verso, 1983.

3 These artists had met Stevenson at Birket Foster's house in Surrey.

4 These works include Emmerson's *This is my House and this my little wife* RA 1870, *A Foreign Invasion* RA 1871: Orchardson's *Toilers of the Sea* RA 1870: Holl's *No Tidings from the Sea* RA 1871: Watson's *Fishermen's Cottages, Cullercoats* and *A Prize* OWCS 1870, *Limpet Gatherer* OWCS 1871, *At Cullercoats* OWCS 1872: Marsh's *The Missing Boats* RA 1871, *Pilot* OWCS 1871, *The Signal — Breakers on the Bar* RA 1872. All received critical attention in the art press.

5 *Art Journal*, 1862, p.197.

6 ibid., p.157.
7 Charles Baudelaire, 'The Salon of 1846', *Charles Baudelaire: Selected Writings on Art and Literature*, Penguin, 1972, pp.104-7. As a poet and critic, Baudelaire was hugely influential on the proto-modernists of the late nineteenth century.
8 Lübbren, 2002, op.cit., p.41.
9 See for example Michael Ancher's *Will She Clear the Point?* 1879-80.
10 See G Quilley, 'Missing the boat: the place of the maritime in the history of British visual culture', *Visual Culture in Britain* v.1, no.2, 2000.
11 See J A Kestner, *Masculinities in Victorian Painting*, Scolar Press, 1995, p.3.
12 For example, J A Froude, *England's Forgotten Worthies*, 1853; Kingsley, *Westward Ho!*, 1854; *The Heroes*, 1855; Carlyle, *On Heroes, Hero Worship and the Heroic in History*, 1840-41.
13 *Art Journal*, 1870, p.170.
14 *The Athenaeum*, January-June 1870, p.681.
15 ibid., p.680.
16 See for example J Stuart Mill *On Liberty* 1859, Matthew Arnold *Culture & Anarchy*, 1869 and *Poems*, 1853; Thomas Arnold in R Jenkyns *The Victorians and Ancient Greece*, 1980; Walter Pater *Greek Studies*, 1895.
17 *Saved* was also reproduced in *The Graphic*, Dec 1871. The original oil (untraced) was shown at the A.A. exhibition in 1880.
18 In Homer's similar work, *The Lifeline* 1884, the thrill of danger is heightened by added sexual *frisson*, which was not lost on contemporary critics.
19 Art Circle critique, *N.D.C.* 6 January 1897.
20 N Cikovsky & F Kelly, *Winslow Homer*, exh cat, National Gallery of Art, Washington, 1995, p.207.
21 Horton recounts seeing Homer sketching the *Iron Crown* in 'Artist with Craze for Clocks', op.cit.
22 Undated letter, February 1882, quoted in Cikovsky & Kelly, op.cit.
23 *N.D.J.* 19 January 1884.
24 J Millard, 1992, op.cit., p.31.
25 Kestner, op.cit., p.8.
26 It was commissioned by Sir Johnstone Wallace, a self-made man, an iron and coal merchant who became chairman of the Laing Art Gallery and had associations with the Lifeboat Institute.
27 Its genesis remains unknown but is unlikely to have been commissioned since it remained in his studio until his death in 1917.
28 *N.D.C.* 30 April 1910.
29 *Art Journal*, 1910.
30 On New Year's Day 1861 the women of Cullercoats dragged the lifeboat 'Percy' across the fields to St.Mary's Is. to rescue the crew of the 'Lovely Nellie'.
31 Charlton's 'historical' works included pictures of the Egyptian Campaign during the early 1880s, of Queen Victoria's Jubilee processions of 1887 and 1897, and illustrations of the Boer War for *The Graphic*.
32 See Michael Roper & John Tosh eds., *Manful Assertions. Masculinities in Britain since 1800*, Routledge, 1991, p.13, in Kestner, op.cit., p.4.
33 For David's imagery and politics see for example A Brookner, *Jacques-Louis David*, Chatto & Windus, 1980.
34 See Open University A102 for figures.
35 See Tomlinson, op.cit., p.103.
36 See A M Reynolds, *The Life and Works of Frank Holl*, Methuen & Co. Ltd., 1912, pp.83-85, for his daughter's account of the incident which inspired this work.
37 *Art Journal*, 1871, p.173.
38 *The Graphic*, 17 June 1871.
39 G E Campbell 'Frank Holl and his Works', *Art Journal*, 1889, p.53.
40 H V Barnett in *N.D.L.* 19 September 1889.
41 Anderson and Garland sale catalogue, Sept. 1993.
42 The poem reads,
Three wives sat up in the Lighthouse tower,
And they trimmed the lamps as the sun went down;
They looked at the squall, and they looked at the shower,
And the night-rack came rolling up ragged and brown.
This poem was also used as inspiration by Thompson, Jobling and Laura Knight, amongst others.
43 *N.D.J.* 14 February 1891.
44 Notes by Altona, *N.D.J.* 17 February 1891.
45 O.W.C.S. review *Art Journal*, 1893, p.29. See also *Art Journal*, 1874, p.228 in which the critic declares, 'Thus we find a large number of painters who treat watercolour very much as if it were oil.'
46 R Langley, *Walter Langley. Pioneer of the Newlyn Art Colony*, Sansom & Company/Penlee House Gallery, 1997, p.65.
47 See for example D Lowenthal, 'British National Identity and the English Landscape', *Rural History*, vol.2, no.2, 1991.

48 A Corbin, *The Lure of the Sea. The Discovery of the Seaside in the Western World 1750-1840*, trans. J Phelps, University of California Press, Berkeley & Los Angeles, 1994, p.40.
49 See A McClintock, *Imperial Leather. Race, Gender and Sexuality in the Colonial Context*, Routledge, 1995, pp.352-357.
50 G Cubitt ed., *Imagining Nations*, Manchester University Press, 1998, p.10.
51 Corbin, op.cit., p.164.
52 See for example *N.D.C.* 31 August 1881 for a critique of Jobling's *Overhauling the Nets*.
53 It was bequeathed to the Laing by John Lamb, a local collector, in 1909.
54 K McConkey, *The Restless Wave*, Newcastle upon Tyne Polytechnic Art Gallery, 1978.
55 It was for sale for £25 at the Bewick Club in 1885. It was also exhibited at the Walker Gallery in 1909, but was eventually given to the Laing by Mrs Marsh.
56 J Ruskin, *Sesame and Lilies*, 1865, quoted in Kestner, op.cit., p.10.
57 Although untraced, *Sharing the Burden* was graphically described by the *N.D.J.* 3 September 1881.
58 See S Mendus & J Rendall eds., *Sexuality and Subordination*, Routledge, 1989, especially Joanna de Groot 'Sex and Race: The construction of Language and Image in the 19th century', pp.89-130. For discussion on the fetishisation of working-class women in nineteenth-century imagery see McClintock, op.cit., pp.181-203.
59 *Tyneside Daily Echo*, 31 August 1881.
60 *Boston Advertiser*, 4 February 1882, cited in Cikovsky & Kelly, op.cit., p.202.
61 *Boston Herald*, 5 February 1882, in ibid.
62 G Sheldon, 'Sketches and Studies II', *Art Journal*, 1880, p.105, quoted in H Adams, 'Winslow Homer's Impressionism and its relation to his trip to France', in N Cikovsky ed., *Winslow Homer: A Symposium*, National Gallery of Art, Washington, 1990, p.79.
63 'The Fine Arts', *Boston Daily Evening Transcript*, 9 February 1882, in Cikovsky & Kelly, op.cit., p.201.
64 The connotation of images of working-class women with sexual availability is well known, although it most frequently applies to urban working women.
65 McClintock, op.cit., p.359.
66 ibid., p.184.
67 L Fiedler, *The Collected Essays of Leslie Fiedler* vol.1, New York: Stein & Day, 1971, p.150, cited in Christopher Reed, 'The Artist and the Other: the Work of Winslow Homer', *Yale University Art Gallery Bulletin*, Spring 1989, p.75.
68 *N.D.C.* 28 January 1886.
69 *N.D.J.* 19 January 1886.
70 See for example *North Mail*, 6 March 1923.
71 At the Arts Association exhibition in 1878 this latter picture was universally praised for its masterly rendition of stormy seas and convincing figures. See for example *N.D.J.* 10 September 1878 and *N.D.C.* 12 September 1878 for critiques.
72 See *Art Journal* 1877, which also mentioned that this watercolour was a preparatory work for a version in oils. The oil (untraced) was lent to the first Artists of Northern Counties Exhibition in 1905 by the executors of the estate of William Cochrane. The watercolour was owned by C W Mitchell and sold in 1926.
73 *Newcastle Courant*, 25 February 1893.
74 *N.D.J.* 2 March 1893. It seems that almost all Thompson's Academy pictures were Staithes subjects. She all but stopped painting fisherfolk at Cullercoats after her marriage in 1893, perhaps to avoid competition with her husband in the local market. By exhibiting Staithes works at the Academy she was, consciously or not, allying herself with better known artists such as Jackson, Friedenson, Knight and Mackie.
75 These include *Three Girls* 1881-2, *Early Evening* 1881-1907; *A Little More Yarn* 1884 and *Fisher Girls on the Shore, Tynemouth* 1884.
76 See P J Waller, *Town, City and Nation. England 1850-1914*, Oxford University Press, 1983, especially chapter 5.
77 The picture was commissioned by the farmer Fenwick Wilson of Marden Farm, Whitley Bay for £50 and was originally accompanied by a key to identify the girls. It was sold by Wilson's descendants at Anderson & Garland, March 1998, (lot 870).
78 Although Thompson and Jobling married in 1893, she seems to have continued to sign her work with her maiden name up until c.1900. *Haymaking* was donated to the Shipley Art Gallery in January 1920 by the local collector Thomas Reed.
79 *Art Journal*, 1871, p.178.
80 See Tomlinson, op.cit. There are a number of early-nineteenth-century guides which describe Cullercoats as a 'watering' or 'bathing' place.
81 For a discussion of the growth of these resorts see J Walvin, *Beside the Seaside*, Allen Lane, 1978: and J K Walton, *The English Seaside Resort. A Social History 1750-1914*, Leicester University Press, 1983. In 1851 Tynemouth was the only true north-east resort, but by 1881 Whitley Bay had out-stripped Tynemouth in size and by 1911 was the 25th largest resort in England and Wales (a rise of 700%). Factors such as its proximity to the urban/industrial conurbation, increased leisure time for the working classes and increased industrial wages would have been important in this.

82 A Hemingway, *Landscape Imagery and Urban Culture in early 19th century Britain*, Cambridge University Press, 1992, especially chapter 'Growth of Seaside Resorts'. He mentions examples by Francis Holman, Benjamin West, Cristall, Linnell, Cox, Havell, Turner, Prout, De Wint and Constable.

83 Exceptions to this include Whistler's beach scenes of the early 1880s and Stanhope Forbes' *Beach Scene, St. Ives* 1886. However, this type of image was common in French art from Boudin in the 1860s to Monet, Manet and Morisot, in the 1870s and 80s.

84 L Tickner, *Modern life and Modern Subjects. British Art in the Early 20th Century*, Yale University Press, 2000, p.129. She offers a number of examples from Romantic literature but none from Romantic British art.

85 Although undated, this picture must date from after 1908 because of the presence of the Dove Marine Laboratory.

86 See Tomlinson, op.cit., p.103 for a description of pictures by G W Brownlow.

87 Corbin, op.cit., pp.170-171, traces the history of nostalgic childhood beach scenes.

88 Emmerson showed *Children Bathing off Whitley Beach* 1893, at his 1894 exhibition. In Homer's *Children Playing at the Seaside* 1881/2 it is difficult to tell whether they are fisherfolk resting or middle-class leisure seekers. This latter theme had been a significant one for Homer during the late 1860s and early 1870s.

89 *Minding the Bairn* was exhibited at the Artists of the Northern Counties exhibition in 1916, priced £6.

90 This work may well date from c.1916 since it shares many characteristics with his *Women and Children at Staithes* of that year, including size of canvas, colouration and handling.

91 Tickner, op.cit., p.131.

92 These included Ellie Fenwick, Elizabeth Petrie, A J Sticks, Chambers, W T N Boyce, S Brownlow, J Rock Jones, W C Way, J Watson, G A Waterston, G S Wood, R Ventress, F D and F S Ogilvie, C Rutherford, W Redpath, J D Liddell, C George and J W Gilroy, to name but a few.

93 Although early examples are now rare, it is evident from exhibition catalogues that Cullercoats was a regular subject for Horton.

94 *N.D.C.* 2 May 1896.

95 *N.D.J.* 9 May 1896.

96 Horton's writings and notes are full of references to the works of Sickert in particular, but also frequently mention Steer, Rothenstein, Sisley, Monet, Morisot and Whistler.

97 *N.D.L.* 2 May 1896.

98 Many of these buildings were demolished in 1914. See Eric Hollerton, *The Archive Photographic Series, North Shields*, Chalford Publ., 1997, p.33.

99 Atkinson worked for Charles Mitchell and his son at Armstrong Mitchell & Co., so would have had contacts with that patronage circle, perhaps making the transition to professional artist a little easier.

100 *Comical Corner* was bought by South Shields Library from the Royal Academy exhibition in 1935.

101 C Hemming, *British Painters of Coast and Sea*, Victor Gollancz Ltd, 1988, p.68.

102 Corbin op.cit., p.167.

103 Reed, op.cit., p.77.

104 Julius Olsson was a member of the Staithes Group who sent seascapes regularly to the Bewick Club exhibitions from 1888 onwards. He moved to St Ives in 1890, from which period this painting dates.

105 Reed also makes this connection with Homer, see op.cit., p.77. Slater used this style for all his later subjects.

106 Lowenthal, op.cit., p.206.

107 Rosalyn Thomas maintains that the Newlyn pictures were 'an accurate visual survey of Cornish life.' R Thomas, *Frank Bramley*, R A 1859-1915, Usher Gallery, Lincolnshire County Council Education and Culture Services Directorate, n.d., p.8.

108 W J T Mitchell ed., *Landscape and Power*, University of Chicago Press, 1994, pp.5-34, especially pp.15-16.

109 Although Cullercoats fishermen did adopt some new methods, by the 1890s their livelihood was under severe threat. In the period 1850-80 a fisherman could expect to earn £100-150 p.a., but during the 1890s this had dropped to £31-65 p.a. (figures Quinn, op.cit., p.335).

110 This assimilation of PRB techniques into mainstream art practices came within a few years of the emergence of the original brotherhood. J D Watson is perhaps the only Cullercoats artist to have had a genuine connection and affinity with the PRB.

111 For details see Newton, op.cit., chapter 2.

112 For a fuller discussion of this issue see Newton, op.cit., pp.208-210.

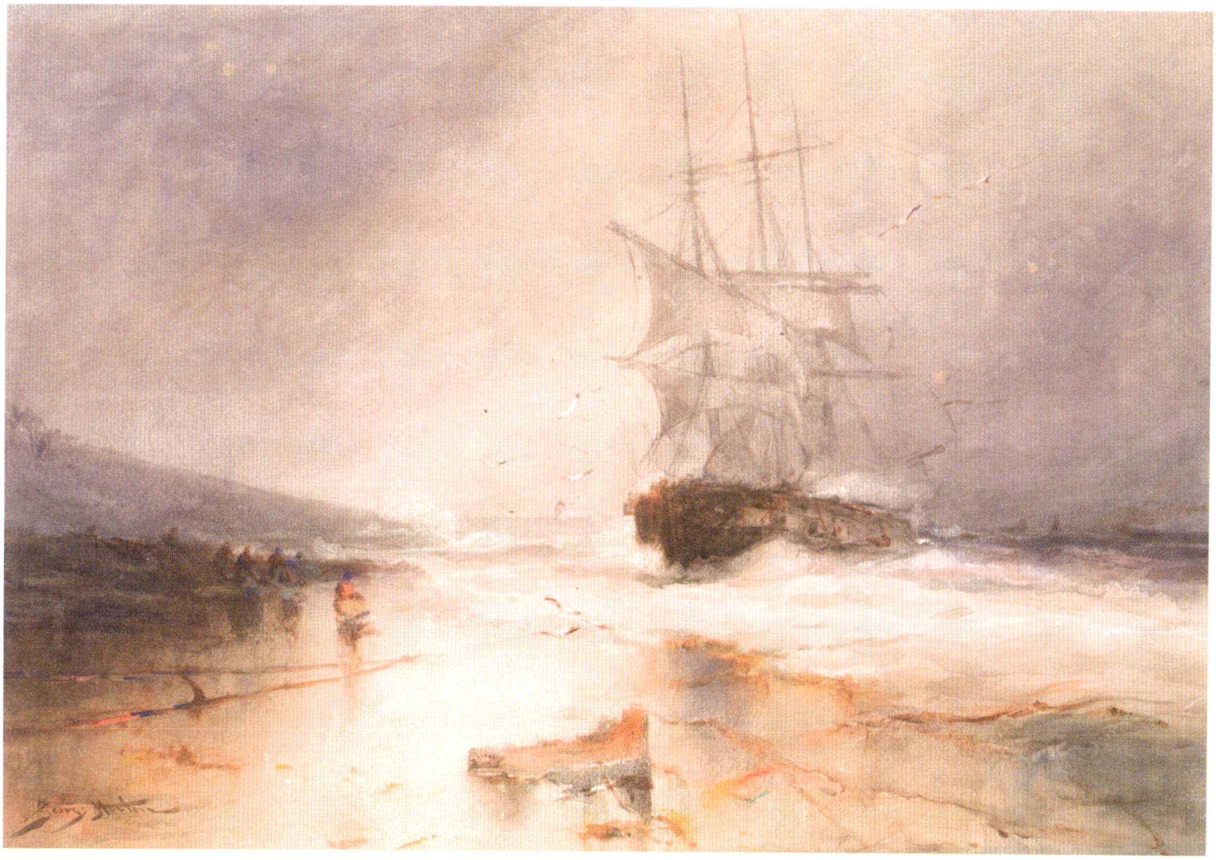

PLATE 1 George Horton, ***Wreck of the Salween*** c.1895; Laing Art Gallery

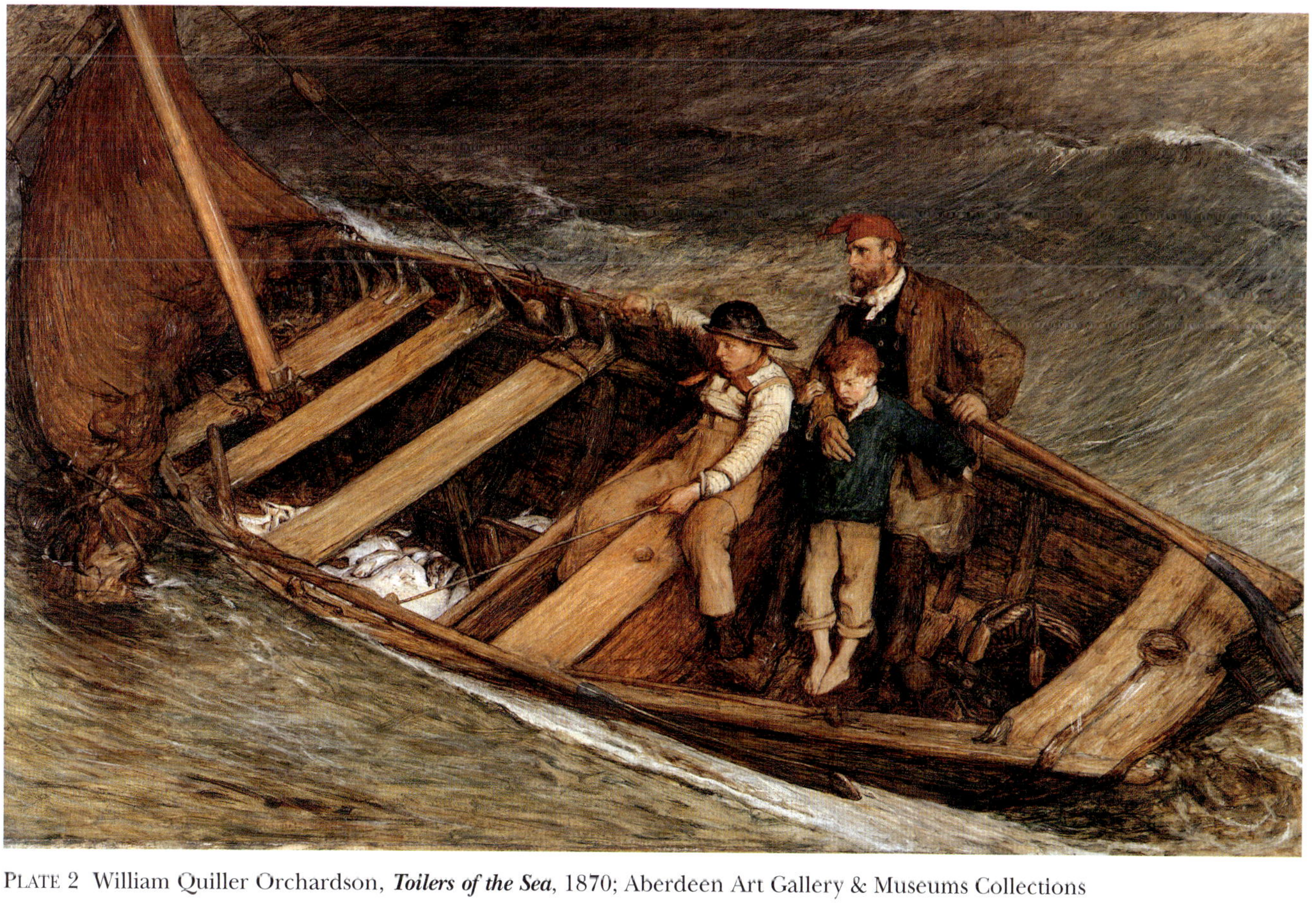

PLATE 2 William Quiller Orchardson, ***Toilers of the Sea***, 1870; Aberdeen Art Gallery & Museums Collections

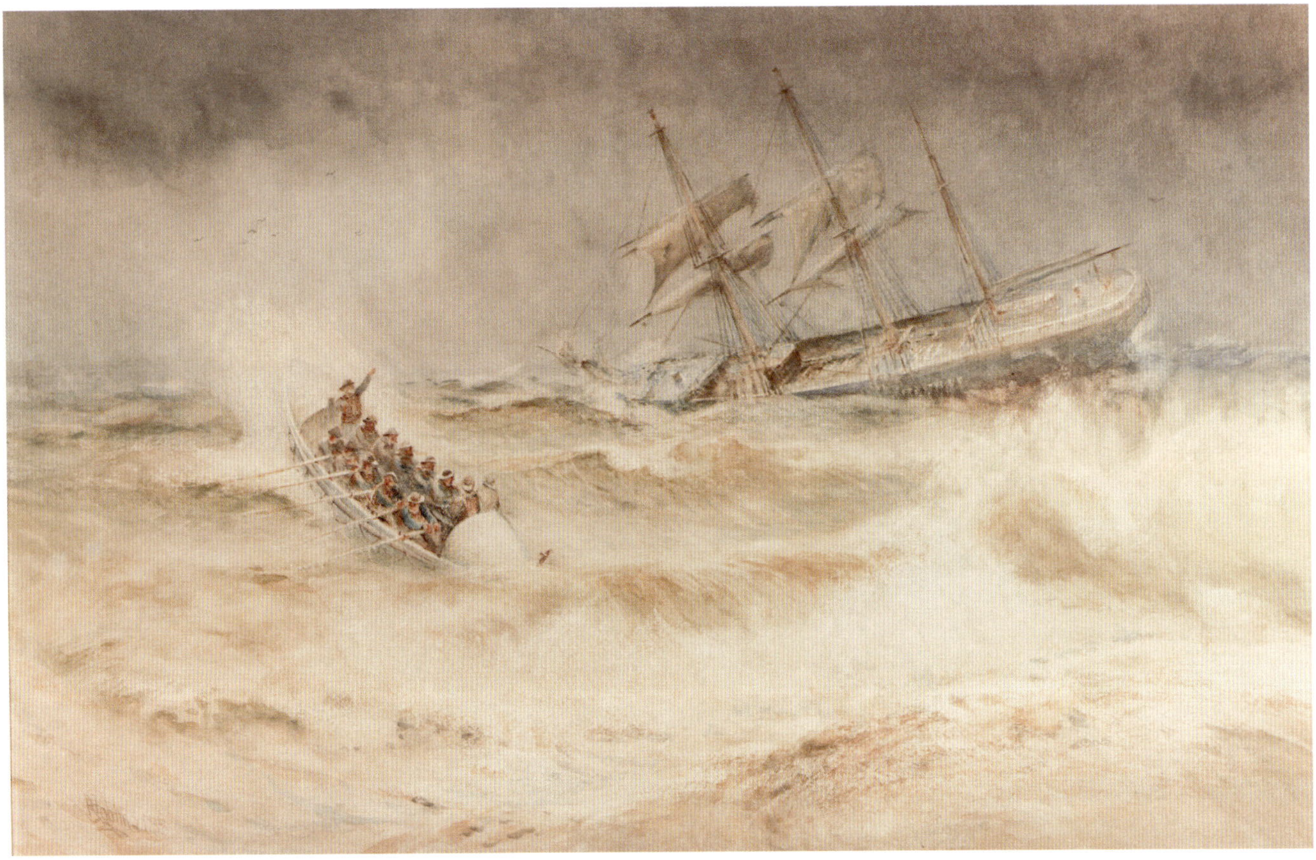

Plate 3 Robert Jobling, ***Wreck of the Iron Crown***, 1882; private collection

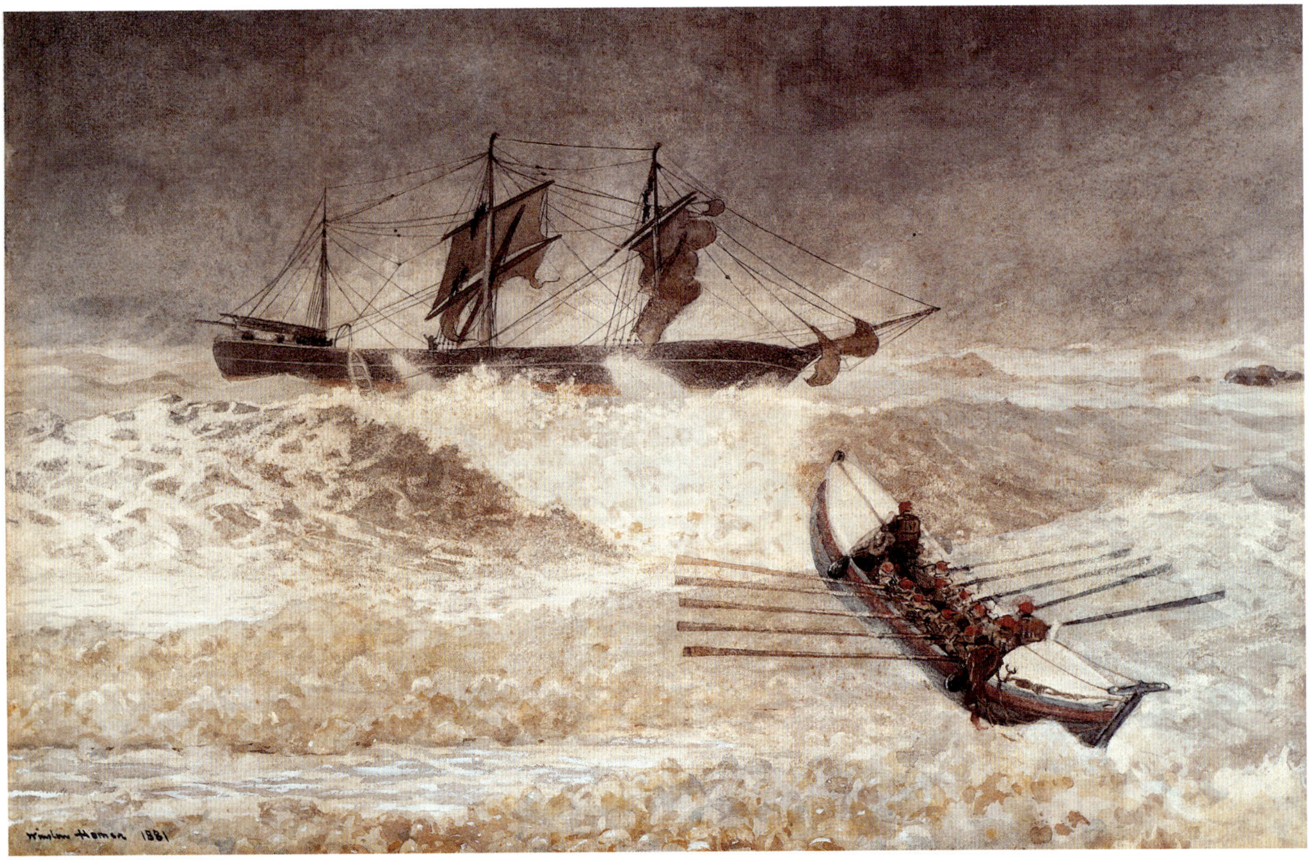

Plate 4 Winslow Homer, ***Wreck of the Iron Crown***, 1881; The Baltimore Museum of Art: Carleton Mitchell Collection, on extended loan to the Baltimore Museum of Art R8613.2

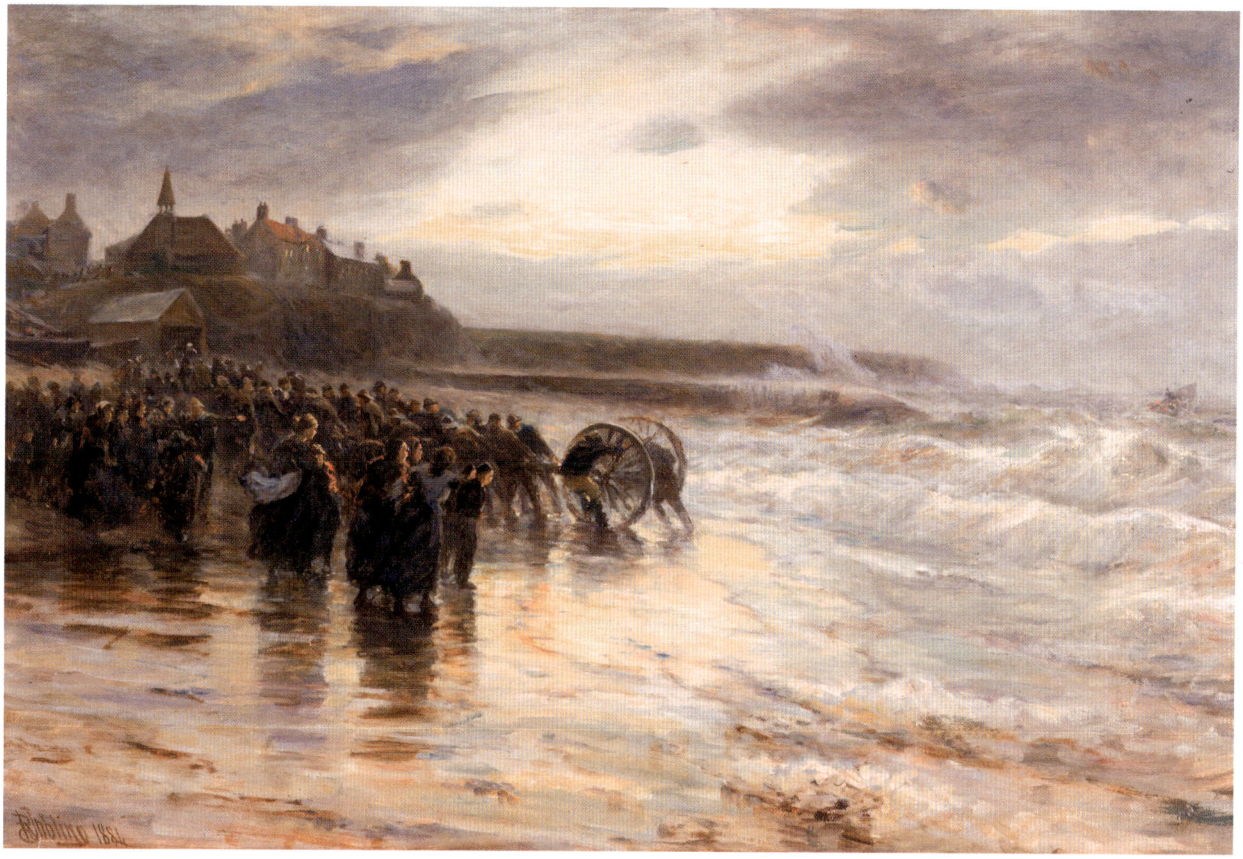

PLATE 5 Robert Jobling, ***Storm – Lifeboat Off***, 1884; Laing Art Gallery

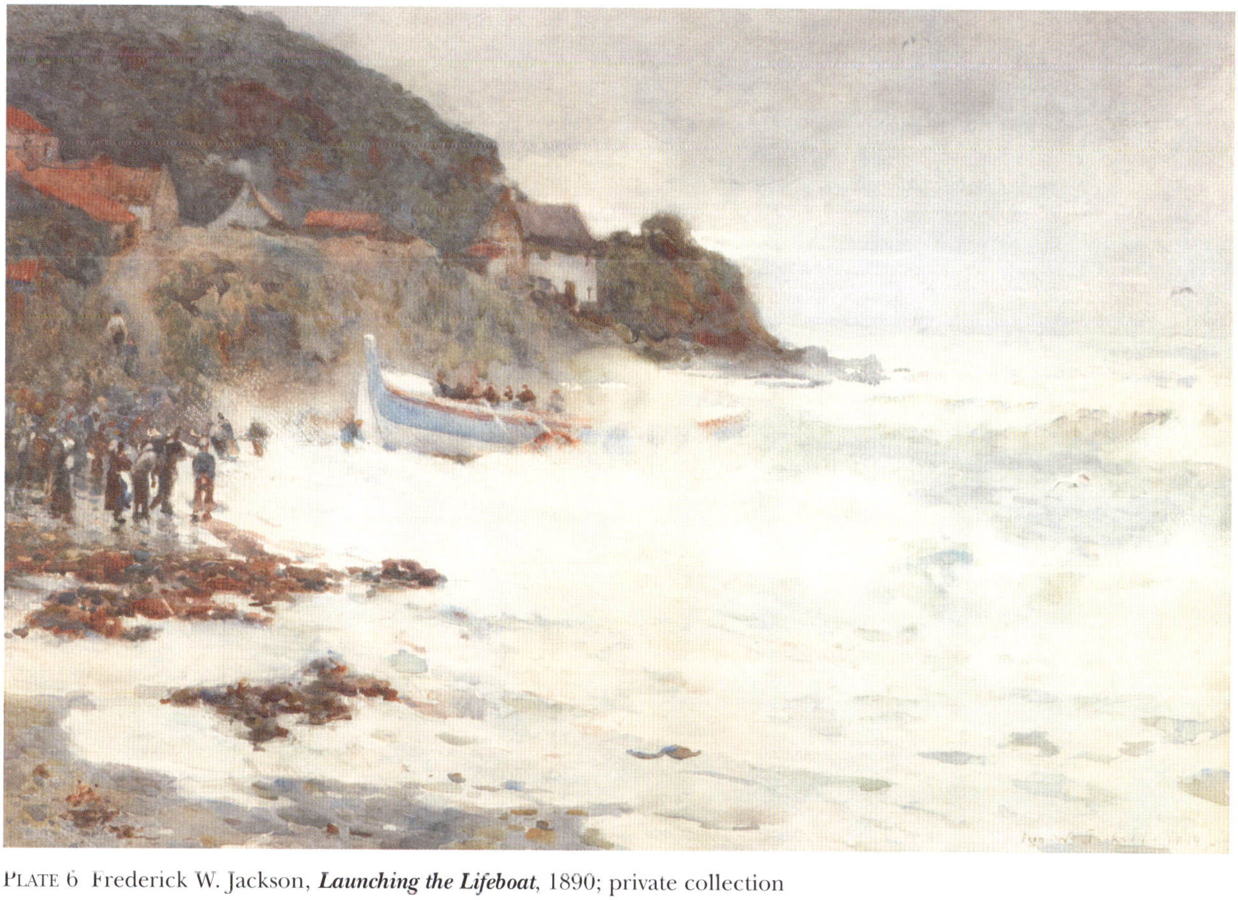

PLATE 6 Frederick W. Jackson, ***Launching the Lifeboat***, 1890; private collection

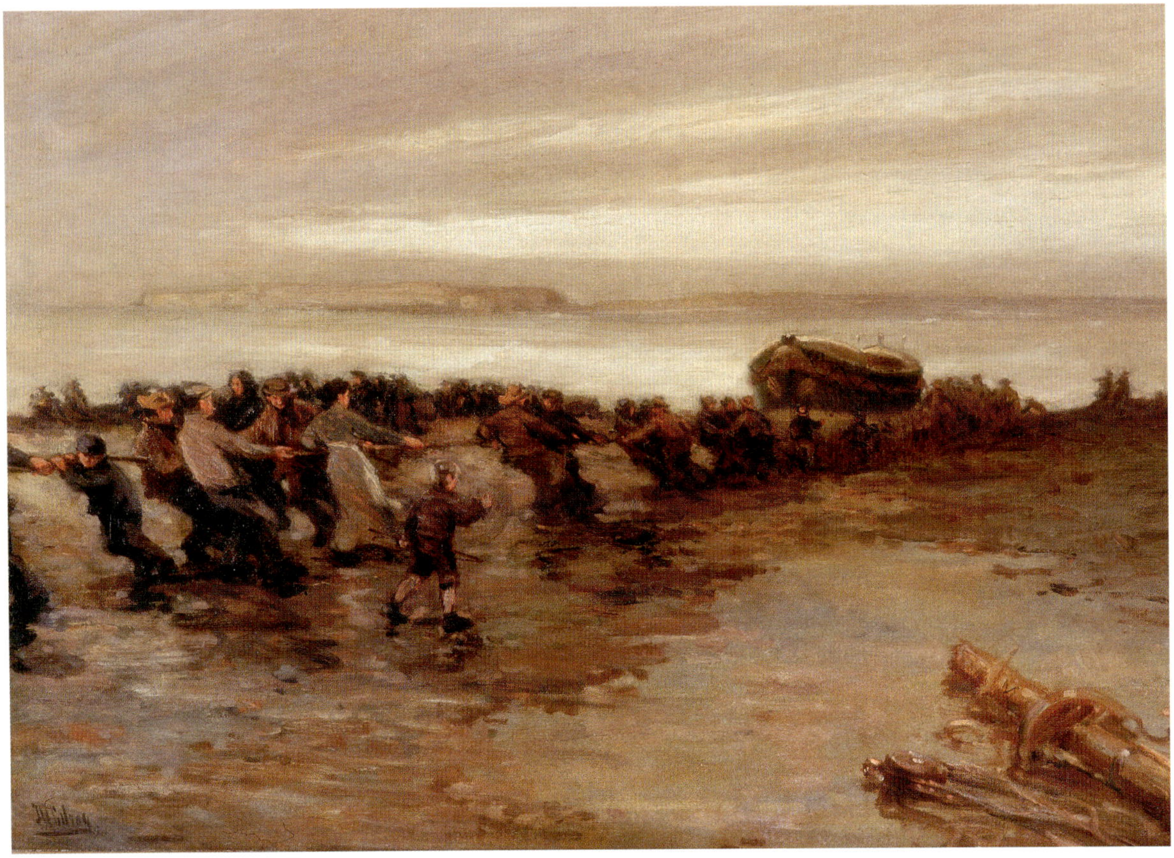

PLATE 7 J. W. Gilroy, ***Hauling up the Lifeboat***, Laing Art Gallery

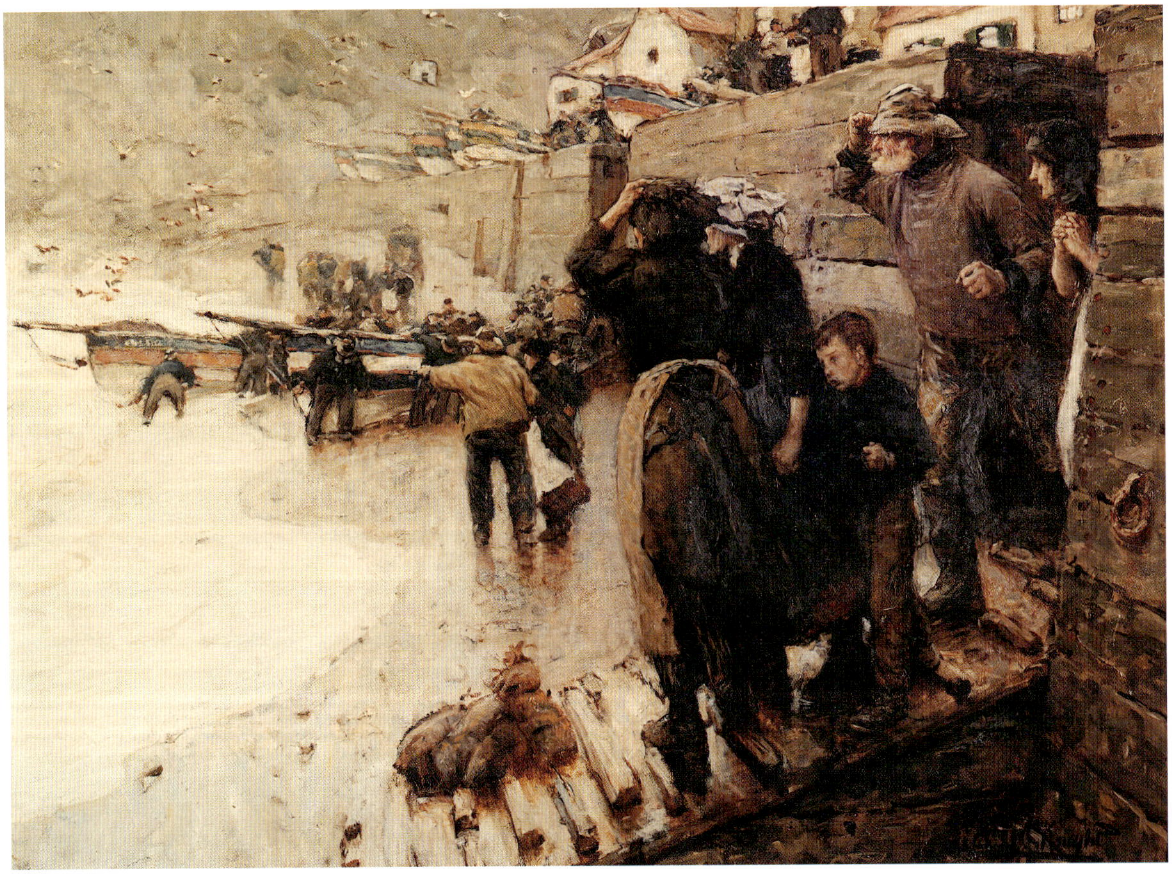

PLATE 8 Harold Knight, ***The Last Coble***, 1900; Nottingham City Museums & Galleries; Castle Museum and Art Gallery Reproduced with permission of Curtis Brown Group Ltd, London on behalf of the estate of Dame Laura and Harold Knight. Copyright © Harold Knight

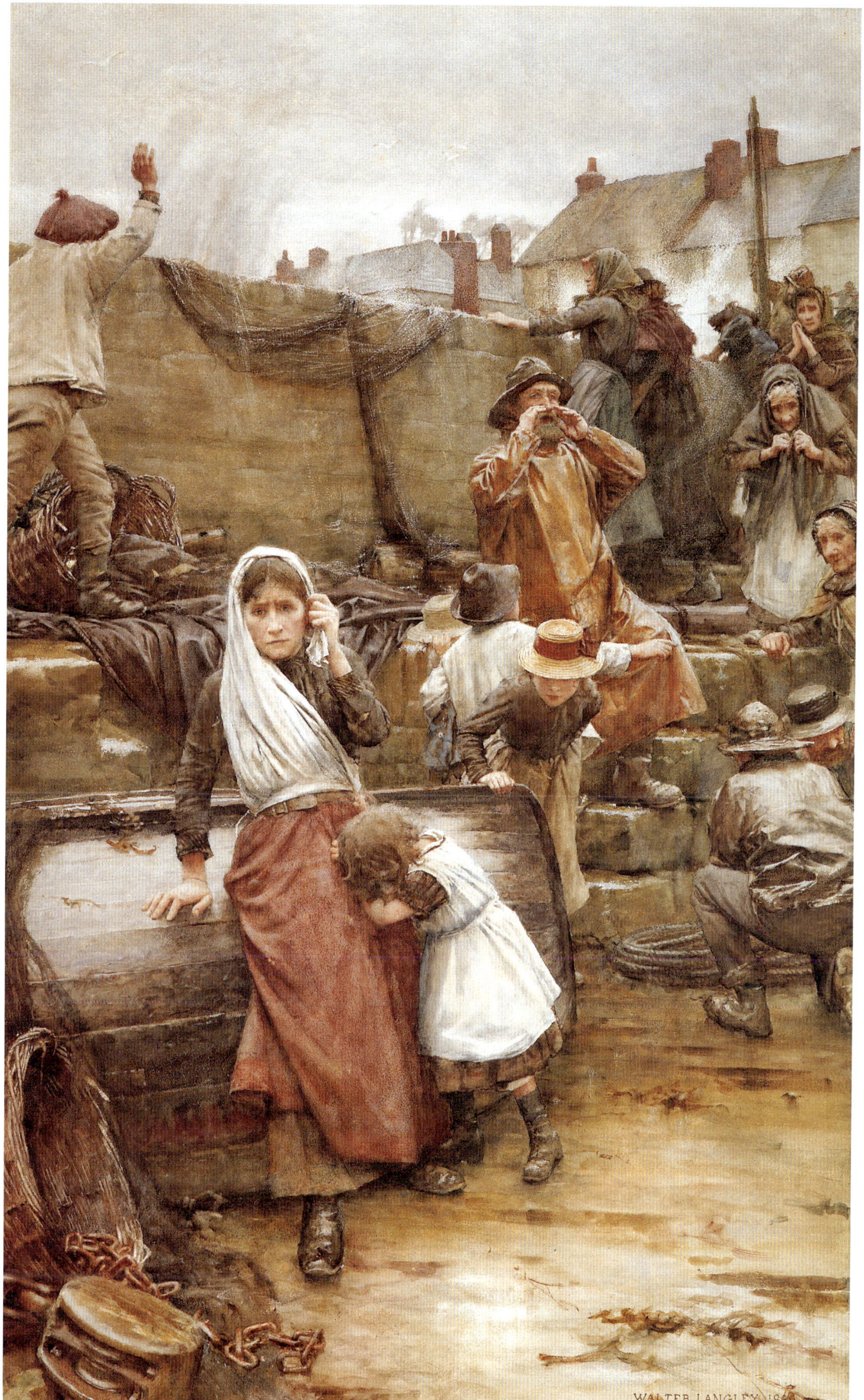

PLATE 9 Walter Langley, ***Disaster! Scene in a Cornish Fishing Village***, 1889; Birmingham Museums & Art Gallery

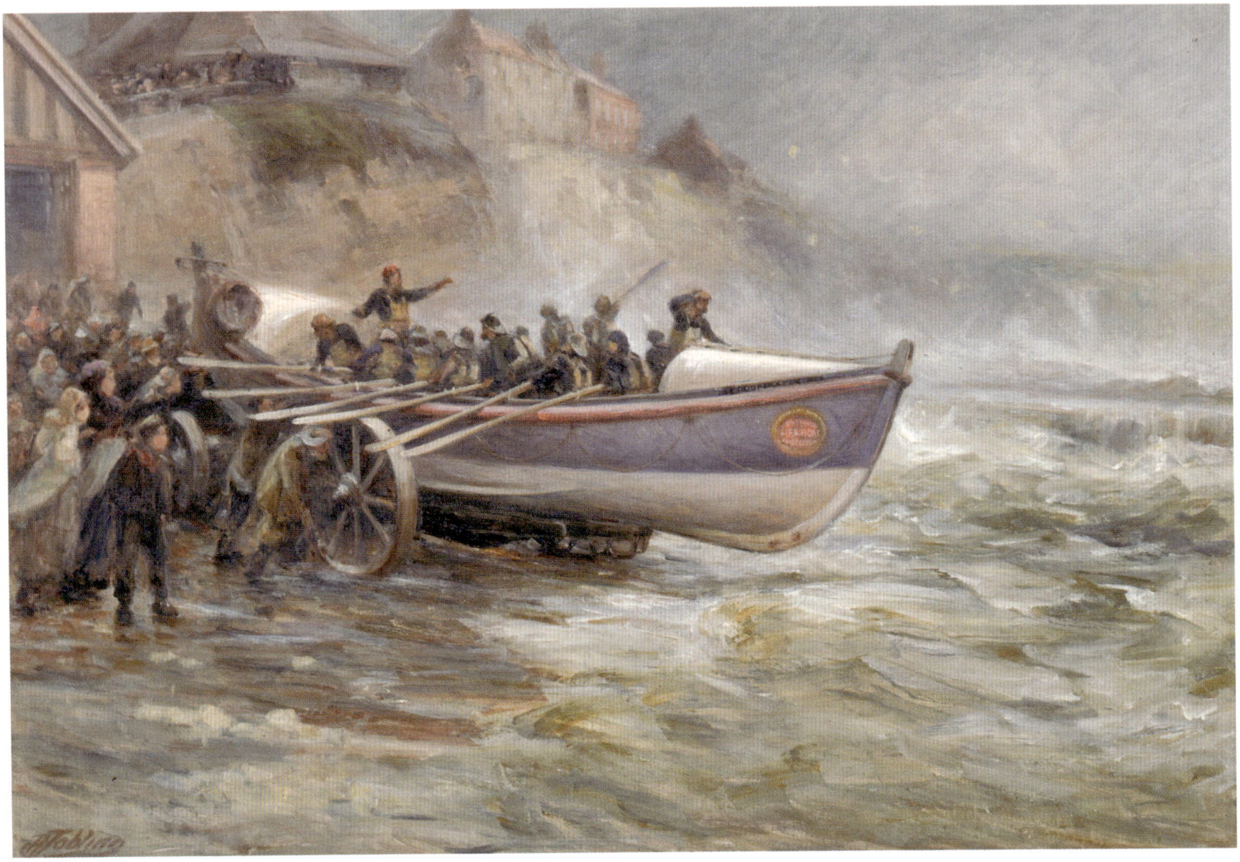

PLATE 10 Robert Jobling, ***Launching the Cullercoats Lifeboat***, 1902; Laing Art Gallery

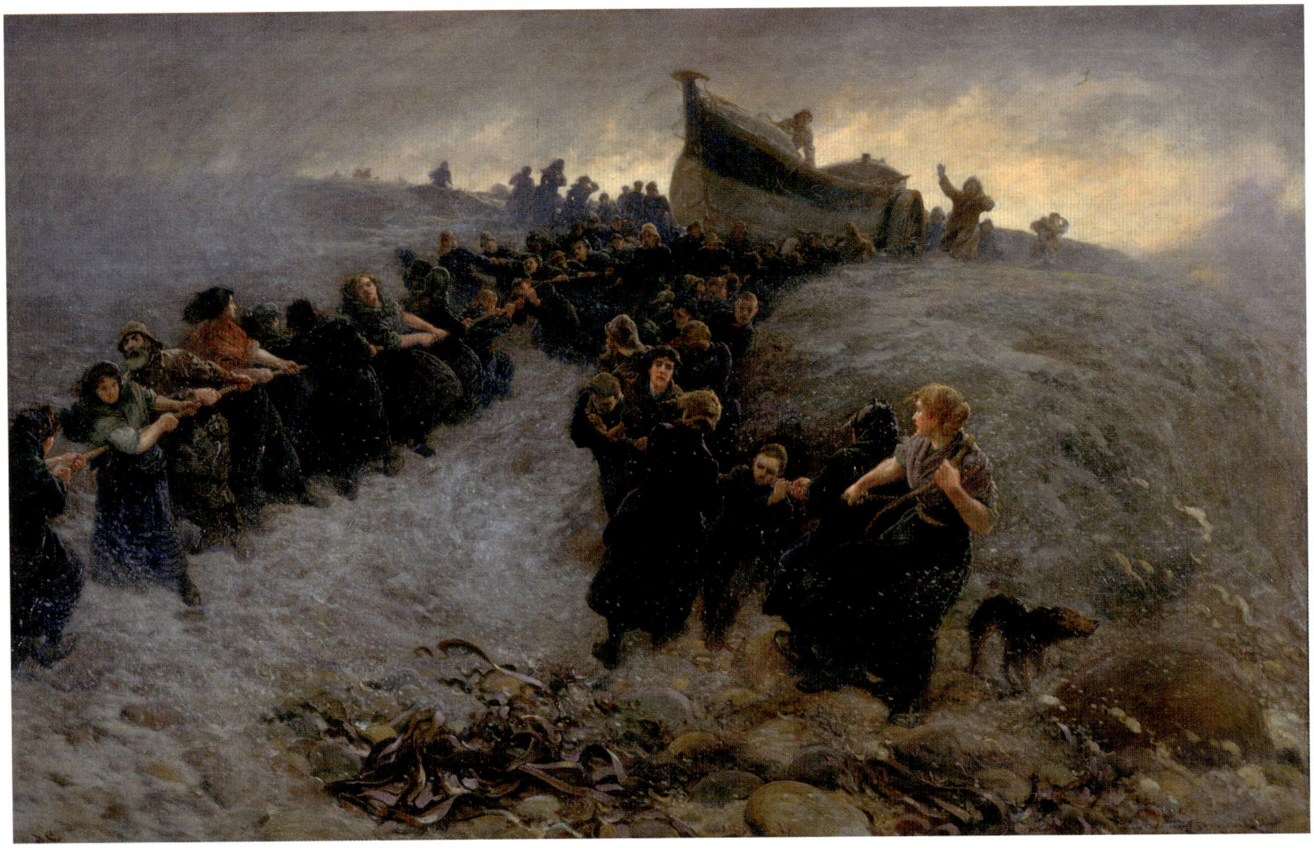

PLATE 11 John Charlton, ***The Women***, 1910; Laing Art Gallery

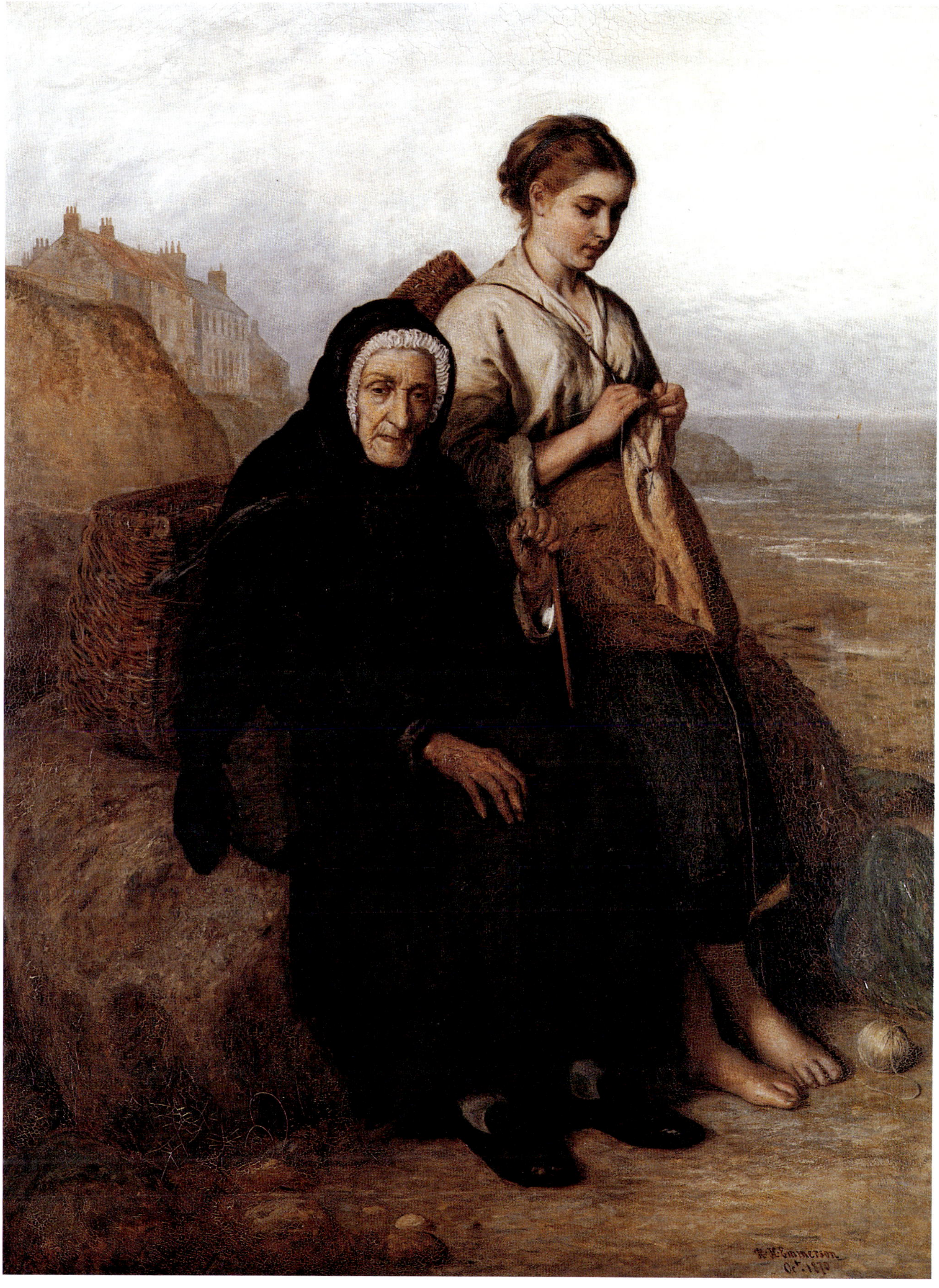

PLATE 12 Henry Hetherington Emmerson, ***Waiting for the Boats***, exh. 1870; private collection; photograph courtesy Anderson & Garland Auctioneers

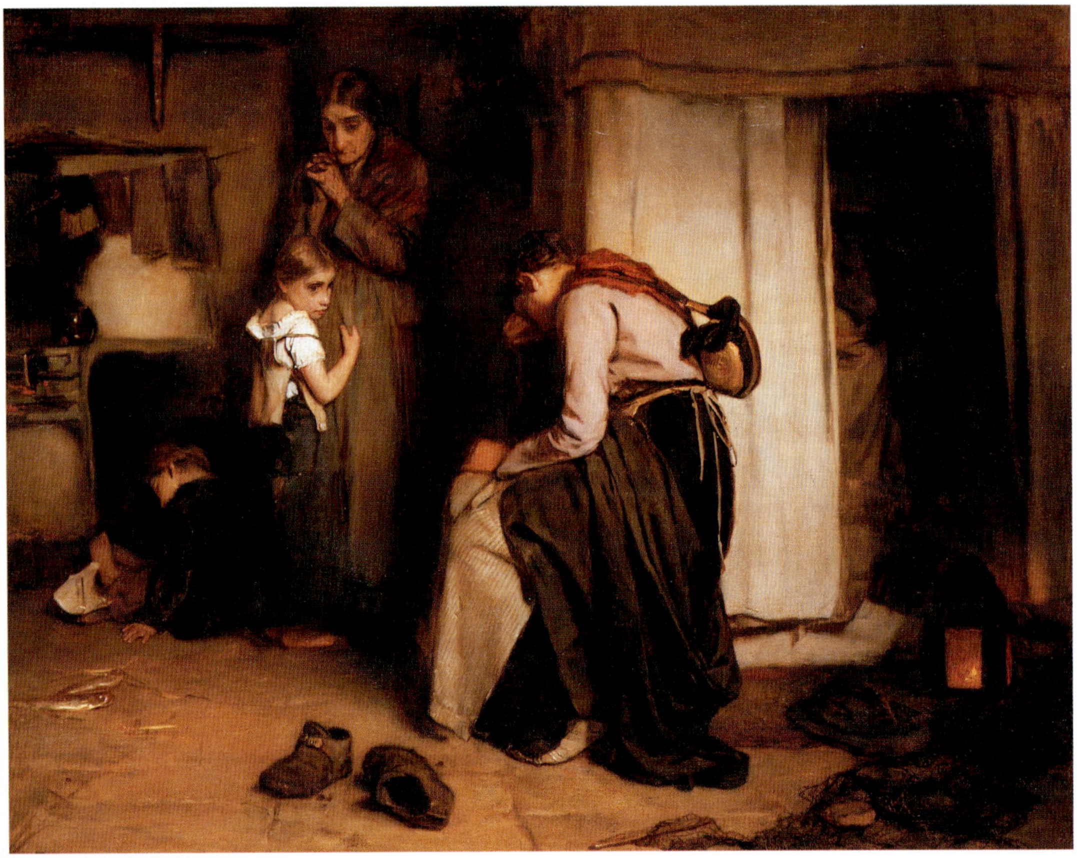

PLATE 13 Frank Holl, ***No Tidings from the Sea***, 1871; Courtesy The Royal Collection

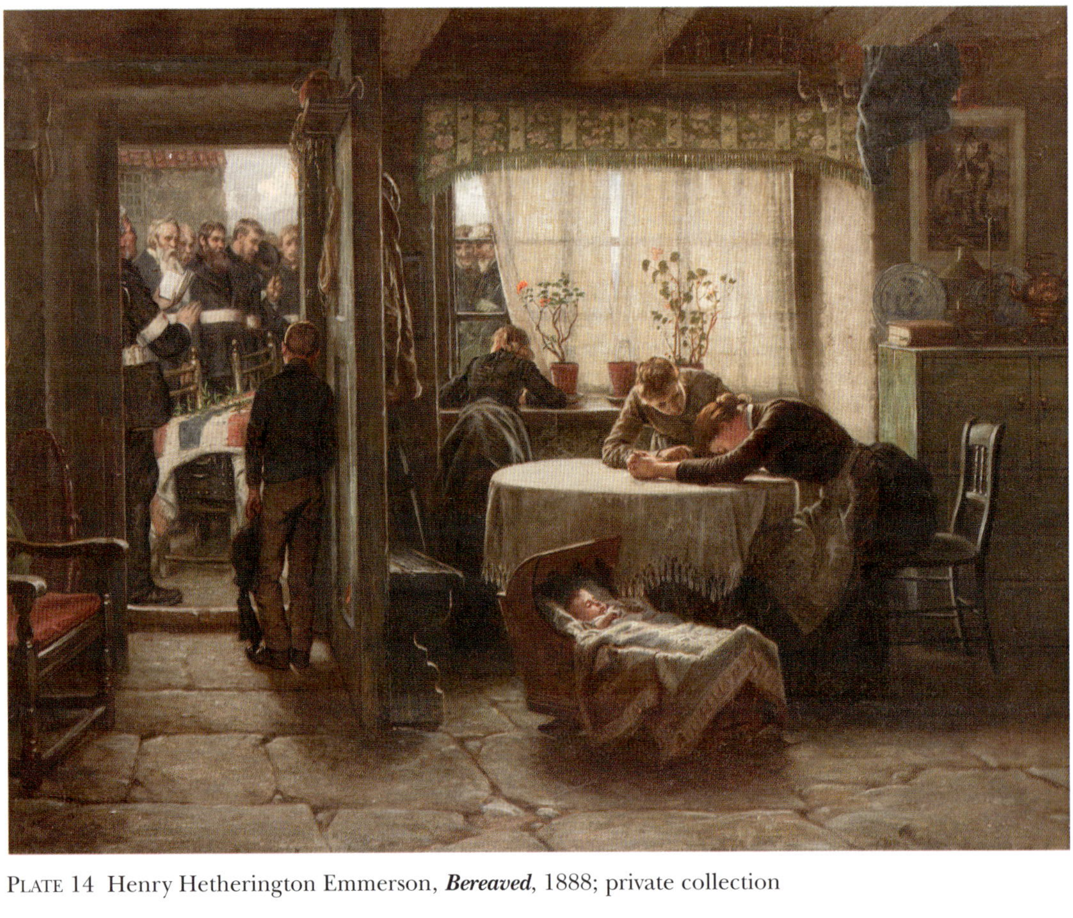

PLATE 14 Henry Hetherington Emmerson, ***Bereaved***, 1888; private collection

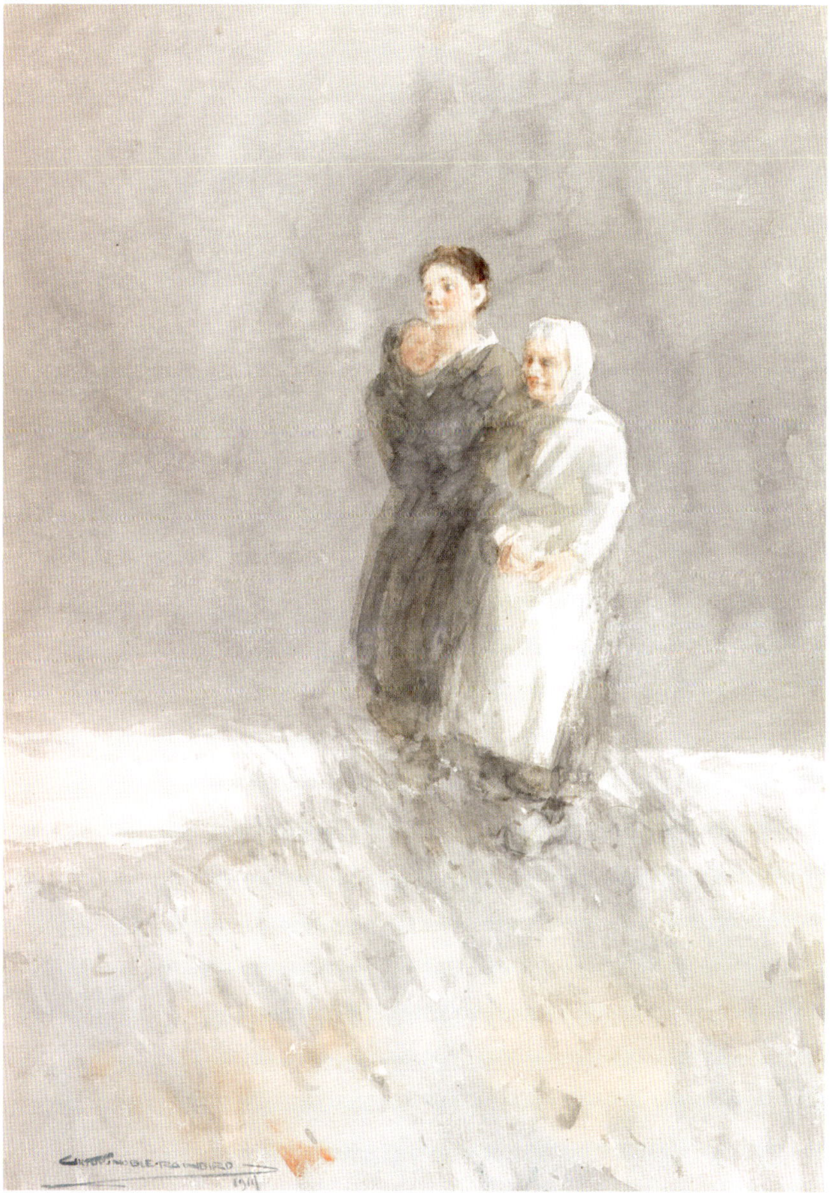

PLATE 15 Victor Noble Rainbird, ***Waiting***, 1919; private collection

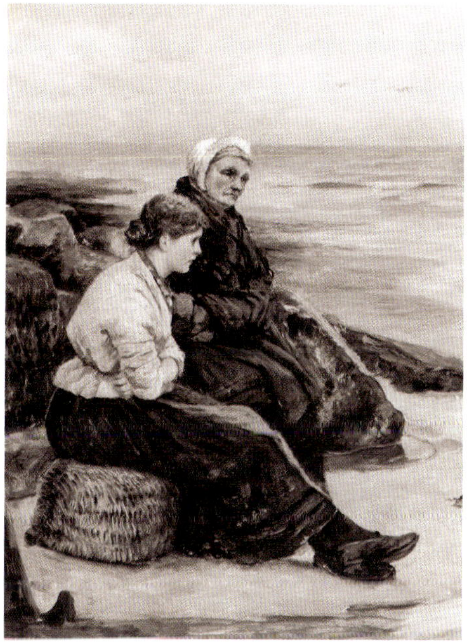

PLATE 16
Robert Jobling, ***Old Betty Laidler and Mary Lisle***, 1886; private collection; photograph courtesy Anderson & Garland Auctioneers

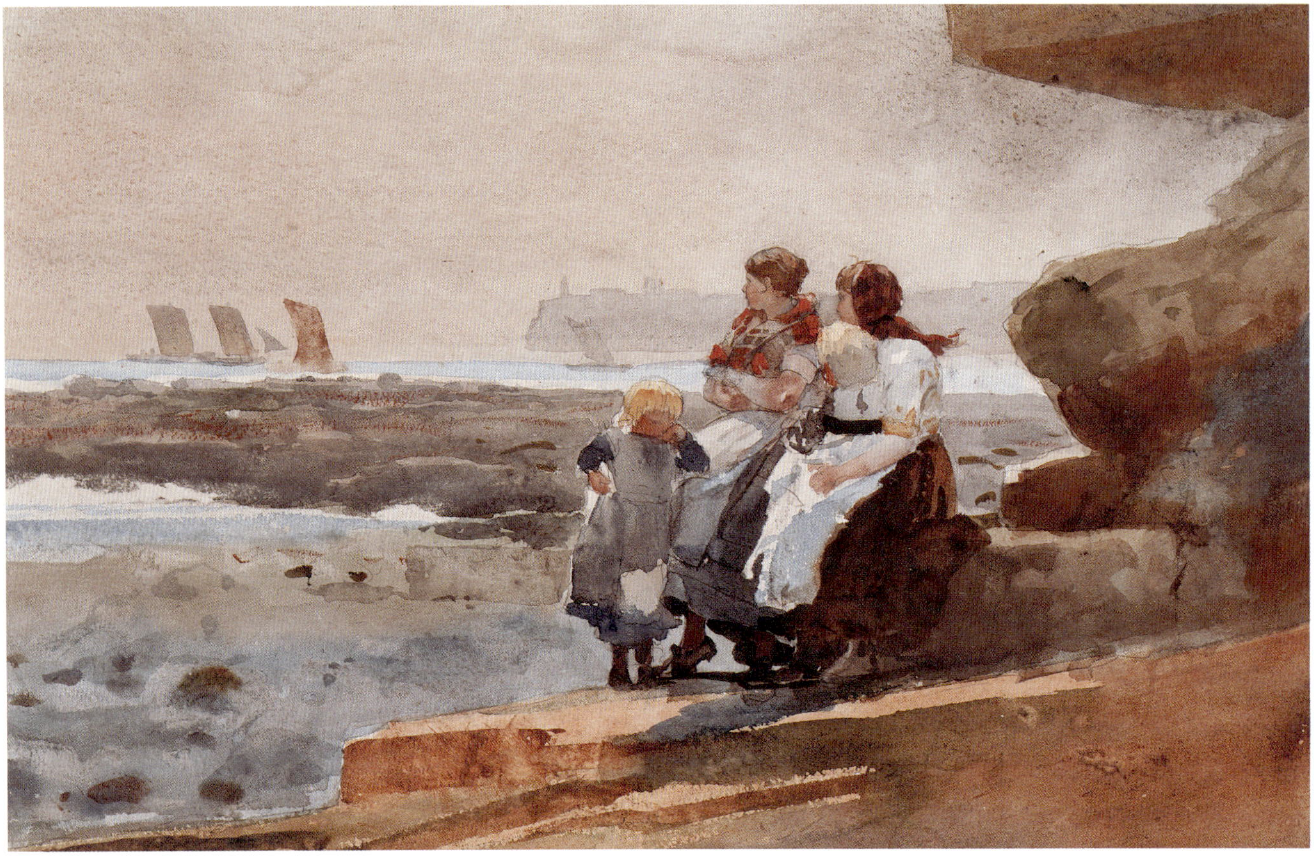

PLATE 17 Winslow Homer, ***Under the Cliff, Cullercoats***, c.1881; gift of an anonymous donor

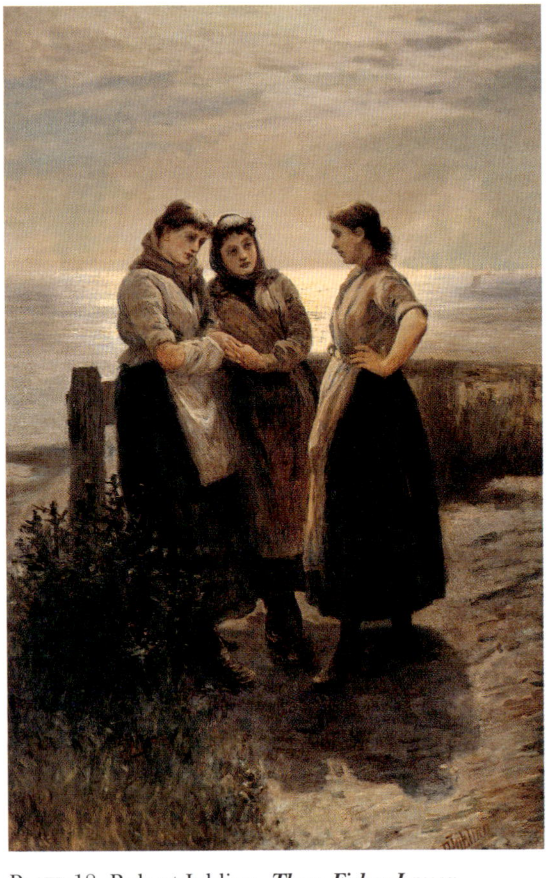

PLATE 18 Robert Jobling, ***Three Fisher Lasses***; private collection

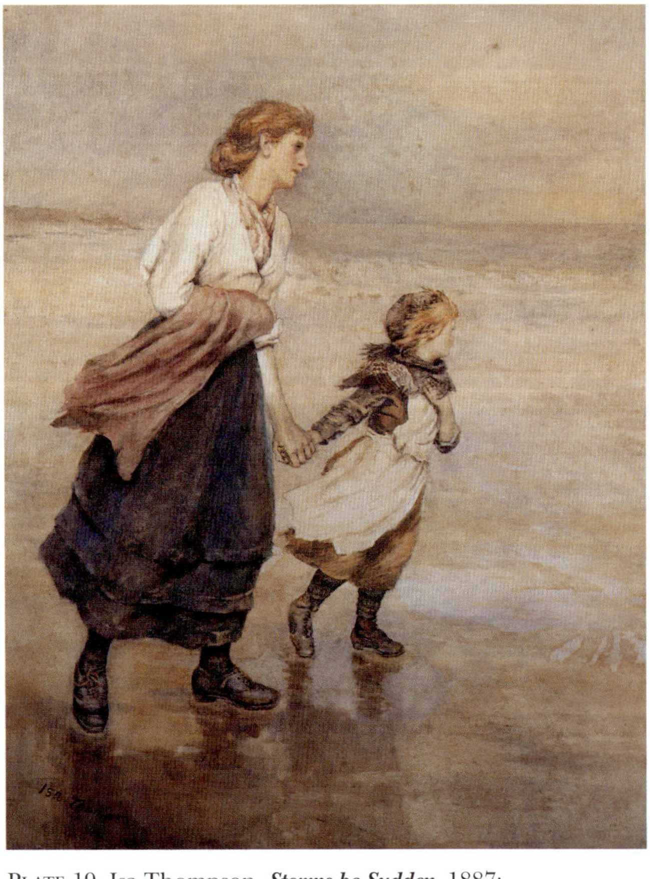

PLATE 19 Isa Thompson, ***Storms be Sudden***, 1887; Mr. & Mrs. P. Whitwam

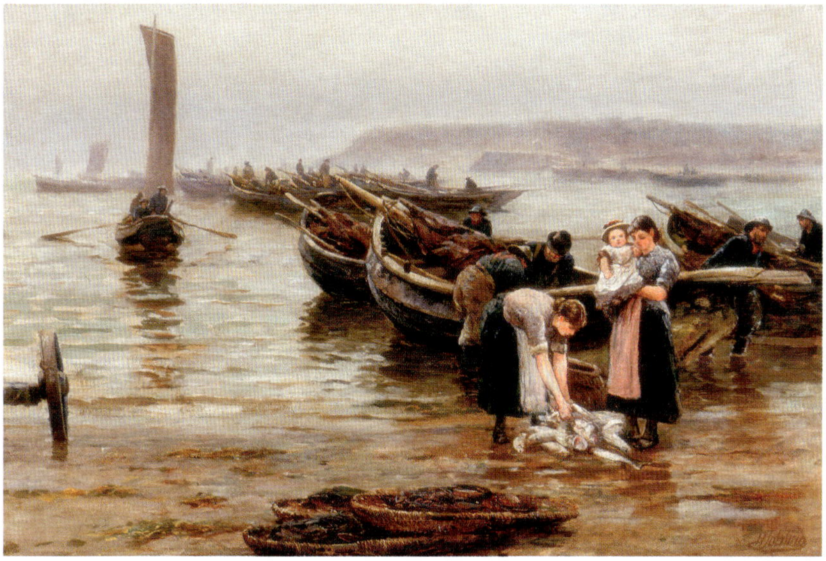

PLATE 20
Robert Jobling, ***Sea Fret***, exh.1884;
Laing Art Gallery

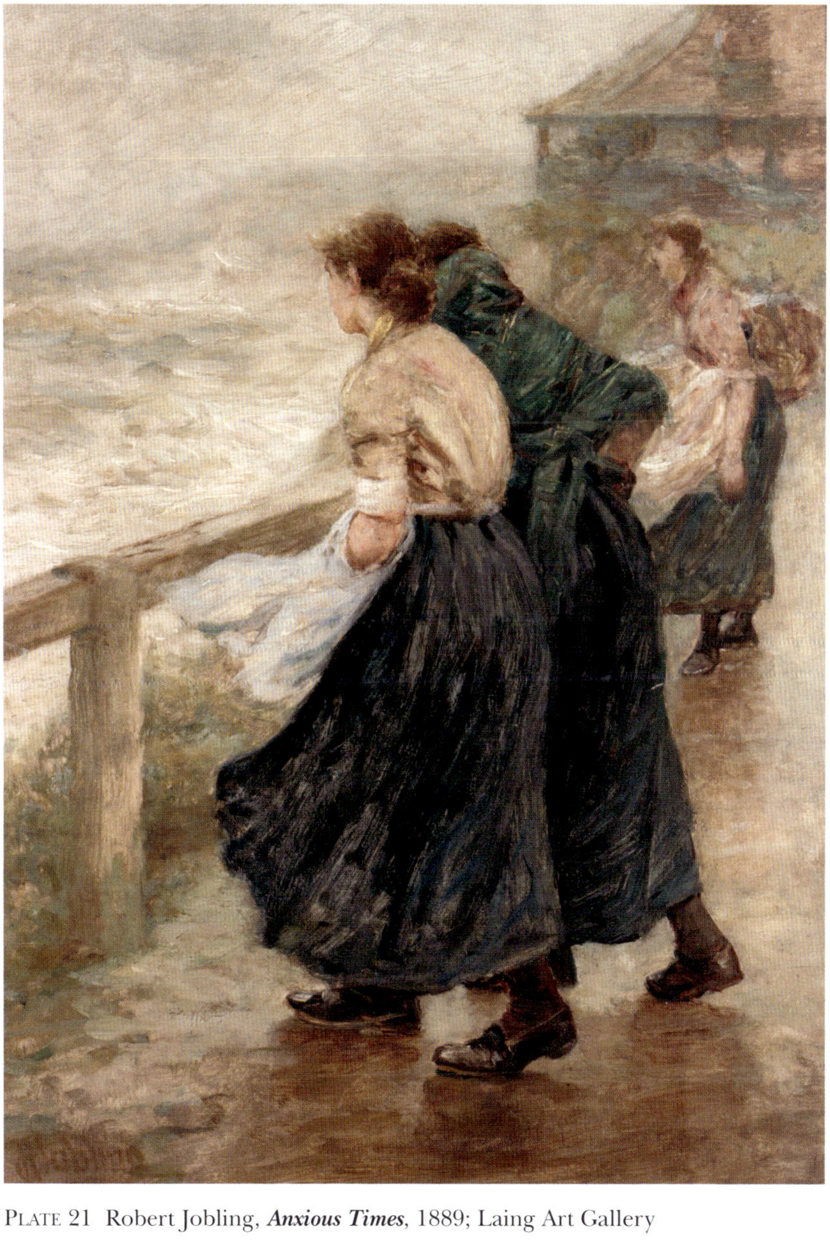

PLATE 21 Robert Jobling, ***Anxious Times***, 1889; Laing Art Gallery

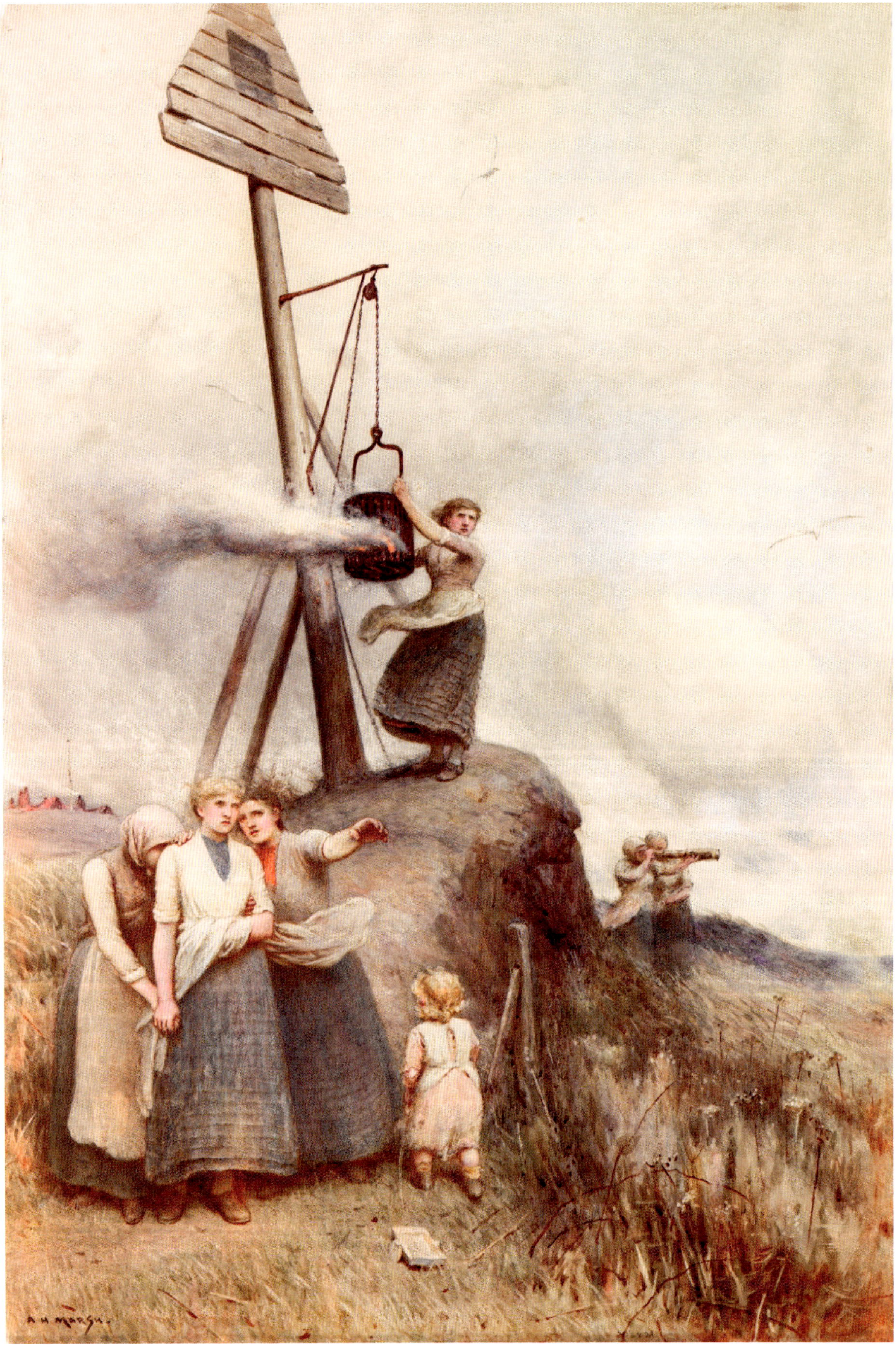

PLATE 22 Arthur Hardwick Marsh, ***Lighting the Beacon***, 1887; Laing Art Gallery

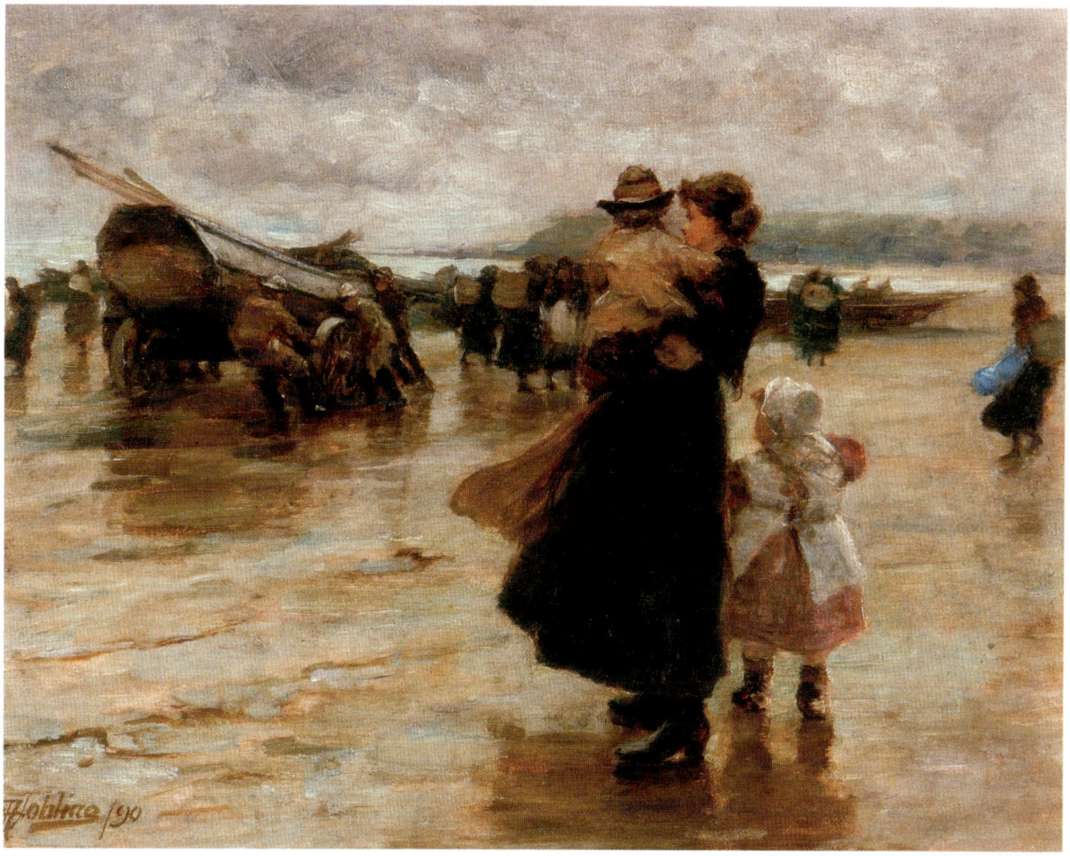

PLATE 23 Robert Jobling, ***Hauling up the Boats***, 1890; Laing Art Gallery

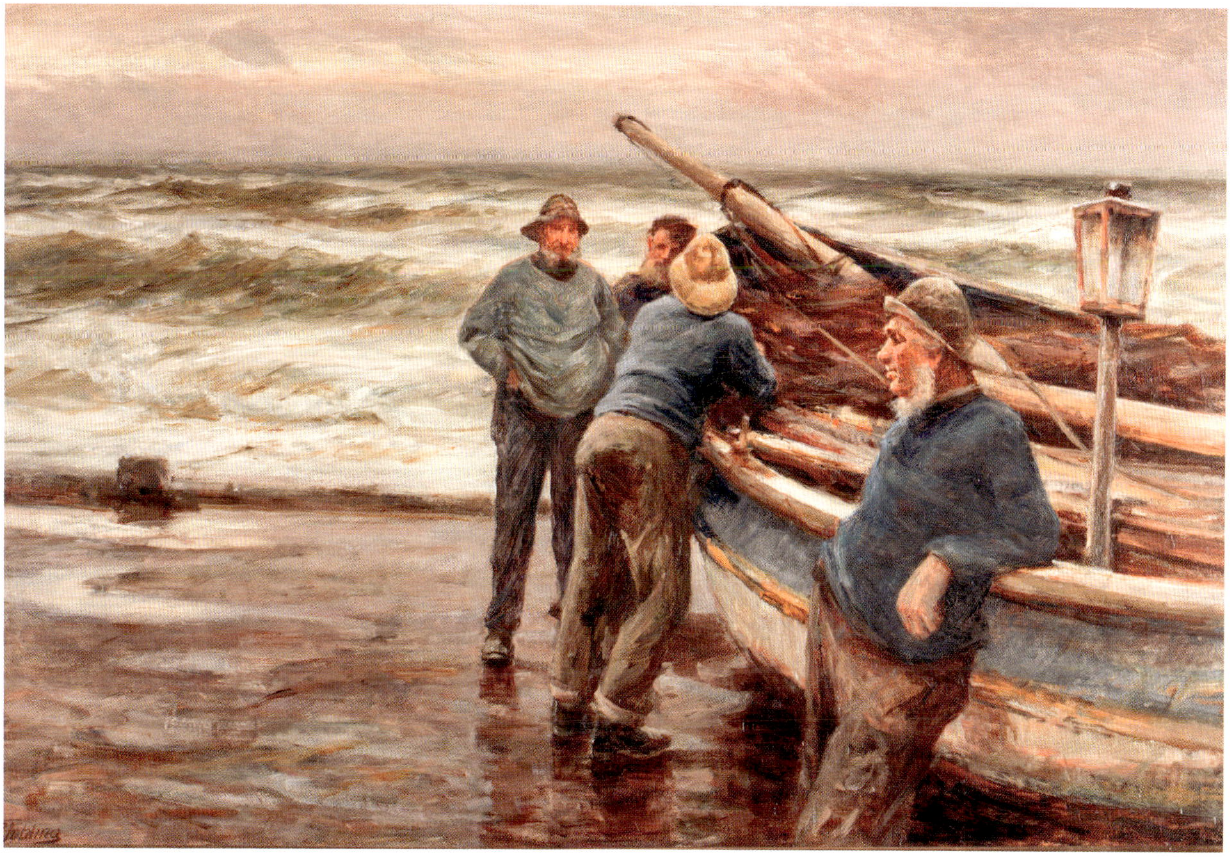

PLATE 24 Robert Jobling, ***Fishermen at Staithes***; private collection

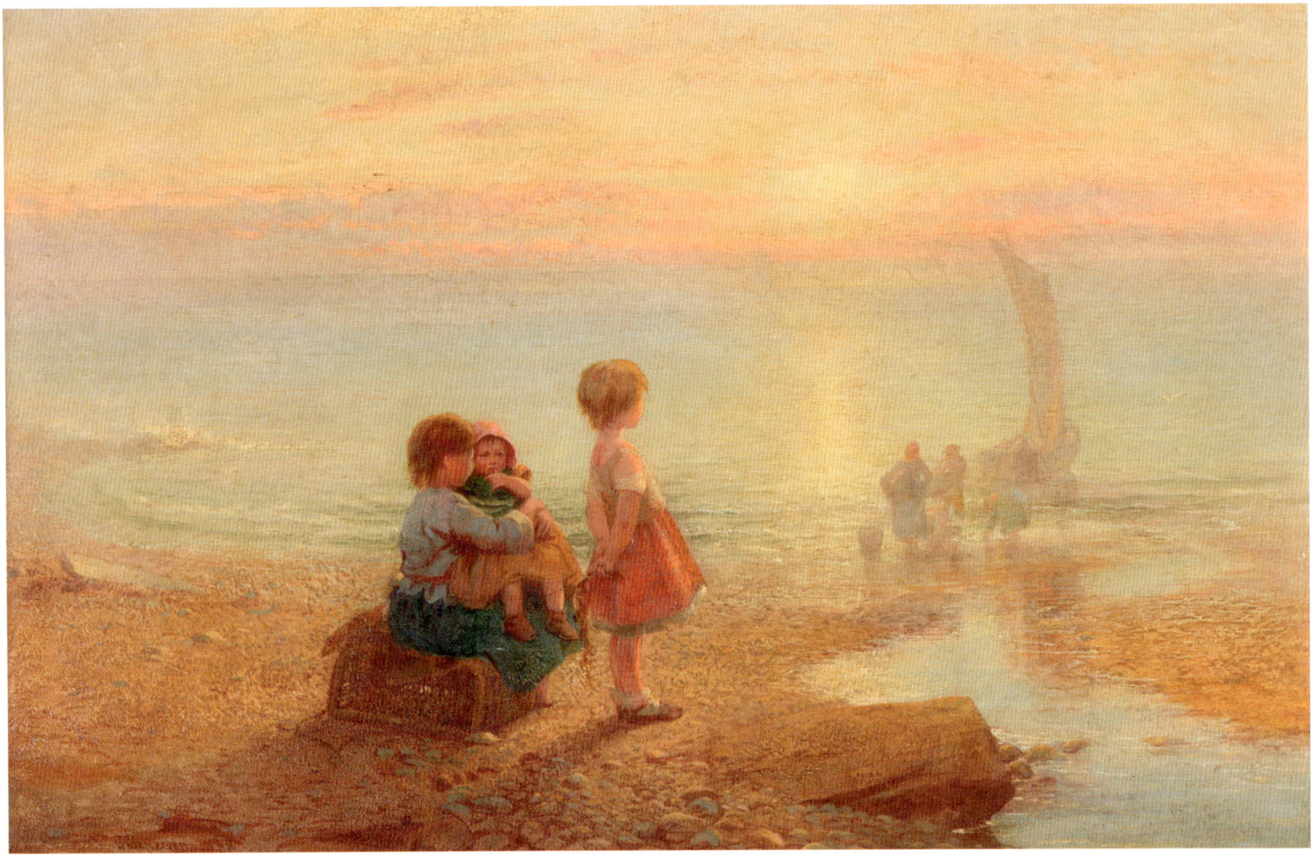

PLATE 25 Henry Hetherington Emmerson, ***Early Morning off the Coast***, 1888; Laing Art Gallery

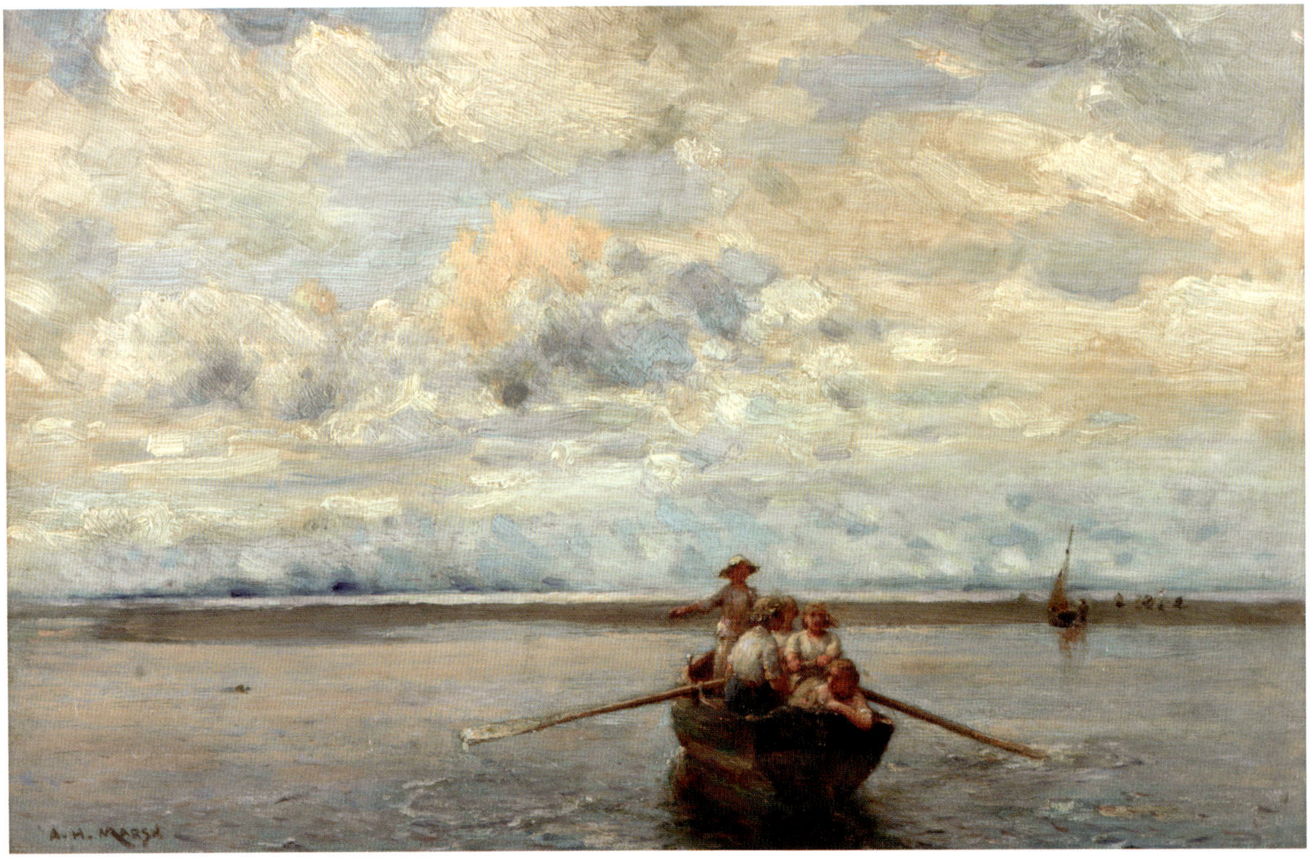

PLATE 26 Arthur Hardwick Marsh, ***Cockle Gatherers***, 1885; Laing Art Gallery

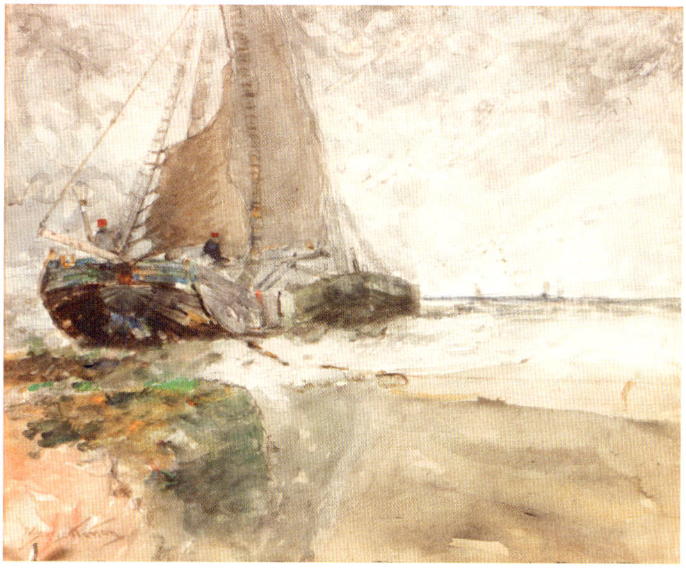

PLATE 27 George Horton, ***Coast Scene with Beached Fishing Boats***; South Shields Museum and Art Gallery

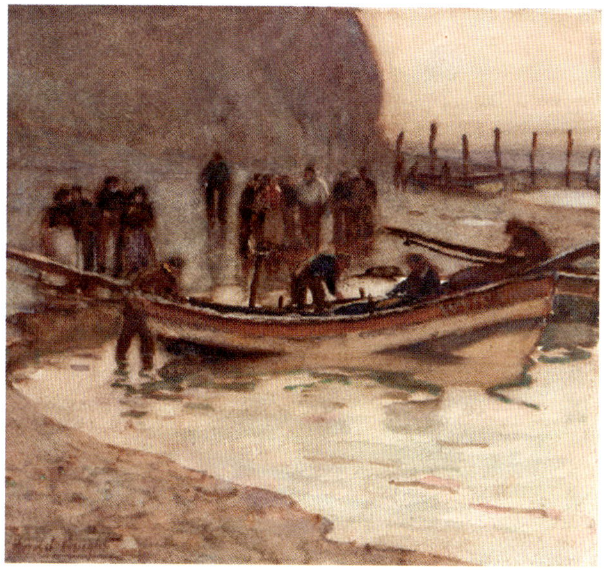

PLATE 28 Harold Knight, ***Fishing Boats, Evening***; Laing Art Gallery; Reproduced with permission of Curtis Brown Group Ltd, London on behalf of the estate of Dame Laura and Harold Knight. Copyright © Harold Knight

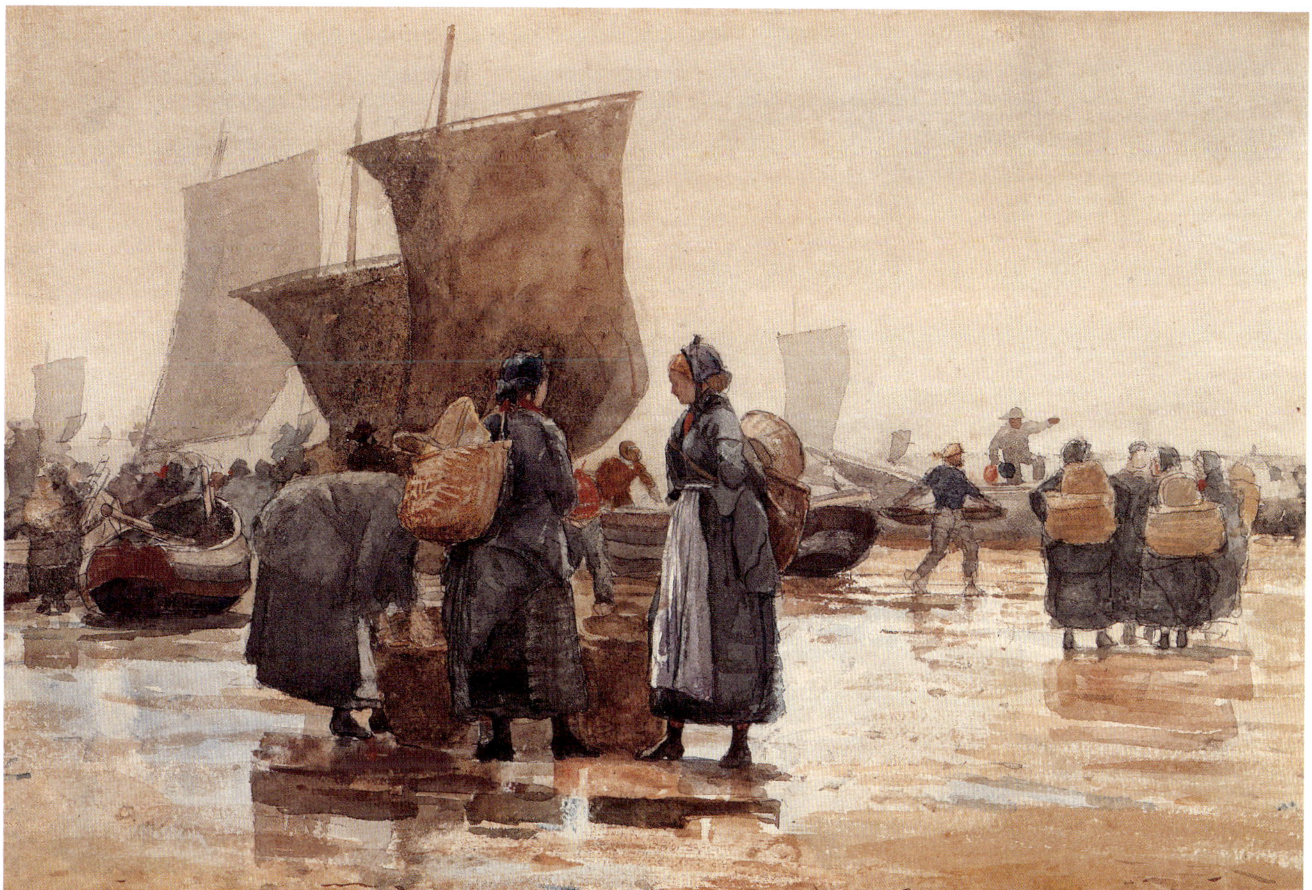

PLATE 29 Winslow Homer, ***Fisherfolk on the Beach at Cullercoats***, 1881; gift of an anonymous donor © Addison Gallery of American Art, Phillips Academy, Andover, Massachusetts. All Rights Reserved.

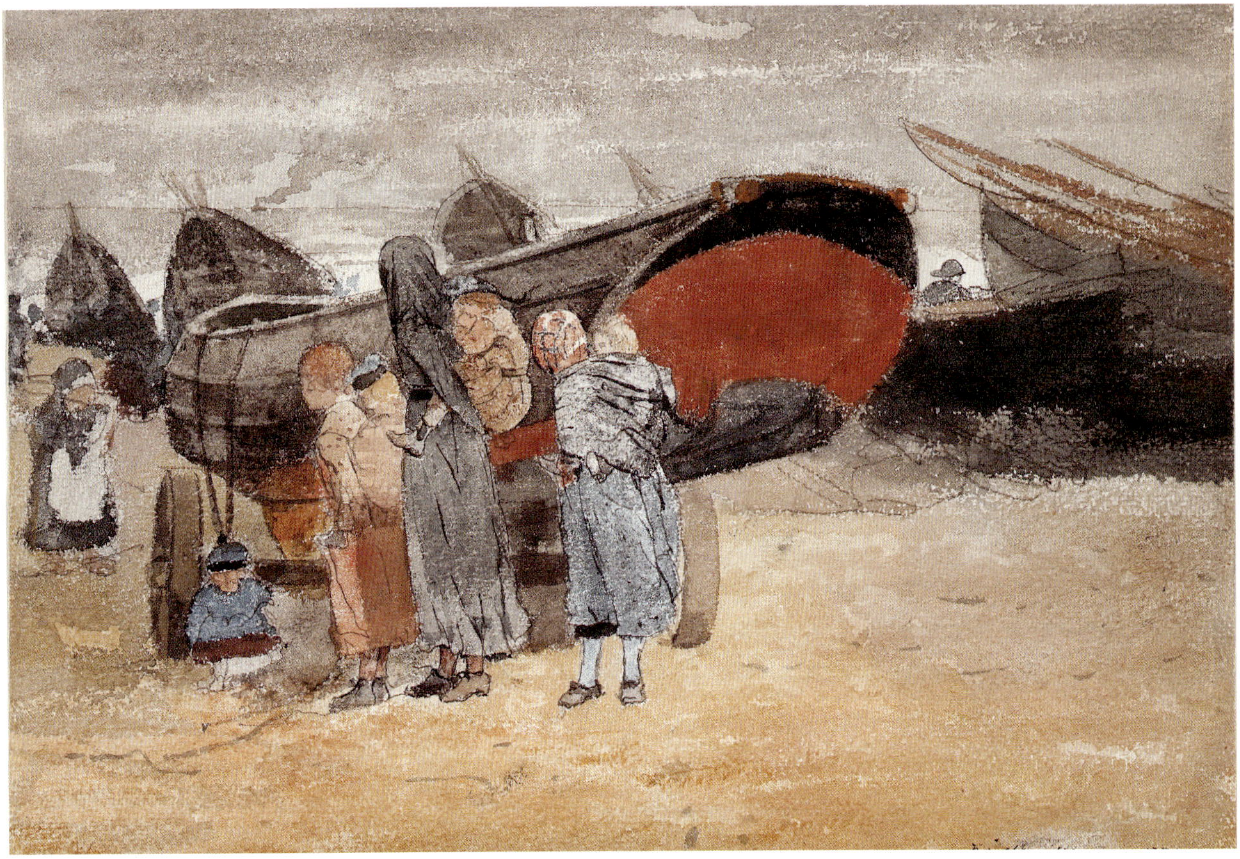

PLATE 30 Winslow Homer, ***Coast Scene with Boats on the Beach***, 1881; Courtesy, Museum of Fine Arts, Boston. Bequest of John T. Spaulding, 1948 (48.725) © 2003 Museum of Fine Arts, Boston

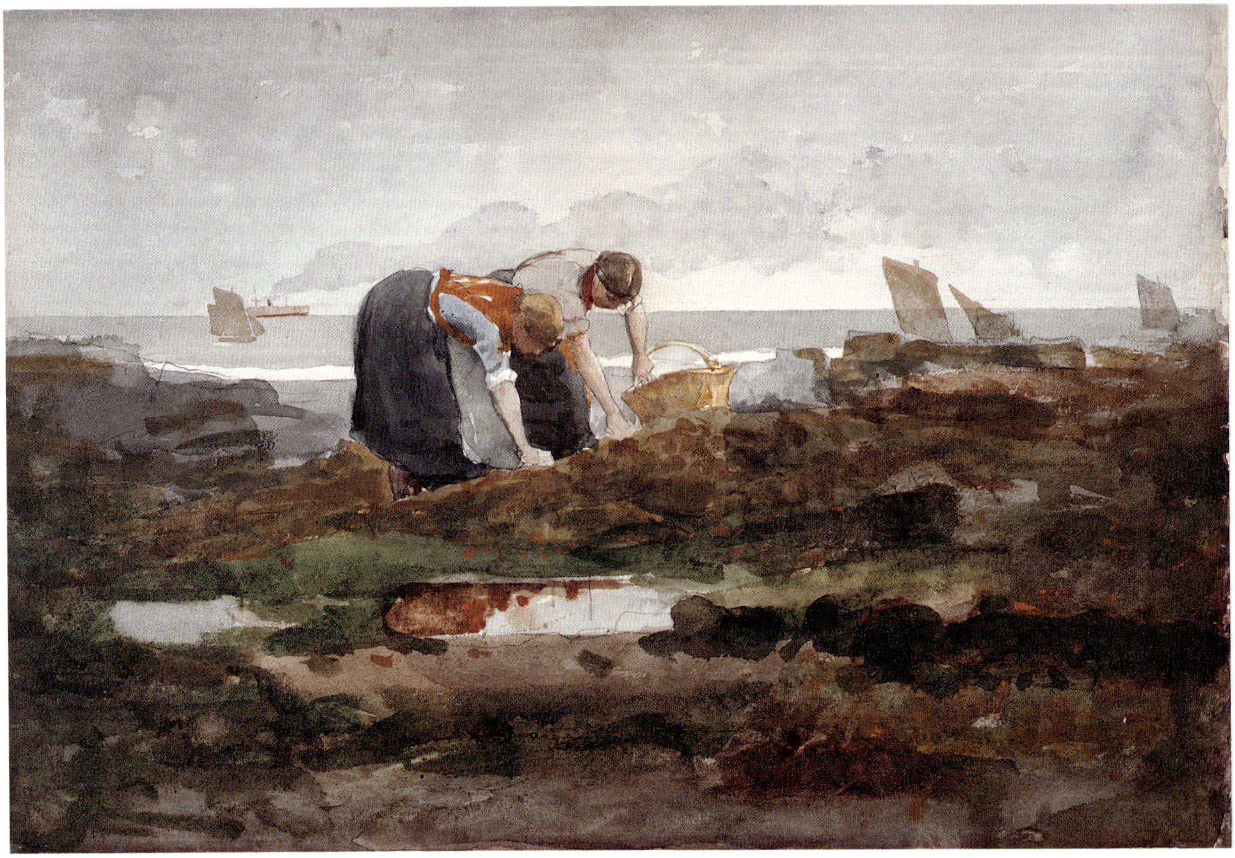

PLATE 31 Winslow Homer, ***The Mussel Gatherers***, c.1881-1882; The Baltimore Museum of Art: Gift of Alvin and Fannie B. Thalheimer BMA 1956.226

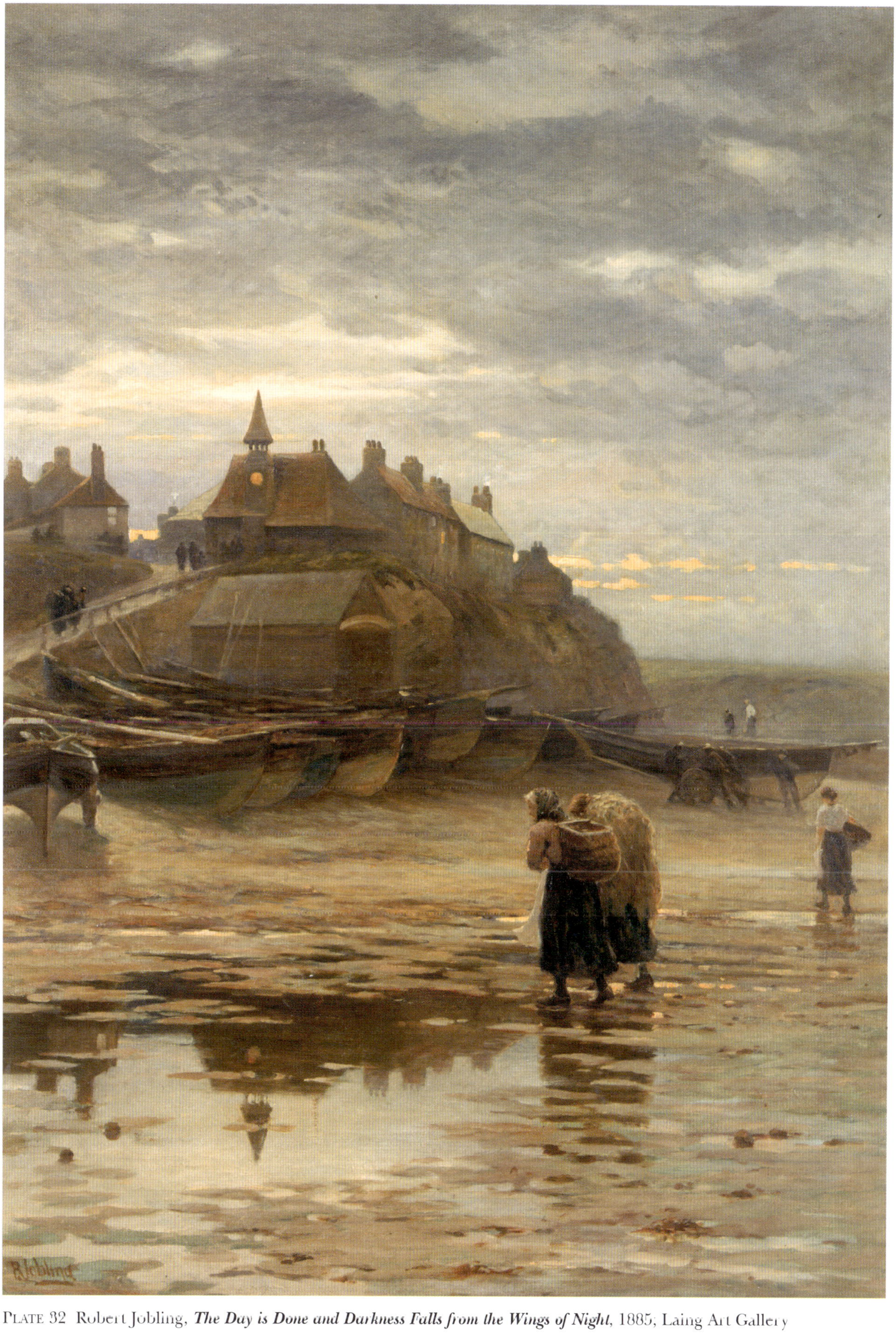

PLATE 32 Robert Jobling, ***The Day is Done and Darkness Falls from the Wings of Night***, 1885, Laing Art Gallery

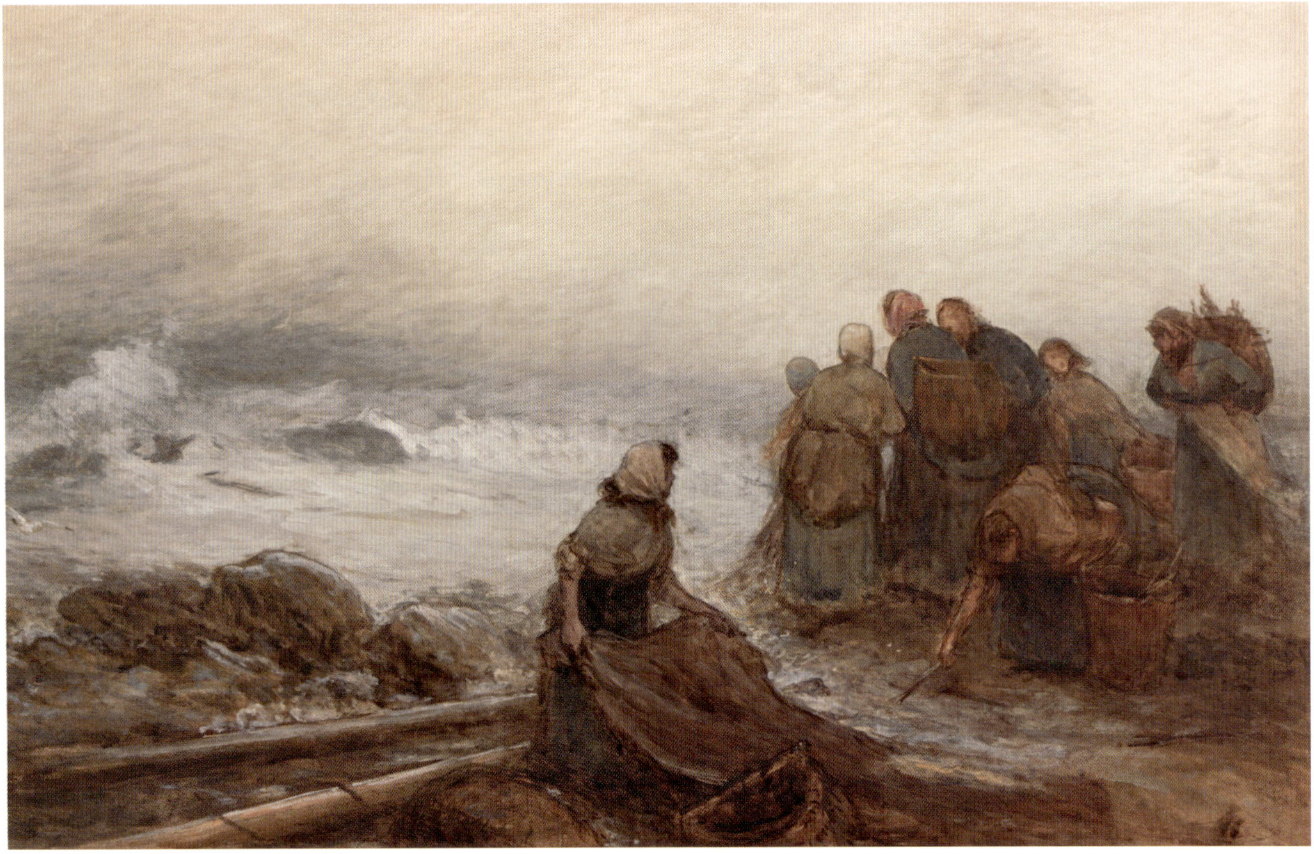

PLATE 33 Arthur Hardwick Marsh, ***Harvest of the Sea***, 1877; Laing Art Gallery

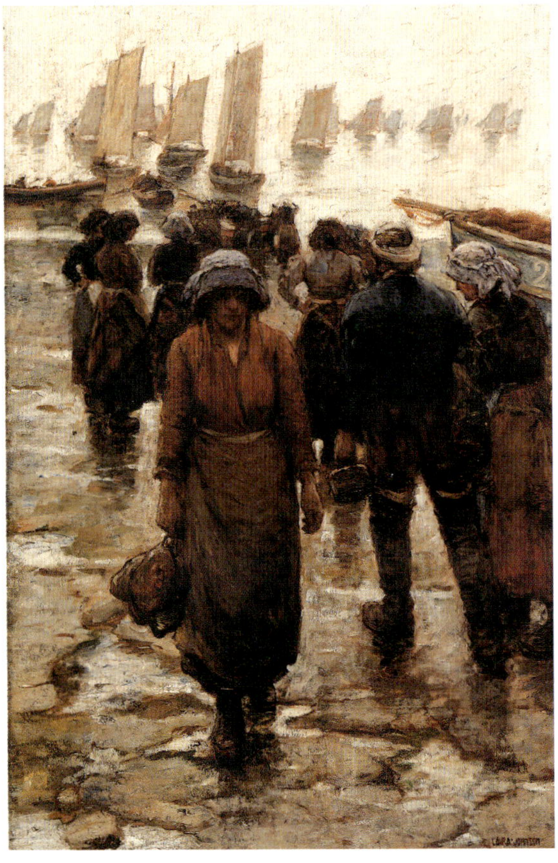

PLATE 34
Laura Johnson (Knight), ***The Fishing Fleet***, 1897-1903; Bolton Museums, Art Gallery & Aquarium, Bolton MBC/Reproduced with permission of Curtis Brown Group Ltd, London on behalf of the estate of Dame Laura and Harold Knight. Copyright © Dame Laura Knight

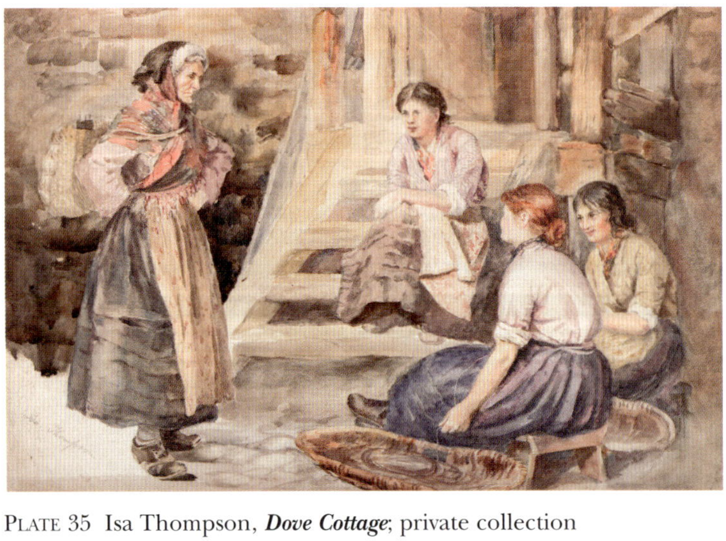

PLATE 35 Isa Thompson, ***Dove Cottage***; private collection

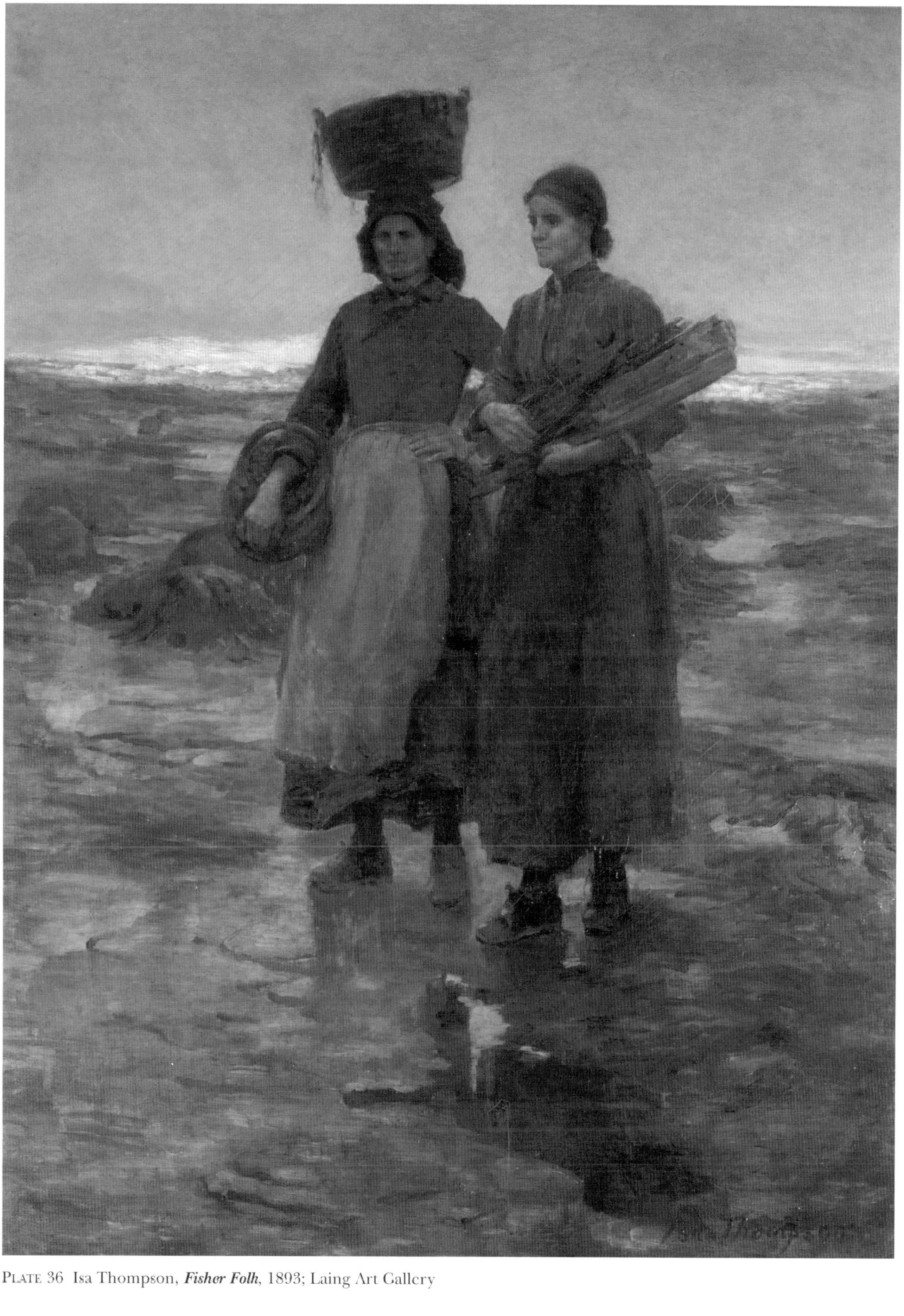

PLATE 36 Isa Thompson, ***Fisher Folk***, 1893; Laing Art Gallery

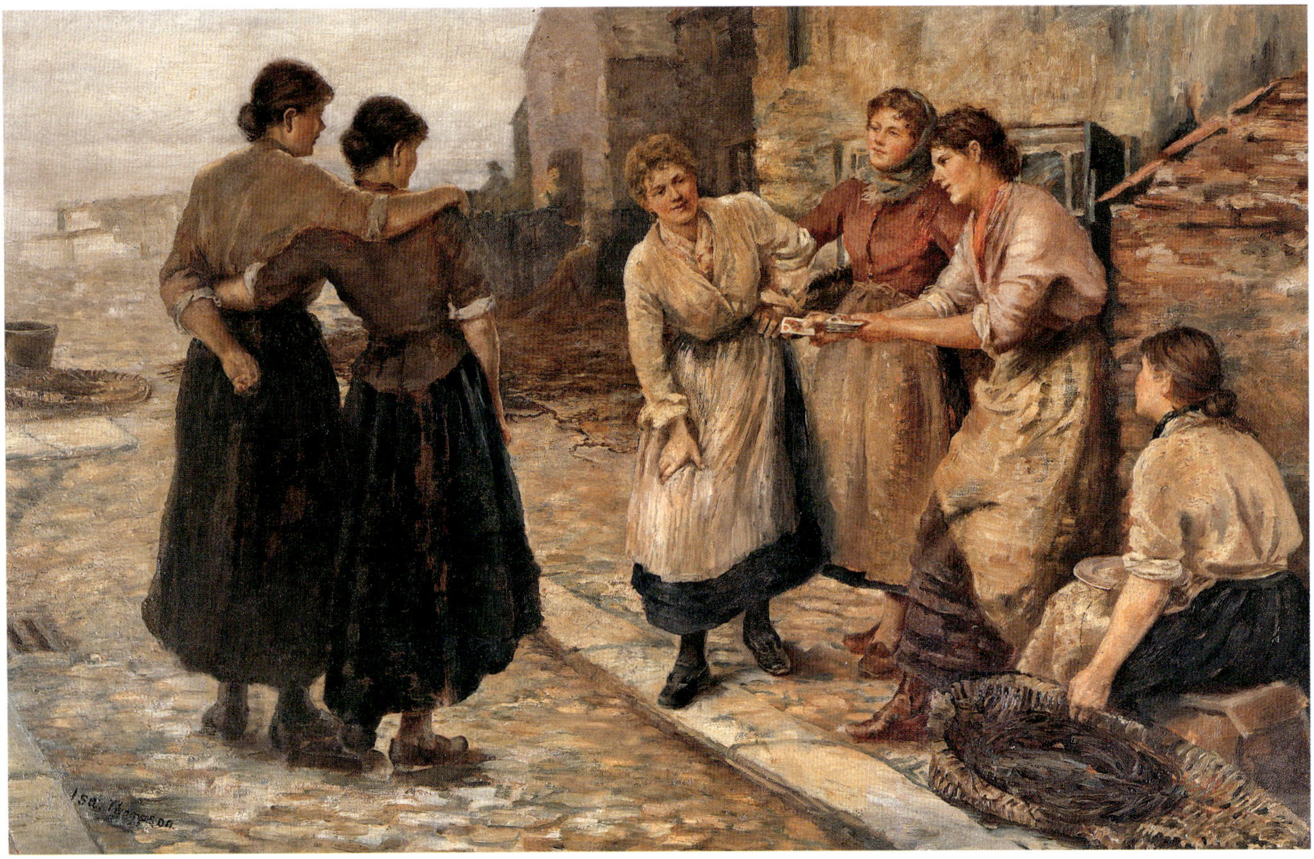

PLATE 37 Isa Thompson, ***Fortune Telling***, 1887; private collection

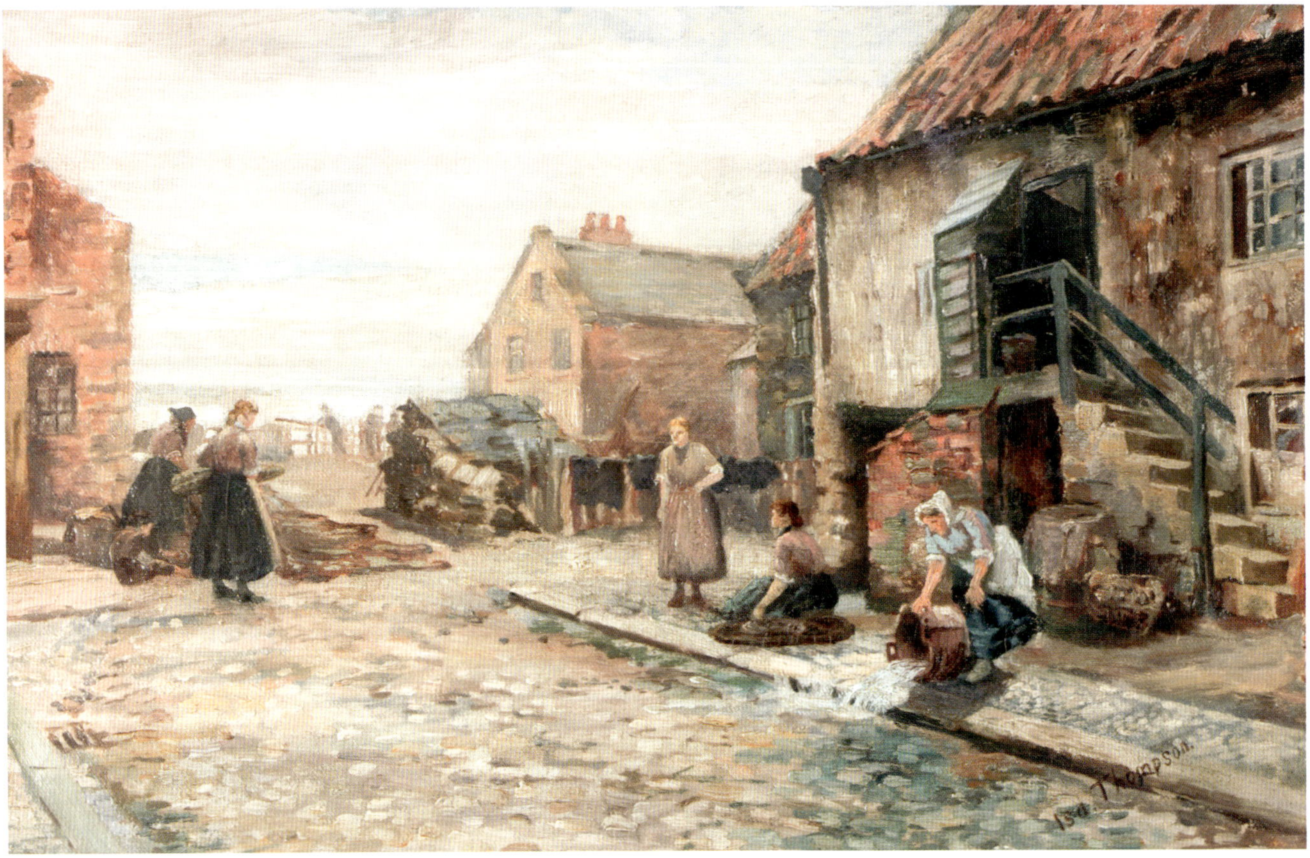

PLATE 38 Isa Thompson, ***Women in the back lane, Cullercoats***; private collection

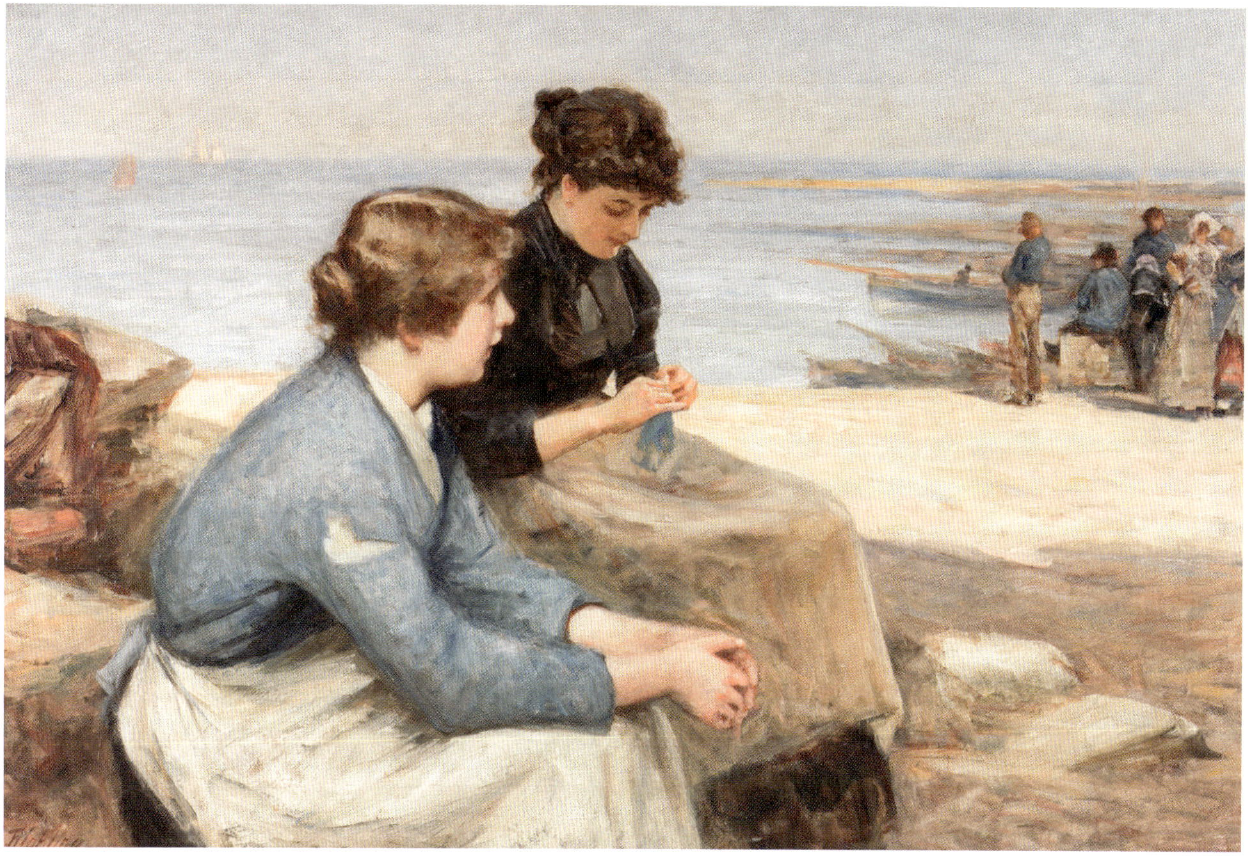

PLATE 39 Robert Jobling, ***Awaiting Sweethearts***; private collection.

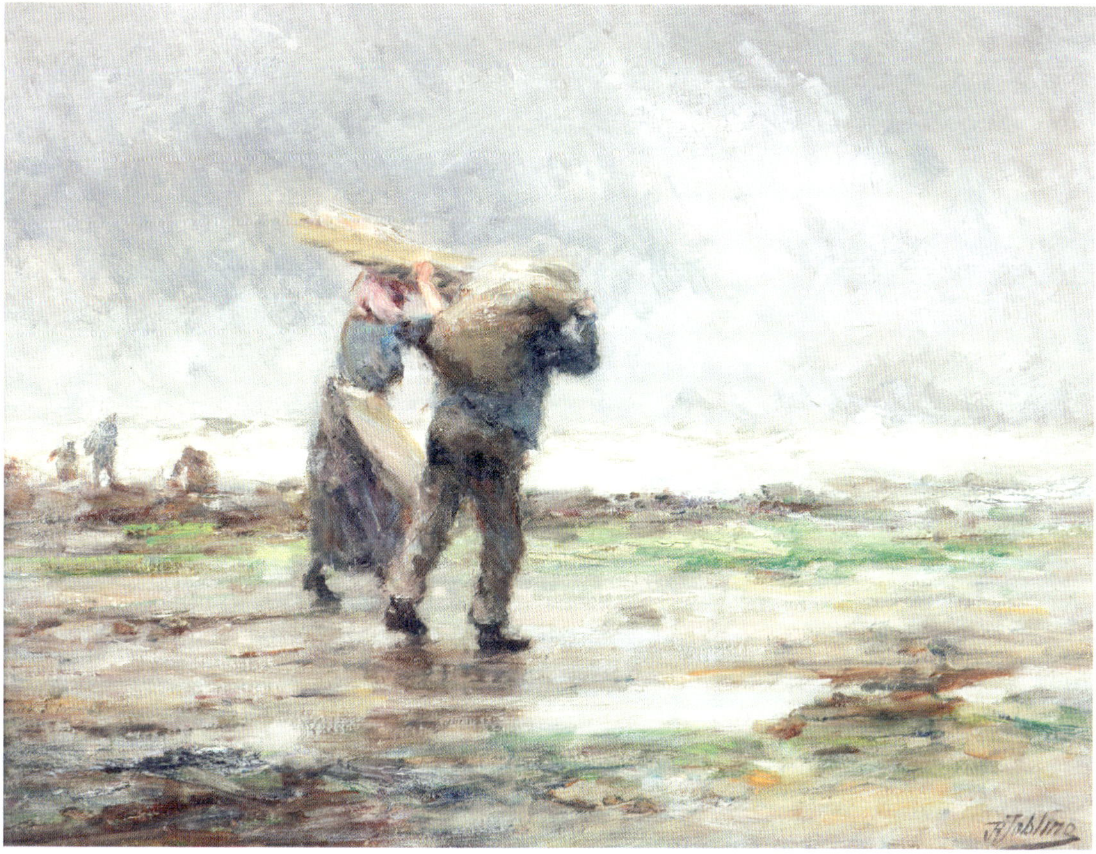

PLATE 40 Robert Jobling, ***Winter Fuel***, 1910; South Shields Museum and Art Gallery

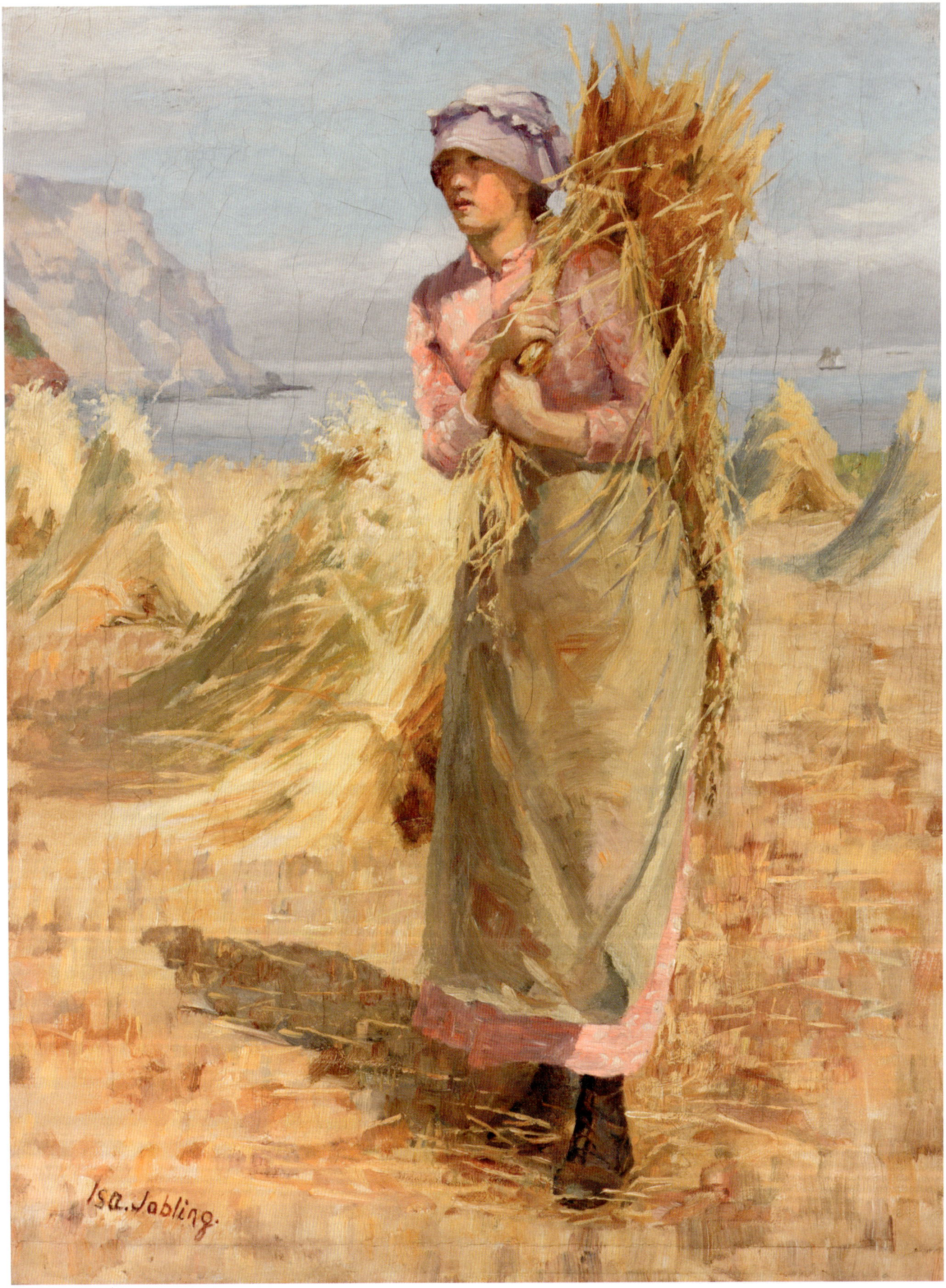

PLATE 41 Isa Thompson, ***Haymaking***, post 1900; Shipley Art Gallery, Gateshead

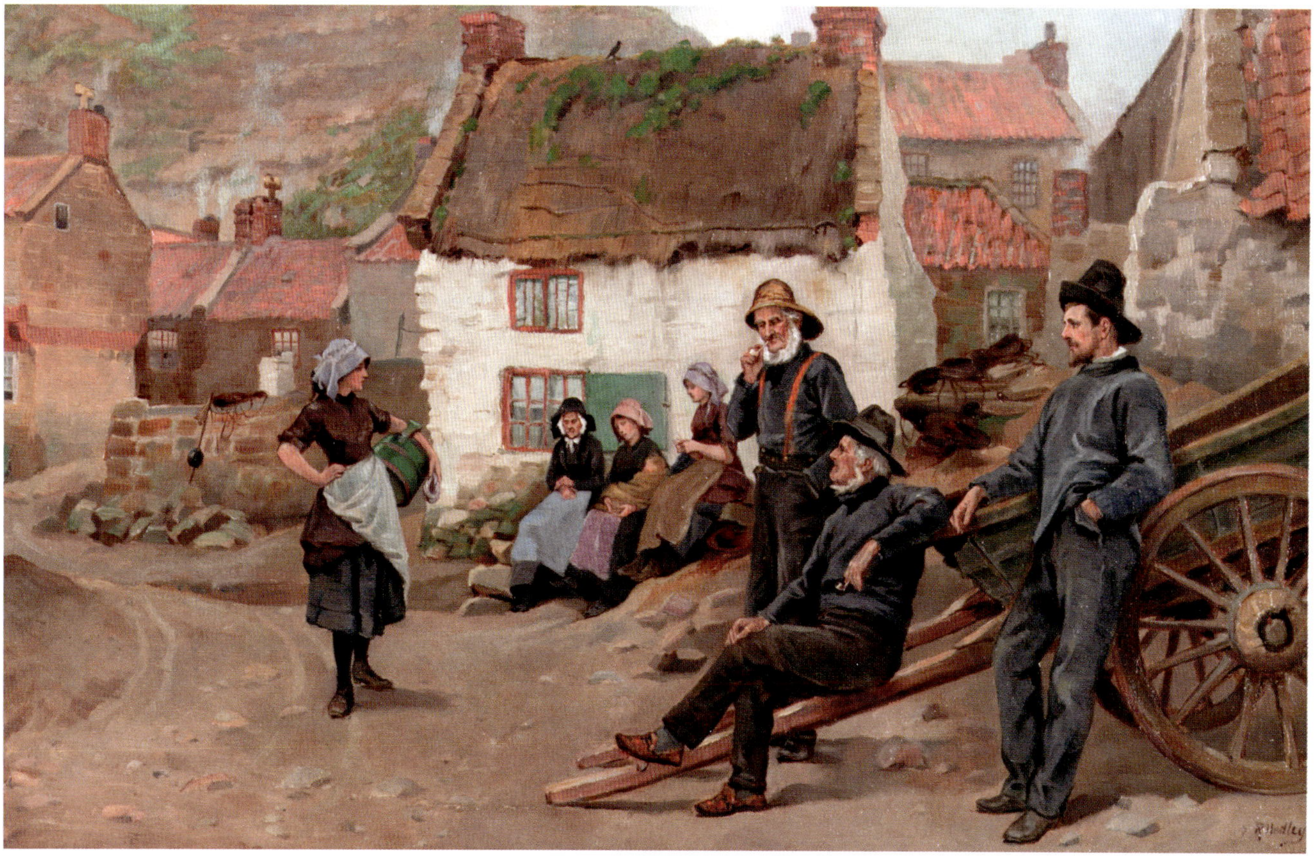

PLATE 42 Ralph Hedley, ***Fisherfolk at Staithes***, 1886; private collection

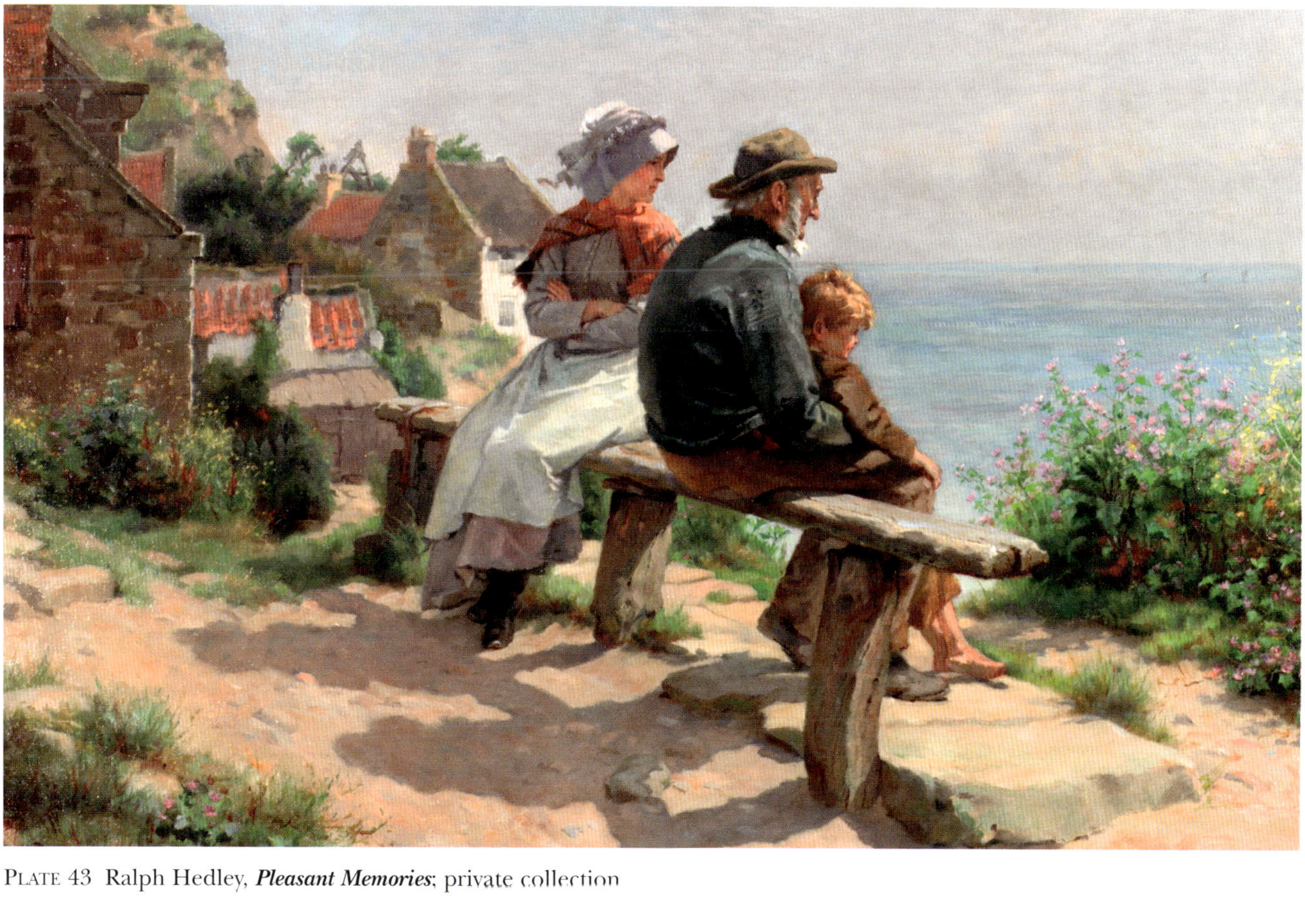

PLATE 43 Ralph Hedley, ***Pleasant Memories***; private collection

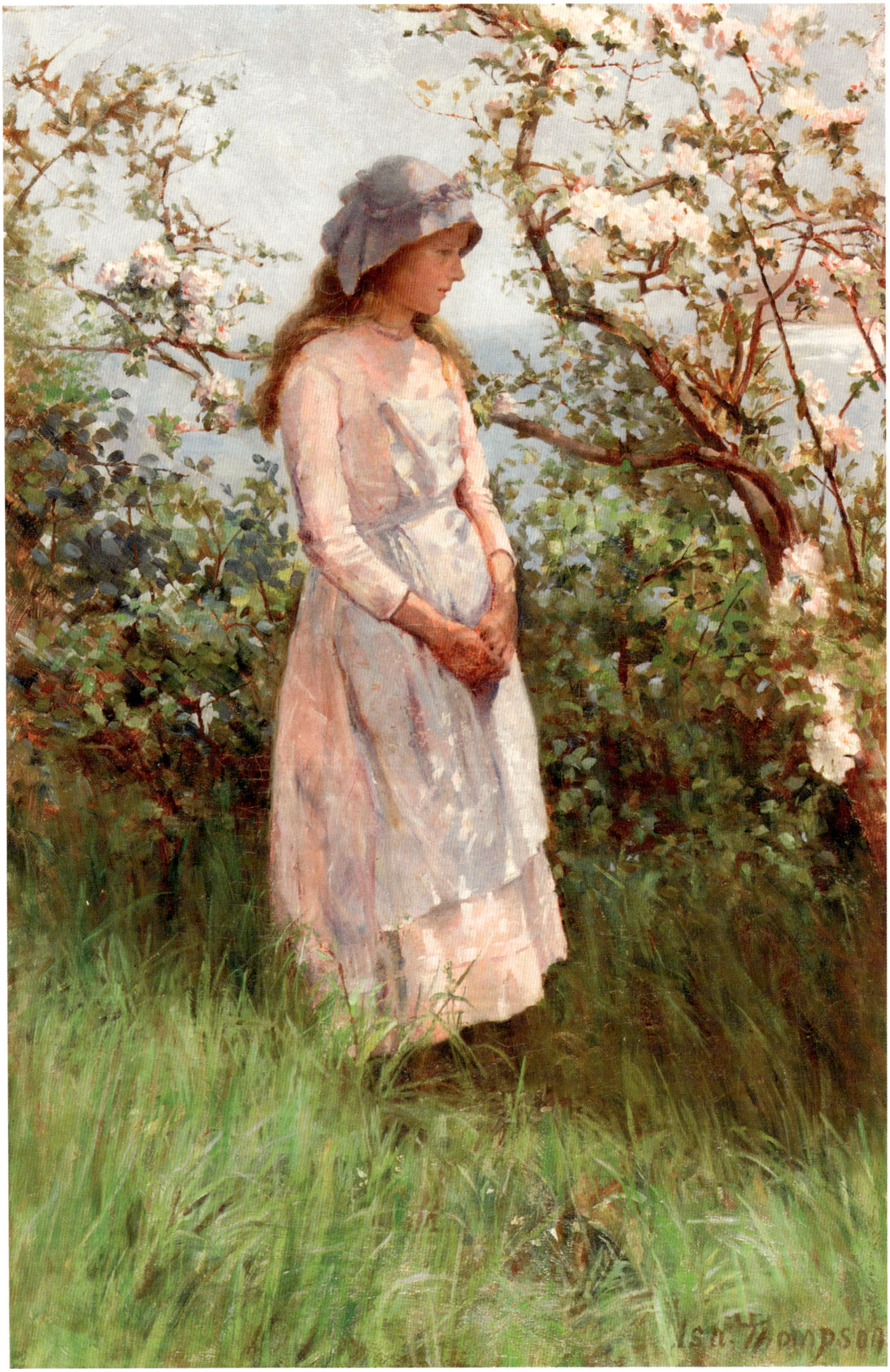

PLATE 44 Isa Thompson, ***Blossom***, 1892; private collection

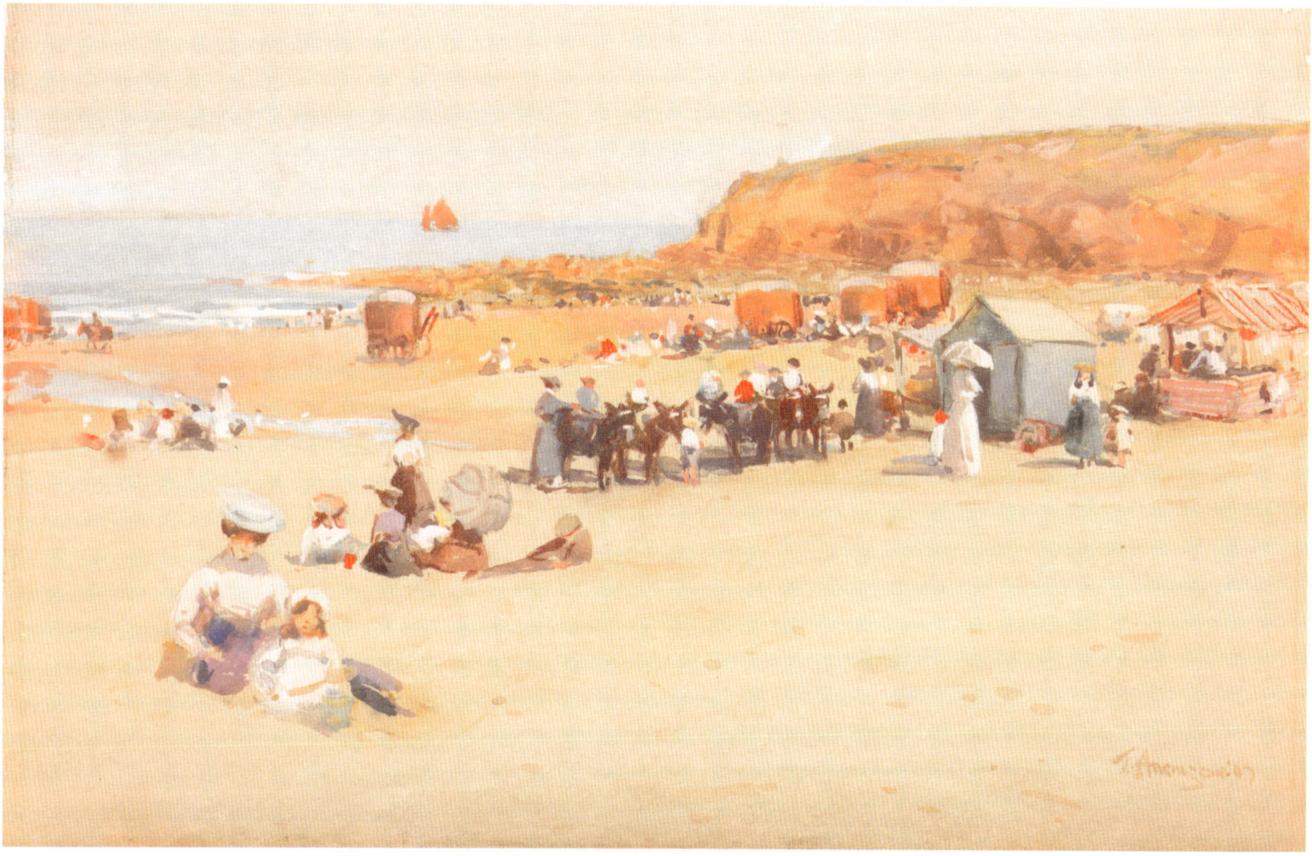

PLATE 45 John Atkinson, ***Tynemouth Sands***, 1907; Shipley Art Gallery, Gateshead

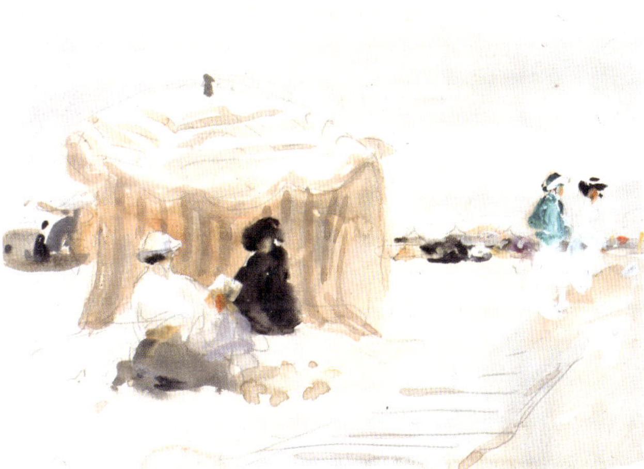

PLATE 46 Fred Mayor, ***The Bathing Tent***; Laing Art Gallery

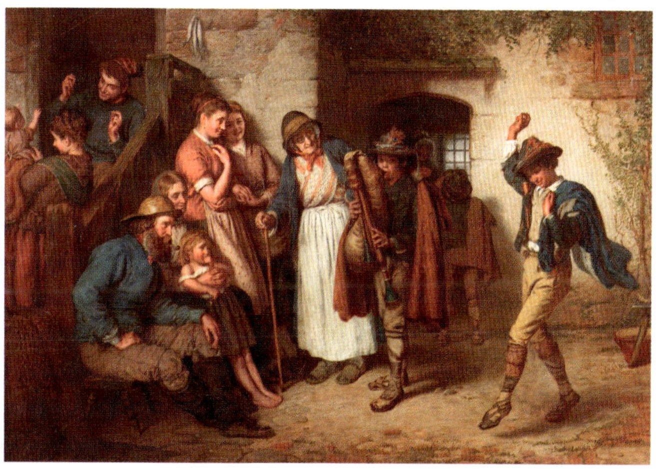

PLATE 47 Henry Hetherington Emmerson, ***A Foreign Invasion***, exh.1871; Laing Art Gallery

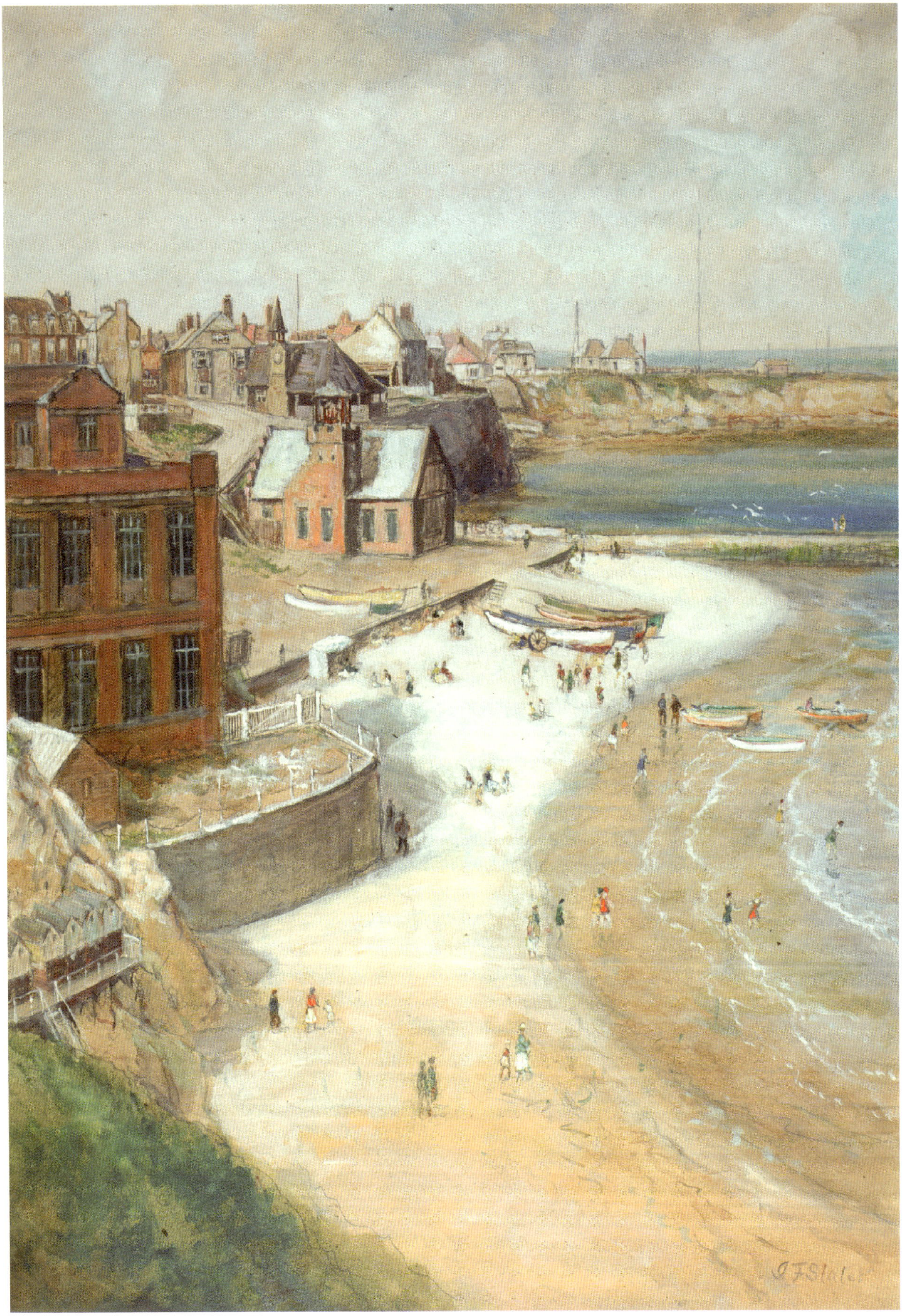

PLATE 48 John Falconer Slater, ***Cullercoats***, Laing Art Gallery

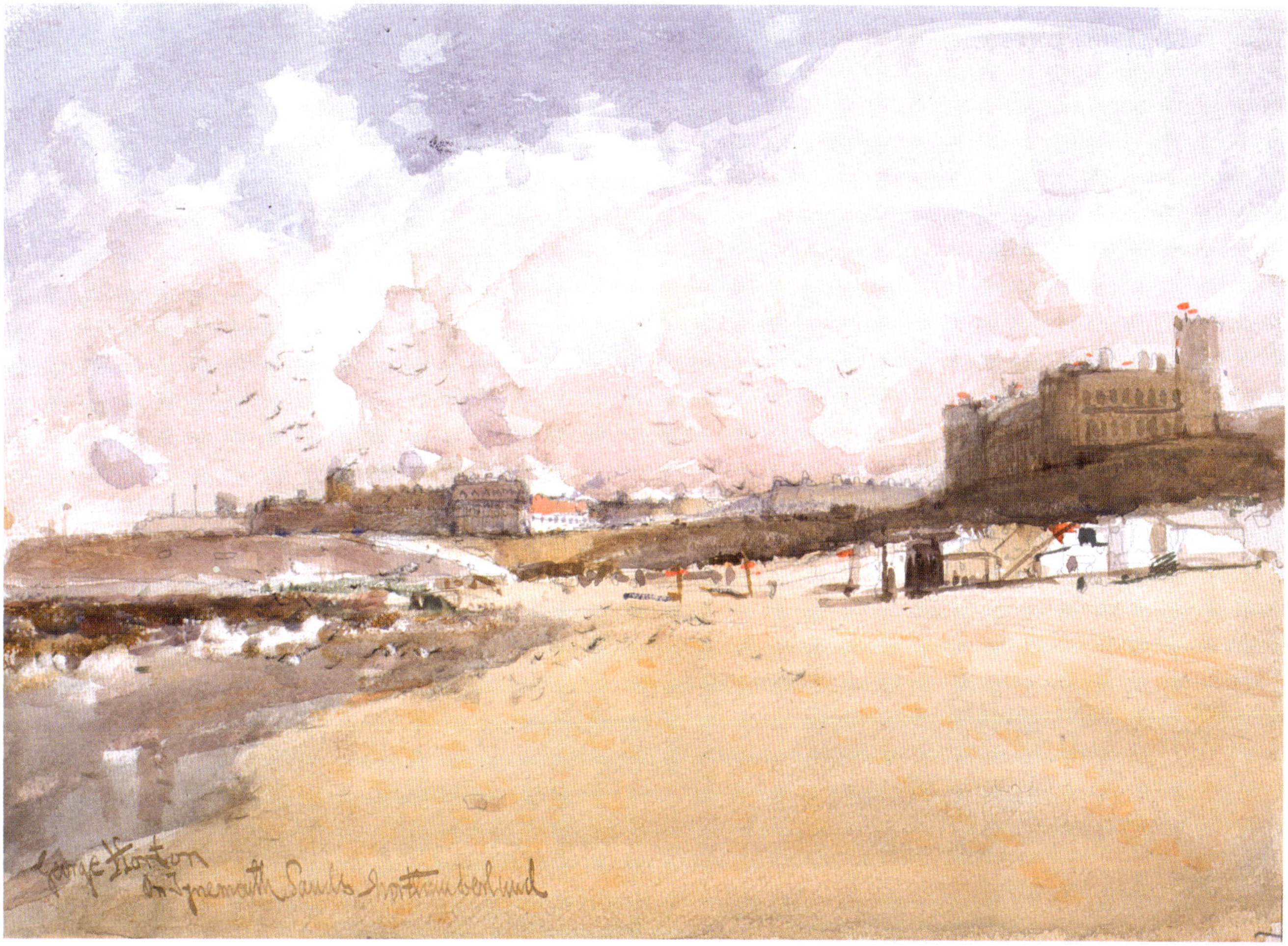

PLATE 49 George Horton, ***On Tynemouth Sands***; Laing Art Gallery

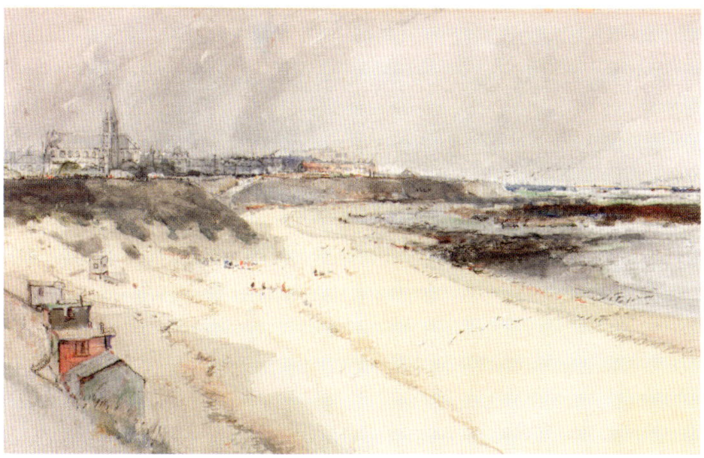

PLATE 50 George Horton, ***Tynemouth***; Alan Dodd

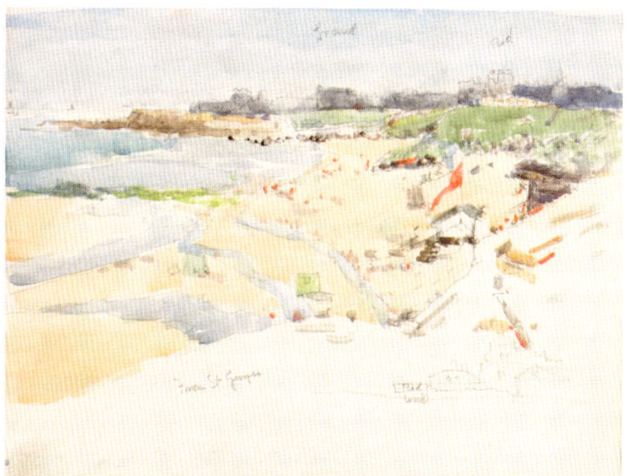

PLATE 51 George Horton, ***From St Georges***; Tyne & Wear Archive, reproduced courtesy D & M Redpath

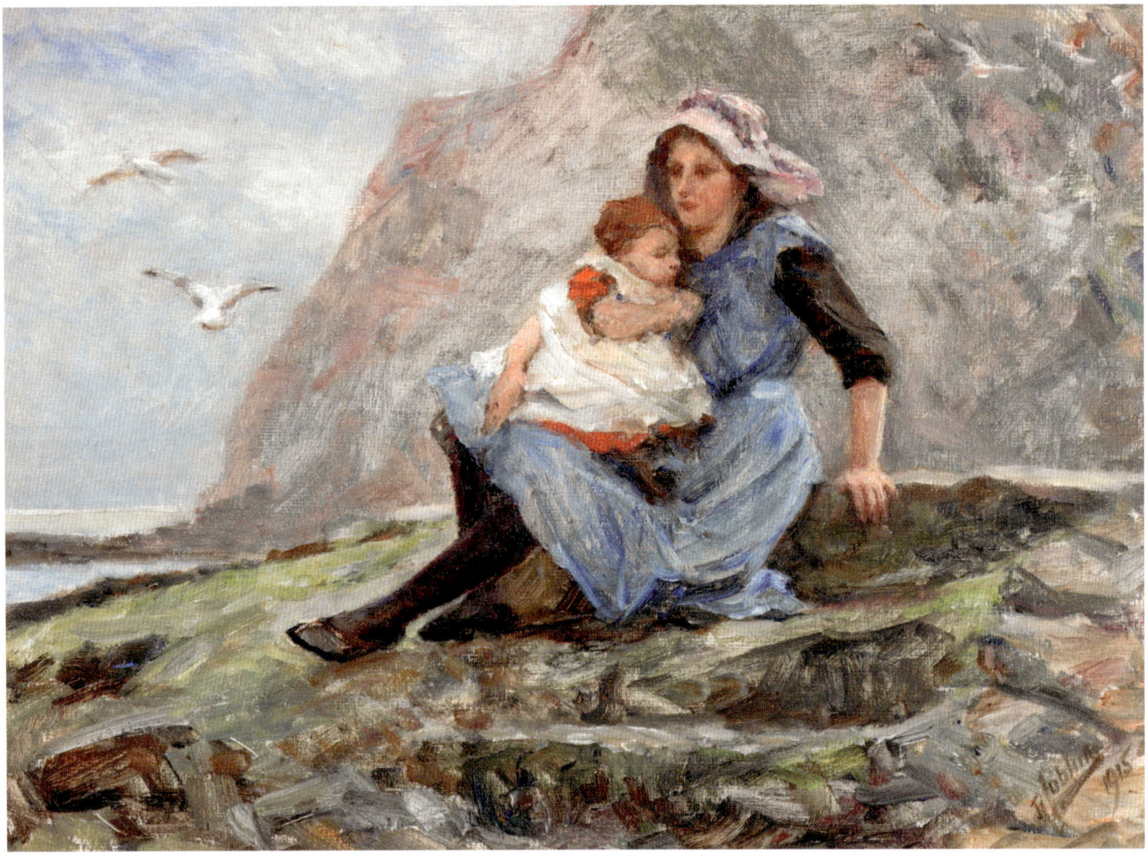

PLATE 52 Robert Jobling, ***Minding the Bairn***, 1915; private collection

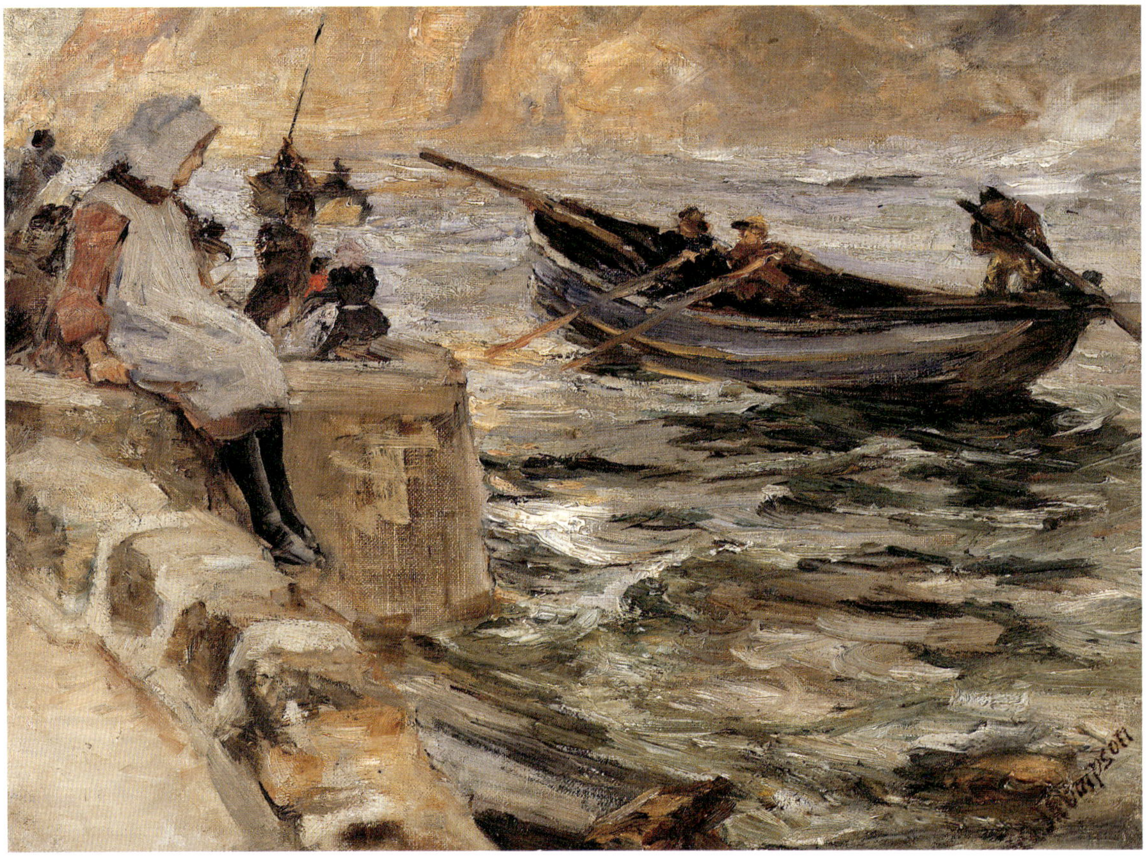

PLATE 53 Isa Thompson, ***Girl on the Quay at Staithes***; private collection

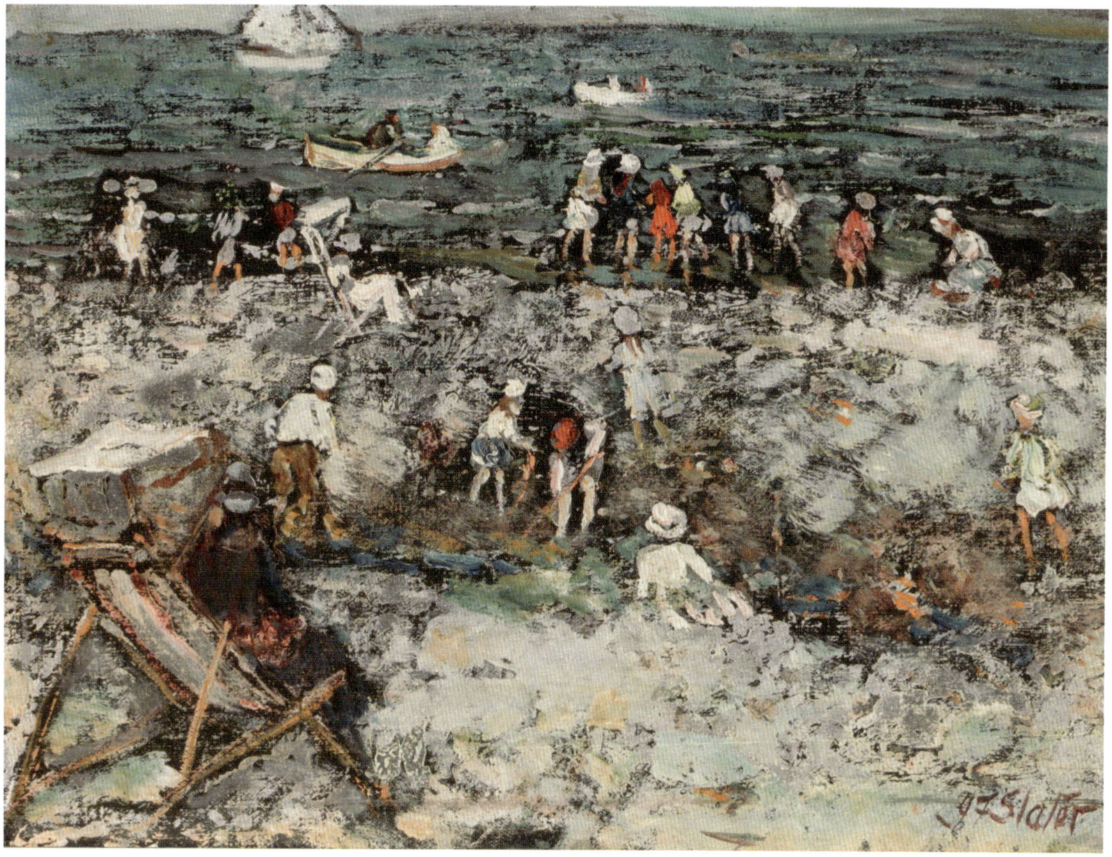

PLATE 54 John Falconer Slater, ***Beach Scene***, c.1920; private collection

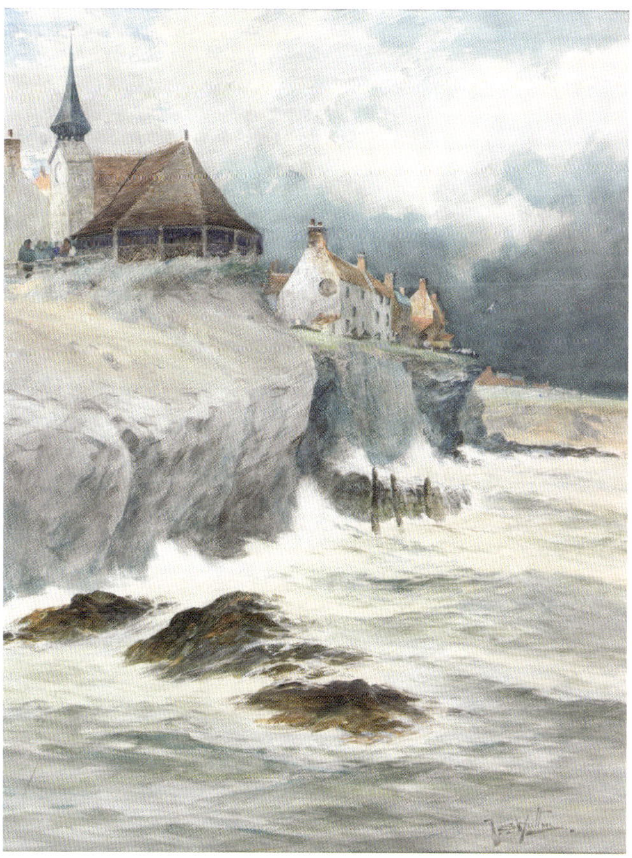

PLATE 55 Thomas Swift Hutton, ***Cullercoats***; South Shields Museum and Art Gallery

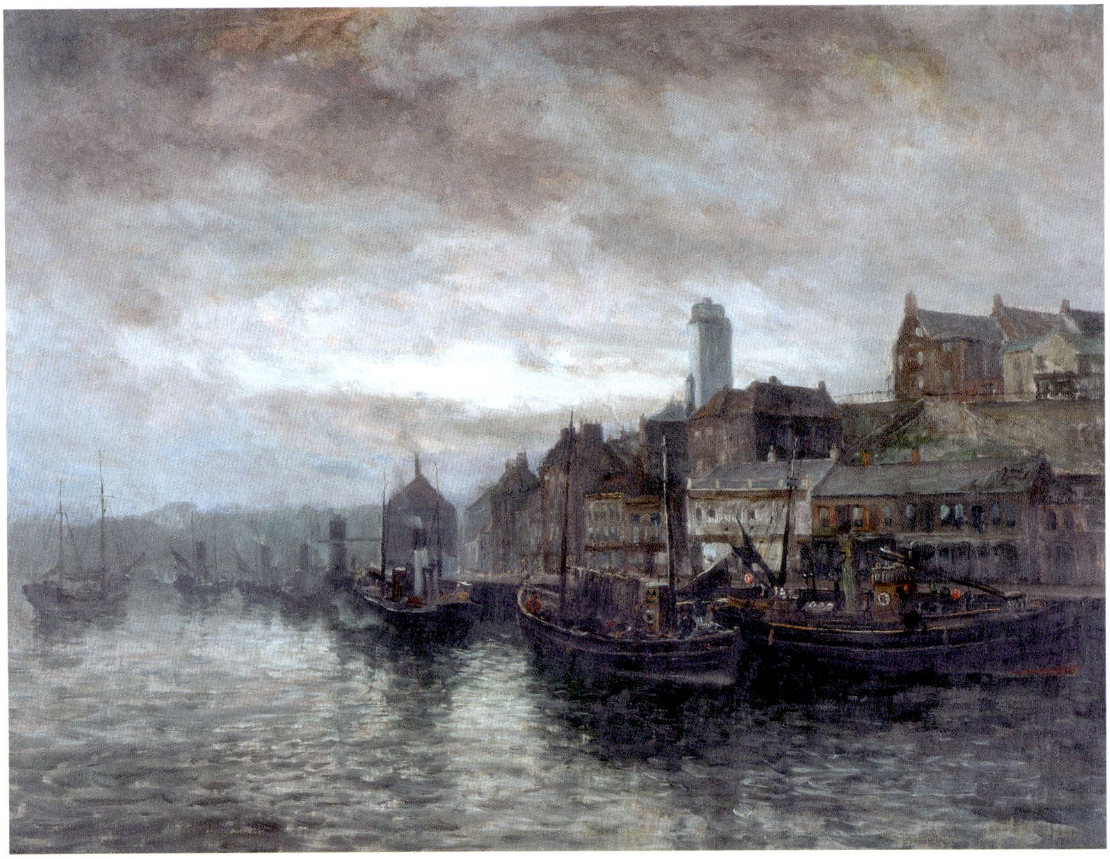

PLATE 56 John Falconer Slater, ***Quayside at North Shields***; Laing Art Gallery

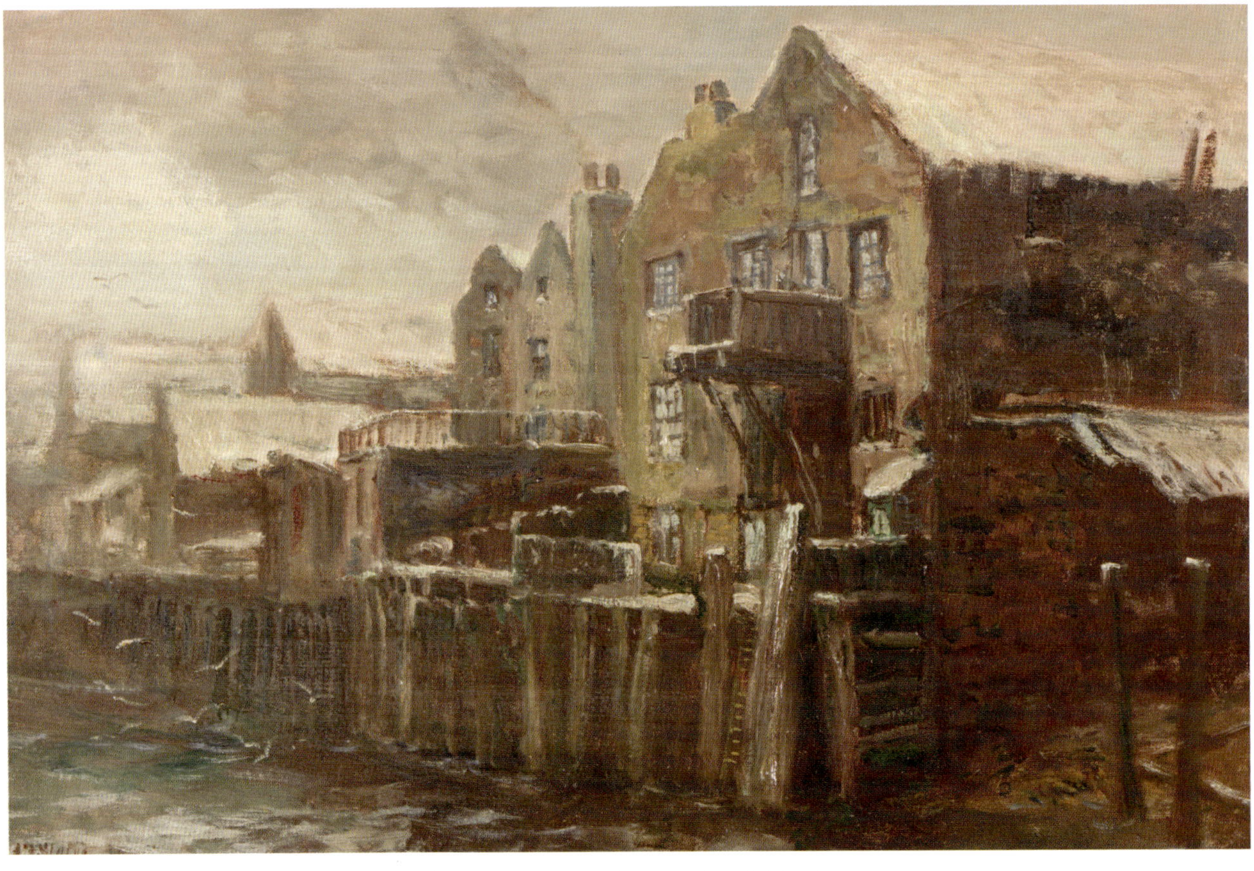

PLATE 57 John Falconer Slater, ***North Shields River Frontage, Snow***; Walter S Wood

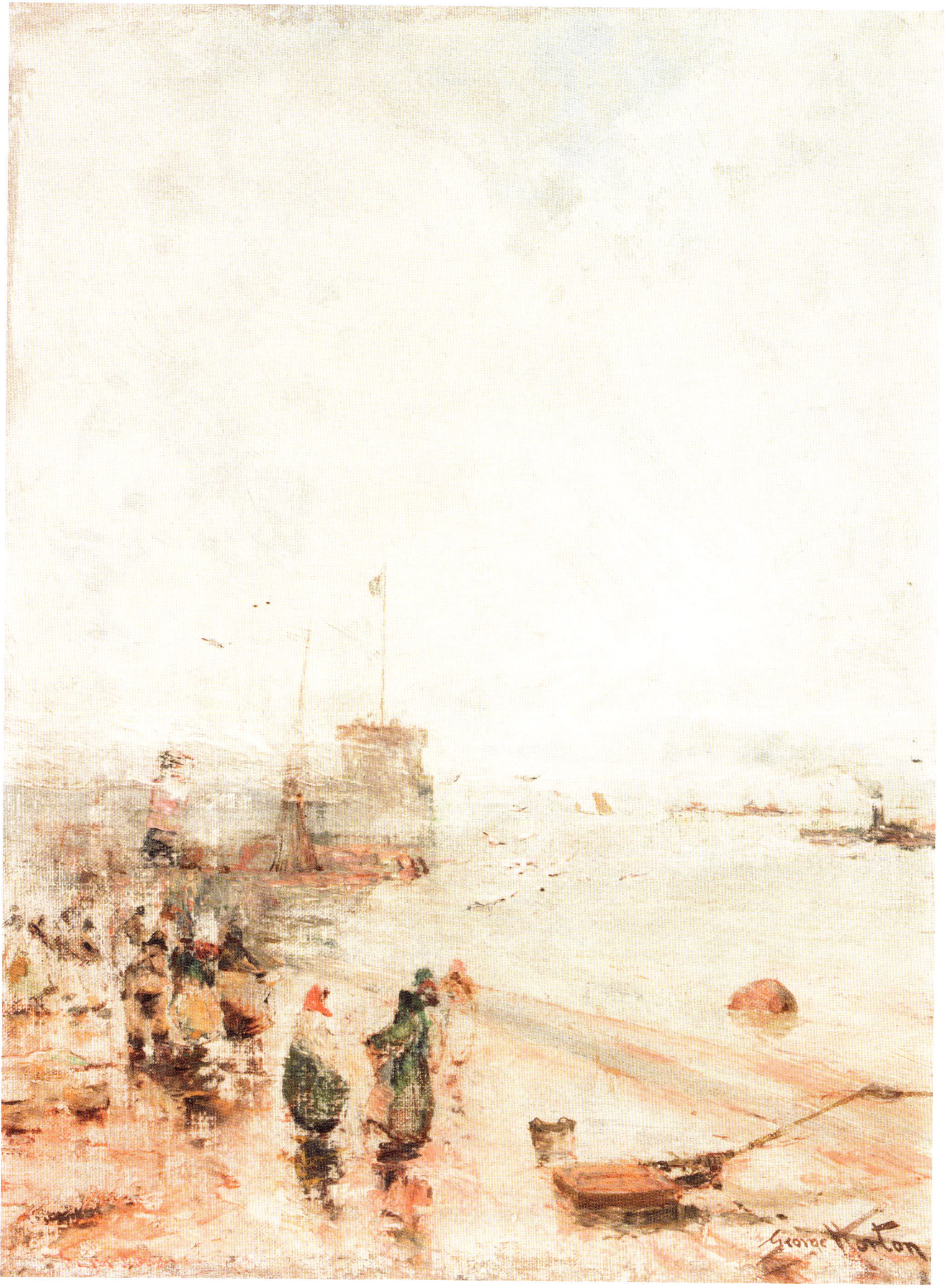

PLATE 58 George Horton, ***Fish Quay, North Shields***, 1896; South Shields Museum and Art Gallery

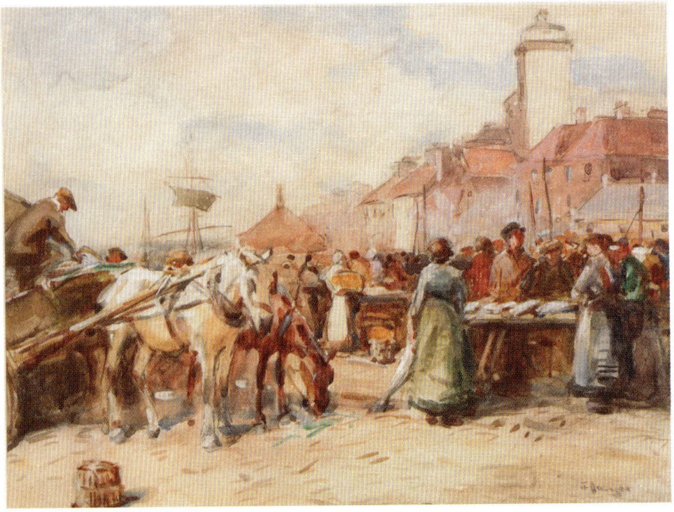

PLATE 59
John Atkinson, ***Fish Quay, North Shields***;
private collection

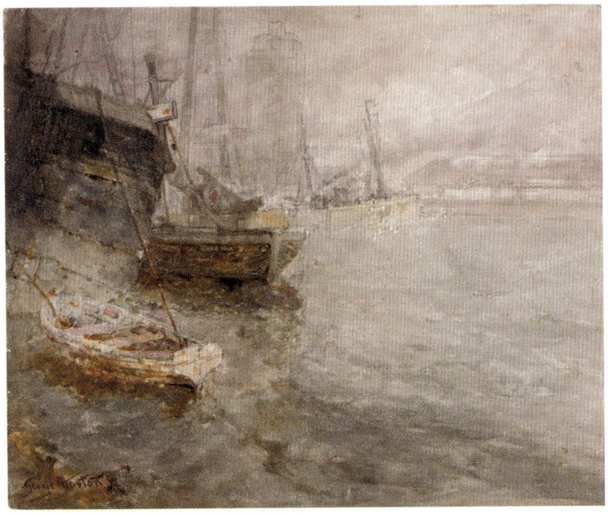

PLATE 60
George Horton, ***Fish Quay***;
Laing Art Gallery

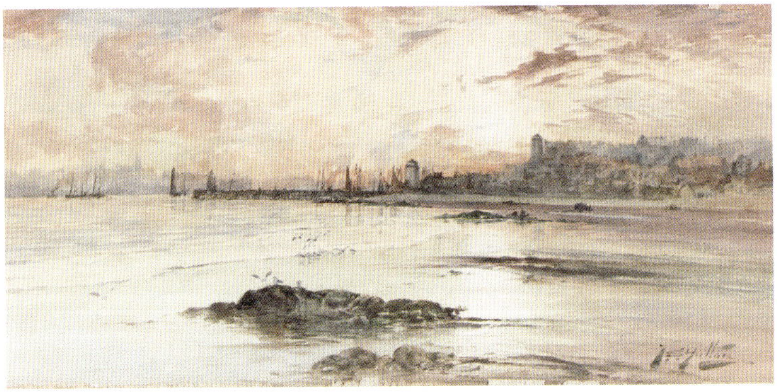

PLATE 61 Thomas Swift Hutton, ***Mouth of the Tyne, North Shields***;
Laing Art Gallery

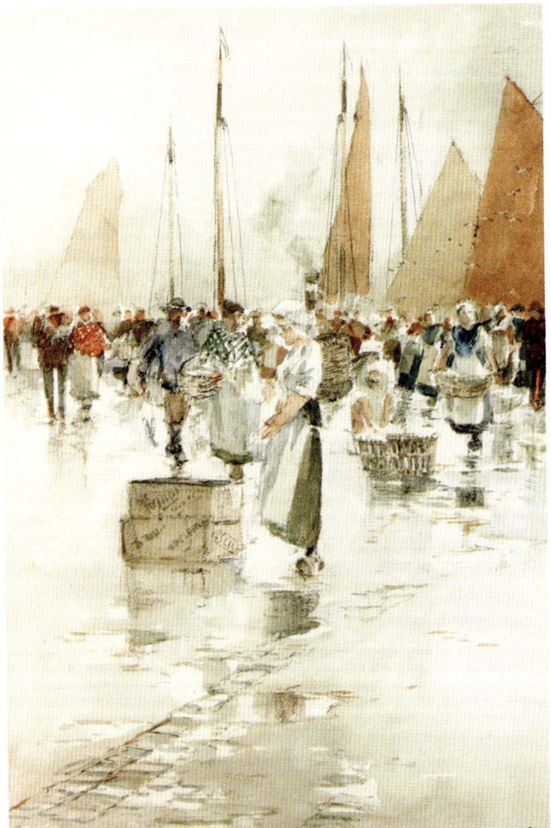

PLATE 62 Victor Noble Rainbird, ***Fish Market***;
Laing Art Gallery

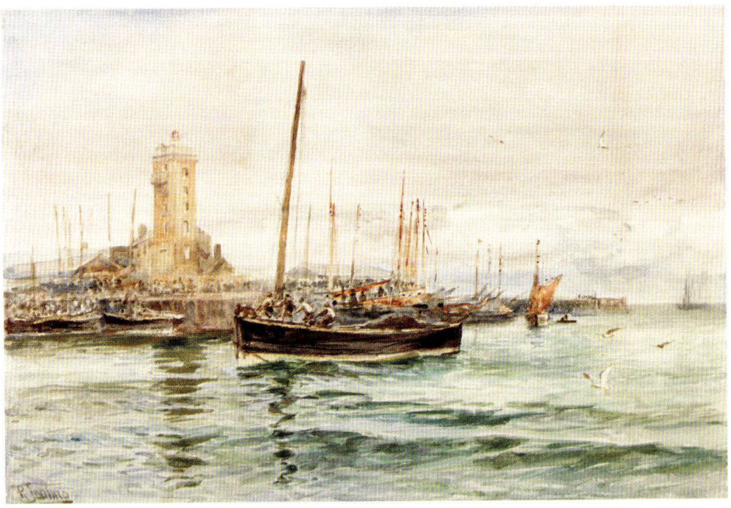

PLATE 63 Robert Jobling, ***Low Lights, North Shields***,
1901; Laing Art Gallery

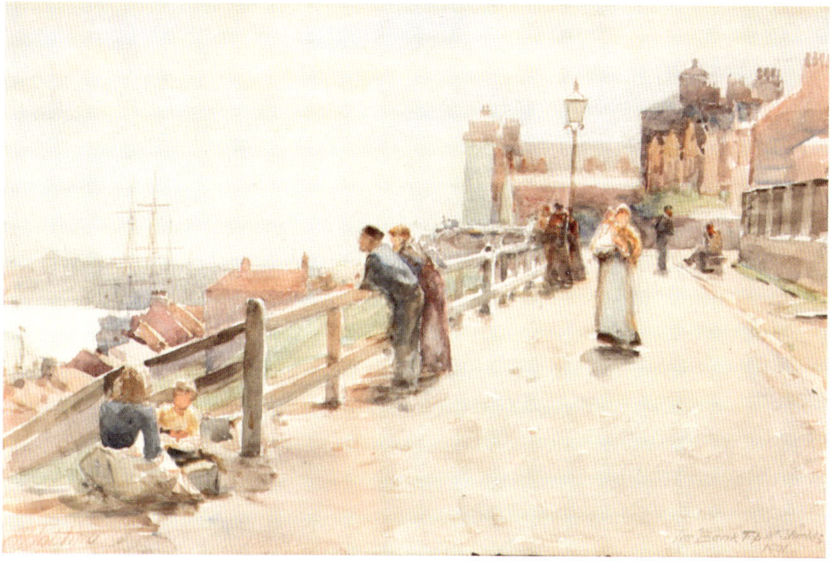

PLATE 64 Robert Jobling, ***Bank Top, North Shields***, 1901; Laing Art Gallery

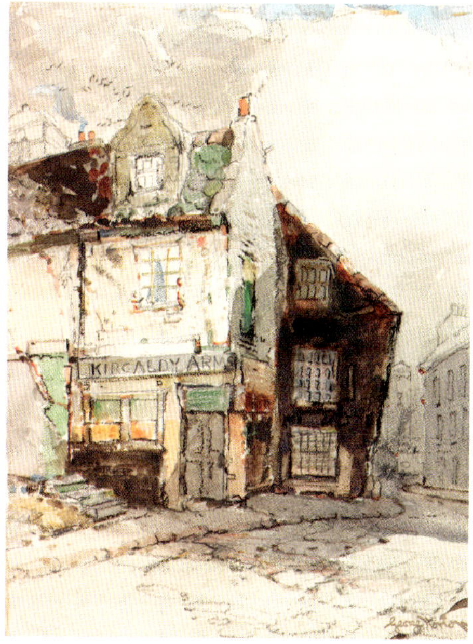

PLATE 65 George Horton, ***Kirkcaldy Arms***; Laing Art Gallery

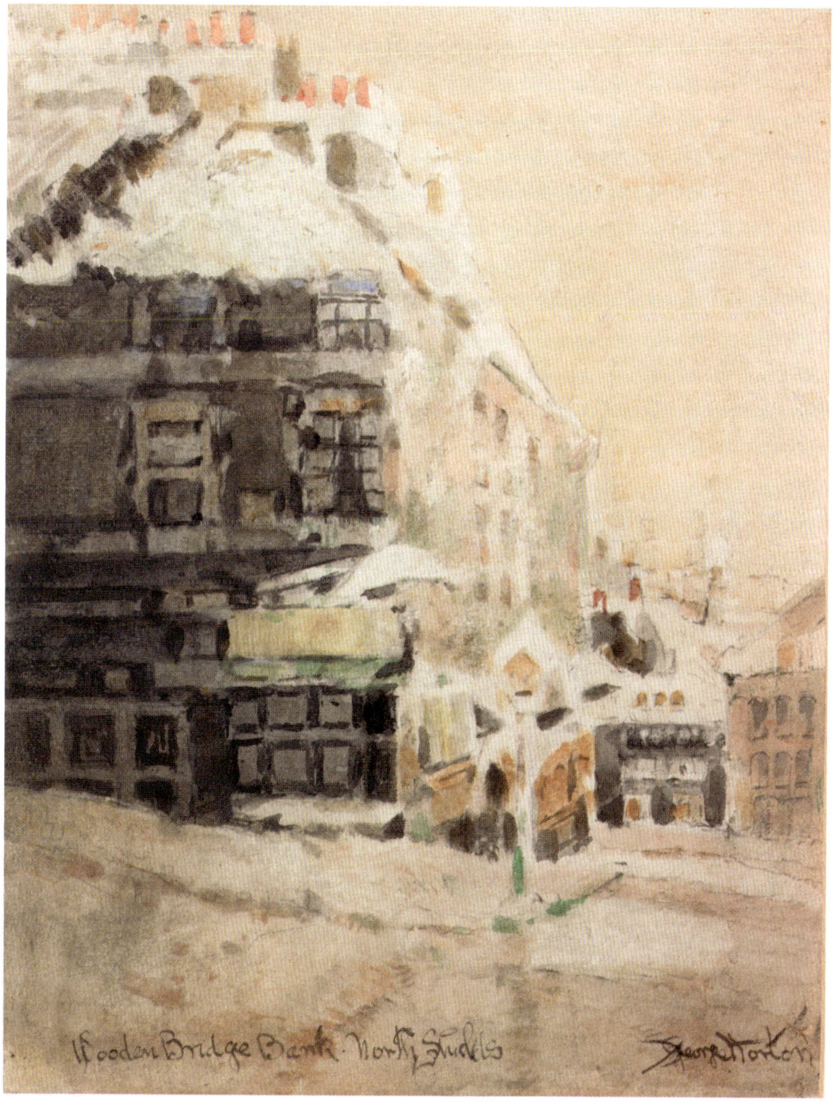

PLATE 66 George Horton, ***Wooden Bridge Bank***; private collection

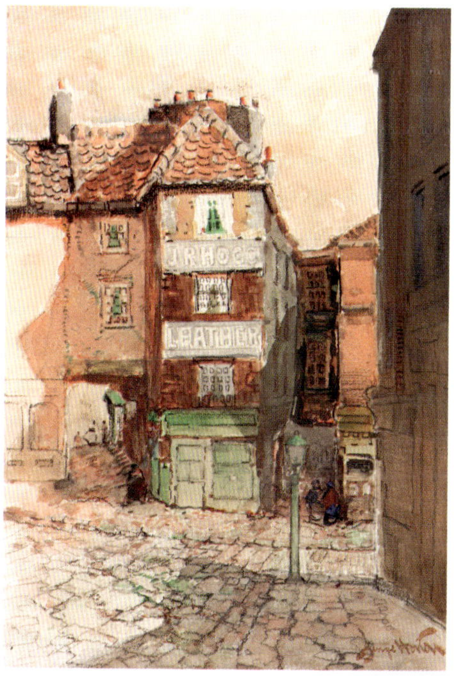

PLATE 67 George Horton, ***J R Hogg's Shop***; Laing Art Gallery

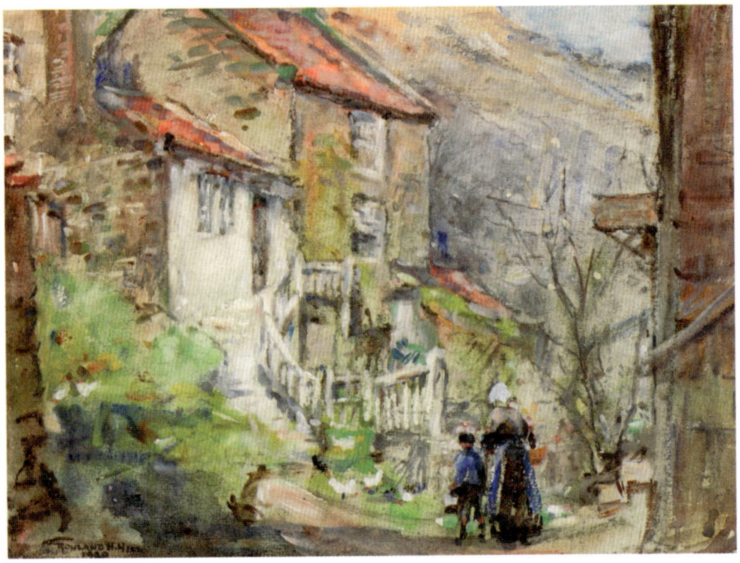

PLATE 68 Roland Henry Hill, ***Runswick Cottages***; South Shields Museum and Art Gallery

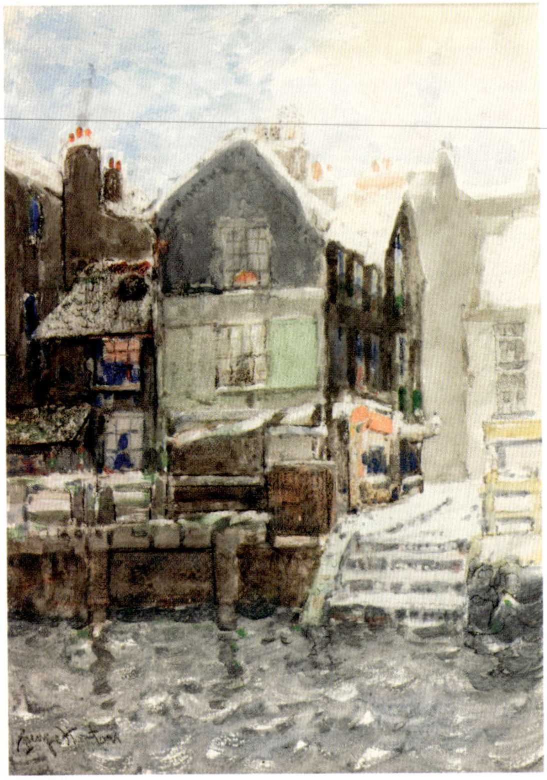

PLATE 69
George Horton,
Comical Corner, South Shields, 1935;
South Shields Museum and Art Gallery

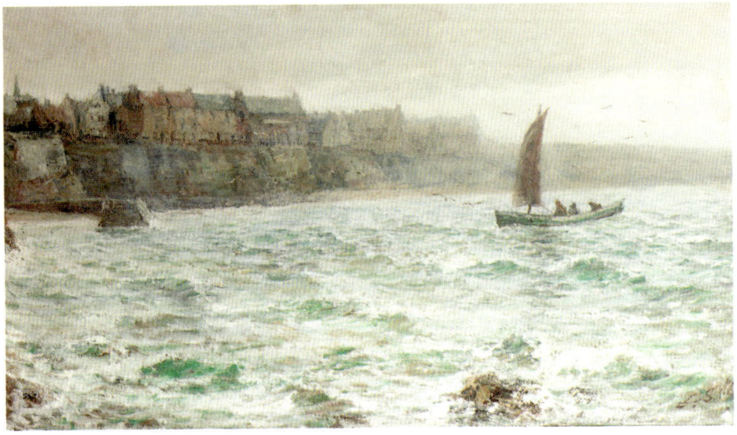

PLATE 70 John Falconer Slater, ***Cullercoats Bay***; private collection

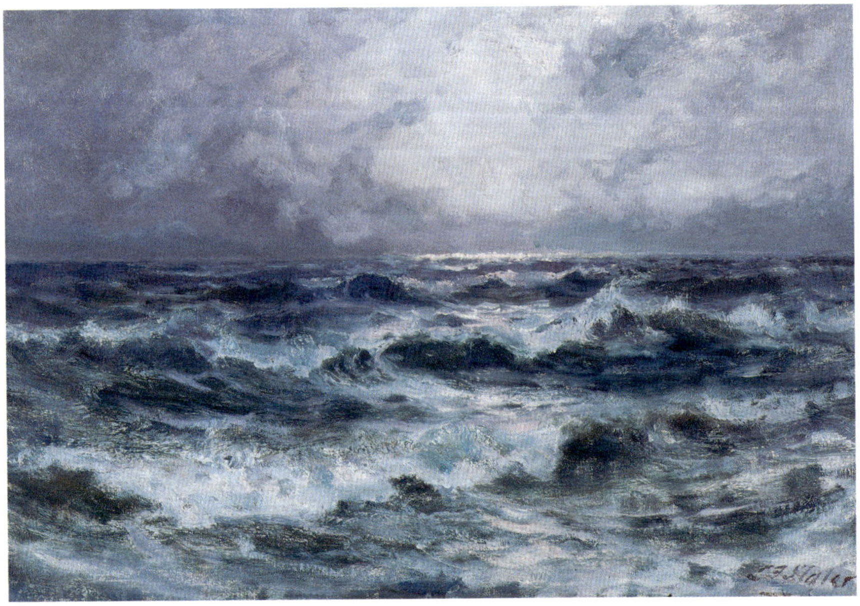

PLATE 71 John Falconer Slater, ***Seascape***; Laing Art Gallery

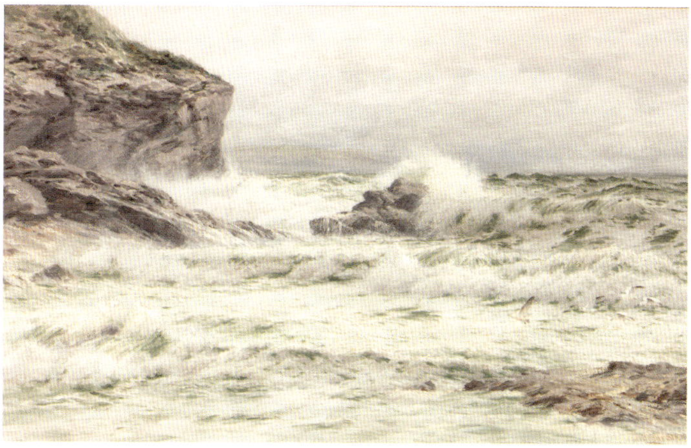

PLATE 72 Harry Sticks, ***Breakers, Whitley Bay***, 1915; Shipley Art Gallery, Gateshead

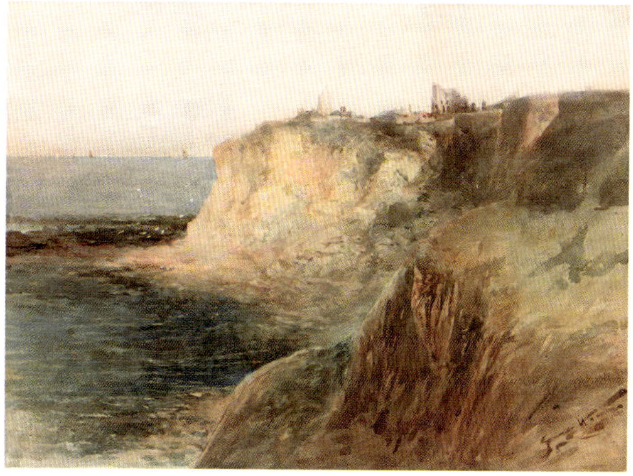

PLATE 73 George Horton, ***Tynemouth from King Edward's Bay***; Laing Art Gallery

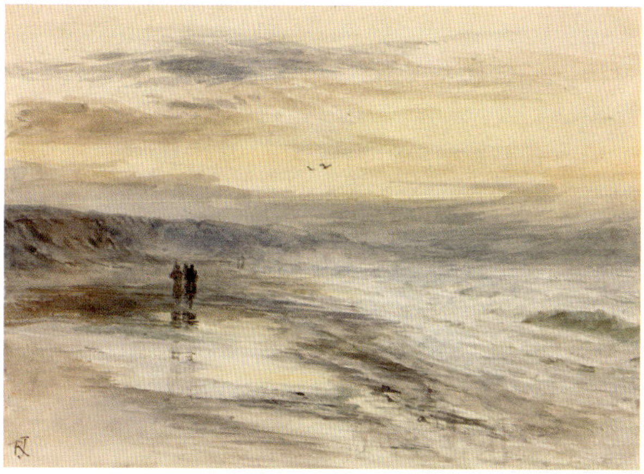

PLATE 74 Robert Jobling, ***Dusk***; Laing Art Gallery

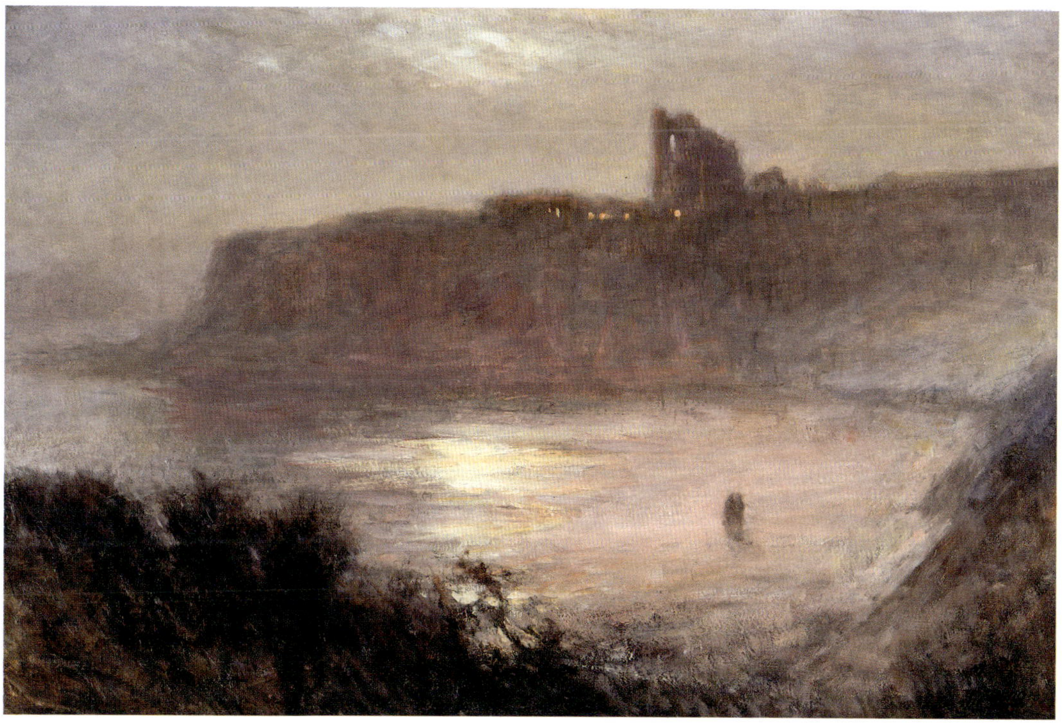

PLATE 75 Robert Jobling, ***Moonlit Bay***, 1909; Laing Art Gallery

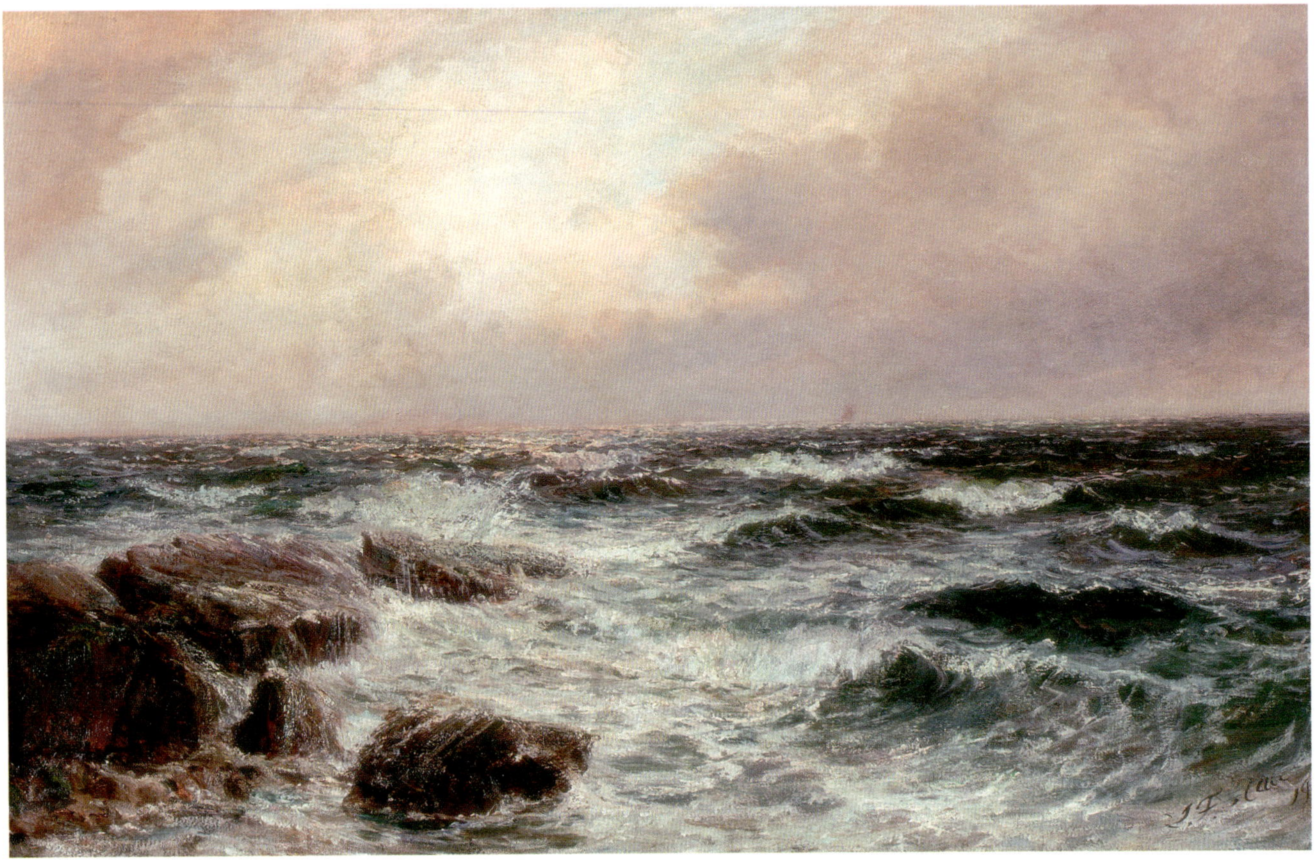

PLATE 76 John Falconer Slater, ***Seascape***, 1905; Laing Art Gallery

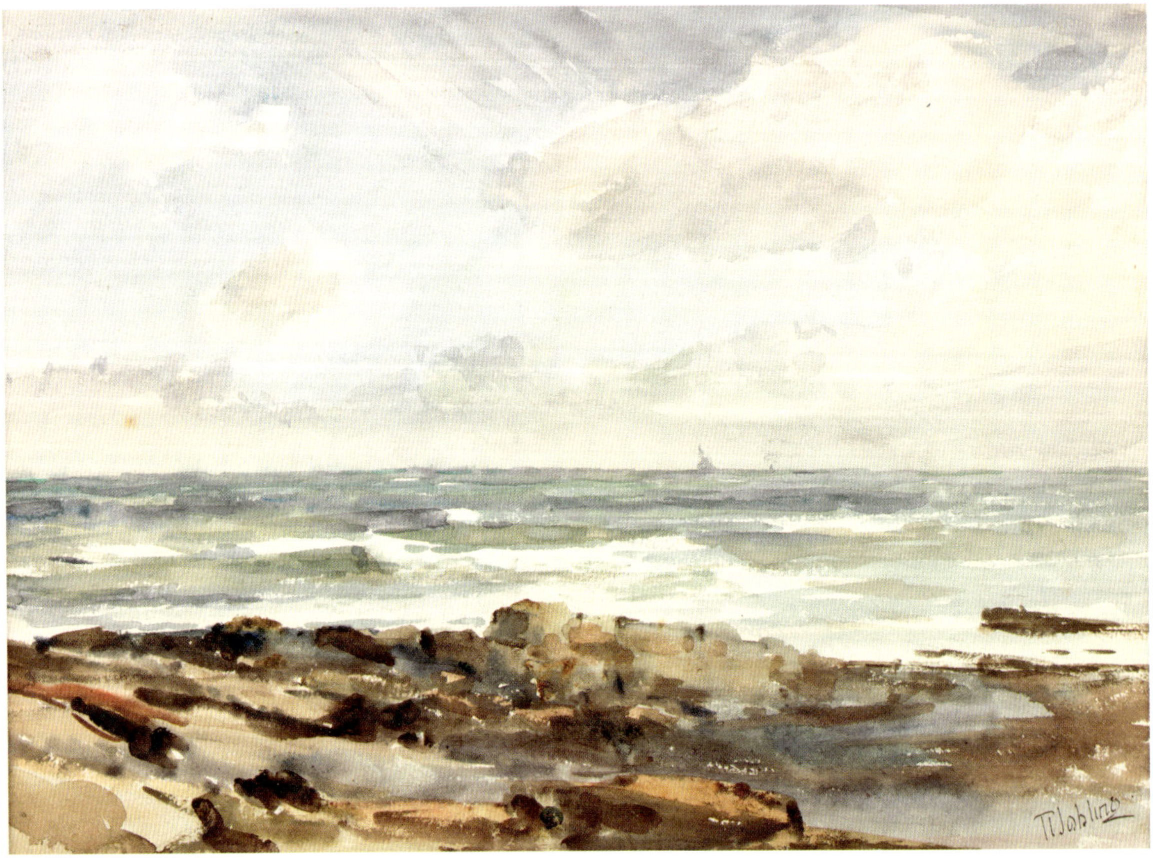

PLATE 77 Robert Jobling, ***Seascape***; Laing Art Gallery

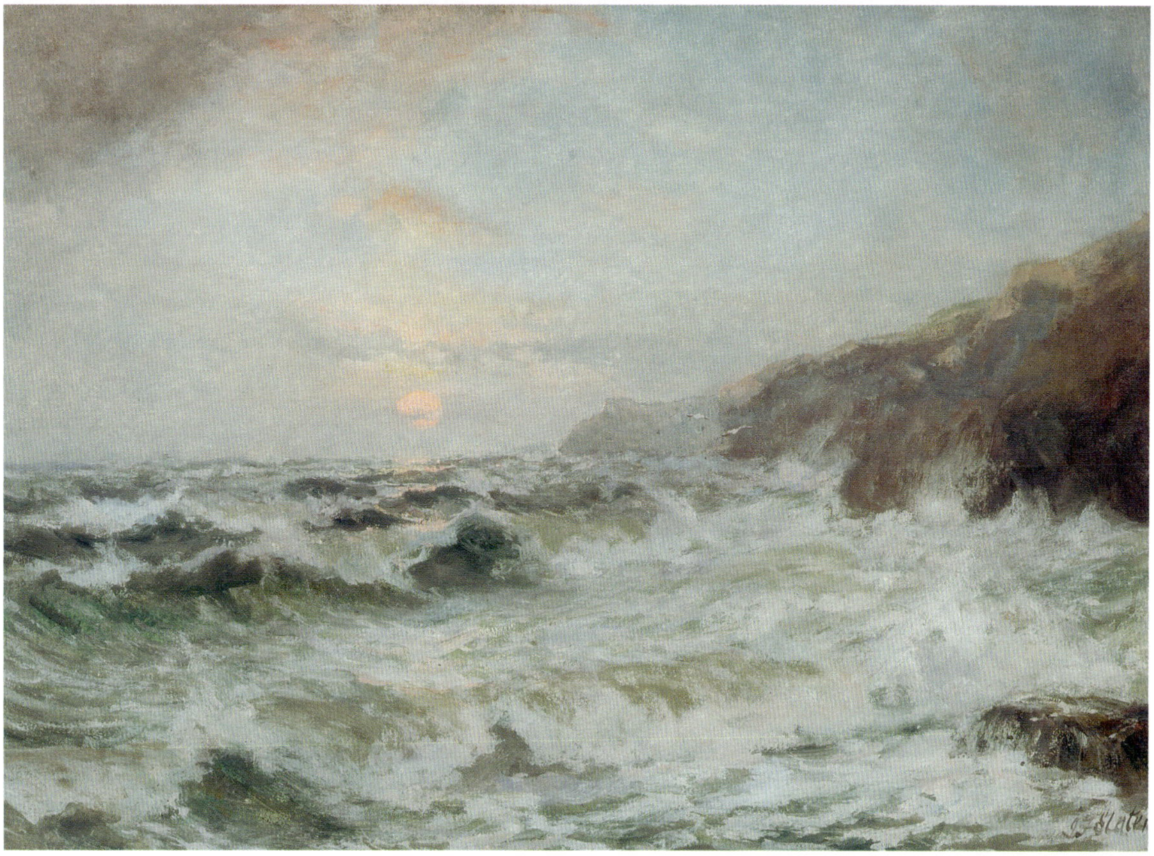

PLATE 78 John Falconer Slater, ***Seascape***; Laing Art Gallery

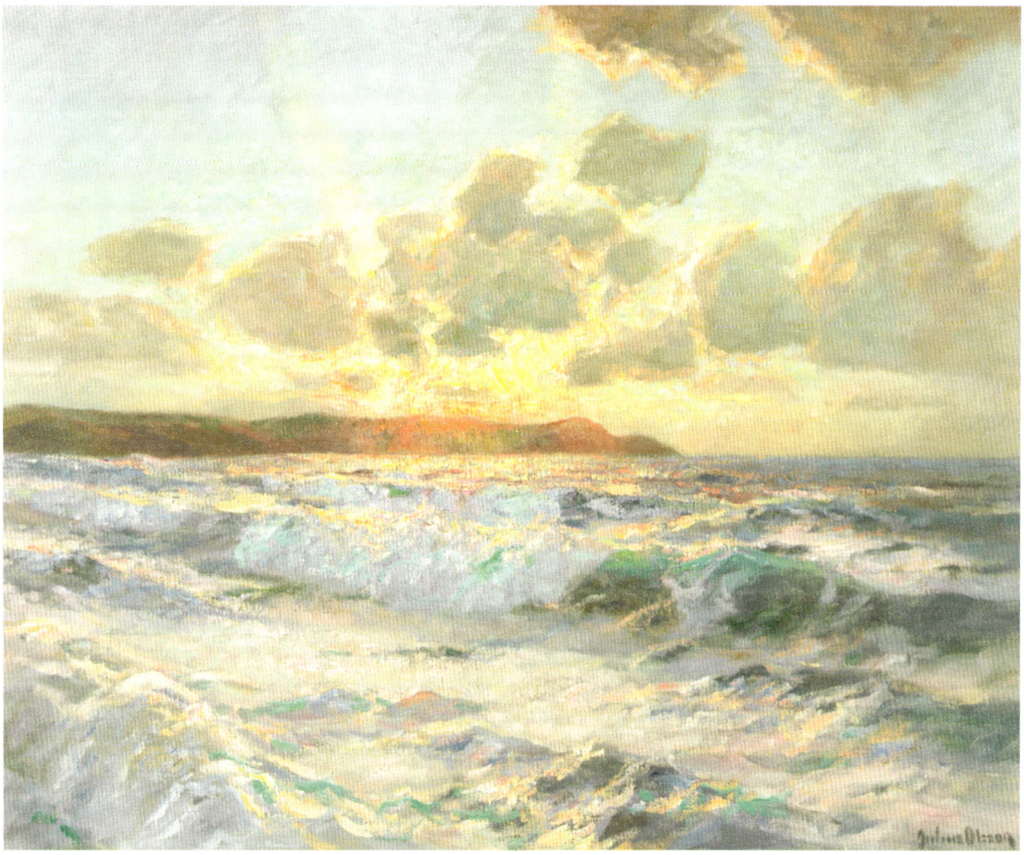

PLATE 79 Julius Olsson, ***Off Cornwall***; Sunderland Museum and Winter Garden

Main Artists at Cullercoats

Stephen Brownlow (1828–1896)

Trained Newcastle School of Art under William Bell Scott.

1866	Lodged (or had studio?) at Mary Lisle's, 127 Back Row, Cullercoats.
1879	Slater's Directory: 1 St. Nicholas Buildings, Newcastle — studio.
1887	Bulmer's Directory: 70 Parker St., Newcastle — home.
1887	Jubilee Exhibition catalogue: 23 New Bridge St., Newcastle — studio.
1888	Ward's Directory: 22 New Bridge St. — studio.

Work

South Shields Fine Art and Industrial Exhibition 1877. Arts Association and Bewick Club exhibitions until his death, his subjects usually drawn from Cullercoats or the river Tyne. He was a close friend of Robert Jobling, going on sketching trips with him.

John Chambers (1852–1928)

1879	Arts Association catalogue: North Shields.
1890	Kelly's Directory: 5 Frank Place, North Shields (occupation — master mariner).
1891	Ward's Directory: 3 Queen St., Newcastle — studio.
1892	South Shields catalogue: Trinity House, North Shields.
1893	South Shields catalogue: 29 Washington Tce., North Shields.
1897–8	Ward's Directory: 58 Borough Rd., North Shields.

Work

South Shields Fine Art Exhibition, 1877: Arts Association, 1879 and Bewick Club exhibitions: South Shields Art Club Exhibitions 1893, 1894, 1911 & 1912: Artists of Northern Counties exhibitions.

John Charlton (1849–1917)

Trained at Newcastle School of Art and then to London where he shared a studio (and had lessons from?) J D Watson, c.1865.

1870	Royal Academy catalogue: 15 Grey St., Newcastle — studio.
1873–9	Kelly's Directory: 8 St.Mary's Place, Newcastle — studio.
1874	onwards: resident in London. Early 1880s in Africa and Egypt as war artist, covering colonial campaigns. He lived primarily in London for the rest of his career, but kept a house at Cullercoats.
1890	Kelly's Directory: 44 Beverly Tce, Cullercoats.
1904	Ward's Directory: 44 Beverly Tce, Cullercoats.

Work

Primarily a painter of animals and hunting scenes, but also did battle pictures and commissioned by Queen Victoria to paint the Royal Procession during her Jubilee celebrations in 1897. *The Women* 1910 and the follow-up, *The Lifeboat* 1911, are only known large-scale Cullercoats pictures by him. Continued to contribute regularly to Arts Association, Bewick Club and Artists of Northern Counties exhibitions throughout his career. Royal Academy 1870–1917: Glasgow Institute 1881–87.

Henry Bewick Emmerson (1861–1897)

1881	Census: 16 John St. Cullercoats.
1882	Son's birth certificate: Haven View House, Cullercoats. Occupation — Artist.
1886	Kelly's Directory: 2 Cheviot View, Whitley Bay.
1887–8	Electoral Register: 18 John St. Cullercoats.
1889–90	Ward's Directory: Station Road, Cullercoats.
1890	Son's birth certificate: 2 West View Buildings, Cullercoats.
1892	Ward's Directory: 5 Nun St., Newcastle — studio(?)
1894	*Shields Daily News* (wife-beating trial): 36 Jackson St. North Shields.
1897	Died in Bulawayo, South Africa.

Work

Specialised in pictures of animals. Showed at Arts Association 1882, Gateshead Fine Arts Exhibition 1883, and at the Bewick Club exhibitions until at least 1892.

Henry Hetherington Emmerson (1831-1895)

1844–8	Government School of Design, Newcastle under William Bell Scott.
1848	studied in Paris.
1848–9	studied at Leigh's School in London.
1856	moved to Whickham.
1857	moved to Ebchester.
1858	moved to Bywell.
1865–6	3 John Street, Cullercoats. (Census 1871).
1865	Ward's Directory: 63 Grainger St. Newcastle — studio.
1867	Ward's Directory: 65 Grainger St. Newcastle — studio sharing with Robinson Elliott.
1873–8	Royal Academy catalogues: Tosson Tower, Rothbury (Lord Armstrong's estate).
1881	Census: 16 John St. Cullercoats. (This became No.25 after 1924).
1884–5	Millard: 22 New Bridge St. Newcastle — studio with S.Brownlow, J. Dickinson and T. Stanton Bowman. This confirmed in 1887 Bulmer's Directory.

Work

Royal Academy 1851–1893. First Cullercoats works shown at Central Exchange Gallery, Newcastle in 1870. Exhibited at Arts Association, Bewick Club, South Shields, and Tynemouth art clubs. Exhibition at Hellyer Bros Gallery, South Shields 1894 and posthumous exhibition 1895.

Hugh Percy Emmerson (1865–1919)

1871 Census: 3 John St., Cullercoats.
1881 Census: Tosson Tower, Rothbury (Lord Armstrong's estate).
1889 Electoral Register: 1 John St., Cullercoats.
1891 Census: 16 John St, Cullercoats.
1899 South Africa (2nd Boer War). Died there 1919.

Work
Varied subject matter, including landscape, genre, still life and portraiture. Showed at Bewick Club 1884–86, 1888, 1890, 1893: Jubilee Exhibition 1887: South Shields Model Yacht Club Exhibition 1890 & 1892.

Ralph Hedley (1850–1913)

1873 Ward's Directory: 11 Neshams Buildings, New Bridge St., Newcastle — sculptor.
1879 Kelly's Directory: 24 Milton St., Newcastle — studio?
1888 Ward's Directory: 28 New Bridge St., Newcastle — studio.
1890 Kelly's Directory: 28 New Bridge St., Newcastle — studio & St. Mary's Pl. — woodworking shop.
1891–2 Ward's Directory: 11 New Bridge St. — studio.

Work
Go! And God's will be done (Royal Academy 1891) is his most significant Cullercoats work. Exhibited at the Bewick Club, Art Circle, South Shields and Tynemouth art clubs and Artists of the Northern Counties exhibitions. Other significant exhibition venues included Royal Scottish Academy 1878–82: Walker Art Gallery 1888–1905: Oldham Art Gallery 1891–1904: Leeds Art Gallery 1892-1900: Manchester 1892–1904: Nottingham Castle 1900-1905: Derby 1901-1914: Bath 1901 & 1907.

Bernard Benedict Hemy (1845–1913)

1863 35 West St., Gateshead — the family home.
1892 South Shields Art Club catalogue: Penman St., North Shields.
1897-8 Ward's Directory: 59 Cleveland St., South Shields.

Work
Exhibiting locally from 1877 onwards, his subjects usually taken from the coast and along the Tyne.

T M Hemy (1852–1937)

1881 Census: appears as T. Henry — he and his wife Annie are listed as marine artists, with a son named Charles Napier (after his brother?). Address given as 7 Alexandra Tce., Whitley Bay.
1881 Arts Association catalogue: 72 Lovaine Place, Newcastle.
1882 Arts Association catalogue: The Valley House, High Coniscliffe, Darlington.
1885 Bewick Club catalogue: 32 Alma Square, Abbey Road, St. Johns Wood.

Work
Specialised in dramatic marine works such as *Women and Children First* (Royal Academy 1887). Royal Academy 1874–1898: Glasgow Institute 1874–1898: Royal Institute 1887: Artists of the Northern Counties 1909–10.

Frank Holl (1845–88)

Always based in the south-east but there are a number of significant 'interconnections' with other artists working in Cullercoats.
1867 Knew Pettie and Orchardson on social basis and therefore probable that he also knew Birket Foster.
1870 Family holiday to Cullercoats. His choice of location may well have been influenced by J D Watson's representations of Cullercoats in *The Graphic* and by recommendation from Orchardson.
1871–2 Introduced to working for *The Graphic* by J D Linton, friend of H H Emmerson.
1872 Moved to Shere in Surrey where visited often by J D Watson.
1877 Member of the Arts Club in Hanover Square, London and the Sketching Club in Fitzroy Square, whose other members included Orchardson, Pettie, Tom Graham, Phil Morris, Abbey, Parsons, Colin Hunter, Macbeth, Watson and MacWhirter — many of them having strong links with the north-east, including having trained with Emmerson at Leigh's.

Work
No Tidings from the Sea 1871, commissioned by Queen Victoria. Royal Academy 1864–88: British Institute 1865: Royal Glasgow Institute 1877, 1882 & 1905: Royal Scottish Academy 1882–86.

Winslow Homer (1836–1910)

Spring 1881 Possibly at room 17 Huddlestone Arms (later the Bay Hotel) — ref. article by Linda Greenley and in Helen Cooper's work on Homer. Most references say Homer had a studio at 12 Bank Top (belonging to Miss J Carrick, also an artist) and lived in a cottage behind the Stone House. BUT:
1881 Census: 12 Bank Top does not appear at all, AND: Miss Jane Carrick is recorded as a visitor of Mr. Alfred W Waagen (merchant) of 71 Holly Ave, Jesmond.
1886 Kelly's Directory: Jane Carrick at 12 Bank Top — teacher of china painting, artist (census 1891), and lodging house (Kelly's, 1893). The position of the cottage in which Homer lived has been placed to the north of the Huddleston Hotel, but this does not match with the records of Stone House at North Shields Library. It seems probable that Homer did not stay continuously at Cullercoats, but returned to America late in 1881, returning to Cullercoats in 1882. The length of his stay is still disputed, although most scholars place him back in America by the end of 1882.

Work
He exhibited a Cullercoats work at the Arts Association Autumn exhibition in 1881 and at the Royal Academy in 1882. He had exhibited at the Royal Academy in 1878.

George Horton (1859–1950)

1859 70 Church Way, North Shields (family home).
1881 Arts Association catalogue: 51 Nile St., North Shields (his father's butchers shop).
1884 Bewick Club catalogue: Percy Arms, West Percy St., North Shields
1887 Jubilee catalogue: 19 Sidney St., North Shields
1893 South Shields Exhibition catalogue: 19 Marine Approach, South Shields.
1896 Royal Academy catalogue: 61 Winchester St., South Shields.
1897 Wards: 2 Clayton St., Newcastle — studio.
1907–12 Royal Scottish Academy catalogues: 23 Winterbottom St., South Shields.
1914 14 Belle Grove Tce., Newcastle.
1919–20 London.
1940–44 14 Belle Grove Tce., Newcastle. His London home was bombed during the war.

Work
Arts Association, Bewick Club and Artists of Northern Counties exhibitions 1881-1950. Royal Academy 1896–1938: Glasgow Institute 1891: Royal Scottish Academy 1902–1912: Paris Salon pre-1914. One-man exhibitions: Greatorex Gallery, London 1922: Brighton 1922: Bolton 1923: Rochdale 1923, Middleburg, Holland 1925: The Hague 1926, Fine Art Society, London 1927.

Robert Jobling (1841–1923)

Up to 1881 85 Corbridge St. Byker (1881 Census).
1879 Kelly's Directory: 1 Shakespeare St., Newcastle — studio.
Late 1881 13 Delaval Rd., Whitley Bay
1887 Kelly's Directory: 57 Beverly Tce., Cullercoats.
1891 Census: 29 Victoria Ave., Whitley Bay.

1901 Academy of Arts, Blackett St., Newcastle — studio (Pen & Palette Club).

Work
Started exhibiting locally c.1866 (Hays & Sons gallery). Exhibited at Central Exchange from 1870 onwards, Arts Association, Bewick Club, Tynemouth and South Shields Art Clubs, Art Circle, Artists of Northern Counties. Regular studio exhibitions from 1885. Glasgow Institute 1874: Royal Academy 1883–1911: Society of British Artists 1883: Walker Art Gallery 1885–88: Staithes Art Club 1902–5. Retrospective Exhibition Armstrong College, Newcastle 1923.

Arthur Hardwick(e) Marsh (1842–1909)

1869 Guest of Alexander Stevenson at 45–6 Front St., Tynemouth. Had met previously at Birket Foster's house in Surrey. Used Emmerson's studio in Cullercoats during stay.
1870 Royal Academy catalogue: Cullercoats.
1871 Royal Academy catalogue: 22 King Henry's Rd., London.
1872–3 Royal Academy catalogue: Tynemouth
1874 Royal Academy catalogue: Whitley
1876 Royal Academy catalogue: 5 Waterloo Place, London.
1877 Slater's Directory: Osborn House, Whitley Bay. (Census for 1871 shows this as a boarding house run by Mary Ann Robinson.)
1878 Royal Academy catalogue: 23 Camden Road, London.
1882-3 Cullercoats. Marsh working for Sowerby's Glass Company — designs shown at Manchester.
1886 Royal Academy catalogue: Alnmouth.
1890 Kelly's Directory: 15 Market St., Newcastle — studio with H V Barnett.
1892-3 Ward's Directory: 14 Otterburn Tce, Jesmond (home).
1896 Royal Academy catalogue: Cullercoats — studio.
1897–8 Ward's Directory: Studio at Cullercoats, living at Jesmond.
1899–1900 Ward's Directory: Mast Lane, Cullercoats — studio.

Work
Exhibited at Arts Association, Bewick Club, Tynemouth Art Club, Art Circle and Artists of Northern Counties 1878–1908.
Royal Academy 1868–1896: Grosvenor Gallery 1879: Old Watercolour Society 1870–1905: Paris Exposition 1876 & 1889: Manchester 1886.

Frank S Ogilvie (1856–1936)

1887 Jubilee Exhibition catalogue: Rosella House, North Shields.
1892 South Shields Exhibition catalogue: 6 Park Rd. Studios, Haverstock Hill, London.
1894 Bewick Club catalogue: 63 Hanley Road, Stroud Green.
1902 Wards 22 Blackett St., Newcastle — studio with T E Macklin. Home — 17 Chester Crescent.
1908 Artists of Northern Counties catalogue: Rosella House, North Shields.
1911 Artists of Northern Counties catalogue: 50 Percy Road, Whitley Bay.
1912 Artists of Northern Counties catalogue: 1 St.Mary's Place, Newcastle (studio?).
1923 Artists of Northern Counties catalogue: 13 St.Thomas Cresc., Newcastle.
1934 Artists of Northern Counties catalogue: Truro House, Hotspur St., Tynemouth.
1935 Artists of Northern Counties catalogue: 15 St.Mary's Place, Newcastle (studio?).

Work
He concentrated mostly on portraiture, securing many local commissions from local dignitaries. Exhibited Arts Association, Bewick Club, Tynemouth and South Shields Art Clubs 1882–1892. Royal Academy 1888–1915: Glasgow Institute 1888 & 1891.

Fred D Ogilvie (1851–1921)

1880 Arts Association catalogue: The Rocks, Tynemouth.
1881 Census: Rosella House, North Shields.
1885 Bewick Club catalogue: 1 Belhaven Tce., Edinburgh.
1890 Bewick Club catalogue: 2 Charing Cross, Glasgow.
1894 Bewick Club catalogue: Farine House, Helensburgh.
1908 Artists of Northern Counties catalogue: 47 Westcliffe Tce., Harrogate
1909 Artists of Northern Counties catalogue: 18 Raglan St., Harrogate.
c.1913 Horton Archive: 22 Spring Mount, Harrogate.

Work
Mostly marine pictures and landscapes. Exhibited Arts Association, Tynemouth Art Club, Bewick Club 1879–1891. Royal Academy 1877–8 & 1909: Glasgow Institute 1887–1900.

William Quiller Orchardson (1831–1910)

Based in London after leaving native Scotland.
1868 Painted Mrs. Birket Foster's portrait (shown at Royal Academy).
1869 Guest of Alexander Stevenson at Tynemouth (see Marsh). Remained lifelong friend of Stevenson, spending many summers at Stevenson's Scottish retreat, Achnacloich, often also with Fred Walker.
1870 Painting trip to Venice with Birket Foster and Fred Walker.

Work
Cullercoats painting *Toilers of the Sea* shown at Royal Academy in 1870 and Royal Scottish Academy 1872 (loaned by Alexander Macdonald of Aberdeen).
Portrait of A S Stevenson 1881 shown at Royal Academy 1882 and Bewick Club 1893.
Portrait of J C Stevenson shown at Royal Academy 1890 and South Shields Loan Exhibition 1911. Exhibited Arts Association 1878–82: Bewick Club 1884, 1887, 1893. Royal Academy 1863–1904: British Institute 1864: Royal Glasgow Institute 1861–1817: Royal Scottish Academy 1848–1917.

Victor Noble Rainbird (1889–1936)

Trained at Tynemouth School of Art, Albion Rd., North Shields; Armstrong College, Newcastle; Royal College of Art, London and Royal Academy School.
Early years at Sidney St., North Shields.
1906 Artists of Northern Counties catalogue: 95 West Percy Street, North Shields.
1911 Artists of Northern Counties catalogue: 71 West Percy Street, North Shields.
1925 Artists of Northern Counties catalogue: The Studio, Newsham, Darlington.
1932 Artists of Northern Counties catalogue: 71 West Percy St., North Shields.
1933 Artists of Northern Counties catalogue: Howard Street, North Shields.

Work
His work included portraiture, religious pieces, designs for stained glass windows and scenes from World War 1, as well as seascapes and urban scenes. He travelled to Holland, Belgium and France. Exhibited at Artists of Northern Counties exhibitions 1905–1933 and South Shields Art Club 1911& 12. Royal Academy 1926 & 1930.

John Falconer Slater (1857–1937)

1882 Returned to the north east from South Africa.
1887 Jubilee catalogue: Stone Villa, Forest Hall.
1895–6 Ward's Directory: 13 Mosley St., Newcastle — studio (with Miss E C Mawson).
1902 Ward's Directory: Woodlands, Killingworth — home.
1906 Artists of Northern Counties catalogue: 13 Mosley St., Newcastle — studio.

1908 Artists of Northern Counties catalogue: 54 Pilgrim St., Newcastle — studio.
c.1910 3 Charles Ave., Whitley Bay.
1911 Artists of Northern Counties catalogue: Howard Chambers, Howard St., North Shields — studio?
1912 Artists of Northern Counties catalogue: 6 South Parade, Whitley Bay.
1913 Artists of Northern Counties catalogue: 15 Esplanade, Whitley Bay — studio.
1914 *Odds and Ends from an Artist's Notebook:* St. Oswin's Ave, Cullercoats — home.
1920 Artists of Northern Counties catalogue: 46 Lish Ave., Whitley Bay — home.
1921 Artists of Northern Counties catalogue: 2 St. Nicholas Buildings, Newcastle — studio.
1925 Artists of Northern Counties catalogue: 19, St. Oswin's Ave., Cullercoats.

Work
Exhibited Bewick Club, Tynemouth and South Shields Art Clubs, Central Exchange, Artists of Northern Counties 1884–1920. Royal Academy 1889–1936.

Isa Thompson (1851–1926)

1871 Census: 5 Graingerville, Newcastle (family home).
1881 Census: Does not appear on this census for Northumberland.
1881 Arts Association catalogue: 6 Wentworth Place, Newcastle.
1884 Bewick Club catalogue: 48–9 Huddlestone St., Cullercoats (res. Paul Wardropper, chemist).
1885 Bewick Club catalogue: 13 Seabanks, Cullercoats. ? Cliff House, 13 Bank Top, Cullercoats (res. Richard Welsh, mariner).
1888 Bewick Club catalogue: 5 Victoria Cresc., Cullercoats (res. Louise Lambert, lodging house).
1889 Royal Glasgow Institute catalogue: St. Oswald's Buildings, Cullercoats (studio?)
1889 Millard: 6 Wentworth Pl/Tce, Newcastle (res. H E Armstrong, doctor). But she does not appear on the census for that address in 1891.
1891–2 Ward's Directory: 15 Market St., Newcastle — studio (Marsh's old one.)
1892 Summer visits to Staithes from at least this date, perhaps earlier.
1893 29, Victoria Ave, Whitley Bay. Marries Robert Jobling and gives up studio in Newcastle.

Work
Exhibited at Arts Association 1881–3, Bewick Club 1884–95, Central Exchange 1892, Artists of Northern Counties 1905–1925.
Royal Academy 1892–1912: Royal Glasgow Institute 1883–97: Royal Scottish Academy 1883–88: Society of British Artists 1885: Walker Art Gallery 1886–93: Staithes Art Club 1902–05.

John Dawson Watson (1832–92)

Spent much of early life and career in Manchester but moved to London in the early 1860s. His sister Frances married Birket Foster in 1864.
1869 Guest of Alexander Stevenson at Tynemouth (see Marsh).

Work
Cullercoats work often reproduced in *The Graphic* and the Boston weekly illustrated paper *Every Saturday* in 1870-71 (when Homer working for the magazine). He painted a *Portrait of H H Emmerson* — information supplied by Mrs. P Bolam.

Exhibited Arts Association 1878-81, Bewick Club 1887. Royal Academy 1853-90: Glasgow Institute 1868-90: Society of Painters in Watercolour 1870: British Institute 1855 & 1962: Royal Scottish Academy 1860.

T J Watson (1847-1912)

Lived and painted with brother, studying at Royal Academy School.
1869 Guest of Alexander Stevenson at Tynemouth.
1871 Royal Academy catalogue: John St. Cullercoats (possibly using Emmerson's studio).
1872 Royal Academy catalogue: 4 Tynemouth Tce, Tynemouth.

Work
Exhibited Central Exchange 1870, Arts Association 1878–81, Tynemouth Art Club 1881, Gateshead Fine Art Exhibition 1883 Royal Academy 1971–1903: Royal Glasgow Institute 1873–82.

Other Artists living in Cullercoats/Tynemouth/Whitley/Shields Area

1836 Isabella Errington, North Shields (d.1890)
1861 James Shotton, North Shields (d.1896)
1865 Thomas Harper, Cullercoats
1871 J R Mather, Whitley Bay
A Lasczky, 18 Grey St., North Shields
1875 J R Mather, 49 Beverly Tce., Cullercoats
J C Wasserman, 50 Beverly Tce., Cullercoats
1879 J L Lambert, 5 Tynemouth Rd., North Shields
Robert Turner, 5 East Parade, Whitley
1881 Susanna M Jones, 18 Duchess St., Whitley
1886 John Surtees, 41 Beverly Tce., Cullercoats
1887 J G Gibbon, 25 Duchess St., Whitley (then 25 Delaval Road, Whitley)
J H Hogg, 3 Pearsons Tce., North Shields
G S Wood, 8 Upper Norfolk St, North Shields (then 35 Alma Place, North Shields)
1891 Charles Frampton, 46 Beverly Tce., Cullercoats
Thomas Rankin Strang, 53 Beverly Tce., Cullercoats
Henry Sawyer, Hawkey's Villa, North Shields
Aaron Watson, 13 Argyle St., Tynemouth
Frank Stocker, 9 Whitley Rd., Cullercoats (Sculptor)
William Sadler, 27 St Marys Place, Whitley (Sculptor).
Esther P Phillips, 29 Grafton Rd., Whitley
Grace E Sewell, 4 New Milfred Tce, Whitley (Teacher of Art)
Edith Thomlinson, 1 Victoria Villas, Whitley (Student of Art)
1892 J D Liddell, 161 Grey St., North Shields
William Urpeth, 12 Alma Place, North Shields
William Turnbull, 52 Beverly Tce., Cullercoats (then 28 Beverley Tce.)
Charles Rutherford, 10 Nile St., North Shields (gallery and studio, 53 Side, Newcastle)
1893 J Smith, 24 Spencer St., North Shields
1895 Hugh Crawhall, 47 Front St., Cullercoats (brother of Joseph Crawhall)
1897 William Cozens Way, 26 Esplanade, Whitley (studio 101 Percy St., Newcastle)
1899 Aaron Watson, 31 Victoria Ave., Whitley (next door to the Joblings)
William Brittain, 46 Percy Rd., Whitley

	J W Clark, 40 Waterloo Place, North Shields
	H Simmons, 18 York Tce., North Shields
1903	T A Hancock, 48 Hotspur St., Tynemouth.
	A J Sticks, 6 Beach Ave., Whitley
	J McColvin, Woodbine Cottage, Gladstone Tce., Whitley
	Mrs. J Sewell, 38 Percy Rd., Whitley.
1906	D W Forster, 10 Cleveland Ave., North Shields
	T A Hancock, 1 Dawson Square, Tynemouth
	D F Hingley, School House, Cullercoats
	Miss E Oliver, Clovelly, Windsor Cresc., Cullercoats
	J E Reid, 8 Promontory Tce., Whitley
	Miss Rooke, 188 Whitley Road, Whitley
	E S Scorfield, Tynemouth Place, Tynemouth
1908	R J S Bertram, 10 Percy Ave., Cullercoats
	E Hodgson, 11 Algernon Tce., Tynemouth
	J Edgar Mitchell, 42 Jesmond Tce., Whitley
	Miss C Ogilvie, Rosella House, North Shields
	FW Reaveley, 39 Eleanor St., Cullercoats
1909	C Baguley, 20 Burnfoot Tce., Whitley
	Miss E A Freeth, Preston Park, North Shields
	Mrs A Layton, 1 Burnfoot, Whitley
	C Nixon, 12 Collingwood Tce., Whitley (later 21 East Parade, Whitley)
1910	H V Charlton, 44 Beverley Tce., Cullercoats
	O F Hingley, Station Road, Cullercoats
	J Pybus, Cleveland Road, North Shields
1913	G W Lisle, 22 Percy Ave., Cullercoats

Artists working at Cullercoats/Tynemouth but not resident

1842	Robert Watson (res. South Shields)
1850	Robinson Elliott (res. South Shields)
1858	Fred Barnard *My Ain Fireside* (Royal Academy 1858) painted at Cullercoats
1870s	C J Spence & John O'Connor
c.1871	Isaac Henzell (uncle of the Hemy brothers)
	H B Richardson (res. Newcastle)
	William Cozens Way
c.1875	G B Sticks (res. Newcastle)
1880s	J Cleet (res. South Shields)
	W H Charlton (res Gosforth)
	John Wallace (res Newcastle)
	John Hodgson Campbell (res Newcastle, studio Pilgrim St., Newcastle)
	James Watson (res Newcastle). Also worked at Runswick/Staithes
	John Atkinson (res Newcastle, then Glaisdale)
1890s	Thomas Eyre Macklin (res 18 Summerhill Tce 1893; studio Newcastle)
	W T N Boyce (res. South Shields)
	H J Sticks (res. Newcastle)
	D F McLea (res. South Shields)
	A Gauld (res. Gateshead)
	Robert Ventress
	Thomas Swift Hutton (res Newcastle)
1900	W G Glendenning
	William Connell
	Edith F Grey
	J W Gilroy
	Jared Dobeson
	Thomas Harrison
	Frank W Corner
	Charles H Jennings
	Samuel J Wild
	Charles F Ogle
	Harry Sticks

List of Illustrations

Black and white

Colour

Selected Bibliography

Allen, B. ed., *Towards a Modern Art World*, Yale University Press, New Haven & London, 1995.

Anderson, B., *Imagined Communities: Reflections on the Origin and Spread of Nationalism*, Verso, 1983.

Anon, *Art Prices Current*, 1907-1914.

Anon, *Royal Academy Exhibitors 1905-1970*, 6 vols., E.P. Publishing Ltd, 1979.

Anon, *Royal Academy Pictures* (vols up to 1920), Cassell & Co. Ltd.

Baile de Laperriere, C. ed., *Royal Scottish Academy Exhibitors* 1826-1990, 4 vols., Hilmarton Manor Press, 1991.

Beam, P.C. et.al., *Winslow Homer in the 1890s. Prout's Neck Observed*, Hudson Hills Press, New York, 1990.

Billcliffe, R., *Royal Glasgow Institute of the Fine Arts 1861-1989*, 4 vols., The Woodend Press, 1992.

Blackburn, H. ed., *Academy Notes*, Chatto & Windus, (several vols.1884-1894).

Casteras, S.P. & Denney, C., *The Grosvenor Gallery. A Palace of Art in Victorian England*, Yale University Press, New Haven & London, 1996.

Charleton, R.J., *A History of Newcastle-on-Tyne*, Walter Scott Publ., c.1885.

Cikovsky, N. ed., *Winslow Homer: A Symposium*, National Gallery of Art, Washington, 1990.

Colls, R. & Dodd, P. eds., *Englishness. Politics and Culture 1880-1920*, Croom Helm, 1986.

Corbin, A., *The Lure of the Sea. The Discovery of the Seaside in the Western World 1750-1840*, transl. J. Phelps, University of California Press, U.S.A., 1994.

Cubitt, G. ed., *Imagining Nations*, Manchester University Press, 1998.

Daniels, S., *Fields of Vision. Landscape Imagery and National Identity in England and the U.S.*, Polity Press, 1993.

Denvir, B., *The Late Victorians. Art, Design and Society 1852-1910*, Longmans, 1986.

Dunbar, J., *Laura Knight*, Collins, 1975.

Faulkner, T. ed., *Northumbrian Panoramas*, Octavian Press, 1996.

Fox, C., *Dame Laura Knight*, Phaidon, 1988.

Fox, C., *Stanhope Forbes and the Newlyn School*, David & Charles, 1993.

Graves, A., *Royal Academy Exhibitors 1769-1904*, 4 vols., S.R. Publ. Ltd, 1970, (reprint from Henry Graves & Co Ltd, 1905).

Grey, H.O., *The Life of Sir W.Q. Orchardson, R.A.*, Hutchinson, no date.

Hall, M., *The Artists of Northumbria*, Marshall Hall Associates, 1973.

Harris, J., *Private Lives, Public Spirit: Britain 1870-1914*, Penguin, 1993.

Hayward, W., *James Hall of Tynemouth*, vol.1, Hazell, Watson & Viney Ltd., 1896.

Hemming, C., *British Painters of Coast and Sea*, Gollancz Ltd., 1988.

Hendricks, G., *The Life and Work of Winslow Homer*, H.N. Abrams, New York, U.S.A., 1979.

Hiley, M., *Frank Sutcliffe. Photographer of Whitby*, Gordon Fraser, 1974.

Hiley, M., *Victorian Working Women. Portraits from Life*, Gordon Fraser Gallery, 1979.

Hollerton, E., *The Archive Photographic Series. North Shields*, Chalford Publishers, 1997.

Holt, Y.H., Russell, F. & Corbett, D.P. eds., *The Geographies of Englishness: Landscape and the National Past 1880-1940*, Yale University Press, 2002.

Hoopes, D.F., *Winslow Homer Watercolours*, Barrie Books Ltd., 1969.

Howell, S., *The Seaside*, Cassell & Collier Macmillan Publ. Ltd., 1974.

Jacobs, M., *The Good and Simple Life. Artist Colonies in Europe and America*, Phaidon, 1985.

Kestner, J.A., *Masculinities in Victorian Painting*, Scolar Press, 1995.

Knight, L., *Oil Paint and Grease Paint*, Nicholson & Watson, 1936.

Knight, L., *The Magic of a Line*, Kimber & Co., 1965.

Lanyon, A., *The Rooks of Trelawne*, Gordon Fraser Gallery Ltd., 1976.

Ledger, S. & McCracken, S. eds., *Cultural Politics at the fin-de-siècle*, Cambridge University Press, 1995.

Longstreet, S., *The Drawings of Winslow Homer*, Borden Publ., U.S.A., 1970.

Lübbren, N., *Rural Artists' Colonies in Europe* 1870-1910, Manchester University Press, 2001.

Mackenzie, J.M., *Propaganda and Empire*, Manchester University Press, 1984.

Mackenzie, J.M., *Imperialism and Popular Culture*, Manchester University Press, 1986.

Mackenzie, J.M. ed., *Popular Imperialism and the Military, 1850-1950*, Manchester University Press, 1992.

Macleod, D.S., *Art and the Victorian middle class*, Cambridge University Press, 1996.

Mastermann, C.F.G., *The Heart of the Empire: Discussions of Problems of modern city life in England* (1901), B.B. Gilbert ed., Harvester Press, 1973.

McClintock, A., *Imperial Leather. Race, Gender and Sexuality in the Colonial Context*, Routledge, 1995.

McCord, N. ed., *Essays in Tyneside Labour History*, Newcastle Polytechnic, 1977.

McCord, N., *North East England. The Region's Development 1760-1960*, B.T. Batsford Ltd., 1979.

McGuire, D.F., *Charles Mitchell*, Newcastle Upon Tyne Libraries & Arts, 1988.

Mendus, S. & Rendall, J. eds., *Sexuality and Subordination*, Routledge, 1989.

Mitchell, W.J.T. ed., *Landscape and Power*, University of Chicago Press, U.S.A., 1994.

Newall, C., *The Grosvenor Gallery Exhibitions. Change and Continuity in the Victorian Art World*, Cambridge University Press, 1995.

Palmer, W.J., *The Tyne and its Tributaries*, (no publ.) London, 1882.

Reynolds, A.M., *Life and Work of Frank Holl*, Methuen, 1912.

Robinson, A., *Poetry, Painting and Ideas 1885-1914*, Macmillan, 1985.

Sinton, A.G.M., *Pen and Palette Club 1900-1990*, (no publ.), Newcastle, 1990.

Slater, J.F., *Odds and Ends from an Artist's Notebook*, Hewitt & Rudge, 1914.

Stevenson, C.B., *The Creation of an Art Gallery*, Laing Art Gallery, 1956.

Tickner, L., *Modern Life and Modern Subjects. British Art in the Early 20th Century*, Yale University Press, New Haven & London, 2000.

Tomlinson, W.W., *Historical Notes on Cullercoats, Whitley and Monkseaton*, Walter

Scott, 1893, republ. F.Graham, 1980.
Waller, P.J., *Town, City and Nation. England 1850-1914*, Oxford University Press, 1983.
Walton, J.K., *The English Seaside Resort. A Social History 1750-1914*, Leicester University Press, 1983.
Walvin, J., *Beside the Seaside*, Allen Lane, 1978.
Welford, R., *Men of Mark 'twixt Tyne and Tweed* (3 vols.), W. Scott, 1895.
Wilkes, L., *Tyneside Portraits*, F. Graham, 1971.
Williams, R., *The Country and the City*, Chatto & Windus, 1973.
Willis, I. Cooper, ed., *A Vernon Lee Anthology*, John Lane, 1929.
Wolff, J. & Seed, J. eds., *The Culture of Capital: art, power and the 19th century middle class*, Manchester University Press, 1988.

Exhibition catalogues

Anon, *Cullercoats Revisited*, Dean Gallery, Newcastle, Nov. 1983.
Anon, *Paintings and Drawings from the Leathart Collection*, Laing Art Gallery, 1968.
Anon, *F.W. Jackson 1859-1918*, Rochdale Art Gallery, 1978.
Anon, *Mark Senior 1862-1927*, Wakefield Art Gallery, 1983.
Anon, *Sir William Quiller Orchardson* R.A., Laing Art Gallery, Newcastle May 1972.
Atkinson, D.S. & Wierich, J., *Winslow Homer in Gloucester*, Terra Museum of American Art, Chicago, U.S.A., 1990.
Cikovsky, N. & Kelly, F., *Winslow Homer*, National Gallery of Art, Washington, 1995.
Fox, C. & Greenacre, F., *Artists of the Newlyn School*, Newlyn Orion Gallery, Arts Council, 1979.
Fox, C. & Greenacre, F., *Painting at Newlyn 1880-1930*, Barbican Art Gallery, 1985.
Gardner, A.T.E., *Winslow Homer. A Retrospective Exhibition*, Museum of Fine Arts, Boston, U.S.A., 1959.
Goodrich, L., *Winslow Homer*, Whitney Museum of American Art, U.S.A., 1973.
Knipe, T. ed., *Winslow Homer. All the Cullercoats Pictures*, Northern Centre for Contemporary Art, Sunderland, 1988.
Langley, R., *Walter Langley. Pioneer of the Newlyn Art Colony*, Sansom & Company/ Penlee House Gallery and Museum, 1997.
McConkey, K., *Impressionism in Britain*, Yale University Press, London & New Haven, U.S.A., 1995.
McConkey, K., *The Restless Wave*, Tyne & Wear Museums, 1978.
Millard, J., A *Romance with the North East. Robert and Isa Jobling*, Tyne & Wear Museums, 1992.
Millard, J., *Ralph Hedley. Tyneside Painter*, Tyne & Wear Museums, 1990.
Moss, B. & R., *John Atkinson 1863-1924*, Moss Galleries, Hexham, 1981.
Moss, B & R., *George Horton 1859-1950*, Moss Galleries, Hexham, 1982.
Phillips, P., *The Staithes Group*, Phillips & Son, 1993.
Quarm, R. & Wilcox, S., *Masters of the Sea*, National Maritime Museum, Greenwich, Phaidon, 1987.
Sellin, D., *Americans in Brittany and Normandy 1860-1910*, Phoenix Art Museum, U.S.A., 1982.
Weisberg, G.P., *Beyond Impressionism. The Naturalist Impulse in European Art 1860-1905*, Thames & Hudson, 1992.

Contemporary Exhibition Catalogues

Annual Spring Exhibition of Watercolour Drawings at Mr. Turner's Gallery of Arts, Newcastle, 1866.
Artists of the Northern Counties Exhibitions, Laing Art Gallery, Newcastle, 1905-1920.
Arts Association Exhibitions, Newcastle 1878-1882.
Bewick Club Exhibitions, Newcastle, 1884-1910.
British Association Exhibition of Works of Art, Newcastle, 1863.
Central Exchange Exhibition, Newcastle, 1878.
Drawings by George Horton, Greatorex Gallery, London, May 1922.
Emmerson Exhibition (posthumous), The Galleries, Newcastle, 1895.
Emmerson Exhibition of Oil Paintings, Hellyer Bros. Gallery, South Shields, 1894.
Fine Art and Industrial Exhibition, South Shields, 1877.
Fine Art and Industrial Exhibition, Gateshead, 1883.
Grosvenor Gallery Exhibitions, 1877-1890.
John Charlton Exhibition, Laing Art Gallery, Newcastle, 1917.
Jubilee Exhibition, Newcastle, 1887.
Laing Art Gallery Inaugural Exhibition, Newcastle, 1904.
Loan Exhibitions, South Shields, 1911, 1912.
Loan Exhibition of Works by F.T. Carter, T.B. Garvie, G. Horton and J.F. Slater, Laing Art Gallery, Newcastle, 1934.
Model Yacht Club Exhibition of Pictures, South Shields, 1888, 1890.
Newcastle Mechanics Institute Exhibition, 1866.
Old Watercolour Society Exhibitions, 1868-1879.
Polytechnic Exhibition, Central Exchange, Newcastle, 1870.
South Shields Art Club Exhibition, 1892, 1893, 1894.
Tynemouth Art Club Exhibition, 1889.
Tynemouth Fine Arts Association Exhibition, 1891.
Watercolour Drawings by George Horton, Corporation Art Gallery, Bolton, July 1923.
Watercolour Drawings by George Horton, Corporation Art Gallery, Rochdale, (1923?).
Watercolour Drawings by George Horton, Lange Voorhout, The Hague, Jan 1926.
Watercolours by George Horton, Fine Art Society, London, Oct. 1927.
Williams,C., *The Lifework of Robert Jobling, Exhibition Catalogue*, Armstrong College Art Gallery, March 1923.

Sales Catalogues

Anderson & Garland Sales catalogues, misc. 1960s-present.
Julia Boyd Sale, Academy of Arts, Newcastle, Oct. 1892.
John Dickinson Sale, Christie's, London, 4 Dec. 1909.
S.H. Fraser Sale, Christie's, London, May 1904.
J. Leathart Sale, Christie's, London, June 1897.
Mrs Mitchell Sale, Anderson & Garland, Sept. 1926.
Oil Paintings, Studies and Sketches by the late H.H. Emmerson, R & W Mack, Newcastle, 1902.
W.W. Pattinson & J.M. Redmayne Sale, Davison & Sons, Dec. 1886.
J.A.D. Shipley Sale, May 1914.
Sotheby's Sale, 21 June 1988 & 21 November 1989.
Percy Westmacott Collection, Christie's, London, 10 May 1918.
Christie's Sale, 18 July 1919.

Journals and Periodicals (Contemporary)

Anon, 'The Lifebrigade Man', *The Graphic*, 1870, p.274.
Anon, 'Newcastle Arts Association', *Art Journal*, 1880, p.339.
Anon, 'Art in the Provinces', *Art Journal*, 1889, p.175.
Anon, 'The Bewick Club and its Founders', *Monthly Chronicle*, May 1889, p.193.
Anon, 'American Painters — Winslow Homer and F.A. Bridgman', *Art Journal*, 1879, pp.154-5.
Armstrong, W., 'The Art of W.Q. Orchardson', *Portfolio*, February 1895.
Campbell, G.E., 'Frank Holl and His Works', *Art Journal*, 1889, p.53.
Charleton, R.J., 'Cullercoats', *Magazine of Art*, vol.9, 1886, pp.456-462.
Charleton, R.J., 'Newcastle-on-Tyne (Old Bits in a New City)', *English Illustrated Magazine*, 1885-86.
Dafforne, J., 'W.Q. Orchardson', *Art Journal*, 1870, p.233.
Dibdin, E.R., 'Lord Armstrong's Collection of Modern Pictures', *Magazine of Art*, 1891.
Dircks, R., 'Northumberland and Some Artists', *Art Journal*, 1904, pp.305-310.
Forbes, S.A., 'A Newlyn Retrospective', *Cornish Magazine*, vol.1, 1898, pp.81-93.
Hill, R.H., 'A Seaside Colony of Painters', *Yorkshire Evening Post*, 30 August 1939.
Horton, G., 'South Holland as a Sketching Ground', *The Studio*, vol.XI, 1897, pp.26-31.
Horton, G., 'Artist with a Craze for Clocks', *Sunday Sun*, 5 March 1939.
Larkins, W.G., 'Reminiscences of Artistic Cullercoats', *Tyneside*, vol.1, no.1, December 1894.
Leicester-Burrows, A., 'Sir William Quiller Orchardson', *The Studio*, July 1910, pp.87-98.
McC.G.M., 'Down Tyneside', *The Graphic*, 23 August 1884.
Meynell, A., 'Newlyn', *Art Journal*, 1889, pp.97-102 & 137-142.
Meynell, A., 'A Group of Great Painters', *Art Journal*, 1890, pp.283-286.

Rensselaer, V.G. van, 'An American Artist in England', *Century Magazine*, vol.5, November 1883, pp.13-21.
Spielmann, M.H., 'John Charlton: Painter of Sport and War', *Magazine of Art*, 1898, p.401.
Stephens, F.G., 'Private Collections of England', *The Athenaeum*, September 13, 20, 27 & October 18, 1873.
Walker, H., 'A Yorkshire Artist and his Work: The Late Joseph Bagshawe', *Yorkshire Weekly Post*, 30 April 1910.
Wasserman, L., 'Where the North wind blows', *Newcastle Weekly Leader*, 25 December 1886, 1, 8 & 15 January 1887.
Wasserman, L., 'Some Fisher Folk', *Art Journal*, 1887, pp.57-60.
Watson, A., 'Newcastle upon Tyne', *The Graphic*, 4 June 1881.
Watson, A., 'After the Herring Pt.I & II', *Magazine of Art*, vol.5, 1882, pp.405-11 & 454-460.
Watson, A., 'The Coaly Tyne', *Magazine of Art*, vol.6, 1883, pp.114-121.
Welford, R., 'Newcastle upon Tyne', *Art Journal*, 1882.
Wood, T.M., 'Some Paintings and Sketches by H.S. Hopwood, R.W.S.', *The Studio*, vol.49, 1910, pp.27-33.

Journals (Other)
Adams, H., 'Mortal Themes: Winslow Homer', *Art in America*, vol.71, February 1983, p.113.
Bell, Q., 'The School of Design at Newcastle', *Durham Research Review*, September 1958.
Burns, S., 'Revitalizing the "Painted-Out" North. Winslow Homer, Manly Health, and New England Regionalism in Turn-of-the-Century America', *American Art*, vol.9, Summer 1995, pp.20-37.
Garnett, O., 'Sold Christie's. Bought Agnew', *Apollo*, vol.137, 1993, p.253-258.
Gerdts, W.H., 'Winslow Homer in Cullercoats', *Yale University Gallery Bulletin*, Spring 1977, pp.18-35.
Hall, M., 'John Atkinson and the Staithes Group Connection', *Antique Collecting*, February 1995.
Hamer, L., 'The Cullercoats Fishwife', *Costume*, no.18, 1984.
Lowenthal, D., 'British National identity and the English Landscape', *Rural History*, vol.2, no.2, 1991, pp.205-230.
Macleod, D.S., 'Art Collecting and Victorian Middle-Class Taste', *Art History*, vol.10, 1987.
Macleod, D.S., 'Private and Public Patronage in Victorian Newcastle', *Journal of the Warburg & Courtauld Institutes*, vol.52, 1989, p.188.
Millard, J., 'The Bewick Club', *Cherryburn Times*, vol.1, nos.6&7, 1989-90.
Moore, S., 'Victor Noble Rainbird', *North East Times*, Christmas 1992.
NcCord, N., 'Some Aspects of Change in the 19th Century North East', *Northern History*, vol.XXXI, 1995.
Phillips, P., 'Early Days and hard times at Staithes', *Art & Antiques*, 1 October 1977, pp.22-24.
Phillips, P., 'Britain's Impressionists', *Art & Antiques Weekly*, 9 June 1979.
Phillips, P., 'Nowhere like it for Painting', *The Antique Dealer and Collector's Guide*, vol.40, no.4, 1986.
Provost, P.R., 'Winslow Homer's The Fog Warning: The Fisherman as Heroic Character', *The American Art Journal*, vol.22, no.1, pp.21-27.
Quilley, G., 'Missing the Boat: the place of the maritime in the history of British visual culture', *Visual Culture in Britain*, vol.1, no.2, 2000.
Reed, C., 'The Artist and the Other: The Work of Winslow Homer', *Yale University Art Gallery Bulletin*, Spring 1989, pp.69-79.
Rich, P., 'Elite and Popular Culture: Patriotism and the British Intellectuals c.1886-1945', *History of European Ideas*, vol.11, 1989, pp.449-466.
Smith, V., 'Some Antecedents of the Department of Fine Art, Newcastle', *Durham University Journal*, vol.14 (new series), 1953.
Wilmerding, J., 'Winslow Homer's English Period', *The American Art Journal*, November 1975, pp.60-69.
Woods, A., 'Doré's London: Art and Evidence', *Art History*, vol.1, no.3, September 1978.
Wright, A.I., 'Bastien-Lepage and English Critical Taste', *Gazette des Beaux Arts*, September 1990, pp.94-104.

Miscellaneous
Allen, S., *Technical Analysis and Treatment of Two Foxed Watercolours by A.H.Marsh attached to secondary supports, with a consideration of their Art Historical Context*, unpubl. M.A. thesis, University of Northumbria, 1989.
Carse, A., *Scrapbook*, Newcastle City Library.
Censuses for Cullercoats, Tynemouth, North Shields, Newcastle, Whitley Bay; 1851, 1861, 1871, 1881, 1891.
Crawhall, J., *Scrapbook*, Newcastle City Library.
Emmerson, H.H., letter to Lord Armstrong, Oct. 1884, Tyne & Wear Archive, acc. no. DF/A/1/14.
Emmerson, H.H., miscellaneous letters to Amy Emmerson, Mrs P. Bolam.
Hedley, R., 'The Schools of Painting Today' manuscript for lecture, and other miscellaneous archive material, Julian Brown.
Horton, G., miscellaneous letters, notebooks, sketches, sketchbooks, etc., Horton Archive, Tyne & Wear Archive, courtesy Mr. & Miss Redpath.
Laing Art Gallery Archive.
Local Newspaper Cuttings and Local Obituaries, bound volumes in Newcastle City Library.
Lübbren, N., *Rural Artists' Colonies in 19th Century Europe*, unpubl. PhD thesis, University of Leeds, 1996.
Millard, J., 'Exhibitions in and around Newcastle 1863-1930', typescript, Newcastle City Library, 1991.
Mitchell, C., *Scrapbook of Newspaper Cuttings, 1868-93*, Newcastle City Library.
Newton, L., *The Cullercoats Artists' Colony c.1870-1914*, unpubl. PhD thesis, University of Northumbria, 2001.
Oxberry, J., 1918 Scrapbook, 'H.H. Emmerson. Notes on his Life and Work', Newcastle City Library.
Pen and Palette Club Papers, 1901-1903.
Quinn, P., *Picturing Locality. Art and Regional Identity in the North East of England 1822-1900*, unpubl. PhD thesis, University of Sunderland, 1997.
Watson, A., *Notes on the Principle Pictures at the Arts Association Exhibition*, Autumn 1879, (no publ.), 1879.
Watson, R.S., *An Address to Members of the Bewick Club*, Tyne Printing Works, 1885.

Acknowledgements

I would like to express my deepest gratitude to those who have freely given their advice, support and practical assistance, without which this exhibition and catalogue would have been considerably poorer. In particular I must thank Jamie Amos, Julian Brown and Alan Dodd for their unbridled enthusiasm and generosity throughout this project. I would also like to thank Abigail Booth Gerdts and Professor Kenneth McConkey for their help and advice on securing the works by Winslow Homer, and my co-curator Ruth Percival for her tireless editorial efforts and infinite patience.

My warmest thanks go to all those private individuals who have loaned pictures and archive material for inclusion in the catalogue and exhibition, but who wish to remain anonymous.

I am indebted to John Millard (Tyne & Wear Museums), Lynda Macleod (Christie's Archive, London), Adrian Osler, Hugh Dixon and Pamela Wallhead (National Trust), Ken Wilson, Eric Hollerton (North Shields Central Library), and John Bullock-Anderson and Marshall Hall (Anderson & Garland). I would also like to thank staff from Newcastle City Library Local Studies department, Leeds City Library, Whitby Library, South Shields Library, National Art Library, Tyne & Wear Archive, Northumberland Records Office, Hatton Gallery Library, Beamish Archive and Northumbria University Library.

Laura Newton

Index

[See also **Main Artists at Cullercoats** and **List of Illustrations**]
Excludes references in footnotes